Information, Democracy, and Autocracy

Advocates for economic development often call for greater transparency. But what does transparency really mean? What are its consequences? This breakthrough book demonstrates how information impacts major political phenomena, including mass protest, the survival of dictatorships, democratic stability, as well as economic performance. The book introduces a new measure of a specific facet of transparency: the dissemination of economic data. Analysis shows that democracies make economic data more available than do similarly developed autocracies. Transparency attracts investment and makes democracies more resilient to breakdown. But transparency has a dubious consequence under autocracy: political instability. Mass unrest becomes more likely, and transparency can facilitate democratic transition, but most often a new despotic regime displaces the old. Autocratic leaders may also turn these threats to their advantage, using the risk of mass unrest that transparency portends to unify the ruling elite. Policymakers must recognize the trade-offs that transparency entails.

James R. Hollyer is a Benjamin Evans Lippincott Associate Professor in Political Economy in the Department of Political Science at the University of Minnesota. Professor Hollyer obtained his PhD in political science from New York University in 2012, his MA in international relations from the University of Chicago in 2006, and his BA in political economy from Williams College in 2003. His research focuses on comparative and international political economy, particularly on transparency, corruption, political accountability, and the effects of international policy on domestic politics.

B. Peter Rosendorff is Professor of Politics at New York University and is editor of the interdisciplinary journal, *Economics & Politics*, and serves on the editorial board of *International Organization*. Professor Rosendorff holds a Ph.D. from Columbia University in economics, a BA (Hons) and BSc from the University of Witwatersrand, South Africa, in mathematics and economics. He is the author of many journal articles, some of which have appeared in *American Political Science Review*, *American Economics Review*, *Quarterly Journal of Political Science*, and the *Journal of Politics*, among others.

James Raymond Vreeland is Professor of Politics and International Affairs in the Woodrow Wilson School and Department of Politics at Princeton University. He received his PhD in political science from New York University in 1999. He currently serves on the editorial board of *International Organization*. He is the author of *The IMF and Economic Development* (Cambridge University Press, 2003) and *The Political Economy of the United Nations Security Council: Money and Influence* (Cambridge University Press, 2014).

Information, Democracy, and Autocracy

Economic Transparency and Political (In)Stability

JAMES R. HOLLYER
University of Minnesota

B. PETER ROSENDORFF
New York University

JAMES RAYMOND VREELAND
Princeton University

CAMBRIDGE
UNIVERSITY PRESS

CAMBRIDGE
UNIVERSITY PRESS

University Printing House, Cambridge CB2 8BS, United Kingdom

One Liberty Plaza, 20th Floor, New York, NY 10006, USA

477 Williamstown Road, Port Melbourne, VIC 3207, Australia

314–321, 3rd Floor, Plot 3, Splendor Forum, Jasola District Centre, New Delhi - 110025, India

79 Anson Road, #06-04/06, Singapore 079906

Cambridge University Press is part of the University of Cambridge.

It furthers the University's mission by disseminating knowledge in the pursuit of education, learning, and research at the highest international levels of excellence.

www.cambridge.org
Information on this title: www.cambridge.org/9781108420723
DOI: 10.1017/9781108355100

First published 2018

Printed in the United States of America by Sheridan Books, Inc.

A catalogue record for this publication is available from the British Library.

ISBN 978-1-108-42072-3 Hardback
ISBN 978-1-108-43080-7 Paperback

To
Jim and Kathleen Dennis, in memoriam
Clive and Daphne Rosendorff, and Nora Scott
Mr. James McGovern III and Bobita Thakuri

Contents

Figures

Tables

Acknowledgments

This study represents the fruit of a collaboration of three good friends, who have received a lot of help from other friends and colleagues over many years. The project began with a conversation during a seminar hosted by the Political Science Department at UCLA back in 2003 and slowly gained momentum through exchanges at NYU. Over the years, we received helpful feedback from participants at various conferences, seminars, and workshops hosted throughout the United States and the world.

In the United States, presentations at the annual meetings of the American Political Science Association, the International Political Economy Society, the Midwest Political Science Association, and the International Studies Association yielded helpful comments and advice. American Universities who hosted seminars that enriched our work include The Ohio State University, Princeton University, Stanford University, Syracuse University, UC Riverside, UC San Diego, University of Southern California, and Yale University.

The institutions based internationally include Academia Sinica (Taiwan), Economic Research South Africa, ETH Zurich (Switzerland), the European Political Science Association meetings (Austria, Germany, Scotland, Spain), the Helen Suzman Foundation (South Africa), the Instituto Nacional de Transparencia, Acceso a la Información y Protección de Datos Personales (Mexico), the Latin American Studies Association meetings (Puerto Rico), London School of Economics (United Kingdom), Université Laval (Canada), National University of Singapore, Tel Aviv University (Israel), University of Nottingham (United Kingdom), University of Stellenbosch (South Africa), and the University of the Witwatersrand (South Africa).

We thank the participants – too numerous to list – at all of these venues. They contributed in various ways to the development of our thinking on transparency and political stability. By sharing their ideas, they helped give us a more global perspective.

For specific suggestions and extensive comments, we thank Luisa Alemany, Ben Ansell, Ben Bagozzi, Daniel Berliner, Christina Bodea, Adam Bonica, Lawrence Broz, Chris Canavan, Christina Davis, José Fernández-Albertos, John Freeman, Jennifer Gandhi, Erik Gartzke, Scott Gehlbach, Emilie Hafner-Burton, Sikyun Cindy Im, Leslie Johns, Michael Laver, Adrienne LeBas, Andrew Little, Helen Milner, Layna Mosley, Megumi Naoi, Tom Pepinsky, Carlo Prato, Stephanie Rickard, Sebastian Saiegh, David Samuels, Jillian Schwedler, David Singer, William Skorupski, Randall Stone, Milan Svolik, Scott Tyson, and Johannes Urpelainen. We also thank the anonymous reviewers of the book manuscript as well as the reviewers of the several papers that contributed to this project.

Special thanks go to the colleagues at our home institutions who have offered advice on the project. From Minnesota, we thank John Freeman, David Samuels, and Jane Sumner. We also thank the Minnesota Supercomputing Institute for access to their resources. From NYU, we thank Neal Beck, Bruce Bueno de Mesquita, Michael Gilligan, Jonathan Nagler, Alastair Smith, and David Stasavage. From Georgetown, we thank Marc L. Busch, Matthew Carnes, Raj Desai, Jenny Guardado, Diana Kim, Marko Klasnja, Paasha Mahdavi, Anna Maria Mayda, Abraham Newman, Irfan Nooruddin, Ken Opalo, Dennis Quinn, Nita Rudra, George Shambaugh, Yuhki Tajima, Jennifer Tobin, Erik Voeten, and Stephen Weymouth, who offered specific suggestions at various workshops.

We are also grateful to students who scrutinized the manuscript for errors and issues of clarity: Camille Afable, Valeria Balza, Samuel Bernstein, Olivia Bisel, Vickie Chang, Marisa Clery, Viviana De Santis, David Deliz, Prashant Desai, Neil Filosa, Willie Hall, Joshua Haney, Camila Hernandez, Ines Jimenez-Ontiveros, Arjun Krishnan, Diana Marin-Melo, Aislinn McNiece, Giulia Nardi Martins, Hanna Niczyporuk, Munir Pavez, Furkan Pehlivanli, Allison Pfotzer, Abigail Reinhold, Elaine Shen, Meghna Sinha, Mike Sliwinski, Jaein Song, Samantha Wulfson, Yuou Wu, and Amy Zhihao Zhang. We also thank Camille Squires and Sapir Yarden, who posed the question to IMF Managing Director Christine Lagarde which we use in the introduction to the book. Most importantly, we thank Claire Chaeryung Lee and, especially, Trellace Lawrimore, who carefully read each page of the manuscript and provided volumes of written feedback. We thank Molly Dunn, Vanessa Hofman, and Praveen Navaratnam for excellent research assistance.

The Arab Spring inspired much of this work, and political protest and regime instability is the central theme of this book. The cover art – detail from the monumental painting by Julie Mehretu, *Cairo* – captures the sense of an ancient, and also contemporary city, both a site of massive political protest, and obscured, perhaps by the winds of the Sahara, but also by government suppression of information and political organization. We'd like to thank the artist, Julie Mehretu, Catherine Belloy and the Marian Goodman Gallery, and The Broad Foundation for permission to use the image.

James Hollyer would like to thank the Niehaus Center on Globalization and Governance and the Benjamin Evans Lippincott Foundation for support. The University of Southern California Gould Center for Law and Social Science, and Gillian Hadfield offered a warm and welcoming environment for Peter Rosendorff, in the Spring of 2017, for which he is grateful.

Finally, we thank the Wilf Family Department of Politics at New York University. Two of us are alumni of the department and the third is a professor there. This book is very much a result of the training, mentoring, and friendship that are hallmarks of the NYU Politics community.

1

A New Approach to the Study of Transparency

Transparency endures as a mantra for many policymakers concerned with improving life in the developing world. Asked how to improve governance in developing countries, the managing director of the International Monetary Fund, Christine Lagarde, has answered emphatically: "Transparency, transparency, transparency!"[1] The international community has lauded efforts of some states, such as Bulgaria, Mexico, and South Korea, for increasing their historic levels of transparency, sometimes even heralding them as economic and political miracles. Other states, such as Argentina, Bangladesh, and Zimbabwe, have lost credibility due to their failure to report credible information about the state's economic activities.

Why are some countries more transparent than others? And what are the consequences – economic and political – of increased transparency? This book seeks to address these questions using an innovative measure of transparency. While we confirm some broadly held views, we also introduce new and surprising findings.

In essence, the book is about the role of the informational environment in political economy. Political action, such as voting or protest, requires coordination across individuals. Coordination, in turn, requires information – not just any information, but shared information. That is, mass political coordination requires information about actors' higher-order beliefs: their beliefs about what other actors believe. The informational environment matters for mass coordinated political action.

The first puzzle we confront in our work is a measurement problem: how to gauge the transparency of economic information. We take advantage of something that usually stands as an obstacle to research: missing data. We observe

---

[1] Georgetown University, Washington, DC, October 2, 2014.

1

that missing data are data. We use patterns of reporting data as a proxy for the publicness of credible economic information.

Using this measure, we find that more transparent countries attract higher levels of investment and that transparency stabilizes democracies. A rich informational environment facilitates economic decision-making and it enables voters to discriminate between good and bad leaders. When elections function better, democracies face fewer protests, enjoy greater legitimacy, and become more likely to survive. Not surprisingly, democracies tend to be more transparent than autocracies.

When it comes to the political stability of autocracies, however, we find less intuitive patterns. As autocratic regimes become more transparent, they face higher risks of upheaval due to unrest among the masses. Increasing the availability of information about government performance enables the masses to more effectively engage in collective protest. Still, autocrats face risks beyond the masses outside the halls of power. They also face risks from within the elite – members of the inner circle of the regime. At the same time as it facilitates mass protest, transparency lowers the risks of coups led by the elite whose loyalty to the regime leadership increases with the risk of mass upheaval. When the masses stand at the gate, the elites must unite behind their leadership to prevent the downfall of the entire regime.

In sum, increasing transparency leads to an uncertain future for the autocratic regimes. On the one hand, it may facilitate mass mobilization, which sometimes results in democratization from below and sometimes causes one autocratic regime to be replaced by a new one; on the other hand, it may simply unite the elites behind their leader, further entrenching the incumbent leadership.

The pages ahead unpack the logic and empirics of these varied effects of transparency on political stability.

This book makes a further contribution by relying on a new measure of transparency – one that eschews subjective opinions about the transparency of countries in favor of using more objective measures from economic data. Indeed, before we can develop arguments about the determinants and consequences of transparency, we first must address a basic question: What does transparency really mean?

Ultimately, transparency concerns the dissemination of information. Many forms of information exist, and they can be disseminated through various channels to different audiences. Thus transparency has many facets. We take an original approach, focusing on *the dissemination of aggregate economic data through international organizations.*

We recognize the value of measuring other forms of transparency and we address them throughout the book. Numerous studies have employed alternate conceptions of transparency (Berliner and Erlich 2015; Berliner 2014; Besley and Burgess 2002; Djankov et al. 2003; Grief 2006; Habyarimana et al. 2009;

Kosack and Fung 2014). These alternative conceptions include the openness of political institutions (Bremmer 2006; Broz 2002; Dahl 1971), freedom of the press or circulation of the press (Adserà, Boix, and Payne 2003; Brunetti and Weder 2003), the presence of freedom of information laws (Berliner 2014; Islam 2006), and access to the Internet (Milner 2006a). These conceptions represent valid approaches for certain theoretical questions.

For our project, we use a narrow conception of transparency – one that focuses on the dissemination of economic data. The dissemination of economic data as a measure of transparency is of central importance to political economy. The availability of aggregate data affects decisions about investment, resource allocation, and consumption. Market participants constantly rely on data measuring the size and growth of the gross domestic product per capita, trade and monetary statistics, unemployment, inflation, and many other economic indicators. These data have inherently political roots because the state has the unique capacity – the required labor power and scope of authority – to collect them. As we will reveal, the availability of credible aggregate economic data has consequences for the performance of the economy and for the stability of the state.

Other measures of transparency, which incorporate political or economic openness, may create a tautological relationship between the effect of transparency and various political or economic outcomes. For example, if the coding of transparency directly incorporates the presence of democratic institutions, a correlation between such a measure and democracy is neither surprising nor interesting. Similarly, if the coding of transparency directly incorporates the ease with which investment flows into a country, the measure cannot be used to test the effect of transparency on investment.

Our measure of transparency is precisely measured and closely corresponds to the theoretical models presented in this book. It narrowly focuses on the degree to which a country has reported aggregate economic data to international organizations and stands apart from the other independent and dependent variables we examine in this book. Indeed, who would think that the provision of national income accounting statistics would lie behind such important phenomena as the emergence and stability of democracy, increased mass unrest and decreased coups under autocracy, and patterns of investment?

An additional reason we focus on the reporting of economic data relates to the dissemination mechanism: international organizations. Credibility lies at the crux of this mechanism. We view international organizations as independent third parties that vet information provided by states, especially from developing countries. A government may release economic data, but international organizations only include the information in their databases if the government has followed the appropriate standards and if the international organization deems the data accurate. Specifically, we obtain our data from the World Bank's World Development Indicators (WDI) data series, which, in turn, takes data directly from national governments or from other international organizations that obtain their data from national governments.

Now, the quality of data that international organizations have is far from perfect, but these organizations do have standards that often exceed those that governments may use if left to their own devices. We thus rely on international organizations that have specific data standards and guidelines for data collection and calculation.[2] We can then generate an approximate measure of the degree to which the aggregate economic data released by governments are credible.

We stress that our measure represents only an approximation of the availability of credible data. We do not directly evaluate the millions of national accounting figures that governments have historically made available (or not). Nor can we directly assess individual citizens' subjective judgments of the credibility of the aggregate economic data that they observe published (or not) by their governments. We do recognize, however, that when data are reported as missing by international organizations, either the national government released excessively manipulated information or the government failed to release any information at all. Thus missing data approximate a more generally held view – both domestically and internationally – that the government failed to report credible information about the economy.

Why do some states provide credible economic data while others fail to do so? *Capacity* stands as one determinant of this kind of transparency – some states are too poor and lack the technology to collect data. Another important determinant is states' *willingness* to disclose. Some states have the capacity to provide data about their country – to the world and to their own citizens – but they choose not to do so. They lack the political will. What then are the consequences of choosing to disseminate (or not) aggregate economic data?

The provision of credible data permits citizens to better coordinate their political behavior and make more efficient economic decisions. These effects of transparency lead to opposing outcomes under democratic and autocratic forms of government. Under democracy, data dissemination makes elections more effective in removing poorly performing incumbents, reduces the incidence of mass protest and irregular removal of leaders, and stabilizes democratic regimes. By contrast, autocratic governments face a risk from revealing

---

[2] For an overview of the various purposes of international organizations, see Abbott and Snidal (1998) and Martin and Simmons (1998). On domestic perceptions of international organizations and the ability of these organizations to influence and inform domestic populations, see T. Johnson's (2011, 2014) work on the subject. See also Bierman and Siebenhuner (2009); Cox and Jacobson (1973); Jinnah (2014); Johnson and Urpelainen (2014); Karns and Mingst (1990); Posner (2009); Reinalda and Verbeek (1998); and Tallberg et al. (2013). The view that international organizations serve to provide credible signals to domestic audiences fits with other work we have pursued with other colleagues, including Mansfield, Milner, and Rosendorff (2002); Hollyer and Rosendorff (2011); Vreeland and Dreher (2014); see also Chapman (2011).

*economic data, which enable citizens to better coordinate protest: mass upris-
ings, which can unseat incumbents and upend autocratic regimes, become more
likely.*

When autocrats provide data about the economic performance of a country, the information can serve as a focal point to help citizens coordinate to
address a collective action problem. Citizens may stage mass demonstrations
or go on strike, especially when economic performance is weak. Obviously,
mass uprisings are problematic for autocrats as these can lead to the downfall
of the regime. Consequently, autocrats have incentives to withhold economic
data from the public.

Autocrats also face other types of threats beyond mass unrest. Autocratic
leaders often risk deposition from inner-circle elites staging coups or engaging
in nonviolent political maneuvers that shake up the leadership. Here we offer
an ironic twist to the logic of data dissemination under autocracy. Precisely
because a more transparent informational environment facilitates mass unrest,
data dissemination can render inner-circle elites more supportive of the regime.
Members of the elite are less willing to take action against their leader as the
regime becomes less stable because everyone in the regime – the dictator and
his inner circle – will all fall together if the masses topple the government.

In essence, transparency can empower a bold dictator to use the prospect
of mass insurrection as a threat to control members of his own regime. In
this part of the story, a cunning strategy motivates transparency: the autocrat
increases the ability of the masses to organize by releasing economic data simply to inspire his inner circle to rally around his leadership. So, for autocrats,
economic transparency acts as a double-edged sword: Loyalty among elites
increases precisely because mass unrest becomes more likely.

Thus, in the ensuing chapters, we make several predictions:

1. Democracies provide more data in general than autocracies.
2. The decision of autocracies to disseminate data depends on trade-offs
   across the need for investment, the risk of mass uprising, and the risk of
   coups from inside the regime.
3. When states provide more data, investment increases.
4. The dissemination of economic data enhances stability under democracy.
5. The dissemination of economic data has more nuanced effects on the
   stability of autocracies – it reduces the likelihood of coups but increases
   the chances of mass unrest.

Behind all of the research in the book – the theories, predictions, and analyses of data – stands our new approach to measuring transparency. Our index
encompasses the reporting of data by national governments to various international organizations on 240 economic variables. Our dataset covers the period
of 1980 to 2010 for 125 countries, for a total of 3,875 country-year observations of data dissemination. Because some data may be more difficult for

states to collect than others and the reporting of some data may better reflect a general tendency to disclose, we treat transparency as a latent (unobserved) predictor of a state's tendency to disclose data. We estimate the index using a Bayesian model based on item response theory (IRT), which enables us to estimate which variables are the most difficult to report and which discriminate the most transparent governments from the least (we explain IRT briefly in Section 1.1.3 and in detail in Chapter 3).

Our measure – which we call the HRV index (following the initials of our last names) – is publicly available through our website (http://hrvtransparency.org). Some researchers may wish to use our measure to examine questions beyond those introduced in this book. Other scholars may wish to use the methodology we develop to generate new measures tailored to specific questions of interest. For example, Copelovitch, Gandrud, and Hallerberg (2018) have used our approach to develop a specific measure of financial openness, which relies on the reporting of 14 financial indicators for 50 countries across the period of 1990 to 2011. Our methodology has great flexibility. A researcher need only identify the key variables of interest, record where the data on these variables have been reported and where they have not, and then apply IRT. Both our specific index of transparency and our methodology to generate the index have wide-ranging applications.

The book therefore makes several contributions: an innovative approach to estimate transparency along with an original index, new theories of the determinants and consequences of transparency, and a set of inceptive empirical findings.

The remainder of this introduction foreshadows the chapters to come. The book is organized into three parts: Part I, Facets of Transparency; Part II, Protest and Stability; and Part III, Why Disclose. We begin by exploring facets of transparency with a focus on our original measure of the dissemination of economic data (Part I). Armed with our measure of transparency, we examine its consequences for political stability (Part II). We find beneficial effects of transparency for the political stability of democracies, while the effect on the stability of autocracies depends on the type of threat to the regime. Part III examines why governments disclose data. First, we show that data dissemination has beneficial economic consequences with a focus on investment. We then present the logic of why democracies have stronger incentives to provide data than do autocracies. Having explored the nuanced consequences of transparency for the stability of autocratic regimes, we complete this section by revisiting the political logic of why autocrats would ever disclose data. The book's final chapter offers advice to policymakers and scholars concerning the benefits and costs of transparency across regime types.

After briefly overviewing each of the three parts of the book, this introductory chapter concludes with a discussion of the different audiences we seek to reach with our research, including the subfields of comparative politics, international relations, American politics, and public choice.

1.1 MEASURING DIFFERENT FACETS OF TRANSPARENCY

People often hail the merits of transparency without critically assessing the type of information in question. Broadly defined, transparency may pertain to any aspect of information transmission, and different aspects of information transmission may likely have different causes and consequences. Part I offers a framework for conceptualizing three key facets of transparency (Chapter 2). We also introduce the details of our own index, which focuses on the disclosure of aggregate economic data (Chapter 3). We do not suggest that our measure is always preferable to others. On the contrary, we suggest that the optimal measure of transparency depends on the theoretical context (Chapter 4). So we offer guidance about which measures of transparency are the most relevant to which theoretical mechanisms.

Our measure does offer certain advantages over other measures of transparency because of the objective and rigorous methodology used to generate the index. Note that these advantages are also context-specific (for an in depth discussion, see Hollyer, forthcoming). "Objective" does not mean "better" for all purposes; rather, the objectivity simply derives from the fact that the measure is constructed following rigorous rules, making the dataset independently reproducible. Our measure of transparency is itself transparent and can be reproduced using the raw data from the World Bank and appropriate computer software.[3]

What can scholars study using data dissemination as a measure of transparency? Our broad area of theoretical interest is political economy and we are primarily concerned with transparent information about the economy as it relates to political order (both domestic and international) and the accountability of governments.[4] Different facets of transparency play important roles in holding governments accountable. Citizens care about (1) their government's choice of policies, (2) the impact of those policies on outcomes in their everyday life, and (3) the outcomes themselves. The first item concerns the transparency of the policymaking process. The second item relates to the transparency of causal connections between policies and outcomes. The third constitutes the transparency of the material conditions under which people pursue their daily lives.

Ultimately, citizens may care most about the third facet of transparency: the policy outcomes. Some policy outcomes are easily observed: Am I employed?

---

[3] Our estimation process involves a stochastic component, but analyses with the data should prove robust to the expected small deviations from exact estimations of the index.

[4] Prominent examples in the literature include models of political responses to economic crises (Alesina and Drazen 1991; Fernandez and Rodrik 1991), the decision to go to war (Fearon 1995), the signing and ratification of international treaties (Hollyer and Rosendorff 2011, 2012; Mansfield, Milner, and Rosendorff 2002), legislative committee assignments (Gilligan and Krehbiel 1987), and the provision of public goods for different ethnic groups in a society (Habyarimana et al. 2009).

Others may be obscured: Are prices at the market impacted by barriers to trade? Moreover, the evaluation of many outcomes depends on the dissemination of information across a broad swath of society: How strong, for example, is the overall performance of the economy? Addressing questions of the last type requires aggregate economic data. So the dissemination of aggregate economic data may represent the key facet of transparency necessary for citizens to hold their governments accountable on the issues that matter most for daily life.

Throughout this book, we focus on the policy-outcome facet of transparency. Aggregate economic data inform individuals about policy outcomes experienced by broad segments of the population. We discuss other facets of transparency in order to distinguish the key dimension of transparency of interest for this book and to show how data disclosure relates to the other aspects of transparency. We also control for other measures of transparency where appropriate in the empirical sections of the book. So, Part I considers three broad categories of measures of transparency: (1) institutional measures, (2) measures of the media market, and (3) the dissemination of data.

1.1.1 Institutional Measures of Transparency

Institutional measures of transparency mainly reflect the openness of the policymaking process. Several studies (e.g., Broz 2002) measure this facet of transparency using the level of democracy (as reflected by the Polity index). Other commonly used institutional measures of transparency reflect the presence of freedom of information laws (FOILs) or the independence of central banks.[5] Information about the policymaking process may be valuable if citizens care about policies themselves – as opposed to the outcomes these policies produce. Or, they might be valuable if the outcomes of a given policy are obviously good/bad for their welfare. Examples might include simple instances of malfeasance: corruption, misappropriation, or inefficiency (see Di Tella and Schargrodsky 2003; Ferraz and Finan 2011).

1.1.2 Measures of the Media Market

A free and vibrant media can have a wide-ranging impact on the spread of information (Arnold 2013). Investigative pieces may relay information on the policy choices of governments to citizens. Media analyses and opinions may help to inform citizens of the mapping between policy choices and policy outcomes. And media reports may convey information on policy outcomes either via anecdotes about individuals directly affected by policy decisions or through the reporting of national data – assuming such data are available.

---

[5] See Berliner (2014); Islam (2006); Chortareas, Stasavage, and Sterne (2002); Keefer and Stasavage (2003); and Dreher, Sturm and De Haan (2010).

Individual news agencies, however, typically cannot invest the resources necessary to document movements in price indexes, levels of economic growth, levels of poverty, or education rates. The media are unable to collect this sort of information for two reasons. (1) The collection of such information often entails enormous fixed costs. (2) The collection of such information is subject to a public goods problem – once one news outlet collects and publicizes information on aggregate outcomes, other outlets may simply reproduce this information (Rodrik 1995). Facing high fixed costs, as well as the specter of free-riding, the mass media simply tend not to collect these measures. They rely, instead, on governments to collect aggregate economic data.

1.1.3 The Dissemination of Data

Aggregate economic data serve to inform individuals of the welfare of the whole society or some large segment of the population. Measures of this facet of transparency tend to focus on government disclosures because, as argued above, the combination of high fixed costs of collection and externalities in information dissemination tend to make the collection of aggregate data a natural monopoly dominated by the government.

Aggregate economic datasets hardly amount to the public's only source of information on policy outcomes. A free and vibrant media may examine the effects of government decisions as well as the decision-making process itself, while social networks allow individuals to share their individual experiences.

However, aggregate data are unique in their ability to summarize information regarding a large number of individual outcomes. Chapter 2 argues that the dissemination of aggregate data is most likely to be valuable when: (1) the public is imperfectly informed as to the optimal policy choice; (2) policy choices do not perfectly map into welfare implications for individuals; and (3) the policy in question affects a broad swath of the public.

The law of large numbers implies that data offer an increasingly precise signal of the appropriateness of government decisions as the level of aggregation rises. If individuals condition (at least partly) their decision to support the government based on outcomes for society as a whole, they need information on an aggregate level. Aggregate data may therefore play a critical role in mobilizing collective action (we discuss the issue of collective action extensively below).

Yet, recall that the government has near monopoly power in its ability to collect such data. If the government's survival in power depends on the release of data that it may control, how can anyone ever trust the data? Credibility is crucial.

Governments, of course, might fake economic data. Repeated lying by the government results in the public discounting any information from the government about the economy. If the government always reports, for example, that the economy is performing well, eventually no one will believe it. Or, if the government adds a few percentage points to economic growth each year, the threshold for what constitutes a "good" versus a "bad" outcome just shifts upward over time. Media outlets may still rely on faulty government information for their publications, but citizens learn to disregard incredible information.[6]

We theorize that some governments are more likely to provide credible economic data to the public and that the provision of such data generates consequences for economic performance and political stability. We must therefore differentiate between instances of credible communication of economic data and incredible communication. Rather than consider only the data provided to the public directly by their governments, we consider data provided by national governments to highly regarded international organizations.

Data available in the WDI represent, in essence, a joint decision between the national government to provide the information and the international organization to publish it. Throughout the book, we focus on the government decision. In what follows, however, we consider each part of the joint decision in turn.

Capacity and Willingness: The Government Decision to Disclose Data

A familiar reaction to our proposed index of data dissemination is that it is not a measure of transparency but rather a measure of state capacity. As countries develop economically, the government's tax base increases, enabling a larger and more sophisticated bureaucracy to collect and disseminate more and better quality economic data.

Following the influential study of Fearon and Laitin (2003: 76), we proxy for state capacity by using economic development as measured by gross domestic product (GDP) per capita (measured in terms of purchasing power parity – PPP). We find a positive correlation between our index and economic development and assure readers that all of the qualitative findings discussed in this book hold when we control for this factor.

We emphasize, however, that capacity is not the only determinant of the government decision to disseminate data. Willingness also matters. As evidence, we show in Chapter 4 that while the HRV index trends upward with GDP per capita, at every level of economic development, democracies tend to report more data than autocracies. In fact, while the relationship between development and the HRV index is positive and monotonic for democracies, the relationship is more complicated for autocracies.

The fact that democracies report data at higher levels than do autocracies at every level of economic development suggests that governments held to account by elections have greater *willingness* to disseminate data than governments whose survival does not depend on elections.

Within the estimation of the HRV index itself, we also find evidence of the importance of willingness to disclose. As presented in Part I of this book, the most discriminating factors across countries' levels of data dissemination relate

---

[6] Regarding the rationality of citizens choosing to discount the lies of government, we recommend the studies of Gehlbach and Sonin (2014) and Shadmehr and Bernhardt (2015).

to politically sensitive aspects of the economy (for example, trade and investment figures). The items that discriminate the least across countries relate to relatively uncontroversial concerns (for example, population size).[7] We would not expect these results if only capacity mattered. Willingness to disclose data on politically sensitive issues appears to play a prominent role in our index.

The intertemporal relationship between transparency and economic factors may also cast light on the relative contribution of capacity and willingness to variation in our measure. If transparency were simply a product of capacity, increases in government capacity – for instance, arising from high levels of economic growth – should translate into higher levels of disclosure. We examine such relationships in Part III of the book. In general, changes in growth today do a poor job of forecasting changes in disclosure tomorrow. In Chapter 10, for instance, we predict variation in transparency within autocratic regimes as a function of a series of time-varying economic characteristics, time-invariant regime characteristics, and the time a given leader has served in office.[8] Neither changes in GDP per capita, GDP, economic growth, openness to trade, nor participation in IMF programs evidence a significant relation with movements in transparency. Changes in government consumption correlate with variations in transparency, and this relationship borders on statistical significance, but it is negative. Greater spending, if anything, translates into lower transparency in autocracies, cutting against a capacity hypothesis. Other than the lagged value of disclosure, the only time-varying factor that correlates strongly with transparency is an indicator for the assumption of power by a new dictator. In this sample at least, politics trumps economics – factors related to the willingness to disclose exhibit a more consistent relationship with transparency than factors relating to capacity.

Moreover, the view that the HRV index proxies only state capacity can make little sense of our major results. High capacity should make states more resilient to mass unrest. Yet for autocracies, mass unrest increases with the HRV index making autocratic governments increasingly likely to fall from power. Meanwhile, the HRV index has the opposite relationship with democracies. The fact that political institutions mediate the effects of the HRV index again suggests the importance of willingness.

Scholars disagree over whether capacity or willingness trumps in the decision to report data.[9] Our extensive examination of patterns of data disclosure and political institutions leads to the conclusion that *both* matter. In order for a

---

[7] We present these discrimination items in detail in Section 3.4.1 and discuss their implications for the willingness–capacity debate in Section 4.5.

[8] Original publication credit for parts of Ch. 10 goes to *Journal of Conflict Resolution*, where the printed article is soon expected (Hollyer, Rosendorff, and Vreeland forthcoming).

[9] On willingness, see Bueno de Mesquita et al. (2003) and Williams (2009). On capacity, see Stone (2008). Studies highlighting the importance of both include Edwards, Coolidge, and Preston (2012); Lall (2016); and Lorentzen, Landry, and Yasuda (2010). For a formal treatment of the impact of low bureaucratic capacity on governance, see Huber and McCarty (2004). For a novel approach to measuring state capacity, see the recently published Lee and Zhang (2017).

government to collect and then report data on aggregate economic outcomes to international organizations, the state must have both the capacity and the willingness to do so.

International Standards: The World Bank Decision to Publish Data

International organizations act as credible third parties for our research purposes because they provide data-collection guidelines for governments and they uphold data-quality standards. Certainly the quality of data provided by international organizations is not perfect.[10] There are known instances where governments sneaked faulty data past the most reputable of international institutions. Nevertheless, the standards upheld by these institutions do lead them to reject poor quality data. When data are poorly collected, incorrectly calculated, or simply faked, international organizations can refuse to publish the data. If faulty data sneak through, they can be rejected retroactively.

In the construction of our index of transparency, therefore, we rely on data reported – or not reported – in the World Bank's WDI data series. The World Bank has organized a comprehensive set of data collected by various international organizations including the International Monetary Fund, the International Labour Organization, the Organization for Economic Cooperation and Development, and various agencies of the United Nations.

These organizations omit data for various specific reasons. Sometimes national governments simply fail to report data to them. Other times, governments do not collect data according to the appropriate international standards. In other cases, international organizations judge nationally reported data to be too far from the truth. The World Bank and International Monetary Fund (IMF) collaborate to establish standards for reporting – the General Data Dissemination System (GDDS) framework. They also monitor the ability of national statistical agencies to adhere to the GDDS through the Data Quality Assessment Framework (DQAF).[11] The DQAF and the GDDS encourage governments to improve the integrity and quality of data on economic and demographic data, providing comprehensive information in an accessible and timely manner.[12]

We note that the World Bank decision regarding publication of data may vary between measures reported in local currency versus US dollars: it engages

---

[10] See, for example, Coremberg (2004); Kaufmann and Bellver (2005); Alt, Lassen, and Rose (2006); Rauch et al. (2011); Irwin (2012); Jerven (2013); Michalski Stoltz (2013); Alt, Lassen, and Wehner (2014); Linsi and Mügge (2017); and Kerner and Crabtree (2018).

[11] See http://data.worldbank.org/about/data-overview/data-quality-and-effectiveness, accessed July 4, 2017. See also the World Bank statements about the World Development Indicators: http://data.worldbank.org/about/data-programs, accessed July 4, 2017. For a critical evaluation of the institutional design and effectiveness of the IMF's Special Data Dissemination Standard (SDDS), see Mosley (2003). For an analysis of the effectiveness of the SDDS using the HRV index, see Cooray and Vadlamannati (2015).

[12] See http://dsbb.imf.org/Pages/GDDS/WhatIsGDDS.aspx, accessed July 4, 2017.

in an additional level of scrutiny when reporting figures in US dollar amounts. For example, the World Bank has explained that "It is possible that a country will have reported values for GDP in local current prices, but not constant – or constant prices but not current. This occurs if there are breaks in series or the originally reported growth rates appear to be unrealistic – or growth estimates are available, but actual current price data are not."[13] When measures are available both in local currency and US dollars, we use the latter in the construction of the HRV index.

One issue that we have thought carefully about is the fact that the World Bank sometimes updates and fills data in the WDI after the original release. For many countries, there is a drop-off in the reporting of data in the final years of the current data series that we used, likely because there had not been sufficient time to fill in all missing data. (For this reason, we exclude the final two years of data in our main regression analyses throughout the book.) We considered using original releases of data by the World Bank instead of the current version available through the WDI website. We decided to use current World Bank data as opposed to original releases of the data in order to take the most conservative approach to transparency. Note that we use the data from the World Bank as a proxy for credible data available to citizens. If data are missing on the original dates of publication, and not subsequently "backfilled" we can be relatively sure that credible data were not available either currently or at the date in question. A less conservative approach would involve using the original releases of data from the WDI. The original releases of data can be obtained on CD-ROM (and are, therefore, not subsequently updated) for years beginning in the early 1990s through 2008. In principle, one could re-create our index for a smaller subset of years as a comparative measure.

We thus acknowledge that our measure may have a tendency to over-report transparency. Of course, such over-reporting should tend to reduce variance and thus bias against finding correlations with other phenomena, such as political stability or economic performance. Given our theory, predictions, and results, we feel confident in the conservative approach that we have used in generating our measure of transparency.

Item Response Theory

For all the care we have taken in thinking about what should go into our HRV Index, we acknowledge that some people may disagree with our decisions and that mistakes may be included for various reasons, as noted above. For these and other reasons discussed in this section, we employ a rigorous approach – which directly addresses potential idiosyncrasies – to estimate our measure of transparency.

---

[13] The quoted text is originally from http://data.worldbank.org/about/faq/specific-data-series, accessed March 5, 2013. The text can now be found through this link: https://web.archive.org/web/20131003011711/http://data.worldbank.org/about/faq/specific-data-series.

Suppose we mistakenly include among our 240 variables some factors that are unrelated to the underlying propensity to report credible data published by the WDI. Maybe the data are so easy/hard to collect that they bear no systematic relationship with the unobserved propensity to report. The IRT estimation procedure is designed to down-weight the importance of reporting (or not reporting) such variables.

Similarly, there may be idiosyncratic instances where data may be omitted from (or included in) the WDI. Perhaps data are mistakenly coded as missing for particularly small values. Alternatively, we have heard stories where very large values used to be mistakenly coded as missing back when computer memory restrictions prevented the entry of an extreme value. The IRT algorithm, again, down-weights the importance of reporting items that are omitted or included in the WDI for idiosyncratic reasons.

IRT enables us to treat a state's tendency to disclose credible economic data as a latent term predicting the availability of data on 240 variables from the WDI data series. Note that we take advantage of something that usually stands as a hindrance to cross-national research: missing data. In our context, missing data *are* data. Either a country reports data on a variable for a given year, or it does not. From this perspective, there are no missing data.

Governments can collect data for some of these 240 variables with ease, while the collection of data for others may prove difficult. Reporting some information may distinguish a country as particularly transparent, while the reporting of other data may not discriminate much across countries. So, we do not rely simply on the percentage of variables reported. Instead, we estimate our latent variable using a dynamic IRT model, which ensures minimal loss of information from collapsing a 240 dimensional observation into a single-dimensional representation. The index has a consistent meaning over time and covers 125 countries from 1980 to 2010.

As we explain in Chapter 3, IRT allows us to go beyond merely *calculating* the amount of data reported. Rather, we *estimate*, using the well-established IRT approach, the propensity of governments to report credible data published by international organizations. The reporting of certain data have greater influence on the overall index if those items are especially predictive of the reporting of other variables. The estimation procedure thus has certain features of which skeptical readers should take note.

HRV Index Advantages

This approach offers several advantages over earlier measures of data disclosure. Our index – the HRV index – provides a precise estimation of a limited but important component of transparency. We emphasize that our measure does not capture all facets of transparency, and our measure of aggregate data disclosure is of most value when examining government accountability with regards to policies with uncertain outcomes.

Our measure is crisply defined, reproducible, and important as an intrinsically interesting outcome variable and also as a potential explanatory variable. We encourage scholars to use it – along with other appropriate measures of other facets of transparency – to test hypotheses about the relationships between transparency and accountability, governance, and democracy.

Before we proceed to use our measure, however, we must emphasize that we envision the HRV index as an *approximation* for the availability of credible data in society. Nowhere in the book do we argue that citizens seeking economic information need to check with World Bank figures. We do not expect the average citizen to look at national account figures at all. Rather, citizens seek to infer the state of the economy (or social welfare) and the government's role therein. We contend that citizens are better able to do so when accurate data are available. This availability of credible data, which correlates with the free flow of information about the economy, also correlates with the publication of data by the World Bank in the WDI. Of course, accessing the availability and credibility of free-flowing information about the economy directly – for a panel dataset of 125 countries would be daunting, if not impossible, to do from scratch – especially going back historically more than 30 years. We employ our measure of the provision of credible data to the WDI, which can be observed, as an approximation of this unobserved quantity.

One insight of this project is recognizing that the World Bank has actually collected the information to generate this proxy variable by choosing to exclude data from the WDI. Missing data represent instances where a national government has failed to report credible information about the economy. Either the national government failed to release information or the government released information that was sufficiently manipulated so that the World Bank (or the international organizations from which the World Bank sources data) chose to omit it. The decisions of international organizations to report data as missing likely indicate that the government failed to report credible information to any audience. After all, if the government reported credible data at the domestic level, there is little incentive to withhold it from international organizations. Thus the HRV index closely approximates the availability of aggregate economic data on a yearly basis for national audiences across the globe.

1.2 TRANSPARENCY, STABILITY, AND HIGHER-ORDER BELIEFS

Having introduced our measure of transparency in Part I, we explore the consequences of releasing economic data for political stability in Part II. Throughout this section, we pay careful attention to confounding factors, selection bias, and endogeneity. Because we use the world as our laboratory, we do not enjoy random or even quasi-experimental settings. We rely on rigorously developed theory supplemented by carefully analyzed data along with key empirical examples.

Our exploration of political stability begins with the observation that governments, whether autocratic or democratic, depend on at least a minimal level of consent from their populace to survive in office. Should large masses of citizens turn out in protest or revolt against their leaders, regimes of any type will rapidly find the polity ungovernable.

Mass demonstrations are, obviously, collective acts; to be successful, they require the coordination and participation of large numbers of citizens. The relevant concern is whether any single citizen can infer the willingness of other individuals to take part in demonstrations against the ruling regime. We call this collective willingness to protest against the government the "distribution of discontent."

The distribution of discontent is not common knowledge across the citizenry. Regardless of the level of dissatisfaction of any individual citizen, she cannot know with certainty the number of her fellow citizens who are similarly dissatisfied. She is also likely to be aware that other citizens cannot perfectly infer her own level of dissatisfaction.

That is, citizens cannot perfectly refine their "higher-order beliefs" – their beliefs about the beliefs held by others – regarding their respective willingness to participate in a protest movement. Part II examines the ways in which the dissemination of macroeconomic data informs citizens' higher-order beliefs about the distribution of discontent under democracy and autocracy, respectively.

1.2.1 Democratic Stability

Thanks to competitive elections, citizens living under democracy enjoy a rich informational environment with respect to the distribution of discontent – even without the dissemination of economic data. Election returns, participation in election rallies, and public statements by candidates and citizens surrounding elections all serve as public signals to the citizenry of the distribution of discontent. It is for this reason that Fearon (2011) argues that democracy is self-enforcing. Should an incumbent fail to heed electoral results, any given citizen is likely to be aware that many others are willing to protest this behavior and demand the incumbent's ouster (see also Little, Tucker, and LaGatta 2015; Weingast 1997). In the presence of free and fair elections, citizens do not need to rely on aggregate economic data to facilitate protest. The distribution of discontent emerges as common knowledge through the electoral process and other forms of information are left to play marginal roles in updating beliefs.

Nevertheless, the subversion of electoral outcomes plagues the history of democratic rule in many countries. Opponents of democracy see voters as misinformed, fickle, or irrational. In low-transparency democracies, voters rely on noisy economic signals or vote according to issues that do not correspond to economic performance. Campello and Zucco (2016), for example, show that reelection prospects in Latin America have, historically, depended on factors unrelated to incumbents' policy choices, and many have observed voting along ethnic lines in other developing regions (Chandra 2004, 2005, 2006). Poorly performing incumbents often win reelection in such settings, and good leaders may lose, leading to lower confidence in the democratic process (Svolik 2013c). In the face of such skepticism, the dissemination of aggregate economic data can play a role in legitimizing electoral rule. Macroeconomic transparency helps inform voters so that they make better individual decisions, voting in favor of high-performing incumbents and against the rascals.

Greater availability of information ensures that democratic institutions better resolve problems of political agency, leading to outcome legitimacy. As citizens' votes align more closely with incumbents' performance, elections work better – whether "better" is defined in terms of selecting "good" types of politicians or inducing "bad" types to act in the public interest. Under transparency, the democratic process better serves its intended role, delivering and retaining public-minded governments in power.

A richer informational environment also makes voters more likely to view their fellows as behaving in an informed manner. As more information is made publicly available, it grows less feasible for anti-democratic forces to rally subgroups of citizens against democratic institutions by claiming that others' votes are ill-informed and illegitimate. Transparency thus vests the democratic process with greater procedural legitimacy.

Both of these legitimizing effects – outcome and procedural – point in the same direction with regard to democratic survival. *Democracies are more likely to endure, and less likely to revert to autocracy, as public information becomes more readily available.* In our empirical examination in Chapter 7 we find that when holding economic growth to its median value, an increase in transparency of one standard deviation reduces the risk of democratic collapse by between 45 and 85 percent.

1.2.2 Autocratic Instability

The informational environment plays a radically different role under autocracy. Elections, if the government holds them at all, do not permit citizens to throw out a poorly performing incumbent government. Citizens struggle to ascertain the distribution of discontent and thus rely more heavily on aggregate economic data if any become available. The theoretical model presented in Chapter 5 reveals that as more information becomes available, underperforming autocrats are more likely to be revealed as such. A richer informational environment thus destabilizes an autocratic regime.

More precisely, data dissemination can destabilize autocracy. If protest is difficult, citizens must have great confidence that their demonstration will prove successful before they are willing to take to the streets. They need to know that masses of other citizens will protest as well. In an environment where public information is scant, this level of confidence is unlikely to ever be attained. So, regardless of their performance, autocratic leaders are unlikely to face much threat from the public.

As transparency about the economy increases, underperforming leaders face greater risks of protest, while the risks faced by those autocrats who deliver economic growth and public goods remain largely unchanged (and low). Hence, the overall probability of regime collapse rises as more public information becomes available. A rich informational environment serves to destabilize autocratic regimes facing threats from their mass publics.

In our empirical examination in Chapter 7, we find that increasing transparency increases the likelihood of (1) autocratic collapse via democratization, (2) autocratic collapse with replacement by a new autocracy, and (3) incidences of mass unrest – specifically demonstrations and strikes against the government. In other words, *transparency hurts the prospects of the survival of autocracy.*

To anticipate some specific findings, we estimate that a one standard deviation increase in the level of transparency (1) increases the chances of democratization by between 38 and 61 percent, and (2) increases the risk of autocratic collapse due to mass unrest by between 40 and 50 percent. Interestingly, while an increase in transparency is associated with an increase in mass unrest, we find that an increase in transparency actually reduces the likelihood of a coup. Compared with the effect on mass unrest under autocracy, transparency appears to have a different effect on coups and leadership shake-ups – findings to which we return below.

1.3 WHY DISCLOSE

Part II shows that the consequences of transparency for regime stability depend on domestic political institutions: transparency stabilizes democracies and destabilizes autocracies. Part III thus examines in rigorous detail the decision of governments to disclose. The section begins with the intuitive and then moves into the counterintuitive. First we show that transparency delivers economic benefits by increasing domestic and foreign investment (Chapter 8). For democracies, we show that beyond the incentive of economic benefits, electoral contestation further incentivizes the government to publicly disclose data (Chapter 9). Chapter 10 tackles a less intuitive question: Why would autocracies disclose data? If autocrats mainly worry about survival in power, the economic benefits of investment may be outweighed by the increased risk of mass unrest brought about by increased transparency. Thus we explore the *political* logic of disclosing data under autocracy. We present a rather shocking and insidious calculus: autocrats disclose in order to encourage mass unrest so as to aggravate fears among inner-circle elites and thus increase their loyalty toward supporting the regime.

1.3.1 Transparency and Investment

Gauging effects on overall economic performance is notoriously difficult to do with precision (Roodman 2007b; Dreher et al. 2013). Economic growth, for example, represents a rather "noisy" measure, which fluctuates for various idiosyncratic reasons. As throughout the book, we again take a narrow and precise approach to estimate transparency's effects. Chapter 8 addresses the effect of transparency on investment.

Analyzing investment patterns lets us focus on the first step in the causal chain going from transparency to economic performance. We propose that greater availability of information on the macroeconomy reduces risk and thus encourages investment. We further argue that the dissemination of aggregate economic data acts as a costly signal from governments to markets of a commitment to investment-friendly policies.

Empirically, we find that an increase in transparency of one standard deviation results in an increase in *domestic* investment (gross capital formation) of between 0.03 and 0.43 percentage points in terms of GDP. Closer examination of our results on domestic investment reveals that they are driven mainly by democracies in the sample. Increasing macroeconomic transparency thus may have more of an effect in democracies where so many more investment decisions come from the private sector. Among autocracies, oil monarchies and former communist states (for example, China and Vietnam) have the highest levels of investment share of GDP, and these states are not the most transparent states (petro-states score particularly poorly). Investment in these states is dominated by the government itself, so our theory does not apply; presumably, governments can make their investment decisions regardless of the data they provide to the public.

We find an effect of transparency on *foreign* direct investment (FDI) for both regime types. We attribute these results to greater confidence that foreign investors can have – in a country's economy and in its policymaking – when more information about aggregate economic activities is available to them. FDI flows are usually private and tend to be controlled by those unaffiliated with the regime. They also represent a fixed commitment of investors – unlike portfolio investment, FDI is not easily liquidated. Hence FDI may be more influenced by transparency than other forms of investment. Indeed, the positive effect of transparency – for both democracies and autocracies – is unambiguous. Specifically, we find that a one standard deviation increase in transparency results in an increase in FDI as a percentage of GDP of between 0.1 and 0.55 percentage points. When we consider absolute flows, we estimate an effect of between \$39 million and \$871 million per year.

We suspect that the economic benefits of transparency are numerous and our focus on investment represents a starting point for inquiry.[14] For a theoretical perspective, we contend that investment is a good place to begin because investors rely on economic data to make assessments about the future, and missing data may stand out to them as a red flag. Moreover, many other economic benefits, such as the long-run growth of the economy, stem from

---

[14] Our study of the correlation between the HRV index and investment follows Shen and Sliwinski (2015), who look at the effect of the HRV index on foreign direct investment (FDI) and Clore and McGrath (2015), who investigate the HRV index and patterns of domestic investment.

investment. Now, there may be other economic benefits that result directly from transparency and we hope that other researchers will use the HRV index to investigate them.[15] Here we seek to stimulate further research on the economic benefits of data transparency.

1.3.2 Why Democracies Disseminate More Data than Autocracies

Citizens and investors have good reasons to seek out data on aggregate outcomes; states have reasons to withhold these data. Regarding citizens and investors, the availability of data enables them to make judgments about the performance of the government and its policies. Citizens can compare outcomes under the present regime to those under previous regimes or to those of neighboring countries and to worldwide averages. These comparisons can help people to calibrate the risks of making financial investments in the country and also to decide whether to support the current political regime or seek to evict it from office.

States may wish to avoid these judgments, if possible. Authority seems to have a natural tendency toward obfuscation. Opacity permits governments to blame questionable policies on others, to obscure the distribution of the payoffs (or "rents") to political supporters, and to engage in outright corruption without detection. The dissemination of information empowers others, while the very collection of economic data entails burdensome costs on governments. All else being equal, governments prefer opacity.

But all else is not equal. Governments face a trade-off between maximizing social welfare and enjoying the benefits of obfuscation. Providing credible data facilitates economic transactions at the same time as it sheds light on the outcomes of government policies. As Stiglitz (2002) argues, governments have incentives both to restrict and facilitate the flow of information.

Some governments have explicit incentives to care more about social welfare than others – and this welfare improves as the economy functions more smoothly. We argue that contested elections incentivize governments to disseminate economic data because the political benefits of improved economic performance outweigh the costs leaders incur when they eliminate opportunities for obfuscation.

Often people simply assume that democracies are more transparent than autocracies. As Shapiro (2003: 200) writes, "democratic leaders can never be entirely free from a commitment to truth-telling." The logic underlying this argument, however, can be called into question. Indeed, their greater vulnerability to public disapproval may make democratic officials more inclined to obfuscate or withhold information than their autocratic counterparts who need worry less about public perceptions.

---

[15] For example, Shambaugh and Shen (2017) show that when inflation and currency crises strike, higher values of the HRV index correlate with shorter and less severe crises.

For instance, Mani and Mukand (2007) and Bueno de Mesquita (2007) argue that democratic governments, more so than authoritarian ones, have incentives to allocate resources to public goods that are highly visible, while suboptimally allocating efforts toward less visible matters. Kono (2006) argues that democratic governments promote the transparency of trade policy areas where they can take actions that please voters, while they actively obscure policy areas where government action goes against the will of the majority. Rejali (2007) makes a related case with respect to human rights, arguing that political regime influences the type of torture techniques a government may employ but not whether they will engage in torture, as democratic governments opt for "clean" techniques that leave no visible trace (see also Conrad, Hill, and Moore 2014).[16] All of these studies, which are supported by empirical evidence, argue that the policymaking of democratic governments is shaped by transparency and, importantly, that democratic governments have incentives to obfuscate evidence.

We thus ask a basic question: Do electoral politics in and of themselves provide any incentives for governments to disseminate data? Or, instead, do electoral politics intrinsically generate incentives for governments to hide information? Chapter 9 builds a theoretical argument as to the conditions under which governments prefer to make information available to their polities about their policy choices. This information allows voters to make informed decisions regarding investment and consumption that raise voter welfare. In electoral systems where the survival of the government depends more strongly on voter welfare – that is, in democracies – the government is more willing to disclose policy information. By so doing, it helps to promote the welfare of voters and thus ensure its continued survival in office.

Our substantive conclusion is straightforward: electoral competition is associated with greater data dissemination. Specifically, the estimated cumulative long-run impact of a shift from autocracy to democracy is to increase transparency levels by roughly 5 units. This is a large marginal effect, equivalent to just under one-quarter the distance from the minimum to maximum observed transparency scores on our index. *Despite any potential electoral incentives toward obfuscation in other circumstances, democratic governments are more likely to release policy-relevant data than are autocracies.* This finding confirms what has often been taken for granted about democracy and transparency.

1.3.3 Why Autocrats Disclose

If governments have a natural predilection for opacity, and autocrats face a particular threat of mass unrest from the disclosure of economic data, why would

---

[16] Relatedly, Rudra and Bastiaens (forthcoming) show that democratically elected governments face constraints making it more difficult for them to raise tax revenue, compared to the ability of authoritarian governments.

an autocratic government ever tolerate transparency? We reexamine in more detail the question of why autocrats choose to disclose aggregate economic data in Chapter 10. We contend that the answer lies in the interplay between mass and elite politics.

Domestically, autocratic leaders face two basic threats that might upend their rule: one from below and one from within. Collective protest by masses of the citizenry constitutes a threat from below. Meanwhile, elites may lie in wait – within the regime – ready to use administrative maneuvers or even carefully calculated violence to replace the sitting leadership.

These two types of threats – mass insurrection and elite-led coups – interact. Elites opposing the leadership from within cannot always disguise their activities. Any action that they take against the leadership may signal to the public the fractured and weak state of the regime, providing a spark for mass protest. Mass unrest carries the potential to displace the regime as a whole – including most, if not all, members of the elite. Before attempting to discipline their leaders, therefore, autocratic elites must consider the implications of their actions for their own continued survival in privileged positions (Besley and Persson 2007; Bueno de Mesquita et al. 2003).

An autocratic leader can more easily cow fellow elites into quiescence when the mass public is particularly capable of mobilization. Increased transparency, and other liberalizing reforms, may therefore reduce the threat that autocratic leaders face from within the regime, even as it increases the threat from below.

This argument fits with the results mentioned above, that transparency increases the likelihood of regime collapse due to mass unrest even as it reduces the risk of coup under autocracy. The argument also suggests that autocratic leaders should increase levels of transparency when facing particularly high threats from within the regime. For example, elites within the ruling class may be more likely to topple the leadership when the leader is new to office or when legitimacy is vested in institutions rather than the personality of the particular leader. Chapter 10 shows, indeed, that transparency rises when autocratic leaders are new to office and is lower in personalistic regimes as compared to other types of autocracies.

Our analyses of the effects of data dissemination lead to nuanced conclusions. Democracies see only benefits, both in terms of financial investment and political stability. But several factors complicate the decision for autocratic regimes to disseminate aggregate economic data. Increasing transparency in this regard can attract investment – but it also introduces competing risks with respect to political stability. If the key objective of an autocrat is survival in power, concerns about stability may dominate their decision. If transparency leads to mass unrest, the regime may prefer not to disclose data. But if a leader can use the threat of mass unrest to shore up loyalty among the ruling elite, it may be worth the gamble.

1.4 IMPLICATIONS FOR POLICYMAKERS

Enhancing the informational environment can encourage normatively desirable outcomes. Better access to aggregate economic data allows investors and voters to make better decisions. Consequently, we find that increases in the dissemination of aggregate economic data serve to increase investment and stabilize democratic rule. Indeed, for democracies, a rich informational environment represents an unambiguous good. Greater information complements democratic institutions and renders them more robust, reducing the threat of transition to autocracy.

For autocrats, improving the informational environment constitutes a risky wager. On the one hand, it raises the risk of mass protest and democratization. But, on the other hand, this risk may insulate leaders against internal threats.

Policymakers recognize the complex political economy of increased transparency under autocratic regimes. In their quest to engender economic development, encouraging autocrats to disclose economic data might have destabilizing effects. If policy goals include democracy promotion, one might welcome this instability as democratic transitions become more likely. But other outcomes remain possible, including the replacement of an old autocracy by another, or even the entrenchment of the current leader against threats from (potentially more desirable) elements within the regime. The possible benefits of transparency may not always be worth the threat to political stability.

In our final chapter, we must, therefore caution against the wholesale embrace of promoting transparency. One might even counsel against the imprudent imposition of transparency standards on precarious autocracies.

1.5 ACADEMIC AUDIENCES: COMPARATIVE POLITICS, INTERNATIONAL RELATIONS, AMERICAN POLITICS, AND PUBLIC CHOICE

We hope that our research on the questions of transparency and political stability reaches several audiences in different subfields of political science. We flag particular insights from this book that may be of interest to scholars who work in the fields of comparative politics, international relations, and American politics, as well as political economists who work in the area of public choice.

1.5.1 Comparative Politics

With our focus on democratization, the most obvious subfield of interest for our work is comparative politics. Our findings speak directly to one of the most well-known correlations within this subfield: the positive relationship between economic development and the survival of democracy (Przeworski et al. 2000). We show that our measure of transparency also correlates with the survival of democracy. The finding holds when we control for economic development, as measured by GDP per capita, measured in terms of purchasing power parity (PPP). Indeed, in our model specifications, we have found the effect of the HRV transparency index to be more robust than the effect of GDP per capita.

Because the HRV index and GDP per capita are correlated themselves, we do not suggest that the democracy–development link is wrong. Rather, we offer a new causal mechanism to explain the connection between economic development and democracy.[17] As democracies develop economically, governments expand their capacity to collect and disseminate aggregate economic data. As we have discussed, the availability of such data improves the individual voting decisions, procedural legitimacy, and outcome legitimacy of contested elections. We suggest, then, that one reason that developed democracies survive is that they enjoy higher levels of macroeconomic transparency.

Our work also speaks to the rich and growing literature on the survival of autocracy.[18] We build on existing theoretical models of authoritarian control, showing specifically how the transparency of the macroeconomic environment influences the likelihood of collective protest. We propose to explain (1) the transition of autocracy to democracy, (2) the replacement of one autocracy by another, and (3) the entrenchment of autocratic rule. Empirically, we offer a measure tightly linked to the theoretical parameter of interest.

For the broader comparative politics audience, our work speaks to ongoing phenomena of great interest. For example, our work has implications to help understand the mass unrest that spread during the Arab Spring in 2010, which was fueled in part by the availability of new technology to share information under authoritarian rule. We have also used our approach to explain more recent events, such as the failed coup attempt in Turkey in 2016.[19] We thus offer the subfield of comparative politics a new theoretical and empirical approach to analyzing the association between information and political stability.

---

[17] The vast literature includes contributions, such as Londregan and Poole (1996); Boix (2003); Boix and Stokes (2003); Epstein et al. (2006); Acemoglu and Robinson (2006); and Acemoglu et al. (2008).

[18] See, for example, Wintrobe (1998); M. Howard (2002); Levitsky and Way (2002); Boix (2003); Boix and Stokes (2003); Gandhi and Przeworski (2006, 2007); Gandhi (2008); Ansell and Samuels (2010); Boix and Svolik (2013); Shadmehr and Bernhardt (2011, 2015, n.d.); Freeman and Quinn (2012); Svolik (2008, 2012, 2013a, 2013b, 2013c, 2015); Casper and Tyson (2014); Weiss (2014); Little, Tucker, and LaGatta (2015); Albertus (2015); and Clark, Golder, and Golder (2017).

[19] See "What makes governments resistant to coups? Transparency with voters," by James R. Hollyer, B. Peter Rosendorff, and James Raymond Vreeland, "The Monkey Cage," *Washington Post*, August 5, 2016, www.washingtonpost.com/news/monkey-cage/wp/2016/08/05/where-are-coups-more-likely-to-occur-heres-what-we-found-after-looking-at-125-countries, accessed July 26, 2017.

1.5.2 International Relations

This research project centers on the data collected and disseminated by the World Bank. Going back to at least 1996, when World Bank President James Wolfensohn articulated "the concept of the Knowledge Bank," this international institution has claimed that one of its principal purposes is to "manage and disseminate" knowledge (World Bank 2011: vii, x). One of the main arguments that Abbott and Snidal (1998: 20) make in their seminal work on why states act through centralized and independent international organizations is that these organizations can serve as a "neutral information provider."

In our work, we take the World Bank and the international relations literature on international organizations at their words, viewing this institution as a data repository and relying on it as a neutral and independent third party that validates the aggregate economic data provided by national governments as credible (on the "credibility hypothesis" of international institutions, see Gilardi 2002; Majone 1994, 1997). Still, we note that World Bank staff and management are members of epistemic communities who shape ideas about how economies should work by deciding which variables and which data to include in the WDI.[20] We thus encourage scholars to critically consider the variables included in the HRV index and offer a methodology to construct alternative transparency indexes based on the reporting of various subsets of variables.

To the extent that we treat the World Bank as neutral and independent repository of data, this book follows the institutionalist approach to international relations – specifically Rosendorff's previous work on trade (with Edward Mansfield and Helen V. Milner) and his work on human rights (with James R. Hollyer). In this body of research, international institutions act as independent third parties that governments can use to convey credible information to domestic constituents. In the work on trade, democratic leaders use preferential trade agreements to credibly convey their commitment to free trade policies (Mansfield, Milner, and Rosendorff 2000, 2002).[21] In the work on human rights, authoritarian leaders use the United Nations Convention Against Torture to credibly convey their commitment to *violate* human rights (Hollyer and Rosendorff 2011).[22] In this book, the World Bank similarly acts as an independent third party conveying the credibility of macroeconomic data.

However, our use of the World Bank runs counter to much work on international institutions. As argued throughout this introductory chapter and the

---

[20] On the social construction of ideas in international political economy, see, for example, McNamara (1998); Barnett and Finnemore (1999); Johnston (2001); Blyth (2002); Darden (2009); and Abdelal, Blyth, and Parsons (2015). Regarding, specifically, the role of epistemic communities, see Haas (1992); Chwieroth (2007); Nelson (2014); and J. Johnson (2016).

[21] See also Milner (1997).

[22] See also Ritter and Conrad (2016); Conrad and Ritter (2013); Vreeland (2008); and Hathaway (2007). For an overview of the literature, see Hafner-Burton (2012).

rest of the book, we use the reporting (or not) of data to the World Bank as a *proxy* for the availability of credible information on the macroeconomy. The World Bank serves as a convenient independent third party for our data, which spans decades across the globe, because of the neutral and independent way it collects information from governments. In theory, however, one could code for the presence of credible data on a country-by-country, year-by-year basis looking at information available from national governments directly. We argue that this is, indeed, what the World Bank does, so there is no need for us to reinvent the wheel. But our primary theoretical interest is the availability of data domestically, and – in a sense – the international organization is epiphenomenal.[23]

1.5.3 American Politics

Sociotropic voting is central to our theory of how transparency of the economy influences the survival of democracy.

From the literature in American politics, going back at least to Hibbs (1982), we know that election outcomes correlate with macroeconomic indicators.[24] But sociotropic economic voting is more of an empirical regularity than a theory.[25] We know that people vote on the basis of retrospective assessments of aggregate economic performance, but the literature has offered limited microfoundations of why an individual rationally chooses to vote according to how society is doing instead of how she is doing. To the contrary, many retrospective voting models simply assume that aggregate economic outcomes approximate how the economy has performed for the median voter.[26]

Previous work suggests that truly sociotropic concerns might stem from a voter's altruistic preferences – a concern for others in society. Instead, they may come from risk aversion – if others are experiencing hardship, perhaps the voter is more likely to experience hardship too.

We offer here a novel approach to understanding what appears to be sociotropic political behavior. Aggregate level outcomes are more informative of the competence or public-mindedness of a leader than are the experiences of any individual. Because each voter knows she will be better off (on average) in the future with a competent leader who pursues the public interest – and because a public announcement of overall conditions provides superior information about the leader – she conditions her vote on both her private well-being as well as aggregated information about overall economic conditions.

---

[23] For discussions, see, for example, Mearsheimer (1994); Gruber (2000); and Drezner (2008).

[24] The comparative politics literature has also studied economic voting. See, for example, Tucker (2006); Duch and Stevenson (2008); and Kayser and Peress (2012).

[25] We are grateful to an anonymous reviewer for this suggestion and the language we use here.

[26] On retrospective voting, see, for example, Bartels (2008); Fiorina (1981); Ferejohn (1986); Stokes (2001); King et al. (2008); and Owen and Quinn (2016).

What may appear as a concern for the broader society is actually individually rational behavior prompted by better information.[27]

1.5.4 Public Choice: Data as a Public Good

An overarching purpose of this book is to draw attention to the importance of aggregate economic data as a public good. Public goods stand as a canonical market failure: because of problems of free-riding, markets famously under-supply them (Rodrik 1991). Political economists have used the logic of public goods to justify a role for the state in the economy.

We commonly hear arguments in favor of government provision of national defense and the protection of property rights, as well as government solutions to a host of externality problems ranging from protecting the environment to promoting research and development. Typically, however, the well-known list of public goods does not include the provision of aggregate economic data.

Given that our book shows just how important aggregate data can be for political stability and economic prosperity, we suggest that the omission of aggregate data from the list of standard public goods is an oversight in the literature. Just as Abbott and Snidal (1998) argue that collecting and dissemination information is a key purpose of international organizations, we argue that the collection and dissemination of information is also a key role for the state to play in the national economy.

Of course, as we proceed through our analyses of the effects of transparency, we remind the reader that any conclusions we draw should remain restricted to a narrow facet of the concept: the dissemination of aggregate economic data. To the extent that our measure does not address other aspects of transparency, we encourage readers to consider our methodology as a model to construct new measures with a similar level of rigor and objectivity.

In the first part of the book, we introduce our transparency measure in detail. We then use it throughout the book to explore the political economy of transparency. We return to wider implications – for scholars and policy-makers, respectively – in our concluding chapter.

---

[27] We thank an anonymous reviewer for highlighting this contribution.

PART I

FACETS OF TRANSPARENCY

> A popular Government, without popular information, or the means of acquiring it, is but a Prologue to a Farce or a Tragedy; or, perhaps both. Knowledge will forever govern ignorance: And a people who mean to be their own Governors, must arm themselves with the power which knowledge gives.
>
> James Madison, *The Founders' Constitution* (1822: vol. 1)

Transparency is multifaceted; it encompasses a variety of dimensions and definitions that have distinct determinants and effects. In Part I of this book, we contend that the optimal measure of transparency depends on the theoretical context. Ideally, theoretical models should specify exact forms of information transmission; empirical measures should precisely capture these specific dimensions; and empirical tests of theories should employ these precise measures (while controlling for alternative information transmission mechanisms). Most empirical work in economics and political science, however, has neglected the distinctions we identify, relying instead on proxies for a nebulous conception of "openness" when testing theories of transparency.

Part I investigates different approaches to thinking about transparency. We also offer a new measure of transparency – one that pertains to the public availability of aggregate economic data. After introducing our new measure – the HRV index – we then compare and contrast alternative forms of transparency.

Chapter 2 offers a framework for the conceptualization of various facets of transparency. We focus on the relationship between transparency (information) and political accountability. We therefore direct our attention to the transparency of (1) policy-making, (2) the causal connections between policies and outcomes, and (3) policy outcomes themselves.

In Chapter 3, we describe in detail our original measure, a specific form of transparency that focuses on the disclosure of aggregate economic data. This measure concerns the transparency of policy outcomes. The formal theories

29

presented in subsequent parts of this book rely on a concept of transparency directly related to our measure of data dissemination. The theoretical concept captures the precision with which the public can estimate aggregate outcomes of policy, such as economic growth, unemployment, and inflation. We thus use the HRV index throughout the book as a measure to test our theories empirically. We do not contend that the data-dissemination facet of transparency is always the most appropriate measure. Instead, we provide a framework that suggests which facets of transparency best reflect different theoretical mechanisms pertaining to political accountability.

We emphasize in Chapter 3 that the HRV measure of transparency has distinctive features from theoretical, methodological, and empirical points of view.

Theoretically, data on aggregate economic outcomes play a central role in political accountability. As argued in Chapter 1, while citizens may view transparency in the policymaking process as important, ultimately they may care most about policy outcomes. Because our index exactly targets the availability of credible economic data made public by governments, it serves as an appropriate measure to test theories pertaining to the transparency of policy outcomes. The HRV index thus captures a key facet of transparency for testing theories of whether citizens seek to hold governments accountable for policy outcomes.

Methodologically, we present a reproducible approach to estimate levels of transparency that avoids subjective judgments. As much as possible, we let the data "speak." In essence, our measure records the frequency with which governments report aggregate economic data to international agencies. However, we fit a measurement algorithm (following item response theory) to assess the extent of disclosure, which statistically assesses whether the reporting of any one variable should be weighted more heavily than the reporting of others. While limited in scope to the dissemination of economic data, compared to most measures of transparency, ours is objective.

Empirically, our measure elucidates certain patterns distinct from those generated by other commonly used measures of transparency, and Chapter 3 explores the empirical validity of the HRV measure. The chapter offers examinations of single countries across time as well as comparisons across countries at particular points in time. We present data from specific countries in Asia (China, Vietnam, and Cambodia), Africa (Zimbabwe, Somalia, and Zambia), Latin America (Argentina), and Europe (Hungary, Poland, Romania, and Bulgaria).

Chapter 4 further evaluates the HRV index empirically by directly comparing it to measures of other facets of transparency. This chapter presents data on freedom of information laws (FOILs), media freedom, the pervasiveness of media penetration, and democracy. The chapter also confronts the question of whether data dissemination is purely a question of state *capacity* or whether state *willingness* to disclose also plays a role.

Here, we show that the Freedom House index (see, for example, Karlekar and Dunham 2014) rates almost all low- and middle-income autocracies as nontransparent. The HRV index, by contrast, suggests greater nuances across autocratic regimes. Turning to high-income democracies, the HRV index of data dissemination rates this group of countries as more transparent than either Freedom House or measures based on newspaper circulation (from UNESCO and made publicly available through the World Bank – see Adserà, Boix, and Payne 2003). We also find that the HRV index correlates more strongly with a wide range of governance outcomes than does media circulation, especially for autocratic regimes.

Concerning the question of capacity versus willingness, we find that both matter. As countries become more economically developed, they are able to supply more data. But at each level of economic development we find that democracies choose to disclose more data than do autocracies. When it comes to missing data, some governments lack the resources while others lack the desire to disclose.

Differences across measures of transparency are not merely academic. Alternative measures can capture contrasting patterns with respect to political institutions, political stability, and economic performance. Part I seeks to arm our readers with a rigorous approach to thinking about measuring transparency. We also introduce our original measure of transparency, which we use in Parts II and III to test new theories of economic transparency and political stability.

2

The Content of Information

What does it mean to say a government is "transparent"? This chapter offers a brief and rigorous framework for the conceptualization of three key facets of transparency as it pertains to political accountability. The chapter also introduces some commonly used measures of transparency as they fit into our typology. We use some mathematical notation here, in anticipation of the game theoretic logic to be presented in Parts II and III of the book. Readers more interested in the empirical measure of transparency, its determinants, and its consequences may wish to skip to Chapter 3 where we describe in detail our original measure of transparency – the HRV index – which focuses on the disclosure of aggregate economic data. However, we encourage readers to familiarize themselves with the mathematical notation presented in this chapter, as well as the various facets of transparency presented here. Such a rigorous understanding of how transparency relates to political accountability can be used to isolate various causal channels through which the information environment can impact political stability.

We begin with a simple heuristic that crystalizes three facets of transparency that pertain to political accountability: (1) the choice of government policies, (2) the impact of those policies on outcomes, and (3) the outcomes themselves. In each case, we emphasize the importance of identifying what type of information is transmitted and to whom it is transmitted.

2.1 A FORMAL HEURISTIC FOR THE STUDY OF TRANSPARENCY AND POLITICAL ACCOUNTABILITY

Let a government choose a policy p from the set $\mathcal{P}$, $p \in \mathcal{P}$. There exists a set of citizens $\{1, 2, \ldots N\}$ denoted $\mathcal{I}$, where an individual citizen is indexed by i.[1] Each individual experiences some outcome y_i which is a function $g(\cdot)$ of the government's policy choice, plus some random noise ϵ_i, which is drawn from some distribution $f(\cdot)$. Let y be an aggregation of the outcomes for some subset $\mathcal{K} \subseteq \mathcal{I}$ of the population. Equations 2.1 and 2.2 express this heuristic mathematically:

$$y_i = g(p) + \epsilon_i \tag{2.1}$$

$$y = \sum_{k \in \mathcal{K} \subseteq \mathcal{I}} y_k \tag{2.2}$$

This model represents, of course, an extreme simplification. The assumption that the functional form of $g(\cdot)$, for example, remains constant across all citizens presupposes that there is a consistent definition of "good" policy. This assumption follows much of the literature on accountability and retrospective voting, but may not hold in many situations. One could instead consider that policies have varying effects for subsets of the population and focus, for instance, on the median voter. For ease of discussion, however, we focus on the simplest case.

We assume that each citizen i is directly aware only of her own outcome y_i. Political transparency may thus further inform citizen i of (1) the policy choice p of the government, (2) the functional form of $g(\cdot)$ mapping policy choices into outcomes, and (3) the outcomes experienced by some set $\mathcal{K}$ of citizens $\mathcal{K} \subseteq \mathcal{I}$ or an aggregation y, thereof. These three facets interact in crucial ways, which we examine in detail below.

In subsequent chapters, we focus on (3), transparency with regard to aggregated outcomes, y. To ease notation in those chapters, we impose some additional structure on the framework above. Specifically, we let individual outcomes be drawn from a symmetric distribution centered at zero with variance s^2. Specifically, let $\epsilon_i \sim N(0, s^2)$. Then the information contained in the aggregate signal is inversely proportional to $\frac{s^2}{|\mathcal{K}|} \equiv \sigma^2$, which we call "opacity." We can thus denote the dimension of transparency used throughout the ensuing chapters of this book as $\frac{1}{\sigma^2} \equiv \alpha$.

Moreover, we distinguish between (a) private knowledge – when individual i knows y_i, and perhaps y, and (b) common knowledge, when individual i knows that everyone else (or some subset of the population) has also observed y. Common knowledge concerns the aforementioned "higher-order beliefs" – beliefs about the beliefs of others. In subsequent chapters, we particularly examine information that is *public* – and hence that generates common knowledge – allowing citizens to update their higher-order beliefs.

---

[1] In this chapter, we treat the set of citizens as discrete, as is consistent with reality. In subsequent chapters, it will be mathematically convenient to consider a continuum of citizens, while otherwise maintaining the same notation.

2.1.1 Transparency of Policy Choices

Consider first information on the policy p adopted by the government. This dimension, often discussed in public discourse, refers to the policymaking process (Ferejohn 1999; Przeworski 2010). Advocacy organizations often call for an open policymaking environment, where citizens can easily find out which policy choices government officials make and why. The benefits to citizens from transparency of policymaking, however, critically depend on the state of knowledge about the effects of policies. If citizens only know p, they can hold governments accountable for bad policy choices only if they can recognize bad policies as such.

The welfare consequences of some policies are straightforward. For instance, there is likely to be little disagreement that corruption and misappropriation on the part of politicians is deleterious to all except, perhaps, those involved in the corruption scheme (though the size of the group of beneficiaries may vary – see Fernández-Vásquez, Barberá, and Rivero 2016). Indeed, advocacy organizations may have procurement policies in mind when calling for policymaking transparency so as to root out bribery, graft, nepotism, and other common forms of corruption (or simple discrimination – see Kono and Rickard 2014). Evidence shows that the release of audits of government policy choices and implementation does lead to an increase in the sanctioning of corrupt governments (Di Tella and Schargrodsky 2003; Ferraz and Finan 2011).[2]

In other circumstances, the relationship between policy choices and outcomes may be sufficiently complex and obscure that information regarding policy choices can play little role in enhancing leader accountability. Average citizens may remain rationally ignorant of the complex relationship between many policy choices and outcomes (Downs 1957) – particularly with respect to the minutiae of budgetary, tax, and trade policies, for example. As another example, witness the rather muted reaction by the US public to disclosures concerning NSA spycraft (via Edward Snowden). Perhaps because the welfare implications of these policies are ambiguous, the US public is less able to ensure government accountability with regards to national intelligence activities.

Putting the above in terms of our model, the implications of information about policy choices p hinge critically on whether the mapping from policies into outcomes $g(\cdot)$ is also known. When this mapping is known with certainty, transparency with respect to policy choices is sufficient to ensure accountability. When such certainty is absent, information on p is less useful – citizens cannot deduce the best policy and so cannot punish politicians for making the wrong choice.

---

[2] Klašnja (2015) shows that incumbents face disadvantages in winning reelection even if the electorate simply assumes corruption because the environment is such that corruption is too easy to commit. On the importance of oversight and monitoring of bureaucracies to curb corruption, see Guardado (2017).

2.1.2 Transparency of the Link between Outcomes and Policies

To make sense of policy choices, citizens need some understanding of how policy translates into outcomes: $g(\cdot)$. If the mapping $g(\cdot)$ is unknown, circumstances exist under which information about policy choices may actually reduce welfare. Prat (2005) presents a model where citizens are uncertain of the mapping $g(\cdot)$ – they have imperfect beliefs over which policies are right and which wrong. Politicians, who are better (but still imperfectly) informed of this mapping, must make a policy choice. Under these circumstances, transparency regarding this policy choice may cause politicians to ignore their private information and cater to the beliefs of the populace. In the event that the policy fails, the politician is less likely to be punished for following the conventional wisdom than for hewing a better but unconventional path.

Similarly, Stasavage (2004) demonstrates that transparency in the conduct of international negotiations may lead to increased posturing by government representatives, even if such posturing reduces the likelihood of finding an optimal compromise. Such posturing may lead citizens to believe that the representative is fighting for their interests, even as it reduces the likelihood achieving an optimal outcome.

Transparent policy-outcome connections can attenuate such problems. If citizens understand $g(\cdot)$, they can pressure governments to choose better policies.

As with information regarding policy choices, however, transparency with regards to the shape of $g(\cdot)$ may prove of little value on its own. This knowledge acts as a complement to knowledge of policy choices in ensuring government accountability. Information as to which policies would be optimal are of little use if the public cannot observe the policies the government actually adopts. Some information about $g(\cdot)$ may also complement the role of transparency with regards to policy outcomes in promoting accountability. To the extent that the public is better aware of what constitutes a feasible outcome, it can better judge whether current outcomes qualify as "good" or "bad."

2.1.3 Transparency of the Aggregate Outcomes of Policy

Consider the availability of information with regards to the welfare of other citizens – that is, information with regard to aggregate *outcomes*, y. The value of such information stands alone from knowledge of other aspects of the policymaking process. If outcomes for other citizens (y_k for $k \in \mathcal{K}$) are (or the aggregate outcome y is) poor, the public can readily infer that policy choices or implementation was also poor. Consequently, there is little disagreement in the theoretical literature that increasing citizen knowledge of policy outcomes improves accountability.[3]

---

[3] For a possible exception, see Ashworth and Bueno de Mesquita (2014). In their article, since high levels of transparency may induce good and bad politicians to pool in their actions in the first

Still, knowledge of what outcomes are feasible is necessary to define what constitutes a poor outcome. And, of course, a principal–agent problem remains because outcomes are a function of policy $g(\cdot)$ and luck $f(\cdot)$. The ability of citizens to draw inferences of government performance based on policy outcomes thus hinges critically on (1) the extent to which factors orthogonal to government decisions influence citizen welfare (that is, the distribution $f(\cdot)$), and (2) the magnitude of the effect of policy decisions on citizen welfare (that is, for any $p_1, p_2 \in \mathcal{P}$, $p_1 \neq p_2$, $g(p_1) - g(p_2)$). As the variance of outcomes rises and the effect of policies on individuals falls, information regarding policy outcomes must be increasingly aggregated to ensure government accountability. The larger the cardinality of $\mathcal{K}$, the higher the level of aggregation of these outcomes, and the more informative is knowledge of aggregate outcomes y.

Consider, for instance, an extreme example where $f(\cdot)$ is degenerate. That is, no factors other than government policies affect outcomes. An example might be the delivery of a government service – if a citizen's social security check fails to arrive, this can only be attributable to a failure by a branch of government. No additional information is necessary for citizens to attribute this failure to the government.

On the other hand, the overall economic well-being of any given citizen is attributable to many factors beyond the government's control. Knowledge of y_i, therefore, tells an individual citizen i little about the government's performance. The distribution of $f(\cdot)$ may be more or less dispersed – as the level of dispersion rises, the amount of information conveyed by the outcome for any one citizen (y_i) diminishes. As the distribution of $f(\cdot)$ grows more disperse, the need for aggregation rises.

For instance, to deduce the government's contribution to economic performance, citizens require more highly aggregated information than when evaluating performance with regards to the delivery of public services (for a related discussion, see Duch and Stevenson 2008). Such aggregate information provides value beyond that contained in any given citizen's personal experiences.[4] We can think of this principle as a "law of large numbers effect" with regards to aggregate information on policy outcomes. Knowledge of y may be more informative than knowledge of y_i.

We do not contend that the "law of large numbers effect" fully solves the informational problems faced by the populace. Even if aggregate economic

---

period of a two-period game, high levels of transparency may inhibit the screening out of bad politicians – with questionable welfare effects.

[4] This discussion relates to the literature on sociotropic versus "pocketbook" voting in American Politics (Kramer 1983; Markus 1988). Note further that the disclosure of increasingly accurate economic data would provide greater information not only regarding the average effectiveness of government policies on individual welfare, but also more information regarding the distribution of these effects. Such data might reflect particularly poor (strong) performance in certain sectors, geographic locations, or provide information about changes in the income distribution.

outcomes are fully known, assessing government responsibility for these outcomes is a difficult task. For instance, economic well-being may fluctuate with a variety of shocks orthogonal to government policy. But, shocks to aggregate level measures are the sum of a variety of similar shocks at the individual or regional level. Our contention is that – in practical settings – the effects of such shocks on aggregate-level outcomes is likely to be smaller than those on individual-level outcomes, such that the provision of aggregate-level data enables citizens to draw better (though still imperfect) inferences about the appropriateness of government policies.

Aggregate information may also facilitate collective action. Collective action on the part of members of the populace is often hindered by uncertainty over the willingness of others to participate in collective activities (Kuran 1991; Lohmann 1993). This issue has particularly important implications for the accountability of autocrats, as severe collective action problems typically inhibit methods of disciplining such governments. Because aggregate information with regards to outcomes provides insight into the experiences, and thus into the beliefs, of others, it may play a critical role in shaping the incentives for collective action (Morris and Shin 2002; Lohmann 1994; Shadmehr and Bernhardt 2011; Casper and Tyson 2014).

2.2 COMMON KNOWLEDGE AND HIGHER-ORDER BELIEFS

In the previous section, we focus on what citizens know about policies and outcomes. Here, we consider another dimension of transparency: its publicness. The degree to which information is public informs citizens not just about their own beliefs about policies and outcomes, but also about their beliefs about the beliefs of others about policies and outcomes. We call these "higher-order beliefs."

Any type of information may vary in the degree to which it is publicly available. By "public information" we mean the degree to which any piece of information constitutes *common knowledge*. This concept of public information has two prerequisites. (1) It must be available to all citizens. (2) All citizens must be aware of the fact that this information is known to all others (and know that all others are similarly aware of this fact).

The first aspect of public information is straightforward. The degree to which information shapes citizen behavior depends on the set of citizens to whom it is made available. If only a small minority of citizens can access information – regardless of the content – the broad citizenry cannot hold the government to account. Information can only shape the behavior of those citizens who can access it.

The second aspect of the publicness of information involves more subtle "higher-order beliefs." Recall that higher-order beliefs refer to the beliefs individuals hold about the beliefs of others. Information that is known to be known by others helps citizens to form an understanding of their shared beliefs. As

Morris and Shin (2002) note, public information serves not only to cause citizens to update their own beliefs about the performance of the government, it also allows these citizens to update their beliefs about how widely these beliefs are shared. Public information thus plays a dual role: it informs citizens both about reality and about how others might perceive this reality.

As we explore in later chapters, the importance of each aspect of publicness varies depending on the political institutions used to hold leaders accountable. Under democracies, where the fate of incumbents depends critically on elections, only the first aspect – the breadth of the availability of information – is crucial to hold governments to account. Citizen strategies in the voting booth are likely to be largely free of strategic considerations – each citizen acts according to the information she has available. Thus, the pertinent question is: How many citizens are well informed? Citizens' beliefs about government performance are made common knowledge through election outcomes.

By contrast, under autocracy, where governments may be held to account only through the coordinated collective action of a multitude of citizens, the second aspect – the degree of common knowledge – plays a bigger role. In situations characterized by strategic complementarities, higher-order beliefs are crucial: The willingness of citizens to participate in collective action (especially if such action is risky and dangerous) is contingent on their beliefs that others are also willing to participate. Consequently, information that is known to be public plays an outsized role in such activities (Morris and Shin 2002).

Because the breadth of information alone matters in democracy, while higher-order beliefs matter so much in autocracy, the effect of the dissemination of aggregate economic data has distinct effects on the stability of these different regime types. We explore these effects in later chapters – for now we delve into the empirical measurement of the different facets of transparency discussed in this section.

2.3 OPERATIONALIZING TRANSPARENCY

Having introduced the above forms of information pertaining to political accountability – that is, transparency with respect to (1) policymaking, (2) the connection between policy and outcomes, and (3) the outcomes themselves – we now consider the relationship between this typology and commonly used measures of transparency. We focus our attention on cross-national indexes of transparency.

Specifically, we examine three types of measures: First, we consider *institutional* measures of transparency, by which we mean measures of access to information regarding government decision-making. These measures include the presence/absence of freedom of information laws (FOILs), the disclosure of debate minutes (for example, of the board meetings of central banks), and measures of the "openness" of political institutions (often collapsed into measures of democracy). Second, we consider measures of the *media market*. In particular, we focus on measures of media freedom (Freedom House scores) and media circulation (newspaper circulation figures). Finally, we examine indexes that measure the *dissemination of data* by governments. Here we refer to aggregate (often economic) data that only governments have the capacity to collect and share. Our HRV index, which we fully present in the next chapter, falls into the last category.

2.3.1 Institutional Measures

Institutional measures of transparency reflect the extent to which citizens can access information on the decision-making processes of governments or governmental bodies. Broz (2002: 866–867) provides a clear definition of this type of transparency: "Transparency in the political system means that public decisions are made openly, in the context of competing interests and demands, political competition, and sources of independent information."

Broz (2002) measures this form of transparency using the level of democracy, as captured by the Polity index. The other most commonly used class of such measures reflects the presence/absence of FOILs (Berliner 2014; Islam 2006). Alternative measures of institutional transparency may reflect the openness of specific institutions. For instance, measures of central bank transparency – which typically capture the disclosure of board minutes, the publication of bank forecasts, and/or the discussion of past forecasting errors (for example, Stasavage 2003b) – also capture this aspect of information transmission (see also Chortareas, Stasavage, and Sterne 2002). Broadly speaking, people sometimes call the rules governing the transparency of policy-making "sunshine" policies.[5]

In terms of our categorization, such transparency most closely reflects public disclosure of the policies adopted by the government (p). FOILs and open decision-making processes provide citizens with information on the actions implemented by governing bodies (and, in the case of central banks, forecasts of how these policies are likely to change). They do not typically involve information on policy outcomes, as experienced by targeted citizens, nor information on the mapping between policies and such outcomes.

In terms of the breadth of availability, these measures vary. Legislative debates and central bank disclosures are typically directed to a relatively broad audience. On the other hand, disclosures mandated by FOILs are typically targeted at the specific party who initiated the freedom of information request. Though, the resultant information may be disseminated more widely by these

---

[5] For a micro level study of such "sunshine" policies, see Veeraraghavan (2015), who studies the effectiveness of India's countrywide National Rural Employment Guarantee Act in the state of Andhra Pradesh. He finds that government officials and bureaucrats can manipulate the incentives of citizens to take advantage of the act so that it results in more "flashlight" than "sunlight," in that transparency is directed toward some government actions but away from others. See also Berliner and Erlich (2015).

parties, who are often members of the press. Moreover, the availability of a FOIL might make policymakers more open *ex ante* with respect to the policy-making process.

Higher-order beliefs concerning these measures may also vary. All members of the investor community, for instance, are likely to be aware that others within this community are analyzing central bank press releases. By contrast, citizens who follow legislative debates remain uncertain about the attentiveness of other citizens (or they are relatively certain that most people are not attentive at all).

Since institutional measures of transparency primarily reflect disclosure of government policy choices (like p in our model), the value of such information depends on (1) the extent to which citizens are aware of the mapping between policies and outcomes and (2) the breadth with which such information is publicly disseminated. It therefore follows that institutional measures of transparency are most likely to be useful in holding governments to account for the relatively simple examples discussed above (for example, corruption). Institutional transparency may also be more valuable when disclosures are disseminated widely. FOILs, for instance, are likely to be of greatest use when a free and vibrant press is present to both file requests and make any releases available to the broader public.

2.3.2 The Media

The most commonly used measures of transparency reflect the performance and penetration of the media – with good reason. A free and vibrant press may convey information on all aspects of the policy process to the public. With or without the help of FOILs or open political institutions, investigative pieces may relay information on the policy choices of governments to citizens. (Though, naturally, institutional transparency and the media are complements in this regard.) Analyses and opinions, disseminated by the media, may help to inform citizens of the mapping between policy choices and outcome $g(\cdot)$. A functioning marketplace of ideas may help citizens to understand which of the policy options available will achieve the most desirable results. Finally, the media may play a role in conveying information on policy outcomes. Members of the press may contact parties affected by a given policy and air their stories to the broader public.

While there are no aspects of the policy process on which the media is wholly unable to provide information, there is one type of information that it is usually incapable of providing on its own: aggregated information on policy outcomes.

Individual news agencies typically cannot invest the resources necessary to document movements in price indexes, levels of economic growth, levels of poverty, or education rates. The media are unable to collect this sort of information for two reasons: (1) The collection of such information often entails enormous fixed costs. Indeed, the collection of census data often involves work-forces that number in the tens or hundreds of thousands (and, in some instances, even in the millions).[6] (2) The collection of such information is subject to a public goods problem (Rodrik 1995). Once one news outlet collects and publicizes information on aggregate outcomes – whether this information is in the form of qualitative assessments or quantitative data – others may simply reproduce this information. Since much of the benefit from the publication of information flows to entities other than the original source, news agencies underinvest in its collection. Since the fixed costs to gathering aggregate measures of welfare are high, the mass media tends not to collect these measures.

Still, because the media may relay information on a variety of aspects of the policymaking process, the presence of a vigorous press may play an important role in government accountability across an array of policy dimensions. Not surprisingly then, the most commonly used measures of transparency reflect the performance and penetration of the media. Typically these measures reflect one of two aspects of media operations: (1) the extent to which the press is free to report on stories of its own choosing (for example, Freedom House's Freedom of the Press index), and (2) the breadth of the populace the press is able to reach (for example, newspaper circulation per capita figures from the World Bank). Strength across both of these dimensions is necessary for the media to fulfill its central role.

Consider Freedom House's Freedom of the Press index as an example of the first type of a media measure. This index reflects subjective expert judgments of (1) the laws and regulations that constrain media content, (2) the degree of political control over the media, and (3) the structure of media ownership. Countries that score well on this index possess a relatively unconstrained press. A high score on the Freedom of the Press index, however, is no guarantee that information becomes common knowledge.

Other measures therefore focus on the ability of the press to reach a broad segment of the population. The most commonly used such indicators measure newspaper circulation figures, although some scholars also use Internet access in this regard. High degrees of media penetration, however, may be driven by the pervasiveness of state-run media outlets, which offer biased coverage of government actions.

The appropriate media measure, therefore, varies with the scope of the analysis and the importance of the breadth of dissemination. If governments can be held accountable by an informed subset of the population, then the Freedom of the Press measure is more relevant. On the other hand, if it is critical that information be common knowledge across the population, measures of media coverage are more relevant. In many circumstances, an aggregate index reflecting both freedom and breadth may be preferable. Regardless, a key limitation

---

[6] For instance, the most recent Indian census required 2.7 million workers, who often had to travel enormous distances, to complete the enumeration. See "Heads Up: A National Head Count Should Show Dramatic Changes," *The Economist*, February 24, 2011, www.economist.com/node/18233732?story_id=18233732, accessed July 11, 2017.

facing the press lies in its inability to gather highly aggregated information with regard to policy outcomes.

2.3.3 Data Dissemination

Our final facet of transparency relates to the disclosure of aggregate data on policy outcomes by the government to the public. Cross-national indexes of this facet of transparency typically proxy for governments' release of data to the public by measuring the release of data to international agencies. Such indexes may focus on the missingness of one important piece of data such as GDP or tax measures (see, for example, Bueno de Mesquita et al. 2003) or they may reflect the reporting of a broader array of measures (as in Hollyer, Rosendorff, and Vreeland 2011; Williams 2009). Others have focused on the speed with which certain indicators are reported to international bodies such as the World Bank and International Monetary Fund (Islam 2006).

The release of such data provides information on aggregate policy outcomes. That is, they serve to inform individual i of the welfare of some aggregation y of other citizens $\mathcal{K}$. Moreover, measures of such forms of transparency tend to focus on government disclosures since, as argued above, the combination of (1) high fixed costs of collection and (2) externalities in information dissemination tend to make the collection of aggregate data a natural monopoly dominated by the government.

The release of economic data provides the public with information on policy outcomes. Economic data are hardly unique in this regard. A free and vibrant media may also ease the flow of information about policy outcomes; reporters may examine the effects of government decisions as well as the decision-making process itself. Similarly, social networks may allow those impacted by policy decisions to communicate with one another and with those not directly targeted by policy choices.

Aggregate data are unique in one regard: their ability to provide information regarding a large number of individual outcomes. The dissemination of aggregate data is therefore likely to play a prominent role in accountability in precisely the circumstances when: (1) The public is imperfectly informed as to the optimal policy choice, p.[7] (2) The policy in question affects a broad swath of the public. If policies are narrowly tailored, members of the media or social networks are likely able to discover the policy's effects simply by contacting interested parties. (3) Policy choices do not perfectly map into welfare implications for individuals (the distribution of ϵ_i is not degenerate, e.g., $\epsilon_i = 0 \ \forall \ i$). By contrast, the media or social networks may be as, or more, informative about

---

[7] Recall that we refer to optimality from the perspective of the majority, or of a member of the winning coalition. It is not necessary for all citizens to share policy preferences, though this assumption is often adopted for simplicity in retrospective voting models.

policy outcomes when they affect a small population, and the consequences of policy choices are clear.

When policy choices do not perfectly map into welfare implications for individuals, each individual's welfare represents an imperfect indicator of the "correctness" of the government's decisions. In such situations, individuals should not condition their decision of whether to discipline the government on their individual welfare alone.[8] The weaker the correlation between government policies and individual outcomes, the more important is aggregate information. The law of large numbers implies that data offer an increasingly precise signal of the appropriateness of government decisions as the level of aggregation rises.

These aggregate data may also be critical in mobilizing collective action. As noted above, aggregate data have the power to inform citizens of the experiences – and thus the likely beliefs and willingness to mobilize – of others. Consequently, the disclosure of aggregate information may take on heightened importance in circumstances under which collective action is required for government accountability. For instance, when free and fair elections are absent, the masses may only be able to discipline the government through the threat of protests or strikes.

Government disclosures of aggregate data are typically made broadly available; though, the number of citizens who directly access these data are likely to be small. The information contained in such releases is typically translated into qualitative statements about citizen welfare – for example, the strength of the economic growth or the extent of unemployment – and disseminated via the press and word of mouth. Consequently, this facet of transparency is likely to be complemented by measures of media penetration.

In the next chapter, we develop a measure of transparency based on the public availability of information about the outcomes of government policies – a measure of data dissemination.

---

[8] See Kuran (1991) and Khemani (2007) for related discussions.

3

The HRV Index of Transparency

Missing data often pose a problem for researchers. For political scientists who rely heavily on cross-national datasets, missing data may be the bane of their work. The central insight of this chapter is that missing data are not just a problem to overcome. Missing data stand as a phenomenon worthy of investigation and explanation. Patterns of missing data can serve as an approximation of the availability of credible information in a polity – a measure of transparency.

Broadly defined, transparency concerns the full flow of information within a polity. As the previous chapter explains, though, no single measure can capture all facets of transparency. In much of the theoretical literature on political accountability, policy outcomes drive the decisions of citizens to support or oppose incumbent governments. One might expect scholars therefore to employ a measure of data dissemination that captures the transparency of policy outcomes in their empirical research. So far, however, this has not been the case. While several measures of institutional transparency and media freedom are commonly used in empirical studies, few projects employ measures of data dissemination (for some notable exceptions, see Bueno de Mesquita et al. 2003; Islam 2006; Williams 2009; Hollyer, Rosendorff, and Vreeland 2011; Copelovitch, Gandrud, and Hallerberg 2018; Mahdavi 2017). Perhaps scholars have ignored this facet of transparency in their empirical work because a thorough and theoretically rigorous measure of data disclosure has not been available.

Here, we discuss an index of transparency that attempts to fill the demand for such a measure: the HRV index. We treat a state's tendency to disclose data as a latent (unobserved) term predicting the missingness/non-missingness of data on 240 variables from the World Development Indicators (WDI) data series. This latent term is extracted using a dynamic model grounded in item response theory (IRT), which ensures minimal loss of information from collapsing a 240 dimensional observation into a single-dimensional representation. The index has a consistent meaning over time and covers 125 countries from 1980 to 2010. We believe that this approach offers several advantages over earlier measures of data disclosure, as we elaborate below.

The HRV index provides a precise measure of a limited but important component of transparency. We emphasize, again, that our measure does not capture all the facets of transparency. As discussed above, our measure of aggregate data disclosure is of most value when examining government accountability with regards to policies with uncertain outcomes, particularly over macroeconomic policy. Other measures – whether of the media or of institutional openness – are more appropriate to assess accountability with regards to corruption or specific instances of malfeasance.

Still, our measure is important as both an intrinsically interesting outcome variable and as a potential explanatory variable. We contend that it approximates the availability of credible economic data to citizens and the rest of the world. Both citizens and international organizations source aggregate economic data from national governments. Both citizens and international organizations have means to judge the credibility of the reported data. International organizations systematically collect and report these data – if they are reported and if they meet specific reporting standards. When data are not reported or are judged non-credible, international organizations code the data as missing. This coding thus approximates crucial activities that governments undertake to monitor economic performance. We encourage scholars to use the HRV index – along with other appropriate measures of other facets of transparency – to test hypotheses about the relationships between transparency and accountability, governance, and democracy.

Beyond the contribution of the HRV index, the chapter also offers a new way to think about the measurement of transparency.[1] We treat missing data as *data*. The sophisticated methodology we use to aggregate missing data into a single measure has broad applications beyond the specific index we present here (see Copelovitch, Gandrud, and Hallerberg 2018).

The chapter first presents this methodology and then lays forward empirical features of the HRV index, along with specific cases from Africa, Asia, Europe, and Latin America to give the reader a sense of the face validity of our measure.

3.1 CONSTRUCTION OF THE INDEX

We measure governments' collection and disclosure of data directly, by relying on the presence or absence of reported values from the WDI. The World Bank assembles these data from information provided by other international

---

[1] Note that we first published the index in *Political Analysis* in 2014. See Hollyer, Rosendorff, and Vreeland (2014).

organizations – for instance, the International Monetary Fund, the International Labour Organization, the Organization for Economic Cooperation and Development, and the United Nations. These organizations, in turn, obtain information from country-specific national statistical offices. Originally, therefore, the data come directly from governments.

Why are data missing? In many cases, governments have simply failed to report. In some instances, the World Bank codes observations in the WDI as missing because the information provided by national agencies is deemed questionable. The data may not have been collected according to appropriate international standards, or the nationally reported data may be judged to be too far from the truth. The World Bank reports, for example, that sometimes growth rates claimed by national governments "appear to be unrealistic."[2] In adjudicating what data to include, the World Bank collaborates with the International Monetary Fund (IMF) on the Data Quality Assessment Framework (DQAF) to monitor the quality of national statistical agencies' reporting and adheres to the General Data Dissemination System (GDDS) framework.[3] The GDDS centers on "quality, access, and integrity."[4]

Our measure thus reflects the disclosure of credible information by national statistical agencies. As such, the HRV index possesses a high degree of *content validity* (Carmines and Zeller 1979) with regards to the concept of theoretical interest – the collection and dissemination of aggregate economic data. We should note, however, that while data quality is a continuous concept, the World Bank decision to omit or report data is discrete. Consequently, missingness is not fully indicative of data quality – variation exists in the accuracy of the figures disclosed by the WDI across countries and time.

To be precise, we treat *transparency* as a latent (unobserved) term predicting the presence or missingness of data. We obtain estimates of this transparency term through the use of a Bayesian IRT model. IRT models are a class of procedures drawn from the psychometrics literature, used to reduce the dimensionality of data with minimal loss of information (for a thorough overview, see Van der Linden and Hambleton 1997). Political scientists have used the approach to achieve several different goals, including to estimate the ideal points of legislators (Clinton, Jackman, and Rivers 2004), to refine indexes of democracy (Treier and Jackman 2008; Pemstein, Meserve, and Melton 2010),

---

[2] See https://web.archive.org/web/20131003011711/http://data.worldbank.org/about/faq/specific-data-series, accessed July 7, 2017.

[3] See http://data.worldbank.org/about/data-overview/data-quality-and-effectiveness accessed March 7, 2011. See also the World Bank statements about the World Development Indicators: http://data.worldbank.org/about/data-programs, accessed March 7, 2011. For a critical evaluation of the institutional design and effectiveness of the IMF's Special Data Dissemination Standard (SDDS), see Mosley (2003). See also Vadlamannati, Cooray, and Brazys (2017). Note that the WDI are also updated on an ongoing basis – data that might have been missing in earlier releases is occasionally included in later versions.

[4] From http://dsbb.imf.org/Pages/GDDS/WhatIsGDDS.aspx, accessed July 6, 2017.

to examine support for the United States within the UN General Assembly (Bailey, Strezhnev, and Voeten 2017), and to combine expert estimates of bureaucratic agency ideologies (Clinton and Lewis 2008). We use it to construct an innovative measure of transparency.

3.1.1 The Selection of 240 Variables and 125 Countries

Our index summarizes the tendency to report 240 variables to the WDI.[5] For this index to be a valid indicator of a government's tendency to release aggregate economic data, these variables must be representative of the type of data collected by governments more generally and must not be subject to any arbitrary reporting procedures. In short, the quality of our index is a function of the data that we employ.

The 240 variables used in our model are drawn from the entirety of the WDI, which contains 1,265 variables in total (at this writing). We trim this larger set of variables in the following manner: First, we drop any variable that is not reported by at least one country in every year from 1980 to 2010. We thus ensure that our index has constant meaning throughout the time period that we cover.

Second, we exclude all variables that are – or appear to be – measured for only a subset of countries. For instance, we exclude official development assistance (ODA) measures and variables related to holdings of external debt, since these are only routinely reported for – respectively – low income and highly indebted nations. The data generating process underlying the reporting of these variables systematically differs from that for other data in the WDI, and thus including these variables in our model would be inappropriate.

Third, we exclude any data that are derived from World Bank sponsored surveys (for example, the *Doing Business* surveys) or that is an index compiled by entities external to the country, such as nongovernmental organizations. We also exclude, with one exception (detailed below), variables that are derived from World Bank calculations – for example, growth rates and purchasing power parity (PPP) conversion factors. Our index is intended to reflect *governments'* disclosure of data and we thus attempt to confine our data to variables reported with input from governments.

Fourth, we drop variables that are linear combinations of other variables. For instance, data are reported on the total labor market participation rate, the male labor market participation rate, and the female labor market participation rate – as well as relevant population figures. Of the three labor market participation measures, we include only the female participation rate.

Fifth, we delete multiple references to the same underlying measure that are reported in different units. For instance, national accounts data are typically

---

[5] A complete listing of the variables included in our analysis is presented in the appendix to this chapter.

reported in current US dollars, current local currency units (LCU), constant US dollars, constant LCUs, and purchasing power parity US dollars. When measures are reported in this manner, our first preference is to keep only the variable reported in constant US dollars. If no such variable is available, we then keep only the variable reported in constant LCUs. In all instances, we keep only one such reference. Our preference for reporting in constant US dollars would seem to contradict our third requirement for inclusion. After all, most governments report values in their local currency, conversions are subsequently conducted by the World Bank. We prefer the constant US dollar values, however, as these values incur an additional layer of World Bank scrutiny. The World Bank notes that constant dollar values may be left as missing when "originally reported growth rates appear to be unrealistic."[6]

We also restrict the set of countries included in our analysis. We first exclude any country that did not exist for the entirety of the 1980–2010 period.[7] We do this for two reasons: first, the WDI only includes countries currently in existence. For countries that came into existence after the WDI begins its coverage, values for dates prior to independence are constructed – wherever possible – based on existing data (for example, data from prior rulers and/or information made available by the current leadership based on pre-independence records). Second, rectangularizing the dataset eases the construction of our algorithm (because there is an equal number of observations for each country). For similar reasons, we exclude the two modern countries that are formed by the union of preexisting states during the 1980–2010 period (Germany and Yemen). We do, however, keep countries that fractured during the period covered by the index if the largest constituent portion of that country remained independent. So, we treat Russia as the continuation of the USSR, Ethiopia remains in the dataset after the secession of Eritrea, and Indonesia remains after the independence of East Timor. But we drop states that completely dissolved, such as Czechoslovakia and Yugoslavia. Finally, we drop all micro-states from the dataset – that is, we only include states that maintained a population of 500,000 or more throughout the 1980–2010 period. After dropping states that do not meet these criteria, we are left with 125 countries, each of which is observed for 31 years, for a total of 3,875 observations.

3.1.2 Item Response Theory (IRT)

The clearest exposition of the IRT model comes from the psychometrics literature, where the psychometrician attempts to measure student-ability based on her correct/incorrect answers on a test. The approach assumes that there

---

[6] http://data.worldbank.org/about/faq/specific-data-series, accessed March 5, 2013.

[7] For the dates of independence, we rely on the DD dataset of Cheibub, Gandhi, and Vreeland (2010) and the PWT 7.1 (Heston, Summers, and Aten 2012). We merge the WDI data with these two datasets and drop all observations from the WDI that are not included in both.

exists a latent indicator of student ability that drives the (in)correct answering of questions on an exam.

The IRT model takes into account that some questions are simply more difficult than others. (In our context, some variables are less likely to be reported in general.) IRT models thus estimate a "difficulty" parameter for each question.

Note that not all "difficult" questions equally discriminate across student ability. A poorly worded question, for example, may simply result in all students randomly guessing at answers. Thus the model also takes into account that some questions discriminate across student ability: The strongest students answer them correctly, and the weakest students answer incorrectly. (In our context, some variables may only be reported by the most transparent of countries, while only the least transparent countries fail to report other key variables.) IRT models thus estimate a "discrimination" parameter for each question (or, in our context, each variable).

Applying IRT to data dissemination, our approach assumes that there is a single unobserved term – *transparency* – that drives the reporting of variables to the WDI. Countries that score highly on this term are more likely to report each item in the WDI than countries that receive low scores; though the degree to which reporting/non-reporting reflects transparency varies across each variable in the WDI. There is likely to be variation in the degree to which reporting reflects transparency both because certain variables are more likely to be reported – by all countries – than others, and because certain variables may be reported for idiosyncratic reasons unrelated to transparency. Thus, the reporting/non-reporting of different variables in the WDI provides differing amounts of information about transparency. Our model estimates the degree to which each observation is informative regarding transparency. We can therefore report a single value of transparency for each country-year that reflects the missingness of data across all 240 WDI variables with minimal loss of information.

3.1.3 The IRT Model

Let $z_{j,c,t} \in \{0, 1\}$ denote an indicator equal to 1 if country c reports WDI variable j in year t and equal to 0 otherwise. We then estimate

$$Pr(z_{j,c,t} = 1 | transparency_{c,t}) = logit(\delta_j + \beta_j transparency_{c,t}) \qquad (3.1)$$

where δ_j is the difficulty parameter and β_j the discrimination parameter for item j. The term $transparency_{c,t}$ is the measure of a given country-year's propensity to disclose data that is to be estimated. (The *logit* function is a logistic transformation of the data.) Changes in δ_j reflect the degree to which countries, on average, report a given variable drawn from the WDI. Changes to β_j reflect the degree to which the outcome of one item predicts the outcome of other items (Gelman and Hill 2006). Simply taking the fraction of reported variables as an indicator of the transparency of each country would therefore be approximately equivalent to assuming δ_j and β_j are constant across all variables j reported to the WDI (we discuss this alternative in detail below). Our approach here is thus far more general than simple averaging; it lets the data reveal the amount of information contained in each item (WDI variable).

In our model there are 240 items (variables) j, 125 countries c, and 31 years t. We estimate a system of 240 equations (all of the form of Equation 3.1) with 3,875 observations.

The model represented by Equation 3.1 is only identified up to an affine transformation. Note that we can never observe the actual values of δ_j, β_j, or *transparency*$_{c,t}$. We could therefore multiply all *transparency* values by a constant, and divide all β_j by the same value, and produce the same model. One could similarly manipulate coefficient values to shift the transparency index in any direction. This is obviously a problem. So, to fix the scale and location of the index, we recenter simulated index values – by subtracting the mean and dividing by the standard deviation – in the year 1980 at each iteration of the Markov Chain Monte Carlo procedure explained below (Knorr-Held 1999). Initial values for the index in year 1980, the first year of the time series, are drawn from a diffuse normal prior *transparency*$_{c,1980} \sim N(0, 100)$ prior to recentering. We fix the direction of the index by constraining Cuba to have negative transparency scores and Sweden to have positive transparency scores, using half-normal priors for each. Note that this decision is data-driven: We choose Cuba and Sweden as anchors because, in runs of the model without these constraints, Cuba ranks consistently as one of the least transparent, while Sweden ranks as of one the most.

Because our data are time-series cross-sectional, we encounter an additional modeling difficulty: we cannot treat each observation of *transparency*$_{c,t}$ as independent of the observation *transparency*$_{c,t-1}$. A country's level of transparency is correlated across that country's history. We therefore employ a system of random-walk priors for each value of *transparency*$_{c,t}$ after 1980. Our system of priors is thus *transparency*$_{c,t} \sim N(transparency_{c,t-1}, \frac{1}{\tau_c}) \; \forall t > 1$. τ_c acts as a country-specific smoothing parameter, since the degree to which an estimated value of *transparency*$_{c,t}$ shrinks back toward the prior mean is inversely proportional to the variance of the prior distribution (Jackman 2009). Similar priors are often used in the ideal point estimation literature when working with dynamic data (see, for instance Martin and Quinn 2002). We estimate the parameter τ_c for each country in our data, and give this term a prior distribution $\tau_c \sim Gamma(20, 0.25)$.[8]

We place diffuse normal priors on the difficulty and discrimination parameters δ_j and β_j, such that

$$\begin{pmatrix} \delta_j \\ \beta_j \end{pmatrix} \sim N\left(\begin{pmatrix} 0 \\ 0 \end{pmatrix}, \begin{pmatrix} 100 & 0 \\ 0 & 100 \end{pmatrix} \right).$$

---

[8] A Gamma distribution with a shape parameter 20 and scale parameter 0.25 has a mean of 5 and a variance of 1.25.

These diffuse priors ensure that the posterior estimate of each discrimination and difficulty parameter is overwhelmingly determined by the data. This approach allows the data to speak as to which WDI variables contain the most information on transparency.

We estimate this model employing a Markov Chain Monte Carlo (MCMC) algorithm run from JAGS 3.3.0.[9] The model is estimated using two chains of 10,000 iterations each, the first 5,000 of which serve as a burn-in period.[10]

---

[9] JAGS, or "Just another Gibbs sampler" is a computer program that can simulate Bayesian models using Markov Chain Monte Carlo algorithms (see Plummer 2003). Markov Chain Monte Carlo (MCMC) algorithms involve a series of random draws. (Yes, think of the roulette wheels, craps dice, and blackjack and poker tables in the Monte Carlo casinos where James Bond gambles in *Casino Royal*. Actually, seasoned gamblers might get a better picture of MCMC from the blackjack and poker tables because in card games, random draws are not independent – they depend on previously drawn cards. With MCMC, the random draw of the current number is conditioned on a set number of previously drawn numbers – hence a "chain" of draws.)

[10] Gelman-Rubin convergence diagnostics reveal that the model converges. Of the 4,480 parameters in the model, the highest-valued Gelman-Rubin statistic is 1.079. We report convergence statistics for all variables in the appendix of Hollyer, Rosendorff, and Vreeland (2014). To assess model fit, we rely on posterior predictive checks (Gelman et al. 2000). We sample repeatedly from the posterior distributions of all *transparency*$_{c,t}$, difficulty (δ_j), and discrimination (β_j) terms to generate the predicted probability that a given country c reports data on a given variable j in a given year t, which we denote $p_{j,c,t}$. We calculate the deviation between these predicted probabilities and the observed data and express this deviation in a single measure. Specifically, we construct a measure analogous to Herron's (1999) expected percentage correctly predicted (ePCP), which we term the total expected percentage correctly predicted (TePCP). The TePCP is defined as follows:

$$TePCP = \frac{1}{JCT} \sum_{j=1}^{J} \sum_{c=1}^{C} \sum_{t=1}^{T} [z_{j,c,t} p_{j,c,t} + (1 - z_{j,c,t})(1 - p_{j,c,t})]$$

where $J = 240$ denotes the total number of items in the model, $C = 125$ denotes the total number of countries, and $T = 31$ denotes the total number of years. As noted above $z_{j,c,t} \in \{0, 1\}$ denotes whether variable j is reported by country c in year t. The TePCP thus takes on a value in the open unit interval, and a notional value of 1 would indicate perfect predictive power. We run 500 simulations, sampling repeatedly from the posterior densities of each model parameter, to generate 500 TePCP values. These values reveal that the model fits the data well: the average TePCP score is 0.796, and 95 percent of all TePCP scores fall between 0.795 and 0.796. By way of comparison, we fit a model consisting only of constant terms – that is, the difficulty parameters δ_j. This is roughly equivalent to assuming that each observation of $p_{j,c,t}$ is equal to the empirical frequency with which a given variable j is reported in the WDI data (the fraction approach). This process produces a mean TePCP of 0.707 with 95 percent of all observations falling between 0.706 and 0.708. Thus, the IRT model results in a roughly 30 percent marginal reduction in error. We additionally explore whether a two dimensional IRT better fits the data. The two dimensional model only modestly improves model fit, producing an average TePCP of 0.8381, with 95 percent of all values falling between 0.8378 and 0.8383. We present a graphical comparison of the simulated TePCP values from each model in the appendix to Hollyer, Rosendorff, and Vreeland (2014).

3.2 THE VALUE OF ITEM RESPONSE THEORY

At its core, our index reflects the degree to which governments have reported data. One might wonder, therefore, why we do not simply use as our measure the fraction of the 240 variables reported in each country-year. Such a fraction approach would certainly be computationally simpler than using IRT. Plus, it is intuitive. Indeed, previous studies (Hollyer, Rosendorff, and Vreeland 2011; Williams 2009) compute analogous measures of data disclosure based on the fraction of variables reported to the WDI or other international datasets. Given the computational intensity of the IRT approach, it is reasonable to ask whether there is any value-added in fitting an item response model to these data rather than relying on the fraction of reported observations.

In theory, the IRT model offers a substantial advantage over simply computing the fraction of variables reported to international agencies. The fraction approach assumes that the reporting of any one variable is equivalent to the reporting of any other. The IRT approach, by contrast, allows each variable to contribute differentially to index values – the contribution of each variable to the index depends on the extent to which the reporting of this variable is correlated with the reporting of other variables. As highlighted in our discussion of the psychometrics literature, the model adjusts for the fact that some variables are simply much more commonly reported than others (through the difficulty parameters, δ_j), and for the fact that the reporting of certain terms is more predictive of a general tendency to disclose than the reporting of other terms (through the discrimination parameters, β_j).

Nonetheless, it is possible that each item contained in the WDI is as informative as any other. If this is the case, the IRT approach would be roughly equivalent to simply computing the fraction of variables reported. The IRT approach certainly allows for this possibility – the difficulty and discrimination parameters (δ_j and β_j) could be estimated as identical across all items, j. In such cases, it might be advisable to rely on the simpler and less computationally intensive approach rather than going through the trouble of fitting an IRT model.

We can assess this empirical possibility in two ways: First, we can simply compare the HRV index values to those based on the fraction of the 240 variables in our model that are reported. Second, we can examine the estimates of the difficulty and discrimination parameters (δ_j and β_j) from the item response model. If these values differ significantly across items, then the IRT is a more appropriate model for these data than the raw frequency of reporting.

First, we make the comparison. Figure 3.1 contains a scatter plot, together with a lowess regression line, of mean HRV index values against the fraction of the 240 WDI variables used in our analysis reported by a given country in a given year.[11]

---

[11] Lowess curves, used throughout this chapter, are smoothed curves "locally weighted" by the scatter plot data. The line depicts the least squared distance smoothed across rolling averages of bins of several observations.

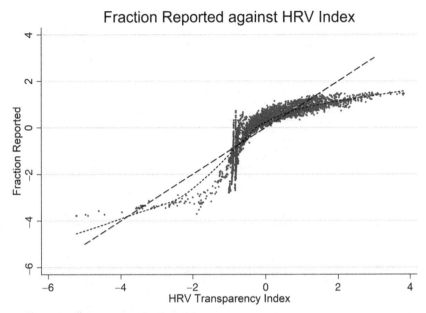

FIGURE 3.1. Fraction reported against mean HRV index scores. The fraction of the 240 variables used to construct the HRV index reported in a given country year plotted against the HRV transparency index scores computed using IRT. Both measures have been standardized by subtracting the mean and dividing by the standard deviation. A 45 degree dashed line runs through the origin. The dotted line depicts the lowess curve fitted to these values. Compared to the fraction of data reported, the HRV index depicts greater variation among observations receiving extreme scores, while it reveals less variation for observations in the middle.

We have standardized both variables by, for each observation, subtracting the variable mean and dividing by the variable standard deviation. It is immediately apparent from Figure 3.1 that these two measures are strongly related – the raw correlation between the mean HRV index score and the fraction of variables reported is 0.84. However, the scatter plot in Figure 3.1 departs substantially from the dashed 45 degree line that represents what would be a perfect correlation. Notably, the slope of the fitted lowess curve is substantially less than one for nearly all values of the HRV index. This implies that the HRV index is more sensitive to variations in reporting than is the fraction of variables reported: Relative to the mean, high-scoring countries do better on the HRV index than they do on the fraction of variables reported, while low-scoring countries do worse. The relationship between the two terms is also nonlinear – the fitted lowess line is sigmoid shaped. The IRT approach thus detects greater variation among countries receiving relatively extreme scores than does the fraction reported measure; and it finds less variation for countries with middling (slightly below average) scores.

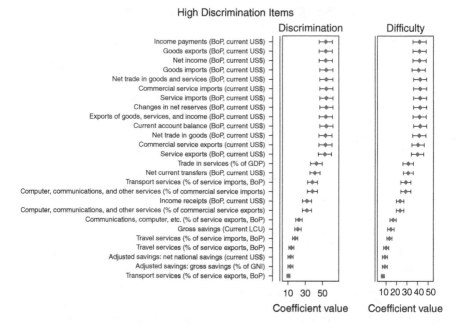

FIGURE 3.2. Parameter estimates, highest discrimination scores. Discrimination and difficulty parameters, and 95 percent highest posterior density intervals, for the 25 items with the highest discrimination parameter scores. Parameter values are plotted on the x-axis and mean estimated values are denoted by diamonds. Ninety-five percent highest posterior density intervals are denoted by whiskers. Item names are noted on the y-axis.

Next, consider the estimates of the difficulty (δ_j) and discrimination (β_j) parameters for the 240 items in our model. The fraction approach would implicitly set these parameters to constant across all variables examined. So, if the estimates of these parameters from our model vary little across items, one might conclude that the IRT model is unnecessary.

In fact, the estimates of these parameters vary considerably. Point estimates for the difficulty parameters vary across items from a minimum of -3.8 to a maximum of 42 (with a standard deviation of 10.4). Point estimates of the discrimination parameters vary from a low of -0.18 to a high of 54.8 (with a standard deviation of 13.3). Figures 3.2 and 3.3 plot these estimates along with their 95 percent highest posterior density intervals for the 25 most and 25 least discriminating items in our data.[12]

Examination of these parameters provides further insight into the validity of our index. If our measure of transparency is to be relevant to political processes, it must reflect the disclosure of *politically relevant* data. If the most discriminating items are systematically obscure politically irrelevant variables, one might

---

[12] The appendix to this chapter presents the complete set of plots for all 240 items.

Low Discrimination Items

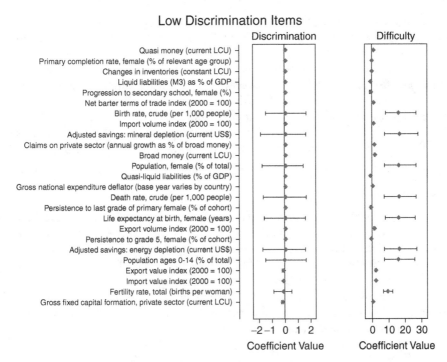

FIGURE 3.3. Parameter estimates, lowest discrimination scores. Discrimination and difficulty parameters, and 95 percent highest posterior density intervals, for the 25 items with the lowest discrimination parameter scores. Parameter values are plotted on the x-axis and mean estimated values are denoted by diamonds. Ninety-five percent highest posterior density intervals are denoted by whiskers. Item names are noted on the y-axis.

conclude that our index reflects bureaucratic technocracy, rather than public data disclosure.

The most discriminating items overwhelmingly relate to trade and investment. These variables are reported relatively frequently and those countries that fail to report these items typically do not report much at all. Standout items include measures of the current account balance, goods and services exports and imports, and changes in reserves. Scholars of international political economy have long studied the political implications connected to changes in these variables, which relate to open economy politics. Key constituencies can be identified as winners and others as losers from changes in these indicators – and the politics have proven contentious.[13]

---

[13] Factor models predict that relatively abundant factors win from expansion of trade and capital movements, while relatively scarce factors lose. Sector models identify key constituencies as export-oriented, import-competing, and dealing in financial services. Newer theories identify constituencies at the firm-level as winning or losing from globalization. (See,

By contrast, the least discriminating parameters consist of population measures, measures of the money supply, and a variety of detailed measures related to education (for example, the pupil-to-teacher ratio). The highly discriminating items are thus composed of measures with clear political relevance. A handful of the less discriminating items (for example, the education items) may be politically relevant in some settings. But, the majority of these items (fertility rates, population values, values of M3 as a percentage of GDP) are unlikely to be at the center of political concern. We therefore conclude that our index reflects the disclosure of politically relevant data and not merely of technocracy.

3.3 FACE VALIDITY

The HRV index, developed using IRT, illuminates patterns of transparency that a simple fraction approach would not. Moreover, we find the estimates of the difficulty and discrimination parameters encouraging. The most highly discriminating items included in our index fit with our intuitions about which aspects of the economy are most contentious. To further assess the validity of our index, however, we now go beyond the items encompassed by the index and consider some simple descriptive patterns that the index produces. We begin with broad comparisons across sets of countries and then present some specific countries in more detail.

3.3.1 Comparisons across Countries and Time

We first examine the estimated values of the transparency index in the 1980 cross-section. We report estimated index values and 95 percent highest posterior density intervals for the 25 lowest scoring countries in Figure 3.4 and for the 25 highest scoring countries in Figure 3.5. As can be seen from the estimates, nearly all the highest scoring countries are members of the Organisation for Economic Co-operation and Development (OECD). The lowest scoring countries consist of the Soviet Union, Cambodia, Guinea, Laos, Mongolia, and Guinea-Bissau – all states we would expect to score poorly on transparency during this period.[14] We can also see that the highest scoring country in this period (Spain) differs significantly in its score from other high-scoring countries such as the United Kingdom. This differentiation is even more dramatic among low scoring countries. The Soviet Union is significantly less transparent

for example, Rogowski 1987; Frieden 1991; Simmons 1994; Oatley 1999; Clark and Hallerberg 2000; Mosley 2000; Broz and Frieden 2001; Scheve and Slaughter 2001; McGillivray 1997; Moene and Wallerstein 2006; Broz, Frieden, and Weymouth 2008; Walter 2008; Nooruddin and Rudra 2014; Baccini, Pinto, and Weymouth 2017.) For an introduction to open economy politics, see Lake (2009).

[14] Note that we label the Soviet Union in our dataset (and thus in Figure 3.4) as the Russian Federation because we treat the contemporary Russian state as the successor to the Soviet Union.

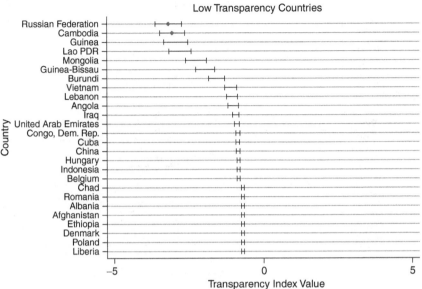

FIGURE 3.4. Low scoring countries, 1980. A cross section of the 25 lowest scoring countries on the HRV index from 1980. Country names are plotted on the y-axis. Index scores are plotted on the x-axis. Mean predicted transparency index values are indicated by diamonds, while the whiskers denote 95 percent highest posterior density intervals. Countries are plotted in ascending order of mean HRV index score.

than Guinea which is, in turn, significantly less transparent than Mongolia. Contrasting the sets of countries presented in Figures 3.4 and 3.5, we see that our index values coincide with commonly held notions about which states are most and, respectively, least transparent. Scrutinizing the rank ordering within each figure, we see that the index can discriminate among the high and low scoring countries. We are further able to differentiate between countries not only at the extremes – as plotted in Figures 3.4 and 3.5 – but also in the middle range of transparency scores.

The general correspondence between HRV scores and common preconceptions not withstanding, the examination of these data does yield a few surprises. Figure 3.4 reveals, for instance, that several first world countries – particularly Belgium and Denmark – score poorly on the HRV index. Both countries actually experience substantial volatility in HRV scores over time. Denmark exhibits variation in the frequency of data disclosure over time – whether measured in terms of HRV scores or of the fraction of variables that are reported. Denmark regularly oscillates between periods of high and low disclosure, with particularly large changes in the mid-1980s and mid-2000s. Belgium, on the other hand, exhibits consistently low levels of disclosure until 2002 when reporting

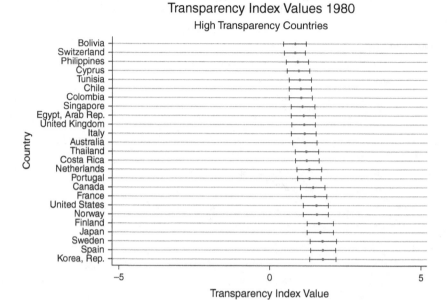

FIGURE 3.5. High scoring countries, 1980. A cross section of the 25 highest scoring countries on the HRV index from 1980. Country names are plotted on the y-axis. Index scores are plotted on the x-axis. Mean predicted transparency index values are indicated by diamonds, while the whiskers denote 95 percent highest posterior density intervals. Countries are plotted in ascending order of mean HRV index score.

jumps dramatically. Interestingly, upon further scrutiny, we have discovered that the Belgian case actually fits into a broader pattern. Belgium represents an extreme example of volatility in European HRV scores around the time of the introduction of the euro (for existing EU members when the euro was first introduced) and around the time of accession (for countries that joined later). We discuss the latter group in greater detail below.[15]

3.3.2 Specific Country Examples

In addition to comparing across countries cross-sectionally, we examine longitudinal variation in our estimates to assess their validity. Based on anecdotal accounts, the level of transparency in many countries in our sample should shift over time. We present our estimates of the level of transparency in several such

---

[15] The group of stable and developed democracies who were members of the EU when the euro was first introduced is not of central interest for this project. We are concerned with developing democracies and autocracies because of our focus on political instability. We flag the data-reporting irregularities of the established EU states around the time of the introduction of the euro for other scholars to consider in their research.

countries below. We begin with examples of countries from Asia before turning to examples from Africa and Latin America, and we conclude with examples from Europe.

Beginning with Asia, China stands out as, perhaps, the country with the most growing interest around the world. The economic and (to a lesser extent) political liberalization of the People's Republic of China since the late-1970s and early-1980s through the present is well known and widely discussed.[16] This liberalization has proceeded to such an extent that some authors refer to China as exemplifying "authoritarian deliberation" under which information is provided to the public, whose opinion is consulted in the policymaking process (He and Warren 2011).[17] One might therefore expect levels of transparency to increase over the 1980–2010 period.

Figure 3.6 demonstrates that – at least according to our measure – such an increase in transparency has indeed taken place in China. In particular, HRV scores jump dramatically between 1981 and 1984. This change coincides both with the Sixth Five-Year Plan, which focused on economic reforms to develop trade and make use of foreign capital, and with entry into the IMF and the World Bank (see Fewsmith 2001; Naughton 2006; Lipscy 2017; Fravel forthcoming).

Like China, Vietnam also experienced enormous economic and political changes over the 1980–2010 period. These changes included substantial economic liberalization, the creation of (relatively) more representative institutions, and the establishment of diplomatic relations with nations with which it had been estranged. The 1986 Party Congress is widely seen as ushering in the period of liberalization (Fforde and de Vylder 1996; Riedel and Turley 1999). The process of economic and political liberalization continued throughout the 1990s and early 2000s (Malesky 2008, 2009; Gehlbach and Malesky 2010). One might therefore expect that Vietnam would grow substantially more transparent over time, particularly after 1986.

Figure 3.7 plots our predicted transparency index scores and 95 percent highest posterior density intervals for Vietnam over time. Predicted levels of transparency increase substantially. In particular, there are large jumps in the 1984–1986 period, corresponding to the Party Congress.

---

[16] On the opening of China's political system, see Landry (2008). On accountability in China see L. Tsai (2007) and Birney (2014). Kelliher (1997) notes that the Chinese discussion of local self-government largely focused on the replacement of corrupt officials with competent political outsiders. Interestingly, the slight drop in transparency in 2004 corresponds with China's Ministry of Civic Affairs initiative for "transparency in village affairs," which is supposed to involved budgetary transparency, but the measures have been seen as "ineffective, surface-level formalities" (Looney 2012: 246–248). For in depth studies of limitations to the economic and political liberalization of China, see Wallace (2016) and Weiss (2014).

[17] China's liberalization has also given rise to a greater openness to foreign influence. For a discussion of these changes, with specific reference to investment and climate change, see Lewis (2007: 163–165).

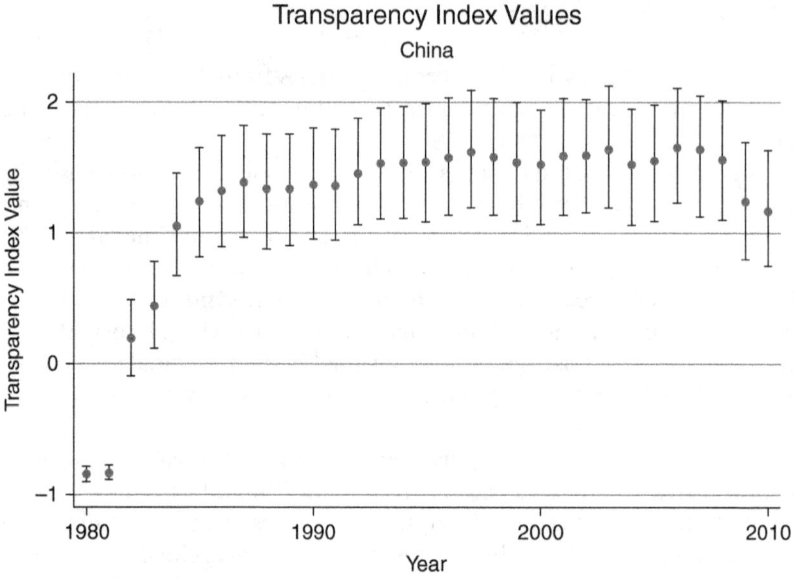

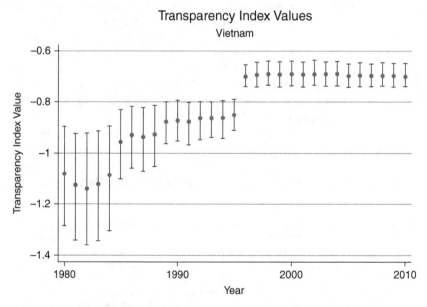

FIGURE 3.6. China HRV scores over time. A longitudinal plot of China's HRV index scores from 1980 to 2010. HRV index scores are on the y-axis, while time is measured on the x-axis. Circles denote mean predicted index scores. Whiskers denote 95 percent highest posterior density intervals.

FIGURE 3.7. Vietnam HRV scores over time. A longitudinal plot of Vietnam's HRV index scores from 1980 to 2010. HRV index scores are on the y-axis, while time is measured on the x-axis. Circles denote mean predicted index scores. Whiskers denote 95 percent highest posterior density intervals.

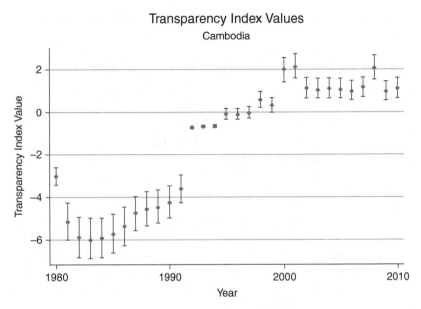

FIGURE 3.8. Cambodia HRV scores over time. A longitudinal plot of Cambodia's HRV index scores from 1980 to 2010. HRV index scores are on the y-axis, while time is measured on the x-axis. Diamonds denote mean predicted index scores. Whiskers denote 95 percent highest posterior density intervals.

Additional increases are visible in the mid-1990s, following the introduction of a new constitution in 1992 and Vietnam's increasing integration with the global economy over this period.

Cambodia experiences a similar (roughly) monotonic increase in HRV scores over time (Figure 3.8). This secular rise in levels of disclosure is consistent with broader political and economic trends in the country. From 1979 to 1989, Cambodia was subject to Vietnamese occupation and civil war. The government of the People's Republic of Kampuchea battled elements of the former Khmer Rouge as well as royalist factions, and also the Khmer People's National Liberation Front (Ear 2007). The Paris Peace Agreement terminated hostilities in 1991, and led to the establishment of the United Nations Transitional Authority in Cambodia, under whose auspices multiparty elections were held in 1993 (Roberts 2003). The cessation of hostilities is accompanied by a large and significant jump in HRV scores. During the civil war period, Cambodia's HRV scores hover in the bottom first percentile among all country-years, but between 1991 and 1992 they jump up to the 25th percentile.

The 1993 elections produced a victory for the royalist party; though, opposition from the former-Vietnamese backed Cambodian People's Party (CPP), under the leadership of Hun Sen, led to the formation of a power sharing coalition (Vander Weyden 2000). In practice, the CPP proved able to consolidate control under the veneer of the coalition government, and the coalition continued to function from 1993 until 1996 (Vander Weyden 2000). This period is marked by slight increases in HRV scores. In 1996 and 1997, tensions between the CPP and royalists led to clashes and eventually to the exile of the leader of the royalist camp (McCargo 2005; Vander Weyden 2000). However, elections were again held in 1998 (in which the CPP won a majority), which were deemed free and fair by the international community (Vander Weyden 2000). Since that time, the CPP has solidified its control – McCargo (2005: 106) describes it as a hegemonic party not unlike the PRI in pre-2000 Mexico. Its political control has not been subject to substantial challenges and it has pursued industrialization, urbanization, and membership in the World Trade Organization (Heder 2005; Roberts 2003). During this period, HRV scores rose, before stabilizing at levels similar to those of China.

Next, consider some examples from Africa. From the 1970s through the 1980s, Tanzania was a single party state run by the Chama Cha Mapinduzi (CCM) party, an amalgam of the TANU party that pushed for independence on the mainland and the Afro-Shirazi party that did the same in Zanzibar. The CCM advocated the socialist principles and import-substituting growth strategy espoused by the founding father of the nation, Julius Nyerere. In the 1980s, this system came under increasing strain due to chronic current account imbalances, IMF pressure, and the international collapse of communist states (Kiondo 1992; Mmuya and Chaligha 1992; Vreeland 2003c). In 1992, the CCM agreed to open the political system to multiparty elections. Tanzania also embarked on a system of significant economic liberalization during the early 1990s (Hoffman 2011).

Figure 3.9 plots our predicted transparency scores and 95 percent highest posterior density intervals for Tanzania over time. An abrupt and significant upwards shift in transparency values is noticeable in 1990, followed by further improvements throughout the early 1990s. These shifts coincide nearly perfectly with the period of economic and political liberalization.

Other examples from Africa demonstrate that the trend toward rising transparency is not universal in our index. A number of countries have experienced substantial declines. For instance, Zimbabwe experienced increasing levels of unrest and trade union-led opposition to the ZANU-PF government beginning in the mid-1990s. General strikes were held in 1996 and met with police intimidation (Van der Walt 1998). This period also saw the forced confiscation of white-owned farms setting off a precipitous economic decline and hyperinflation in the early and mid-2000s.[18] Levels of political repression increased dramatically prior to the 2008 elections pitting the incumbent Robert Mugabe against a strong opposition led by Morgan Tsvangirai and Simba Makoni. The Mugabe regime began to plan – and to implement – its repressive strategy in

---

[18] For an overview of political developments in Zimbabwe during the mid- and late 1990s, see Sithole (2001). On the collapse of business–state relations see Taylor (2007: 30–34).

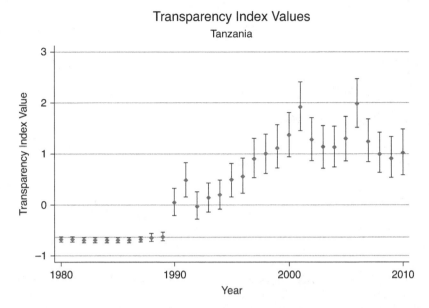

FIGURE 3.9. Tanzania HRV scores over time. A longitudinal plot of Tanzania's HRV index scores from 1980 to 2010. HRV index scores are on the y-axis, while time is measured on the x-axis. Diamonds denote mean predicted index scores. Whiskers denote 95 percent highest posterior density intervals.

2007. This period saw dramatic clashes between pro-regime forces and opposition figures, including the beating of Tsvangirai by riot police (Meredith 2007: 238–239).

Figure 3.10 plots the HRV index scores for Zimbabwe over time. A large and significant drop in HRV index scores is visible in 1995 – during the initial period of labor strikes and protests. Zimbabwe's levels of transparency remain steady at low levels throughout the remaining years of the index, during the period of Mugabe's increasingly authoritarian rule.

The case of Somalia depicts a still more dramatic decline in HRV index scores (see Figure 3.11). Throughout the 1970s and 1980s, Somalia was ruled by the nominally communist government of Mohamed Siad Barre. Following a military defeat to Ethiopian forces in 1978, the Siad Barre government maintained control by relying on a system of clan-based patronage.[19] This government is associated with moderate to low HRV index scores of between −0.6 and −0.75. By the late 1980s, this government faced increasing armed domestic opposition and infighting between clans once supportive of the government. Unrest grew such that, in 1991, Siad Barre was forced to flee Mogadishu in a tank, taking with him the foreign exchange reserves of the central bank (Prunier 1996: 45).

[19] For an overview of the rise and fall of the Siad Barre regime, see Prunier (1996).

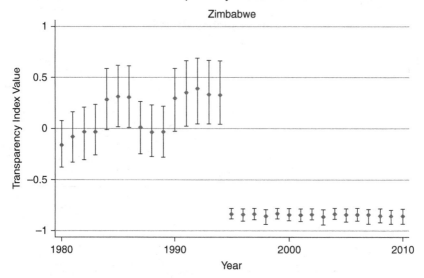

FIGURE 3.10. Zimbabwe HRV scores over time. A longitudinal plot of Zimbabwe's HRV index scores from 1980 to 2010. HRV index scores are on the y-axis, while time is measured on the x-axis. Diamonds denote mean predicted index scores. Whiskers denote 95 percent highest posterior density intervals.

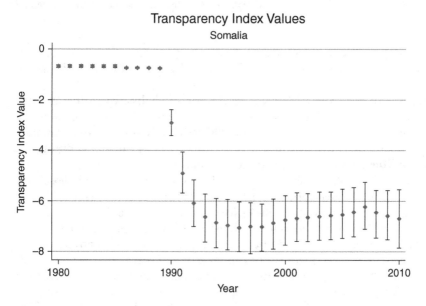

FIGURE 3.11. Somalia HRV scores over time. A longitudinal plot of Somalia's HRV index scores from 1980 to 2010. HRV index scores are on the y-axis, while time is measured on the x-axis. Diamonds denote mean predicted index scores. Whiskers denote 95 percent highest posterior density intervals.

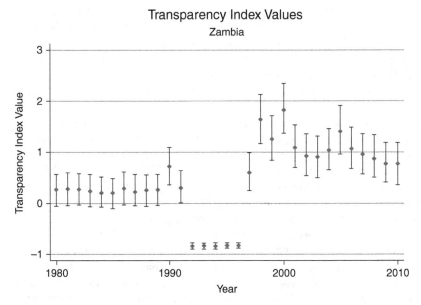

FIGURE 3.12. Zambia HRV scores over time. A longitudinal plot of Zambia's HRV index scores from 1980 to 2010. HRV index scores are on the y-axis, while time is measured on the x-axis. Diamonds denote mean predicted index scores. Whiskers denote 95 percent highest posterior density intervals.

The collapse of the government ushered in a period of civil war during which Somalia became the paradigmatic example of a failed state. The collapse of the Siad Barre government coincides perfectly with a dramatic fall in Somalia's HRV index score. In 1990, Somalia's predicted HRV score falls from −0.75 to −2.9. The following year sees another dramatic drop to −4.9, followed by further declines. Somalia's transparency score stabilizes around values of −6.7, among the lowest in our sample.

Changes in HRV scores over time are not always monotonic within countries. Take, for instance, the case of Zambia. As depicted in Figure 3.12, Zambia's HRV values are fairly constant at middling levels throughout the 1980s. There is a large and significant drop, however, in levels of data disclosure in 1992. Estimated disclosure values remain low for five years, before increasing again in 1997, after which they stabilize at values slightly greater than those during the 1980s period.

Zambia's decline in transparency scores during the early and mid-1990s coincides nearly perfectly with the first term in office of President Frederick Chiluba. Chiluba was elected in Zambia's first democratic elections in 1991 (Opalo 2012: 88). He replaced the single-party government of Kenneth Kaunda, which had been in power since 1964 and which banned opposition parties before the 1973 elections (Bratton 1992: 82–83). Kaunda's government relied heavily on a system of patronage to maintain political support during years of economic stagnation owing to the declining price for copper, the country's largest export (Bratton 1992). An attempted coup in 1990 and widespread strikes in 1991 forced Kaunda to agree to multiparty elections, in which Chiluba's MMD party won a sweeping victory, with 75 percent of the vote and 125 of 150 seats in the legislature (Baylies and Szeftel 1992; Posner and Simon 2002).

It may seem surprising that the introduction of multiparty democracy was associated with a *decline* in disclosure levels in Zambia. In other instances of democratic reform, such as in Tanzania and Eastern Europe (see below), increasing democracy led to substantial increases in HRV scores. Yet, Chiluba's first term in office was marked by low levels of protections for civil rights and economic upheaval. Bratton (1998: 59) remarks that "[Zambia] stands as perhaps the clearest example of the trend of declining quality of second elections in the sub-Saharan region." Upon entering office, Chiluba dismissed the chiefs of many state-owned enterprises and official news agencies, ostensibly as part of the MMD's economic reform program (Baylies and Szeftel 1992). In practice, the state was centralized under executive control and patronage, such that Van de Walle (2002) classifies the government as a "dominant executive" nondemocracy (see also von Soest 2007). Following a 1991 IMF loan (via the Rights Accumulation Program), austerity measures and price liberalization were adopted, which – coupled with a major drought in 1993 – caused GDP per capita to fall by roughly 3.3 percent per year between 1991 and 1996 (Posner and Simon 2002; Rakner, Van de Walle, and Mulaisho 1999). Little progress was made on promised privatization plans (Rakner, Van de Walle, and Mulaisho 1999). Before the 1996 election, Chiluba altered the constitution to ban Kaunda (due to his foreign parentage), and the election employed disputed voter roles (Posner and Simon 2002; Rakner, Van de Walle, and Mulaisho 1999).

By the late-1990s, however, some aspects of policymaking began to change for the better. Strained relations with the international community led to the application of more stringent conditions with regard to loan programs – notably through access to the IMF's Enhanced Structural Adjustment Facility. The rate of privatizations increased, and discussions began regarding the privatization of copper mining (Rakner, Van de Walle, and Mulaisho 1999). In 2000, Chiluba was forced to abandon attempts to amend constitutional term limits and stepped down from office. Consistent with these developments, measures of disclosure rebounded to – and then slightly exceeded – earlier levels.

Another example – this one from Latin America – shows again that movements in the HRV time series are not strictly monotonic. Argentina experienced massive swings in the level of economic liberalization between 1990 and 2010. In the early 1990s, the Menem government introduced policies to curtail the hyperinflation that had run rampant throughout the 1980s. These reforms included the introduction of dollar convertibility and a currency board,

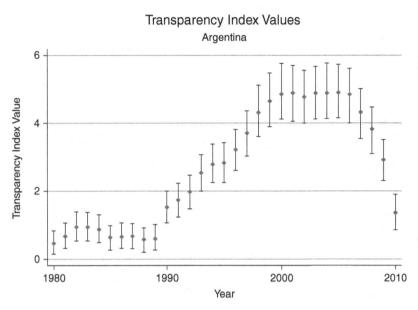

FIGURE 3.13. Argentina HRV scores over time. A longitudinal plot of Argentina's HRV index scores from 1980 to 2010. HRV index scores are on the y-axis, while time is measured on the x-axis. Diamonds denote mean predicted index scores. Whiskers denote 95 percent highest posterior density intervals.

as well as large-scale privatizations and market liberalization. Through such liberalizing policies, Menem secured the support of the business – particularly the export-oriented business – community (Treisman 2004). The policies implemented by Menem remained largely in effect until the 2001 Argentine debt crisis and the subsequent election of Néstor Kirchner in 2003 (Saiegh 2004). Particularly relevant for data dissemination: Kirchner's successor and wife – Cristina Fernández – seized control of the (previously apolitical) National Institute of Statistics and Censuses (INDEC) in 2007. Since that time, inflation statistics have been systematically doctored – largely to reduce government payments inflation-linked debt – leading the IMF to censure Argentina's noncompliance with the Fund's rules governing the reporting of statistics in February of 2013.[20] As one of the first acts of his newly elected administration in 2015, President Mauricio Macri restored the political independence of INDEC.[21]

---

[20] See "Motion of Censure," *The Economist*, February 9, 2013, www.economist.com/news/americas/21571434-fund-blows-whistle-motion-censure, accessed July 11, 2017.

[21] See "Argentina's new, honest inflation statistics," *The Economist*, May 25, 2017, www.economist.com/news/americas/21722694-end-bogus-accounting-argentinas-new-honest-inflation-statistics, accessed July 11, 2017.

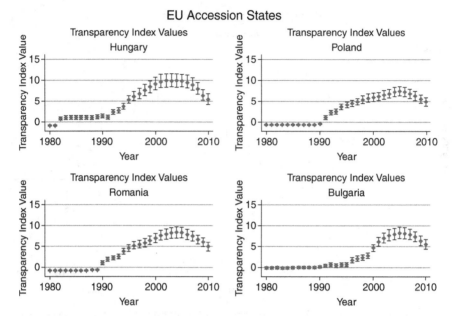

FIGURE 3.14. HRV scores and EU accession. Longitudinal plots of HRV scores for the Eastern European states admitted to the enlarged EU from 1980 to 2010. HRV index scores are on the y-axes, while time is measured on the x-axes. Diamonds denote mean predicted index scores. Whiskers denote 95 percent highest posterior density intervals. Values on the y-axis are common to all time series.

We present plots of Argentina's HRV scores over time in Figure 3.13. Transparency levels in Argentina exhibit a clear nonmonotonicity. Scores begin a dramatic increase in 1991 – the year in which the Convertability Plan was introduced – and these gains continue throughout the 1990s. Transparency plateaus during the debt crisis before declining sharply in the late 2000s. The first year of this decline is 2007 – the same year in which Fernández took control of the statistics institute.

We turn to Europe for a final set of cases (see Figure 3.14). We focus our attention on what might, at first, seem an oddity with the HRV index. In recent years, Eastern European countries – including Bulgaria and Romania – have been among the most transparent states in our index. While these strong performances with respect to data disclosure contrast with often mixed or poor records in regards to other forms of governance, we note a consistent relationship between data disclosure and EU accession. All Eastern European accessor states in our dataset show dramatic increases in HRV scores during the period of application for EU membership, followed by slight declines in more recent years. At their height, these states converge to scores similar to those in the most transparent established EU members. Similar, though more muted, patterns can be seen in Cyprus and in Turkey, during the period Turkey was considering applying for EU membership. These findings are consistent with existing scholarship that has stressed the transformative role played by the EU accession process – particularly in Eastern Europe (Hollyer 2010; Levitz and Pop-Eleches 2009; Vachudova 2005). The convergence of these states with the highest standards of EU disclosure is consistent with arguments that the EU exercises its greatest influence over applicant states and relatively weak member states (Borzel et al. 2007). Recent backsliding is consistent with claims that the EU's influence diminishes once membership is granted (Gray 2009; Hollyer 2010).

3.4 CONCLUSION

This chapter has three main points: First, the HRV index is built on a direct measure of data collection, the publication of information in the WDI. Second, the resultant index scores produce cross-sectional estimates that correlate highly with commonly held notions of transparency and that discriminate well among countries. Third, the HRV index scores seem to move in line with developments within countries over time that one would expect to affect the degree of this form of transparency.

The initial empirical exploration therefore validates the HRV index as a precise measure of transparency associated with governments' collection and dissemination of economic data. But how does our index compare to measures of other facets of transparency? We turn to this question in Chapter 4.

3.5 APPENDIX

> BOX 3.1. Countries included in the HRV index.

Afghanistan	Albania	Algeria
Angola	Argentina	Australia
Austria	Bangladesh	Belgium
Benin	Bolivia	Botswana
Brazil	Bulgaria	Burkina Faso
Burundi	Cambodia	Cameroon
Canada	Central African Republic	Chad
Chile	China	Colombia
Costa Rica	Côte d'Ivoire	Cuba
Cyprus	Dem. Republic of the Congo	Denmark
Dominican Republic	Ecuador	Egypt
El Salvador	Ethiopia	Fiji
Finland	France	Gabon
Ghana	Greece	Guatemala
Guinea	Guinea-Bissau	Guyana
Haiti	Honduras	Hungary
India	Indonesia	Iran
Iraq	Ireland	Israel
Italy	Jamaica	Japan
Jordan	Kenya	Kuwait
Lao PDR	Lebanon	Lesotho
Liberia	Libya	Madagascar
Malawi	Malaysia	Mali
Mauritania	Mauritius	Mexico
Mongolia	Morocco	Mozambique
Nepal	Netherlands	New Zealand
Nicaragua	Niger	Nigeria
Norway	Oman	Pakistan
Panama	Papua New Guinea	Paraguay
Peru	Philippines	Poland
Portugal	Republic of Congo	Romania
Russian Federation	Rwanda	Saudi Arabia
Senegal	Sierra Leone	Singapore
Somalia	South Africa	South Korea
Spain	Sri Lanka	Sudan
Swaziland	Sweden	Switzerland
Syria	Tanzania	Thailand
The Gambia	Togo	Trinidad and Tobago
Tunisia	Turkey	Uganda
United Arab Emirates	United Kingdom	United States
Uruguay	Venezuela	Vietnam
Zambia	Zimbabwe	

3.5.1 List of Countries included in the HRV Index and List of Items used to Construct the Index along with their Discrimination and Difficulty Parameter Estimates

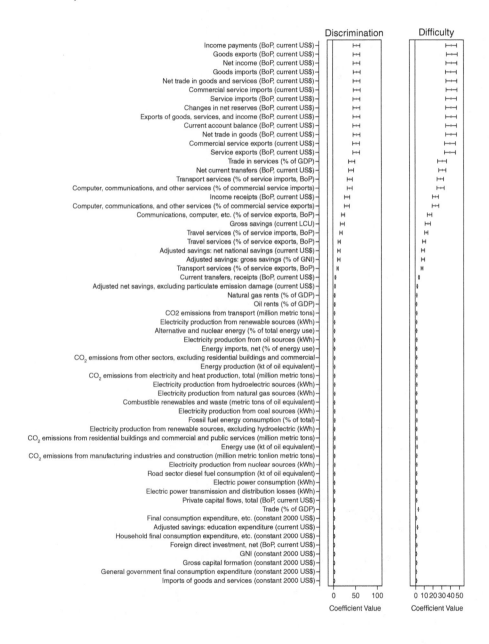

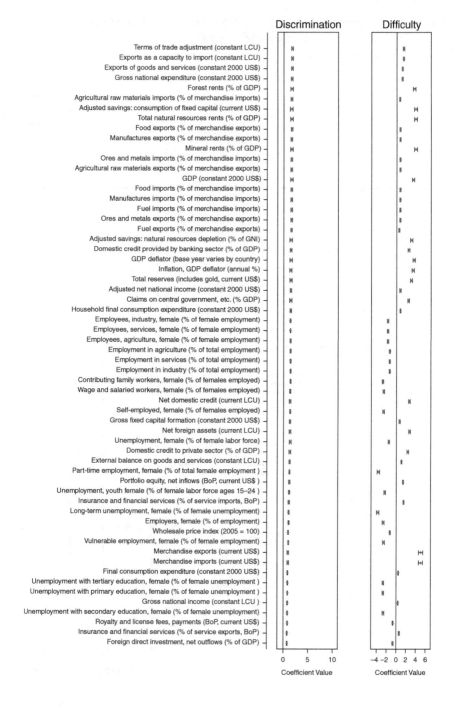

4

Comparing Measures of Transparency

The HRV index represents a new measure of data dissemination. But do we really need another measure of transparency? Other measures of different facets of transparency also exist. If different cross-national measures of transparency were highly enough correlated, then the theoretical distinctions presented in Chapters 2 and 3 would be moot. All indexes would serve as equally strong proxies for the availability of information in a polity. Moreover, it would be nearly impossible to use such indexes in empirical tests to discriminate across precise causal mechanisms. Before proceeding to our original theories about transparency and political stability – and testing them with the HRV index – we must pose a question: How do the various measures of transparency – institutional, media freedom, and data dissemination – correlate with each other?

In this chapter, we study the relationships between various measures of transparency. First, we examine the extent to which measures of these facets covary. We then undertake a more systematic comparison between data dissemination and each alternative measure of transparency in turn. We find substantively important distinctions across the measures. The results of our analysis confirm that the appropriate measure of transparency depends on the theoretical context.

4.1 THE COVARIANCE OF FACETS OF TRANSPARENCY

Table 4.1 presents a correlation matrix of measures of five different aspects of transparency. To measure the dissemination of aggregate economic data, we use the HRV index.

As a measure of institutional transparency, we use a variable capturing the presence of a freedom of information law (FOIL). Our measure of FOILs is drawn from Berliner (2014), who codes the year in which FOILs go into effect

TABLE 4.1. *Correlations between the facets of transparency.*

	HRV Index	FOIL	Freedom House	Newspaper Circ.	Aggregate Media
HRV Index	1.00				
FOIL	0.60	1.00			
Freedom House	0.62	0.55	1.00		
Newspaper Circ.	0.59	0.51	0.57	1.00	
Aggregate Media	0.68	0.60	0.89	0.89	1.00

in a cross-section of countries from 1990 to 2008.[1] We recode these data into a binary indicator {0, 1} that takes the value of 1 if a given country has an effective FOIL in a given year.

As measures of the role media plays in promoting transparency, we begin with two variables. First we include a measure of press *freedoms* as captured by Freedom House's Freedom of the Press index. We scale this index such that 100 indicates the highest possible level of freedom and 0 represents the lowest. This data series runs from 1994 to 2010. Second, we include a measure of media *penetration* as captured by the World Bank's measure of daily newspaper circulation per 1,000 residents. This measure is reported in five year increments from 1980 to 1995 and annually from 1994 to 2010.

Chapter 2 argues that it may be desirable to capture the role of the media in promoting transparency by combining measures of both the media's independence and reach. We apply a simple means to aggregate our two measures of media freedom and penetration to create a third measure of the media. We employ a principal components factor analysis – using the Freedom House and newspaper circulation measures – to create a new measure of media transparency, which we label "Aggregate Media" in Table 4.1. The constituent terms, Freedom House and Newspaper Circulation, are, not surprisingly, highly correlated with Aggregate Media.

Interestingly, the Aggregate Media index correlates more strongly with the HRV index than either media term on its own. Still, the correlation reaches only 0.68. The remaining four measures correlate with one another at intermediate levels. Correlation values mostly fall in the 0.5–0.6 range, implying that variation in one index typically explains 25–35 percent of the variation in the others.

This preliminary analysis reveals that empirical differences exist alongside the theoretical differences across facets of transparency discussed in Chapter 2. We now delve into these empirical differences.

---

[1] Berliner (2014) also codes the year of FOIL passage. Here we concentrate on the year the law goes into effect, as this is a more appropriate indicator of the level of institutional transparency. A law that is on the books, but not yet in effect, is unlikely to directly influence the flow of information to citizens, although one could test for indirect effects.

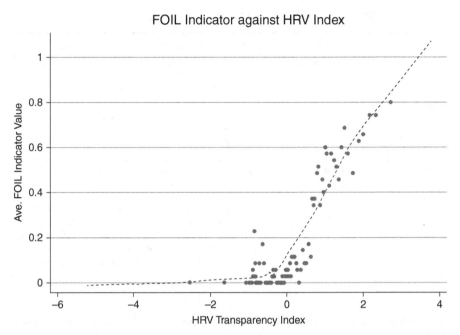

FIGURE 4.1. HRV index plotted against effective presence of FOILs. A scatter plot of an indicator of whether a FOIL is in effect against (standardized) HRV index scores. Observations have been binned – each dot corresponds to a one percentile movement in HRV index scores and the average FOIL presence for all country-year observations within that percentile (22–23 country-years per dot). All country-years with observations on both indexes between 1990 and 2008 are plotted. The dotted line is a lowess smoother (fit to all country-year observations).

4.2 DATA DISSEMINATION AND INSTITUTIONAL TRANSPARENCY

Consider the relationship between data dissemination and institutional transparency as measured by the presence/absence of an effective FOIL (Berliner 2014). Since our institutional transparency measure is binary, and our data disclosure measure continuous, comparisons between the two indexes are not as natural as between two continuous indexes. Figure 4.1 applies one method of comparing these two terms. Here, observations are binned by the level of HRV score – each dot on the scatter plot depicts a one percentile change in HRV score. There are 22–23 country-year observations per dot. The normalized HRV index score is plotted on the x-axis. The average presence of FOILs, which lies within the unit interval, is plotted on the y-axis. The dotted line depicts a lowess curve.

Figure 4.1 depicts a clear relationship between these two facets of transparency. As the HRV scores rise, the fraction of country-years with a FOIL increases sharply. Country-years that score highly on data disclosure are far

TABLE 4.2. *HRV index regressed on FOIL indicator.*

FOIL	2.436	1.839	1.646	1.268
	[1.324,3.548]	[0.824,2.853]	[0.716,2.576]	[0.424,2.112]
Democracy		0.983	0.939	0.719
		[0.569,1.396]	[0.533,1.346]	[0.318,1.121]
GDP per capita			0.013	0.004
			[−0.014,0.040]	[−0.013,0.021]
Democracy ×				0.034
GDP per capita				[−0.038,0.106]
$\hat{\sigma}$	1.245	1.175	1.167	1.159
N	3625	3625	3591	3591

Results of an OLS regression of HRV index scores against Berliner's (2014) indicator for the effective presence of a FOIL, a democracy indicator, GDP per capita (in thousands of PPP USD), and the interaction of GDP per capita and democracy. Ninety-five percent confidence intervals are presented in parentheses. All standard errors are clustered by country, and all observations are weighted by the inverse of the standard deviation of the HRV index score. $\hat{\sigma}$ represents the standard error of the regression.

more likely than average to have a FOIL. However, country-years without FOILs vary substantially in their level of data disclosure.

Table 4.2 examines this relationship more systematically. It reports the results of a regression of HRV scores on the FOIL indicator. We control for potentially confounding factors: an indicator for democracy (we use the DD/ACLP definition of democracy as coded by Cheibub, Gandhi, and Vreeland 2010), GDP per capita in thousands of constant PPP adjusted 2005 US dollars (Heston, Summers, and Aten 2009), and the interaction of these two terms.

Throughout the empirical specifications presented in Table 4.2, the two indexes of interest are positively correlated at standard levels of statistical significance. Neither GDP per capita nor the interaction of GDP per capita and democracy substantially add predictive power to these regressions. Importantly, however, the democracy indicator has a statistically significant positive effect: Democratic countries score more strongly on the HRV measure than would be predicted from FOIL presence alone. Given that both FOIL enactment and data dissemination are the product of government decision-making, these results may be seen as rather surprising. Democratic country-years are roughly 30 percentage points more likely to have a FOIL than autocratic country-years.

4.3 DATA DISSEMINATION AND THE MEDIA

Next we consider the relationship between our measure of data dissemination and indexes of various aspects of media transparency. We consider Freedom

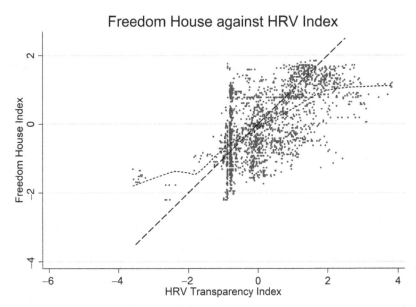

FIGURE 4.2. HRV index plotted against Freedom House scores. A scatter plot of (standardized) Freedom House Freedom of the Press Scores and (standardized) HRV index scores. Each dot corresponds to a country-year observation, and all country-years with observations on both indexes between 1994 and 2010 are plotted. The dashed line runs through the origin at a 45 degree angle. Observations that fall above the line score relatively highly on the Freedom House index as compared to the HRV index. The reverse holds for observations that fall below the line. The dotted line is a lowess smoother.

House scores, newspaper circulation figures, and our aggregation of the two indexes in turn.

Figure 4.2 depicts a scatterplot of HRV index scores against Freedom House scores from 1994 to 2010. Both indexes have been standardized by subtracting the mean index value from each observation and dividing by the standard deviation so that each index is on the same scale with mean zero and standard deviation one. The dashed line follows a 45 degree angle, so the two measures would be perfectly correlated if all observations fell on this line. Observations that fall above the line score relatively highly on the Freedom House index (plotted on the y-axis) as compared to the HRV index (plotted on the x-axis). The reverse holds for observations that fall below the line. The dotted curve represents a lowess smoother that is applied to these data.

A positive correlation between the two indexes is apparent in Figure 4.2. The slope of the lowess curve is positive for the full range of values. Note, however, that the slope flattens at the extremes, suggesting some important differences across the indexes. The HRV index ranks the most transparent country-years

TABLE 4.3. *HRV index regressed on Freedom House scores.*

Freedom House	0.687	0.515	0.424	0.197
	[0.415,0.958]	[0.200,0.829]	[0.111,0.736]	[−0.014,0.408]
Democracy		0.729	0.768	0.477
		[0.171,1.287]	[0.273,1.262]	[−0.012,0.965]
GDP per capita			0.027	0.004
			[−0.010,0.064]	[−0.014,0.021]
Democracy ×				0.073
GDP per capita				[0.002,0.144]
$\hat{\sigma}$	1.496	1.500	1.469	1.420
N	2120	1870	1870	1870

Results of an OLS regression of HRV index scores against the Freedom House index, a democracy indicator, GDP per capita (in thousands of PPP USD), and the interaction of GDP per capita and democracy. Ninety-five percent confidence intervals are presented in parentheses. All standard errors are clustered by country and all observations are weighted by the inverse of the standard deviation of the HRV index estimate. $\hat{\sigma}$ represents the standard error of the regression.

more highly, relative to other observations, than does Freedom House – and it ranks the least transparent country-years less highly.

So, the two indexes broadly agree on which countries should receive relatively high and low transparency scores – but the magnitude of the difference between high/low-scoring countries and mean index values is far greater in the HRV index than in the Freedom House measure. Meanwhile, Freedom House assigns a wide range of scores to country-years that rank in the middle of the HRV index.

Perhaps this disparity across the midrange reflects differences in the way the two indexes evaluate laws and institutions versus practices. Roughly one-third of the Freedom House index is determined by questions relating to legal protections for freedom of speech.[2] These laws may vary greatly, though they may not reflect great differences in government behavior. Thus, Laos, Fiji, and Papua New Guinea have similar HRV scores in 2004 – but Laos receives a far lower (less transparent) Freedom House score than the others do. The legal environments differ greatly, but all collect and report similar amounts of data. By contrast, Saudi Arabia and Tunisia receive identical Freedom House scores in the same year – both have similar legal protections for the freedom of speech – but Saudi Arabia receives a substantially lower HRV index score.

Table 4.3 explores the relationship between these two indexes more systematically. HRV index scores are regressed on the Freedom House index. Again, we control for our measures of democracy, GDP per capita, and their interaction. To adjust for measurement error in the HRV index data, we weigh all

---

[2] See www.freedomhouse.org/template.cfm?page=350&ana_page=376&year=2011, accessed July 14, 2016.

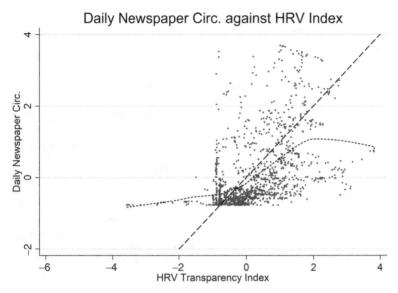

FIGURE 4.3. HRV index plotted against daily newspaper circulation. A scatter plot of (standardized) World Bank Daily Newspaper Circulation per 1000 residents and (standardized) HRV index scores. Each observation corresponds to a country-year, and all country-years with observations on both indexes between 1997 and 2004 are plotted. The dashed line runs through the origin at a 45 degree angle. The dotted line is a lowess smoother.

observations in these regressions by the inverse of the standard deviation of the HRV index predictions.

The results confirm that the two indexes are positively correlated. We can also see that – perhaps somewhat surprisingly – the HRV index remains correlated with democracy even after controlling for Freedom House scores. Democratic countries consistently receive higher (autocratic countries lower) scores on the HRV index than they receive on Freedom House's measure. This result holds despite Freedom House's explicit focus on the protection of a core democratic principle – freedom of the press – and HRV's lack of an analogous focus. High income democracies perform particularly strongly on HRV relative to Freedom House – possibly due to top coding in the latter index.

Next, we consider the relationship between data dissemination and newspaper circulation. Figure 4.3 depicts a scatter plot of the HRV index against newspaper circulation. Both measures have been standardized by subtracting the mean value from each observation and dividing by the standard deviation. The dashed line corresponds to a 45 degree angle, while the dotted line is a lowess smoother plotted over the data.

Figure 4.3 indicates that both indexes broadly agree on a set of low scoring countries. Countries with high scores on the HRV index, however, vary greatly

TABLE 4.4. *HRV index regressed on daily newspaper circulation.*

Newspaper circ.	0.006	0.004	0.004	0.003
	[0.004,0.009]	[0.002,0.007]	[0.000,0.007]	[−0.001,0.006]
Democracy		1.118	1.090	0.735
		[0.633,1.604]	[0.619,1.562]	[0.366,1.103]
GDP per capita			0.010	−0.005
			[−0.030,0.051]	[−0.025,0.016]
Democracy × GDP per capita				0.047
				[−0.026,0.121]
$\hat{\sigma}$	1.366	1.282	1.287	1.269
N	1447	1447	1439	1439

Results of an OLS regression of HRV index scores against the World Bank's Daily Newspaper Circulation per 1000 residents, a democracy indicator, GDP per capita (in thousands of PPP USD), and the interaction of GDP per capita and democracy. Ninety-five percent confidence intervals are presented in parentheses. All standard errors are clustered by country and all observations are weighted by the inverse of the standard deviation of the HRV index estimate. $\hat{\sigma}$ represents the standard error of the regression.

in their daily newspaper circulation numbers. The two indexes are correlated, though the disagreement over which countries are highly transparent is greater than between Freedom House and the HRV values.

Table 4.4 presents the results of a regression of HRV index values against daily newspaper circulation numbers.[3] The two indexes are related to one another – though the strength of the correlation drops with the inclusion of controls. Several systematic discrepancies between the two indexes are apparent. In particular, democracies are ranked as more transparent by the HRV index than by daily newspaper circulation numbers. This strong democratic performance on the HRV index holds regardless of the level of income. This finding meshes well with the theoretical expectation that high newspaper circulation numbers may be driven by a pervasive state media in autocracies. These findings are important since our theoretical expectations about the role of transparency relate not simply to the volume but also to the quality of information relayed to the public.

We also compare data dissemination to the aggregate measure of media transparency, constructed through the principal components factor analysis of the Freedom House and newspaper circulation variables. The resultant Aggregate Media measure by construction has a mean of zero and a standard deviation of one – it correlates with both Freedom House and newspaper circulation at a level of 0.89. Figure 4.4 plots this measure (on the y-axis) against

[3] These values have not been standardized. To adjust for measurement error in the HRV index, all observations have been weighted by the inverse of the standard deviation of the HRV index estimates.

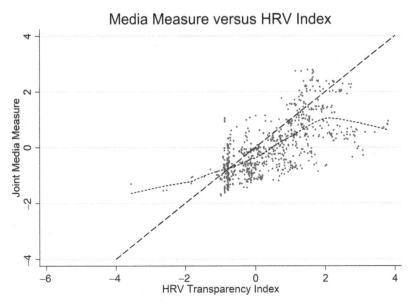

FIGURE 4.4. HRV index plotted against Aggregate Media measure. A scatter plot of Aggregate Media scores and (standardized) HRV index scores. Each observation corresponds to a country-year, and all country-years with observations on both indexes between 1997 and 2004 are plotted. The dashed line runs through the origin at a 45 degree angle. The dotted line is a lowess smoother.

standardized HRV index scores (on the x-axis). The dashed line is a 45 degree angle through the origin, representing a perfect correlation; the dotted line is a lowess smoother applied to the data.

Figure 4.4 confirms that the relationship between the Aggregate Media measure and the HRV index is stronger than the relationship between HRV scores and either of its component parts – as seen in Table 4.1. Both indexes broadly agree on high- and low-scoring country-years, and variation in one index is highly predictive of variation in the other throughout the range of possible scores. However, the slope of the lowess curve is substantially less than one throughout the graph, implying that HRV again ranks high- and low-scoring country-years as more extreme (relative to the average country-year) than does the Aggregate Media index. Moreover, the lowess curve flattens at extreme values of both indexes, suggesting that the HRV index finds greater variation among highly opaque and highly transparent countries than does the Aggregate Media measure.

Table 4.5 examines deviations between these two indexes in greater detail. It reports the results of regressions of HRV index values on the Aggregate Media index, a democracy indicator, GDP per capita, and the interaction between the

TABLE 4.5. *HRV index regressed on aggregate media measure.*

Media Measure	1.288	1.113	1.003	0.880
	[0.619,1.957]	[0.470,1.755]	[0.579,1.427]	[0.343,1.417]
Democracy		0.498	0.535	0.424
		[−0.105,1.101]	[−0.119,1.188]	[−0.122,0.971]
GDP per capita			0.011	0.001
			[−0.038,0.061]	[−0.022,0.025]
Democracy ×				0.025
GDP per capita				[−0.089,0.140]
$\hat{\sigma}$	1.526	1.515	1.513	1.510
N	728	728	728	728

Results of an OLS regression of HRV index scores against an aggregate media measure, a democracy indicator, GDP per capita (in thousands of PPP USD), and the interaction of GDP per capita and democracy. All observations are weighted by the inverse of the standard deviation of the HRV index estimate. Ninety-five percent confidence intervals are presented in parentheses. All standard errors are clustered by country. $\hat{\sigma}$ represents the standard error of the regression.

last two terms. As in the previous regressions, we adjust for measurement error in the HRV index by weighting all observations by the inverse of the standard deviation of the predicted HRV value.

Not surprisingly, the results reveal that the HRV index correlates with the Aggregate Media measure. As is true with both the Freedom House and newspaper circulation measures, democracies tend to systematically receive higher HRV scores than aggregate media scores. Coefficients on the democracy term hover just below levels of statistical significance (p-values range from 0.104 to 0.127), perhaps due to multicollinearity.

Systematic differences between measures of data dissemination and measures of media transparency, therefore, exist. In particular, democracies tend to systematically disclose more data (relative to autocracies) than one would predict from differences in the media across these regime types. This discrepancy may reflect the extent to which the decision to disclose aggregate economic information fundamentally lies with the government, whereas the functioning of the media market lies only partially under the control of the government. Moreover, countries tend to vary more – particularly in the extremes – on levels of data disclosure than in the functioning of the media. Extreme observations on the HRV index tend to depart more radically from average observations than extreme observations on any of the media indexes we examine.

4.4 TRANSPARENCY, CAPACITY, AND WILLINGNESS

Throughout our exploration of the relationships across different measures of transparency above, we control for two key variables: democracy and level of economic development (as measured by GDP/capita). The correlation between level of economic development and democracy is well known, and, as discussed above, some would argue that this political regime is itself an indicator of institutional transparency (Broz 2007).

We have much more work before us to understand the relationship between transparency and democracy. We return to the issue with more theoretical and empirical rigor in Parts II and III of the book.

Before concluding this chapter, however, we wish to discuss further the nexus of economic development, democracy, and transparency, particularly as they relate to the capacity and willingness of a government to collect and disseminate internationally acceptable economic data.

Note that while only a few studies have employed data availability as a variable, those that do implicitly disagree as to the processes that drive this form of transparency. Bueno de Mesquita et al. (2003), Hollyer, Rosendorff, and Vreeland (2011), and Williams (2009) treat missing data as a reflection of governments' *willingness* to disseminate data. Stone (2008), by contrast, treats missing data as a reflection of state *capacity* – under the assumption that missing data results from states' inability to gather and disseminate information.

We suggest that this facet of transparency should not be viewed in contradistinction to state capacity. Nor does data dissemination only reflect the willingness (whether primitive or induced) of a government to provide information. In our view, dissemination is a reflection of *both* the willingness of a government to provide information and its ability to do so. In related work, Edwards, Coolidge, and Preston (2012: 7) find "strong support for a link between regime type and transparency, and some support for economic variables shaping transparency decisions" (see also Lall 2016). Lorentzen, Landry, and Yasuda (2010) – analyzing subnational governments in China – reach a similar conclusion that transparency is a function of both capacity and willingness.

Evidence for this claim can be seen in Figure 4.5. This figure plots normalized HRV index scores (on the y-axis) against the natural logarithm of per capita GDP for both democracies and autocracies. Per capita GDP is an often-used proxy for state capacity. In their highly influential study of civil war, for example, Fearon and Laitin (2003: 76) argue that per capita income proxies "for state administrative, military, and police capabilities." Figure 4.5 presents separate lowess curves for democracies and autocracies.

Note that the democracy curve has a positive slope at every level of per capita income: as society's economic capacity increases, so does the availability of data. The curve for autocracies is more complicated: it slopes upward, then flattens before sloping downward. The difference between the democratic and autocratic patterns strikes us as important. Examining the different patterns of data disclosure – and their effects – across democratic and nondemocratic countries dominates the rest of the book.

Taken together, the data presented in Figure 4.5 suggest that data dissemination is not simply a reflection of state capacity. We make three observations:

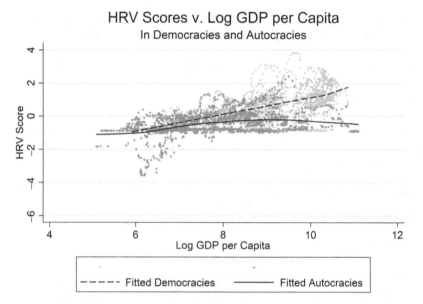

FIGURE 4.5. HRV scores versus log GDP per capita. Scatterplots, and fitted lowess lines, of standardized HRV scores against the natural log of GDP per capita. All HRV index scores have been standardized by subtracting the index mean and dividing by the index standard deviation. Autocracies are plotted as dark gray points, democracies as light gray points. The dashed line is the lowess curve fit to democratic observations. The solid line is the lowess curve fitted to autocratic observations.

1. The lowess curve for democracies is consistently above that of autocracies, suggesting that democratic regimes are more transparent, controlling for income. Apparently, for every level of economic development, democracies are more willing to disseminate data than are their autocratic counterparts.
2. The slope of the lowess curve is steeper for democracies than for autocracies. Although low-income democracies report at similar rates as low-income autocracies – both are constrained by a lack of capacity – democracies become significantly more likely to report as income rises. This relationship is likely attributable to a greater incentive on the part of democracies to report – incentives that we examine carefully in Part III.
3. Contrary to what one would expect if dissemination were simply a function of capacity, the relationship between transparency levels and income in autocracies is largely flat and shows signs of a slight nonmonotonicity. Reporting rises in income for relatively poor autocracies, but this relationship breaks down – and there is some evidence that disclosure even declines – for more wealthy autocracies.

Furthermore, recall that the most discriminating variables from the IRT model used to estimate the HRV index primarily relate to politically sensitive aspects of the economy – notably, trade and investment figures. The least discriminating primarily relate to politically uncontroversial concerns – population size, for example. State capacity is required to collect data on all of these variables, but the politically sensitive variables play a greater role in our index. These results suggest that disclosure is a political decision, not simply a reflection of bureaucratic capacity. Finally, note that our broad analysis is also consistent with the narrower focus of Ross (2006), who finds that "high-performing authoritarian states" tend to report child mortality and economic data infrequently, despite relatively high per capita income levels and low mortality rates. When it comes to the decision to disclose data, political will matters.

From the point of view of citizens, it may not matter whether missing data result from an incapacity or an unwillingness to disclose. In the absence of disclosure, citizens are less able to draw accurate inferences about government behavior. Regardless of whether their government is *unable* or *unwilling* to collect and disclose data, they are equally uninformed. This is not to say the question of whether willingness or capacity has a greater effect on disclosure is unimportant. To the contrary, this question is central to political science and we offer a dependent variable which scholars can use to test various hypotheses about what causal mechanism dominates under different circumstances.

Indeed, one can easily attribute the rankings of certain states on our index to either their capacity or their willingness to disclose data. For instance, Cuba receives low transparency scores throughout the period covered by our index. In the early 1980s, Cuba's per capita GDP was nearly twice that of the median country (according to the Penn World Table data) and the government had vastly expanded education provision – from levels similar to prevailing rates of the developing world in the 1950s and 1960s, to rates similar to those of the developed world in 1980 (Barro and Lee 1996). In short, Cuba possessed a relatively high level of state capacity, but *chose* not to disclose data to the WDI. By contrast, Somalia experienced precipitous drops in its HRV score in 1990 and 1991 – coinciding with the collapse of the Siad Barre government and the outbreak of civil war. It is probable that we can attribute most of the decline in transparency in this instance to the loss of state capacity as Somalia became the paradigmatic example of a failed state.

More generally, we find that the HRV index correlates with GDP per capita (again, often cited as a proxy for capacity), regime type, and their interaction in a manner that cuts against the claim that data dissemination simply reflects states' capacity or willingness to disclose. Our analysis reveals that HRV scores correlate strongly with income, but only under democratic rule. Poor (capacity-constrained) democracies disclose data at similar levels to poor autocracies, but rich democracies disclose substantially and significantly more data than do rich autocracies. In states that possess both the ability (again, proxied by income) and the willingness (proxied by democracy) to disclose, disclosure is high. In states where either factor is lacking, rates of disclosure are low.

4.5 CONCLUSION

It may well make sense to think of some countries as more broadly open than others – different facets of transparency are correlated with one another. Nevertheless, significant discrepancies also exist. Data disclosure is more closely linked to regime type than are the other facets of transparency – high-income democracies, in particular, seem to score more highly on this facet than on other aspects of transparency. Moreover, countries appear to vary more widely in the extent to which they disclose data than in aspects of their media markets and the extent of institutional transparency. We exploit these differences as we proceed through the book to identify empirically the causal mechanisms that we lay out in our theoretical models.

Importantly, we find evidence that data disclosure does not appear to be driven entirely by the capacity of a state to collect data, but also depends on the willingness of a state to disseminate credible data. We suspect that democracies may be more willing than are autocracies to share data with the public because of the consequences of doing so for political stability. Disseminating aggregate data generates common knowledge among the citizenry about the performance of the government. When the survival of the government depends on elections, the consequences for stability are quite different than when survival depends on the loyalty of an inner-circle elite.

Armed with the HRV index of transparency, we are now prepared to explore these consequences throughout the rest of the work. In Part II, we present a new theory of transparency and political stability. In Part III, we examine the incentives of democracies and autocracies to disclose data.

POLITICAL (IN)STABILITY

> More than petards or stilettoes, therefore, words – uncontrolled words, circulating freely, underground, rebelliously, not gotten up in dress uniforms, uncertified – frighten tyrants. But sometimes it is the official, uniformed, certified words that bring about the revolution.
>
> Ryszard Kapuściński, *Shah of Shahs* (1985: 103)

Survival – as the goal of political leaders – has become a canonical assumption in political science. Just as economists assume that individuals seek to maximize the utility associated with consumption (and firms, profits), political scientists often assume that governments seek to survive in power. Whether they do so by winning elections, by paying off an inner circle of elites, or by quelling the masses through fear, we assume that all governments share this common goal of surviving in power. There are, of course, exceptional leaders throughout history who have voluntarily stepped down from power, including Presidents George Washington (1797) and Nelson Mandela (1999) (see Cogley 2013). We treat such exceptional leaders as deviations from the rule.

How does transparency impact the survival of political leaders? We contend that the answer depends crucially on political institutions. As argued by Bueno de Mesquita et al. (2003), political institutions shape the very logic of political survival. Autocrats typically depend on the loyalty of key inner-circle elites to maintain power – mass unrest does not often take down an autocrat because collective action problems typically hinder threats to their rule from below. Indeed, tight control of information helps keep the masses at bay. Under democracy, by contrast, elections enable the masses to express their will. In order to survive in power, democratic governments must win over and maintain the support of the masses by winning regular elections. Autocratic and democratic leaders face different threats and opportunities from changes to the informational environment.

Part II explores the logic of how the informational environment impacts the likelihood of political survival under autocracy and, alternatively, under democracy. We maintain our focus on the dissemination of data on aggregate economic outcomes, specifically looking at how this form of transparency impacts the decisions of average citizens to continue to support or oppose political leaders and regimes. In these three chapters, we emphasize how the informational environment impedes or enables collective action.

We begin by exploring the impact of the informational environment on the survival of autocracies. In Chapter 5, we scrutinize how transparency affects the decisions of the masses of citizens (we examine elite decisions – which are quite distinct – in Chapter 10). We then turn to an examination of democratic regimes. We are concerned both with the removal of democratically elected leaders and also with the survival of the institution of democracy itself. Chapter 5 thus speaks to the large literature in the field of comparative politics on autocratic survival, democratic transitions, and regime breakdowns. A partial list of such recent works includes Acemoglu and Robinson (2000); Rosendorff (2001); M. Howard (2002); Levitsky and Way (2002); Boix (2003); Boix and Stokes (2003); Acemoglu and Robinson (2006); Ansell and Samuels (2010); Freeman and Quinn (2012); Clark, Golder, and Golder (2017).

We highlight some elegance in the mathematics in Chapter 5. We apply the exact same theoretical model to autocracies and democracies – save for the presence/absence of contested elections, which determine the fate of the government under democracy. Though the models are otherwise identical, we reach opposite conclusions about the impact of transparency on the survival of political regimes.

Specifically, we find that transparency makes mass unrest more likely under autocracy, while we find that transparency renders the masses more supportive of the political regime under democracy. In other words, the introduction of democratic elections into our model does not merely attenuate the effect of transparency – the effect actually flips. The chapter's key finding is that transparency provokes unrest under autocracy while quelling it under democracy.

We then turn to testing the theory empirically in Chapters 6 and 7. The theory generates many empirical implications and we examine a plethora of outcomes. Chapter 6 presents empirical examples alongside descriptive data while Chapter 7 examines the data more rigorously using regression analysis. In each chapter, we consider the effect of increasing transparency first on autocratic instability and then on democratic stability.

Looking at autocracies, we show that regime breakdowns leading to democratization become more likely with increased transparency. We then consider autocratic breakdown more generally, looking at instances where mass unrest may have caused either democratization or the replacement of one autocratic regime by another. Finally, we look more specifically at the actions of masses and elites under autocracy, showing that transparency increases the likelihood of mass anti-government demonstrations and strikes, but not of revolutions, coups, or assassinations. These results bolster our confidence in the exact mechanisms identified by our theory in Chapter 5.

Turning to democracies, we show that, in contrast with autocracies, regime stability increases with transparency. Democracy becomes less likely to break down with an increase in data disclosure. Again, we then test our theory more specifically, examining the exact mechanism by which democratic leaders are removed from office. With an exclusive focus on leader removal through domestic means (as opposed to foreign intervention), we show that regular, electoral removals become more likely with increased transparency, while irregular, extraconstitutional leader removal is more likely under opaque democracies.

Throughout the empirical work in Chapters 6 and 7, we take three approaches. First, we present illustrative examples from history. Examples in this part of the book draw on representative experiences of countries in Africa, Asia, Europe, and Latin America (Chapter 6). Second, we present basic patterns in the data, showing the descriptive relationship between our index of transparency and each of several measures of instability (also in Chapter 6).

Finally, we introduce econometric rigor to our analysis, addressing alternative explanations for the observed descriptive patterns (Chapter 7). We introduce control variables, account for trends over time, and incorporate country-specific idiosyncrasies in our empirical models. Generally, the predicted effects of the HRV index are statistically significant at conventional levels – in some cases outperforming variables widely accepted as predicting regime (in)stability in the literature (including GDP per capita). We thus conclude with robust statistical evidence that transparency, as measured by data disclosure, causes mass unrest that topples autocratic regimes, while transparency consolidates democracy.

5

Transparency and (In)stability

The Theory

Toppling a political regime requires dangerous collective action. Governments can crush small protests with ease. Protestors may be jailed, tortured, disappeared, or killed. Under a vicious government, similar fates may await their families and loved ones. As dissatisfied with a regime as a citizen may be, she does not want to participate in a failing movement to overthrow the government. The coordination of mass discontent thus stands as an obstacle to mass movements – especially under autocracy. Autocrats count on fear of retribution to keep the masses from taking to the streets.

We therefore take an approach inspired by the global games literature to examine the effect of transparency on mass unrest. Global games, first developed by Carlsson and Van Damme (1993), examine the strategic actions of individuals who receive (potentially) correlated signals about the state of the world. Economists have employed these models to explore different types of collective action problems, such as bank runs, currency crises, and commodity bubbles (Morris and Shin 1998; Angeletos and Werning 2006; Hellwig, Mukherji, and Tsyvinski 2006). Political scientists have used these models to explain problems of authoritarian control, revolutions, and democratic consolidation (Svolik 2008, 2012, 2013a, 2013b, 2013d, 2015, Boix and Svolik 2013; Shadmehr and Bernhardt 2011, 2015, n.d.; Casper and Tyson 2014; Little, Tucker, and LaGatta 2015; Little 2016, 2017).[1]

---

[1] Our theoretical model, while grounded in a global games informational structure, departs from most of the global games literature in a technical assumption: classical formulations of global games exhibit the property of two-sided limit dominance (Morris and Shin 2001). For some realizations of their private signal, citizens have a dominant strategy: protest or not protest. By contrast, we treat protest as a "pure" coordination game, incorporating problems of incomplete information and a global games informational structure. Hence, unlike in classical global games, multiple equilibria exist in our model. Moreover, we assume away issues of free-riding in protest in order to focus on problems of coordination. In making this assumption, our model is more

In our model, citizens receive signals about the state of the economy. These signals can be associated with more or less "noise," depending on the level of transparency. Intuitively, a highly noisy signal is one that conveys little credible information to citizens about the true performance of the economy – government announcements bear little relation to reality. A more accurate signal conveys a clearer and more credible reflection of aggregate economic performance. We operationalize this noise in our theoretical model below as a random draw from a normal distribution centered on zero. This distribution may have high or low variance. Under low levels of transparency, the signal can be so noisy that the citizens have little idea of how the economy is really performing – they only know their personal experience. When transparency is high, however, citizens have a more accurate picture of aggregate economic performance. Thus, transparency serves to inform citizens of the experiences – and beliefs – of others outside their family or immediate social circle. After receiving this signal, citizens choose whether to actively engage in protest, attempting to topple the political regime.

We organize the chapter as follows. First, we explain how our approach to regime stability relates to the broader literatures on autocracies and democracies. This transitions literature – which focuses on the survival of autocratic regimes, the emergence of democracy, and the breakdown of democracy – constitutes, arguably, some of the most important work in the field of comparative politics. We also provide in this section an overview of the game theoretic models to come. Thereafter, we present the mathematical models themselves. We begin with the bare-bones model for autocratic governments, showing how enhancing the informational environment encourages mass unrest. Then we introduce contested elections into that model, showing how democracy changes the effect of transparency on the willingness of the masses to support the political regime. We conclude by emphasizing the importance of political institutions for understanding the effect of transparency.

5.1 (IN)STABILITY AS A GLOBAL GAME

5.1.1 Autocratic Instability

Autocratic governments, despite their seemingly unconstrained authority, live in the shadow of mass political unrest. At any given moment, the public may reject the existing political order and – by taking political action, such as striking

---

directly comparable to treatments of political accountability in environments of incomplete information (Banks and Sundaram 1993; Besley 2006; Fearon 1999). In adopting this "pure" coordination game approach, we further dispense with the assumption, common in this literature, that some citizens have a dominant strategy of protesting (for another exception, see Bueno de Mesquita 2010).

or protesting in the streets – impose substantial costs upon their government, sometimes even ousting the leadership or upending the regime.[2]

Those citizens who would participate in mass unrest against their political leadership face, of course, a critical problem. While strikes and protests that draw widespread participation might force the hands of their rulers, the government can easily crush rebellions that do not achieve a certain threshold of support among the citizenry. Autocrats have proven willing to use violence and impose considerable costs on protest participants. Only efforts involving large masses of citizens can successfully unseat a government.

The willingness of any one citizen to participate in anti-regime mobilizations therefore depends on the willingness of others to similarly participate (Bueno de Mesquita 2010; Casper and Tyson 2014; Little 2012; Little, Tucker, and LaGatta 2015; Kuran 1991; Lohmann 1993; Shadmehr and Bernhardt 2011). Participation in mobilization is subject to strategic complementarities: A given citizen grows more willing to engage in protest as she believes others are similarly willing to mobilize.

What enables citizens to form shared beliefs in a manner that allows for protest? We focus on the presence or absence of publicly observable information on governments' economic performance. Publicly observable information plays an outsized role in interactions characterized by strategic complementarities, since such information allows citizens to not only update their beliefs about government performance, but also to update their higher-order beliefs – their beliefs about the beliefs held by other citizens (Morris and Shin 2002).[3]

The dissemination of aggregate economic data can inform citizens of the underlying "distribution of discontent" with the autocratic regime. When such information is more widely available, each citizen has a better sense of whether discontent is widely shared – and hence whether others are willing to mobilize against the government. Publicly observable economic information facilitates the formation of shared expectations about the likely success of mass mobilization, rendering such mobilization feasible where it would be nearly impossible absent such information. *We, therefore, contend that the availability of public economic information helps individuals solve their collective action problem and so renders autocratic regimes more vulnerable to threats from the citizenry.*

The threat that mass mobilization poses for autocratic leaders and ruling cliques – and the importance of attempts to repress or co-opt the masses – has played a prominent role in writings on authoritarian regimes.[4] The

---

[2] There are no female autocratic leaders in our dataset, and so (for the purposes of clarity) we assign the masculine pronouns for the leader and feminine pronouns for the citizens/voters. We also use the masculine pronoun for democratic leaders.

[3] For an early application of higher-order beliefs in a different setting, see Przeworski (1998).

[4] See, for example, Wintrobe (1998); Rosendorff (2001); Boix (2003); Acemoglu and Robinson (2006); Gandhi (2008); Przeworski (2009); Svolik (2012); Girod, Stewart, and Walters (2016); and Colgan and Weeks (2015).

findings from our model thus speak to an expansive literature on mass unrest and autocratic stability. Models of autocratic rule often assume that leaders are constrained by the threat of mass unrest, and must employ co-optation or repression to deal with this threat. We suggest that the severity of these pressures depends on the informational environment. In an environment with little information available to the masses, lower levels of co-optation or repression may be necessary for autocrats to maintain power.

A recent literature on mass protest and collective action similarly emphasizes the informational problems involved in coordinating protests (Shadmehr and Bernhardt 2011).[5] Like these studies, our theoretical treatment of transparency and mass unrest builds on the mechanics of global games (Carlsson and Van Damme 1993; Morris and Shin 1998, 2001). Our depiction of the role of transparency owes particularly to Morris and Shin (2002), who emphasize that public information plays a dual role in the presence of strategic complementarities, causing observers to update (1) their own beliefs and (2) their higher-order beliefs about the beliefs of other players.

We focus on how publicly observable information regarding the economic performance of the sitting government shapes the incentives for protest. We contend that citizens are more likely to mobilize when they perceive that the ruling clique is mismanaging the economy, either as a result of its attempts to extract rents or simply as the result of incompetence (Haggard and Kaufman 1995; Przeworski et al. 2000).

As in the Morris and Shin (2002) model, publicly available information can (1) confirm or refute citizen perceptions of economic mismanagement and (2) inform citizens about others' beliefs regarding the extent of mismanagement. Each individual knows that public information is also available to her fellow citizens. Thus public information allows her to better judge others' perceptions of the ruling elite. As citizens become more aware of one another's perceptions, they become better able to judge the willingness of others to mobilize in protest.

The incentives to engage in unrest aimed at unseating the leadership are highest when the sitting regime has revealed itself to be either predacious or incompetent – that is, when its economic performance is poor. As more public information on economic performance becomes available, citizens can better assess the performance of the government. Citizen perceptions align more closely with economic reality. And each citizen is aware that these beliefs are shared.

---

[5] Many of these pieces stress the importance of mechanisms for disseminating information, hence easing the coordination of protest. For instance, revolutionary vanguards may serve to inform the broader public about the extent of discontent with the regime (Bueno de Mesquita 2010; Shadmehr and Bernhardt, n.d.). Authoritarian elections may serve a similar purpose (Egorov and Sonin 2012; Little, Tucker, and LaGatta 2015). Protests may serve to resolve informational problems among the elite, facilitating coups (Casper and Tyson 2014). Edmond (2013), Lorentzen (2014), and Shadmehr and Bernhardt (2015) all consider environments in which elites manipulate or censor information in the shadow of the threat of unrest.

Consequently, as transparency rises, the economic performance of the sitting government translates more readily into manifestations of popular unrest. Transparency strengthens the relationship between economic outcomes and mass unrest.

Our theory also posits that transparency eases mobilization in general and that transparency can destabilize the ruling regime regardless of economic performance. The latter claim is true when mobilization against the regime is sufficiently costly or where the threshold of participation necessary for success is high – reasonable expectations in most authoritarian countries. Individual citizens must be convinced of mobilization's likely benefits before they are willing to take to the streets. This requisite level of certainty is only likely to be reached when the informational environment is rich.

The autocratic model thus makes two predictions regarding the informational environment: (1) transparency increases the likelihood of unrest and (2) the effect of transparency is exacerbated by poor economic performance.

5.1.2 Democratic Stability

The logic of political survival changes in important ways when governments must win elections to retain power. We view democracy as an equilibrium in which elections determine the fate of incumbents (Przeworski 1991, 2005; Weingast 1997). Since constitutions cannot be enforced by external actors, democratic institutions must be self-enforcing (Hardin 1999: 86). Democratic rule can be maintained only as long as all politically relevant actors comply with the rules of the game.

Citizens may take action against their democratically elected leaders – particularly if they perceive that democratic institutions have proven ineffective in disciplining their leaders.[6] Citizens who become disenchanted with democracy may alternatively support anti-democratic factions or elites who challenge democratic institutions. Democracy may certainly be overthrown by members of the elite via a coup or autogolpe.

Democratic regimes thus face many of the same threats as their autocratic counterparts. Democracies differ from autocracies, however, because of the role of elections. Crucial for our study, *elections carry informational value.*

Recall that under autocracy, transparency serves to inform citizens' higher-order beliefs about the "distribution of discontent." Under autocracy, elections

---

[6] For instance, many Egyptians pointed to the Morsi administration's incompetence and consolidation of power as causes for the protests that ultimately led to his ousting. See "Egypt's Tragedy," *The Economist,* July 6, 2013, www.economist.com/news/leaders/21580462-muhammad-morsi-was-incompetent-his-ouster-should-be-cause-regret-not-celebration-egypts, accessed July 11, 2017. Thai protesters similarly claimed that democracy proved an insufficient means of limiting the claimed abuses of the Shinawatra government. See "A Symbolic Exercise," *The Economist,* February 2, 2014, www.economist.com/blogs/banyan/2014/02/thailand-s-election, accessed July 11, 2017.

are either absent or sufficiently heavily manipulated to be uninformative of this distribution.[7] Under democracy, as Fearon (2011) observes, the electoral process serves to directly inform citizens of the distribution of discontent with the sitting leadership (see also Hyde and Marinov 2014; Little, Tucker, and LaGatta 2015; Luo and Rozenas 2018, forthcoming). Citizens observe election returns, in addition to popular participation in election events, which directly serve as an indicator of the extent to which discontent with the government is shared. Thus, *regardless* of the level of transparency, citizens in democracies have a great deal of information about the willingness of their fellows to engage in protest against the sitting leadership.

So what role does transparency play under democracy? *We contend that transparency enhances the effectiveness of elections in addressing "adverse selection" problems in government.* Adverse selection occurs when the electorate mistakenly reelects a bad leader or throws out a good one. When they enjoy better access to credible information about the aggregate economic outcomes of governmental policies, voters are more likely to remove underperforming leaders via the ballot box – and to keep the good ones in office. Moreover, citizens know that their fellows are likely to be well informed and voting in a sensible manner. Consequently, transparency increases popular satisfaction with democracy and inhibits challenges to the democratic order.[8]

Our theoretical model therefore relates to a vast literature on democratic consolidation. Many contributors to this literature have emphasized the importance of structural factors to democratic survival (Huber, Rueschemeyer, and Stephens 1993; Lipset 1959; Moore 1966; Slater 2009). Most significantly, economic development is strongly (positively) correlated with democratic survival (Przeworski et al. 2000). We include economic factors in our model, but do not focus on them – not because we think structural factors are unimportant, but rather because they are tangential to the mechanisms that are our focus.[9]

---

[7] For purposes of analytic tractability, we dichotomize elections as either informative or uninformative/absent, corresponding to the distinction between democracies and autocracies. In reality, elections may vary continuously in the extent to which they are informative of popular discontent. For treatments on the informational value of autocratic elections see, for instance, Egorov and Sonin (2012), Little (2012), Little, Tucker, and LaGatta (2015), Lust-Okar (2006), Gandhi and Lust-Okar (2009), and Magaloni (2006).

[8] Elections within democratic polities serve other functions too, of course: they are used to hold officials accountable for their policy choices, many of which are intended to redistribute resources across individuals and groups (see, for example, Cavaillé and Ferwerda 2017). Regarding accountability, Fearon (1999) discusses how problems of moral hazard become problems of adverse selection when leaders vary by type. We focus here on the role elections play in removing incompetent leaders rather than on legitimizing redistributional policy choices or on questions of moral hazard.

[9] The empirical specifications presented in the next chapter, however, all control for levels of economic development and for past experiences of democratic collapse.

The informational environment, we contend, has its most direct impact on the shared view across the electorate of the legitimacy of the electoral process.[10] Linz (1978: 17), for instance, argues that "Democratic legitimacy . . . requires adherence to the rules of the game by *both a majority of citizens* and those in positions of authority" (emphasis added). When citizens disregard democratic norms, or hold democratic institutions in low esteem, the democratic order is jeopardized.

Scholars disagree, however, as to what factors promote such legitimation (Jamal 2009). Some scholars emphasize the importance of civil society (Diamond 1994) or associational groups (Schmitter 1992), while others stress the extent of participation in electoral processes (Wright 2008b; Vanhanen 2000). Weingast (1997) emphasizes the populace's role in preventing elite encroachments on democratic freedoms. For democracy to survive, citizens must be willing to act against anti-democratic challengers, increasing the costs associated with coups or autogolpes.

Following Weingast's argument, Fearon (2011) finds that elections can play an informational role, enabling the public to mobilize against leaders who fail to comply with electoral rules. Little, Tucker, and LaGatta (2015) further develop this idea, noting that the conditions under which elections are likely to prove self-enforcing are only likely to be consistent with majoritarian electoral outcomes when elections are free from fraud – a point empirically tested by Hyde and Marinov (2014). Empirical observations from Tucker (2007) and Bunce and Wolchik (2011) – which find that fraudulent election results can give rise to protest – lend weight to these theoretical claims. Our approach similarly centers on the satisfaction of voters with the ability of the electoral process to root out bad leaders.

Our theory perhaps bears the closest resemblance to Svolik (2013c), who argues that democracies (particularly young democracies) can fall into a trap in which citizens' low esteem for democratic institutions encourages the entry of corrupt or incompetent politicians into political life, reinforcing citizens' initially low opinions. Svolik (2013c: 686) terms this danger the "trap of pessimistic expectations," and argues that "[w]hen it occurs, it undermines the public's willingness to defend democracy against attempts to subvert it, thus eliminating a key check on politicians or groups with authoritarian ambitions." Critical to this account is the assumption that monitoring incumbents is costly for citizens.

Building on Svolik's work, our theoretical model examines variation in the availability of information. Government provision of data on aggregate economic outcomes, in a sense, decreases the costs of citizens' monitoring,

---

[10] Our emphasis on the importance of the legitimacy of elections in the eyes of the citizenry is widely shared. Many scholars agree that democracies become consolidated as political actors come to accept the rules of the democratic game (Diamond 1994, 1999; Linz 1978; O'Donnell 1996; Schedler 1998; Schmitter 1992).

which should reduce the susceptibility of democracy to the trap of pessimistic expectations. Our contribution is thus to stress the roles that transparency and elections play in rewarding competent leadership and punishing the bad, thereby stabilizing democracy.

Our model suggests that where large amounts of information on the government's performance is made publicly available – and is known to be publicly available – democratic elections function relatively well. Elections better enable citizens to throw the bums out when the electorate has a clear view of economic performance (Przeworski, Stokes, and Manin 1999).[11] Where such information is absent, however, elections may prove a poor means of redressing adverse selection issues in government. With greater economic transparency, elections function better, which helps democratic regimes garner outcome legitimacy. Moreover, since information is publicly available, citizens recognize that their fellows are also acting in an informed manner in the voting booth. Transparency makes it more difficult to castigate portions of the electorate as irrational or ill-informed, enhancing the procedural legitimacy of democratic rule.

We thus consider a political environment in which the voters, en masse, prefer to reelect competent leaders and evict the incompetent. Each voter has her own sources of information about how well the leader is doing – a private signal – and the public at large has information that is commonly known and shared by all – a public signal.[12] At election time, a voter must decide to reelect or evict the incumbent. More transparency means that the public signal is a more reliable, stronger signal and can be used as a guide for keeping the good guys and evicting the bums.

When the polity is opaque the public signal is not very helpful. A noisy public signal might lead some voters to make the wrong choice on election day. With good luck (specifically, a lucky public signal), bad leaders can hope to win reelection, while good leaders with bad luck can lose. As public information becomes more available – as the polity becomes more transparent and the public signal more informative – citizens can rely on the (increasingly informative) public signal rather than just their private signals. Voting behavior therefore aligns more closely with incumbent performance, such that good leaders win reelection and bad ones do not.

Suppose, however, that a bad leader wins reelection because of a lucky public signal ("lucky" in the sense that the public signal about the leader's economic

---

[11] Alternative models (Barro 1973; Ferejohn 1986) emphasize the importance of moral hazard problems in controlling politicians. However, as Fearon (1999) notes, so long as there is any possibility that some elected leaders are "better" than others (from the perspective of the median voter), elections become a problem of adverse selection rather than moral hazard.

[12] An expansive literature notes the importance of information for improving citizen welfare and resolving agency problems between a populace and its elected representatives (Adserà, Boix, and Payne 2003; Besley and Burgess 2002; Brunetti and Weder 2003; Ferraz and Finan 2008). For recent research on the impact of election laws and media access on electoral integrity, see Frank and Martínez i Coma (2017).

performance is significantly better than warranted by his actions – though not lucky for the public at large). Citizens gain additional information about the incumbent's true type by virtue of the election process itself. Each voter learns of others' evaluations of the incumbent – both directly, through election returns, and indirectly, through the tenor of the elections and level of electoral participation. If bad leaders win reelection, the voters realize this when they see the election returns. In particular, they observe a leader win by a margin narrower than would be expected given the public signal.

When this happens, citizens may choose to take to the streets or otherwise seek to oust the leader through extraconstitutional actions. Elections have lost outcome legitimacy. Even if citizens simply lose faith in democratic institutions, one defense mechanism against anti-democratic elites is removed (Svolik 2013c; Weingast 1997). Elite-led coups and assassinations become more likely right along with mass insurrection. (We find a contrasting pattern for autocracies, explored in detail in Chapter 10.)

Elections thus serve to aggregate the private signals of all citizens, allowing individuals to update their beliefs about the performance of the government in light of others' evaluations. In our model, voters can figure out the incumbent's type with certainty after seeing the election results. Incumbents who perform well in elections, given the *ex ante* public information, can be inferred to be good types; while those who underperform can be inferred to be bad (Fearon 2011). In short, elections act as a means of aggregating the private information of all voters.

Of course, if, at the close of elections, citizens realize they have retained a good leader (or removed a bad one), the electoral system has served its role in screening politicians well. Such results should increase the outcome legitimacy of democracy. Since the probability that a bad type is retained falls in transparency, so too then does the risk of citizen disaffection and extraconstitutional leader removal. In contrast to provoking unrest under autocracy, transparency helps to sustain democracy.

5.2 THE BASELINE (AUTOCRATIC) MODEL

5.2.1 Autocratic Model Primitives

Consider an interaction between a leader, L, and a mass of citizens. The leader is an autocrat and does not face meaningful elections that determine his fate. We denote each citizen as i, where i is indexed over the unit interval $i \in [0, 1]$. One can think of the unit interval as representing 100 percent of the citizens.

Our model is one of adverse selection in government. The leader can be either a "good" type or a "bad" type: $\theta \in \{0, 1\}$, where $\theta = 1$ for good leaders and $\theta = 0$ for bad types. A leader's type may refer to his level of skill as a manager of the domestic economy, his competence as a leader, or his honesty when it comes to the temptations of power. On average, good leaders return better economic performance than bad leaders do, but many other factors also influence the economy besides the leader's type. Recessions may be attributable to governmental mismanagement or to global financial conditions; prosperity can result from the government providing proper public goods – or despite government distortions of market forces.

Citizens do not directly observe L's type, but they do seek to infer it. They wish to remove bad leaders from office, while retaining good types – if they can figure out which type of L is in office.

In our model, L's type is determined at random (by Nature), where $\theta = 1$ with probability p and $\theta = 0$ with probability $1 - p$. Only L knows his type with certainty; citizens can only take an educated guess – they know the value of p, and they can gather information over our two-period game.

During each period when he holds office, L chooses whether to provide a public welfare-enhancing good $G_t \in \{0, 1\}$, where $t \in \{1, 2\}$ denotes the period of play. Here, we keep things simple by letting L's utility from providing the public good (or not) be a function of his type, such that in each period:

$$u_{L,t}(G_t; \theta) = \begin{cases} 1 & \text{if } G_t = \theta \\ 0 & \text{otherwise} \end{cases}$$

$$u_L = \sum_{t=1}^{2} u_{L,t}(G_t; \theta)$$

In words, L has an incentive to match his action to his type. For L of type $\theta = 1$, L maximizes his utility by providing the public good, setting $G_t = 1$; and for L of type $\theta = 0$, L maximizes his utility by not providing the public good, setting $G_t = 0$. (In a later subsection we present a richer model where leaders reap benefits from survival and hence may have an incentive to mislead the public about their type by choosing an action that goes against type. The key qualitative conclusions of the simple model also hold in that more complex version.)[13]

L's choice regarding public goods provision $G_t \in \{0, 1\}$ has implications for the economic outcomes of our citizens. The income of each citizen derives partly from her individual economic activity and also from the public good – if it is provided by L. Formally, we denote the income of each citizen i as $y_{i,t} = G_t \gamma + \epsilon_{i,t}$. Here, γ is a strictly positive constant that represents the value of the public good in terms of a citizen's individual income. If $G_t = 1$, each citizen receives the same amount γ. We model the income from individual activity, $\epsilon_{i,t}$, as a random draw for each separate individual citizen during each separate period from a normal distribution (or "bell curve"): some individuals draw extremely

---

[13] Also, actors do not discount over the two time periods of our model, but the key results are unchanged when including a discount factor.

high incomes and some extremely low, but most draw from the middle. To simplify the math, we center the normal distribution on zero. So, formally, we write $\epsilon_{i,t} \underset{\text{iid}}{\sim} N(0, \sigma_y^2) \,\forall\, i, t$. Note that $\epsilon_{i,t}$ may be more or less tightly distributed around zero, depending on the standard deviation of the distribution, captured by $\sigma_y > 0$.

Each citizen observes her overall income in each period, $y_{i,t}$, but she cannot directly observe the values of G_t or $\epsilon_{i,t}$. So she does not know what type of L is in office. She can take her first period income, $y_{i,1}$, as a signal about the type of government she is facing. Higher values of $y_{i,t}$ suggest a greater likelihood that L is type $\theta = 1$, while lower values suggest type $\theta = 0$. But depending on how tightly $\epsilon_{i,t}$ is distributed around zero (determined by the standard deviation of the distribution, σ_y), individual citizens may receive very different individual signals about L's type. Importantly, even if one citizen receives a low $y_{i,1}$ and suspects that L is of type $\theta = 0$, this does not inform her of what other citizens believe about L's type. In other words, individuals' higher-order beliefs remain uncertain.

All citizens *also* receive a publicly observable signal of the state of the economy, s. The overall state of the economy derives partly from the public good (if it is provided) and partly from exogenous economic forces. We model the exogenous economic forces, again, as a random draw from a normal distribution, but this time we introduce a twist. The standard deviation can take on different values, depending on the level of aggregate economic data provided by the government. Highly transparent governments can release more data and thus the signal about the overall state of the economy can be more precise; low-transparency governments release so little data that the signal is almost as noisy as the one associated with individual income.

We thus model the public signal as: $s = G_1 \gamma + \rho$, where G_1 and γ are as before and $\rho \sim N(0, \sigma_s^2)$. We highlight the standard deviation of the publicly observable signal: $\sigma_s > 0$. More transparent governments release more economic data and so citizens are better able to discern the role of government policies in shaping economic outcomes. Consequently, σ_s shrinks.[14]

Under conditions of high transparency, ρ is more likely to be closer to 0 and s, therefore, more likely to be an accurate signal of whether L is the good type (and set $G_1 = 1$). However, when low levels of transparency prevail, s may be much higher or much lower than the true state of the economy. With high σ_s (low transparency), s is less informative. The standard deviation associated with the signal about the overall state of the economy, σ_s, is thus a measure of the inverse of transparency (that is, a measure of opacity).[15] Since s

---

[14] Citizens, however, are not able to perfectly deduce government competence (Duch and Stevenson 2008). Our contention is merely that, *ceteris paribus*, σ_s falls as transparency rises.

[15] Formally, define transparency as the precision of the public signal – i.e., the inverse of the variance of that signal $\frac{1}{\sigma_s^2}$. σ_s is the square root of the inverse of transparency.

depicts the public disclosure of *aggregate* economic data, we further assume that it is always less noisy than the personal signal associated with individual income: $\sigma_s < \sigma_y$. We also assume that error in this signal of the overall state of the economy is uncorrelated with any given individual's good or bad luck: $E[\rho\epsilon_{i,t}] = 0 \ \forall \ i$.

After receiving signals – both public and private – of government performance, each citizen i may mobilize in an attempt to overthrow the sitting government. We write this political action as $a_i \in \{0, 1\}$, where $a_i = 1$ for citizens who choose to mobilize and $a_i = 0$ for citizens who choose to stay home. Let the proportion of citizens who choose to engage in collective action be $A \equiv \int_0^1 a_i di$. If A exceeds some exogenous threshold $T \in (0, 1)$, the sitting government is removed and replaced by a new L, whose type is drawn with the same distribution as the prior leader. We define an indicator function for the removal of the leader, $R(A)$, as:

$$R(A) = \begin{cases} 1 & \text{if } A \geq T \\ 0 & \text{otherwise.} \end{cases}$$

Note that our model predicts only whether the citizens remove the leader through mass unrest, not how the potential replacement leader is selected. (The selection of the new leader could take place through democratic election or a new authoritarian regime could simply replace the old. We explore both possibilities empirically in the next chapter.)

Mobilizing to overthrow the government is not costless for citizens, but it is not without benefits either – as long as the effort is successful. In our model, engaging in mobilization entails a cost of $\kappa > 0$ for each citizen. If the protest is successful in removing the sitting leader, each citizen who participates in these protests also gains a benefit $\beta > \kappa$. These benefits may be thought of as the psychological returns from participating in the successful overthrow of the *ancien regime*, or as material benefits flowing from the likely favors from any new regime that replaces the old. In either case, β represents a form of "selective incentive" for mobilization (Olson 1971).

Each citizen's utility function is thus equal to the sum of the following (1) her income from each period, $y_{i,1}$ and $y_{i,2}$, (2) if she chooses to engage in the collective action and it is successful (i.e., if $a_i = 1$ and $R(A) = 1$), the benefit of deposing the leader, β, and (3) if she chooses to engage in the collective action (i.e., if $a_i = 1$), regardless of the outcome, the cost of engaging in protest, $-\kappa$:

$$u_i(y_{i,1}, y_{i,2}, a_i; A) = y_{i,1} + y_{i,2} + a_i[R(A)\beta - \kappa].$$

So, to clarify, the game proceeds as follows:

1. Nature chooses L's type $\theta \in \{0, 1\}$, with $Pr(\theta = 1) = p$. The value of θ is revealed to L, but not to any citizen.
2. L chooses whether to provide the public good $G_1 \in \{0, 1\}$.

3. Nature chooses $\epsilon_{i,1}$ ∀ i and ρ; $y_{i,1}$ is revealed to each citizen i, but not to any other citizen; s is revealed to all citizens.
4. Each citizen chooses whether to engage in collective action $a_i \in \{0, 1\}$.
5. If $R(A) = 1$, L is removed and Nature draws a replacement L of type $\theta \in \{0, 1\}$, where again $Pr(\theta = 1) = p$.
6. The sitting L chooses the value of $G_2 \in \{0, 1\}$.
7. Nature chooses $\epsilon_{i,2}$ ∀ i; $y_{i,2}$ is realized for all citizens, and the game ends.

Transparency – which we can now write as $1/\sigma_s^2$ – is thus an exogenous parameter of the model. Assigning different values to $1/\sigma_s^2$ enables us to examine the role that transparency plays in fostering mobilization. All citizens observe the same signal s, and so it informs their higher-order beliefs. A low value of s not only signals to an individual citizen that L is more likely of type $\theta = 0$; she also knows that other citizens observe this too. Now, the relationship between s and $(1/\sigma_s^2)$ is mathematically complex, and a real understanding requires a study of this chapter's appendices. We sketch out the intuition in the pages that follow. To anticipate our key equilibrium of interest, increasingly precise signals (high values of $1/\sigma_s^2$) enable citizens, as a group, to better distinguish between good- and bad-type leaders, and, under plausible circumstances, also make mobilization more likely.

5.2.2 Autocratic Equilibrium

We examine pure strategy perfect Bayesian equilibria (PBE) of this game (Fudenberg and Tirole 1991). However, multiple such equilibria exist.[16] We find two of the equilibria unimportant to analyze in depth: one in which all citizens always mobilize, the other in which no citizen mobilizes. In the former instance (the "all-in" equilibrium), given the strategies of all other players, each individual citizen i prefers to undertake the collective action (setting $a_i = 1$), thus obtaining the benefits $\beta - \kappa > 0$ of participating in the successful mobilization – regardless of her beliefs about the government's type. Similarly, in the latter (the "all-out" equilibrium), given the strategies of all other citizens, each i prefers to set $a_i = 0$ – and thus avoid the cost $\kappa > 0$ of participating in a doomed rebellion, regardless of her beliefs. We do not focus on these all-in/all-out equilibria because they require all citizens to believe, with certainty, that their countrymen all either engage or not engage in political mobilization – and, moreover, it requires citizens to believe that this will be the case regardless of the performance of the incumbent government. The all-in equilibrium strikes us as unrealistic – it is implausible to believe circumstances exist such that citizens are absolutely certain that a successful rebellion will take place,

---

[16] As noted above, while our game follows the global games approach to mass unrest (Angeletos, Hellwig, and Pavan 2007; Casper and Tyson 2014), the game presented here does not satisfy the two-sided "limit dominance" condition (Morris and Shin 1998) – there is no type of government for which political action is a dominant strategy for any signal.

and will do so regardless of how the incumbent government performs in office. The all-out equilibrium is plausible but uninteresting – we want to understand, after all, why men and women rebel.[17] Moreover, both of these equilibria are dominated on welfare grounds by an alternative perfect Bayesian equilibrium (PBE): a cut-point equilibrium.

The players here do not have perfect information. Citizens do not know the leader's type and cannot discern his actions with certainty. Nevertheless, a PBE requires players to have rational and consistent sets of beliefs about what scenarios are possible. Here, the leader's actions are determined by his type, the citizens know that he is type $\theta = 1$ with probability p and type $\theta = 0$ with probability $1 - p$, and they can further update these beliefs after receiving private and public signals about whether L has provided the public good. As they receive these signals, citizens update their beliefs according to Bayes' rule.[18] Each player must have a strategy profile dictating actions that are sequentially rational in the sense that the expected payoff of the action, *given the set of beliefs*, is higher than the expected payoff of taking other actions. Our PBE of interest is one of pure strategies, where each citizen either takes action to mobilize or does not.[19]

In the pure strategy PBE of interest, each citizen i conditions her mobilization strategy on all available information – both her private signal from her individual income, $y_{i,1}$, and on the public signal about the overall state of the economy, s. We further restrict attention to monotone equilibria in which citizens (weakly) interpret signals of higher values of $y_{i,1}$ and of s as corresponding to an increased likelihood of a good type leader ($\theta = 1$). Specifically, we consider an equilibrium in which each citizen i employs a cut-point strategy. She engages in the collective action only when her income is below a certain threshold level. That is, i sets $a_i = 1$ if and only if $y_{i,1}$ is less than some threshold value $\bar{y}$ (Bueno de Mesquita 2010).

As we define below, this threshold value, denoted $\bar{y}(s)$, is a function of the publicly observable signal s and, importantly, of transparency, $1/\sigma_s^2$. Intuitively, the threshold is low when the public state of the economy is strong – so that even citizens with low incomes believe that their low $y_{i,1}$ is just due to bad luck and not due to a bad leader; the threshold is high when the public state of the economy is weak, so that even citizens with high incomes believe that the leader's type is bad. What is more interesting to us is to examine what happens when we change the level of precision (i.e., the level of transparency, $1/\sigma_s^2$) of the public signal about the economy – but we must take several technical steps before we can get to such an analysis.

---

[17] A play on the title of NYU alumnus Ted Robert Gurr's famous book (Gurr 1970).

[18] Thomas Bayes' theorem, $P(A \mid B) = \frac{P(B|A)P(A)}{P(B)}$, was originally published posthumously by his friend Richard Price in 1763. See Bayes and Price (1763) for the original text. For a discussion, see Stigler (2013).

[19] Pure strategies contrast with mixed strategies, where players take action according to some rule of randomized probability, such as a coin toss.

A cut-point PBE in monotone strategies is characterized by three key features: (1) a strategy for L that maps from leader type-space to action-space, $G_t : \{0, 1\} \rightarrow \{0, 1\}$; (2) a threshold defined over all real numbers and $\pm\infty$, $\bar{y}(s) : \mathbb{R} \rightarrow \mathbb{R} \cup \{-\infty, \infty\}$, where political action occurs whenever $y_{i,1} < \bar{y}(s)$ for all i – such that if $\bar{y}(s) = -\infty$, no citizen mobilizes, whereas if $\bar{y}(s) = \infty$, all citizens mobilize; and (3) posterior beliefs of each citizen about the probability that L is the bad type, conditioned on the signals she receives about the economy, $Pr(\theta = 0|y_{i,1}, s)$. We characterize and explain in more detail each of these three features in turn; but first some preliminary definitions are necessary.

Definition 5.1. *Define the threshold $\bar{y}^*(s)$ implicitly by the value of $y_{i,1}$ that solves*

$$Pr(\theta = 0|y_{i,1}, s)\beta = \kappa. \tag{5.1}$$

Intuitively, the threshold is the income that makes any individual indifferent between protesting and not. Individuals will protest when their individual signal is low – below the threshold $\bar{y}^*(s)$ – and will not do so when it is above this threshold. The value of this threshold for the private signal, below which citizens will take to the streets, is – in turn – a function of the public signal s. A strong public signal (high value of s) ensures that citizens must receive a correspondingly worse private signal to motivate protest: $\bar{y}^*(s)$ declines as s rises.

However, for sufficiently extreme values of s, situations will arise in which all citizens either choose to mobilize (if s is sufficiently low) or not to do so (if s is sufficiently high), *regardless* of their private signals. We address this complicating factor in Definition 5.2. The next section will elaborate on the derivation of both $\bar{y}^*(s)$ and $\bar{y}(s)$.

Definition 5.2. *Define*

$$\bar{y}(s) = \begin{cases} \infty & \text{if } \Phi(\frac{\bar{y}^*(s)-\gamma}{\sigma_y}) \geq T \\ \bar{y}^*(s) & \text{if } \Phi(\frac{\bar{y}^*(s)}{\sigma_y}) \geq T > \Phi(\frac{\bar{y}^*(s)-\gamma}{\sigma_y}) \\ -\infty & \text{if } \Phi(\frac{\bar{y}^*(s)}{\sigma_y}) < T \end{cases} \tag{5.2}$$

The value of $\bar{y}(s)$ is the cut-point that characterizes the equilibrium in which all citizens receiving a private signal below the cut-point choose to engage in political action; those with signals higher than $\bar{y}(s)$ stay off the streets. We now propose the three characteristic elements of our cut-point PBE in monotone strategies: (1) the leader's strategy, (2) the cut-point for citizen action, and (3) the posterior beliefs.

Proposition 5.1. *The following strategies and beliefs constitute a PBE.*

1. $G_t = \theta$ *for* $t = 1, 2$
2. $a_i = 1$ *if* $y_{i,1} \leq \bar{y}(s)$ *and* $a_i = 0$ *otherwise, for all* i

3. $Pr(\theta = 0|y_{i,1}, s) = \dfrac{\phi(\frac{y_{i,1}}{\sigma_y})\phi(\frac{s}{\sigma_s})(1-p)}{p\phi(\frac{y_{i,1}-\gamma}{\sigma_y})\phi(\frac{s-\gamma}{\sigma_s})+\phi(\frac{y_{i,1}}{\sigma_y})\phi(\frac{s}{\sigma_s})(1-p)}$ *for all i where ϕ is the*
   probability density function (PDF) of the standard normal distribution.

Proofs are in the appendix at the end of this chapter.

5.2.3 Intuitions behind the Autocratic Model

To develop the intuitions behind the formulas presented above, consider first the leader's decision. The leader always matches his action with his type – this is his dominant strategy. Good leaders maximize both their contemporaneous utility and the probability of retention by providing the public good. Bad types, on the other hand, receive enough utility from withholding the public good today to offset the reduced probability of retention. (These strategies follow from our assumption that the leader maximizes utility by being true to type; we relax this assumption in a model extension presented below.)

Turning to the decision of citizens to mobilize, each citizen receives a private signal – her own income – which informs her of the likelihood of a bad leader. The lower the income, the more likely the leader is bad. All citizens also receive public information s about the aggregate state of the economy. Again, the lower s, the greater the likelihood of a bad leader. Each citizen begins with the belief that the probability of a bad leader is $1 - p$. After receiving both her private and public signals, she computes her posterior beliefs about the type of leader she is facing, using Bayes' rule.

She then chooses to mobilize if her private signal (her income, $y_{i,1}$) is below a certain threshold cut-point, $\bar{y}(s)$. This cut-point is a function of the public signal, s, and of the proportion of citizens needed in an effort to overthrow the leader, T. If the public signal s is, loosely speaking, moderate, the cut-point is intuitive to discern. Each citizen understands that a decision to protest must be based on the expectation that enough other citizens will protest, resulting in the removal of a bad leader. Good leaders, by contrast, do not suffer as high a level of unrest and thus survive. Each citizen's expectation of a successful protest is thus given by her belief that the leader is bad: $Pr(\theta = 0|y_{i,1}, s)$. The expected benefit of protest is $Pr(\theta = 0|y_{i,1}, s) \times \beta$. The expected cost of protest is κ. The threshold that makes an individual citizen indifferent between protesting and not is the particular value of $y_{i,1}$ such that $Pr(\theta = 0|y_{i,1}, s) \times \beta = \kappa$. We call the value of $y_{i,1}$ that satisfies this equality condition $\bar{y}^*(s)$. Thus any individual i protests if her own $y_{i,1} < \bar{y}^*(s)$.

Figure 5.1 demonstrates the individual decision made by any citizen. Recall that there is a continuum of citizens indexed over the unit interval $i \in [0, 1]$. Given the equilibrium threshold, we can compute what fraction of the citizens protest in equilibrium. This fraction, of course, depends on the distribution of the private signals, which, in turn, are a function of the leader's type.

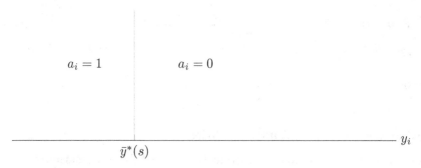

FIGURE 5.1. Individual citizen's decision to protest autocracy. Each individual compares her own private signal $y_{i,1}$ with the threshold $\bar{y}^*(s)$, and protests if $y_{i,1} \leq \bar{y}^*(s)$.

Now consider how the game plays out when L is truly the bad type: $\theta = 0$. L does not provide the public good, and the average individual income of citizens is 0. Still, some individuals are lucky and receive an income greater than zero, while the unlucky receive an income less than zero. The overall distribution of income (and hence private signals about the leader's type) centers on zero. Then, in Figure 5.2, we see that the fraction of the population that mobilizes when in fact $\theta = 0$ is given by the light-gray region, or more precisely, $\Phi(\frac{\bar{y}^*(s)}{\sigma_y})$, where Φ is the cumulative distribution function (CDF) of the standard normal distribution.

If, instead, L is actually the good type ($\theta = 1$), then he provides the public good, which shifts everyone's individual income upward by the value of the public good in terms of a citizen's individual income: γ. Again, some lucky citizens have income greater than the average income of γ, while the unlucky have income less than γ. But the distribution centers on $\gamma > 0$. Compared to when L is the bad type, the income distribution shifts to the right, and the fraction of the population that mobilizes is smaller.

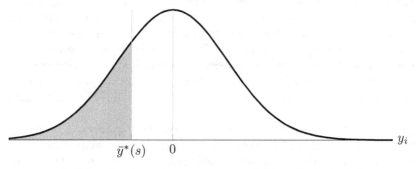

FIGURE 5.2. Political action when an autocratic leader is bad. The light-gray region is the fraction of population that mobilizes, $\Phi(\frac{\bar{y}^*(s)}{\sigma_y})$ when in fact $\theta = 0$, where Φ is the CDF of the standard normal distribution.

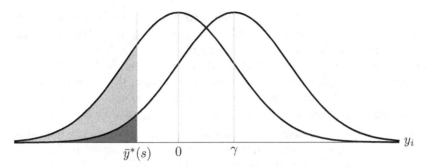

FIGURE 5.3. Political action for both types of autocratic leader. The dark-gray region is the fraction of population that mobilizes when the type is good, $\Phi(\frac{\bar{y}^*(s)-\gamma}{\sigma_y})$ when in fact $\theta = 1$.

Figure 5.3 shows the fraction of the population that mobilizes when $\theta = 1$, which is given by the dark region: $\Phi(\frac{\bar{y}^*(s)-\gamma}{\sigma_y})$. This contrasts with the larger fraction of the population that mobilizes when the leader is the bad type, which is given by the sum of the light region and the dark region in Figure 5.3. The key takeaway from this figure is that for plausible values of $\bar{y}(s)$, we may observe mobilization against either type of leader, but the proportion of citizens who mobilize against a bad leader is greater than the proportion who mobilize against the good type. Bad leaders face a greater risk of mass unrest.

However, $\bar{y}^*(s)$ is defined under the assumption that bad leaders are ousted and good retained. For this to be true, the total number of citizens mobilizing when the leader is, in fact, bad (which is given by the term $\Phi(\frac{\bar{y}^*(s)}{\sigma_y})$) must be greater than T. Additionally, the total mobilizing when the leader is, in fact, good (given by $\Phi(\frac{\bar{y}^*(s)-\gamma}{\sigma_y})$) must be less than T. For intermediate values of the public signal s, some citizens protest, and their numbers are sufficient to depose bad leaders, while good leaders face fewer protestors and survive.

To be thorough, we must also address extreme values of s. For a sufficiently poor value of s, it may be the case that, if all citizens stuck to their strategy of mobilizing for $y_i < \bar{y}^*(s)$, even good leaders would be faced with unmanageable protest – i.e., $\Phi(\frac{\bar{y}^*(s)-\gamma}{\sigma_y}) > T$. Expressed differently, even the dark-gray region of Figure 5.3 would exceed T. Hence, the leader, regardless of his type, would be removed. Citizens, on seeing such a public signal, realize that the toppling of the regime is inevitable. Since the rewards of joining in this (successful) rebellion β are greater than the cost κ, they want to join the bandwagon – regardless of their personal beliefs about the type of leadership they face. The cut-point for mobilization is given by $\bar{y}(s) = \infty$: all citizens i mobilize, regardless of their private signal.[20]

---

[20] Note that this situation is different from the "all-in" equilibrium that we dismissed above (where all citizens take action regardless of the signals they receive). Here, individuals condition their

Analogously, for a sufficiently extreme, and positive, public signal s, if all citizens stuck with their strategy of taking action only if $y_i < \bar{y}^*(s)$, even bad types of leaders would continue to survive in office. The light-gray area in Figures 5.2 and 5.3 would be insufficiently large to oust the leadership. For such a public signal, the number of citizens who believe their government to be bad would be sufficiently low that mobilization is bound to fail, even if this small minority is correct in their assessment – that is, $\Phi(\frac{\bar{y}^*(s)}{\sigma_y}) < T$. Rational citizens should recognize that, following such a strong public signal, opportunities for mobilization are not fortuitous. Given that any action is bound to fail, each i would rather stay off the streets and avoid the cost to mobilization κ. This is true *regardless* of her personal beliefs about the leadership's type. For a sufficiently high value of s, no citizen takes action – the cut-point is given by $\bar{y}(s) = -\infty$.[21]

These strategies give us $\bar{y}(s)$, as laid out in Definition 5.2. For intermediate values of the public signal, citizens take action if (and only if) they believe with sufficient certainty they are faced with a bad leader – and the number of citizens with such beliefs is sufficient to upend the leadership if it is, in fact, bad and insufficient to do so if it is good. For extreme and positive values of the public signal, the number of citizens who are convinced of the pernicious nature of the regime is guaranteed to be too small to successfully ensure its ouster, regardless of the leadership's true nature. Hence no citizen mobilizes, regardless of her private beliefs. For extreme and negative values of that signal, discontent among the public will be so rife that mobilization is bound to succeed. Citizens take to the streets regardless of their private beliefs. Taken together with L's strategy and citizen posterior beliefs, this strategy constitutes the cut-point equilibrium defined in Proposition 5.1.

So far, our analysis of the game establishes (1) if the public signal about the economy is sufficiently bad, all leaders are deposed by mass unrest; (2) if the public signal is sufficiently good, all leaders are retained; and (3) if the public signal is in between these extremes, some citizens protest, and good leaders survive while bad leaders are deposed.

5.2.4 Comparative Statics: Enhancing Transparency under Autocracy

Now we come to the crucial analysis of our model. In this subsection, we consider what happens to citizen incentives to protest when we change the level of transparency. More precisely, we consider the level of mass unrest by the citizens when the public signal s has greater or lesser variance, σ_s.

action on the private and public signals that they receive: the public signal is so low, citizens are all best off taking action regardless of their private signal.

[21] Again, this situation is different from the "all-out" equilibrium that we dismissed above (where no citizen takes action regardless of the signals they receive). Here, individuals condition their action on the private and public signals that they receive: the public signal is so high that citizens are all best off taking no action regardless of their private signal.

Recall that we consider s to be a measure of the aggregate economic data provided to the public. When the variance of s is higher, the signal is noisier – transparency is low, and citizens gain little information about the leader's type from the public signal. To think of it another way, under low transparency (high σ_s), luck plays a bigger role: the public signal s is more likely to be extremely high or extremely low. By contrast, when the variance of s is low, the signal is precise: transparency is high and the public signal helps the citizens better identify the leader's type. Indeed, the public signal is more likely to come from the middle of the distribution and be an on-target message about whether the leader provided the public good, γ.

So, what happens to the likelihood of mass unrest and leader removal as we change transparency? To answer this question, we must shift our focus from individual citizens' incentives to take to the streets, which we discussed above, to the probability the regime is upended.

From our earlier discussion, recall that when the public signal s is sufficiently high, all citizens prefer to stay at home. The leader, regardless of his type, continues to survive in office. Let us call this threshold $\bar{s}$, such that, for all $s \geq \bar{s}$, leaders of all types survive. Conversely, when s is sufficiently low, all citizens take to the streets. The leader regardless of his type, is removed. Let us call this threshold $\underline{s}$, such that for $s \leq \underline{s}$, leaders of all types are ousted. For values of s in between these thresholds, such that $\underline{s} < s < \bar{s}$, we are in the intermediate range of the public signal. Mobilization that takes place is sufficient to unseat bad leaders, but insufficient to usurp good ones – see Figure 5.3.

The formal, mathematical, definitions of $\bar{s}$ and $\underline{s}$ are given by Definition 5.3:

Definition 5.3. *Define $\underline{s}$ implicitly by* $T = \Phi(\frac{\bar{y}^*(\underline{s}) - \gamma}{\sigma_y})$ *and $\bar{s}$ by* $T = \Phi(\frac{\bar{y}^*(\bar{s})}{\sigma_y})$.

In the appendix at the end of the chapter, we demonstrate that $\bar{s}$ and $\underline{s}$ are well-defined.

Consider how these thresholds translate into leader survival, which is also (of course) conditional on the leader's type (θ). If $s \geq \bar{s}$, no leader is removed. If $s \leq \underline{s}$, all leaders are removed. If $\underline{s} < s < \bar{s}$, then a leader is removed if, and only if, he is a bad type ($\theta = 0$). Put differently, bad leaders are removed whenever the public signal $s < \bar{s}$. Good leaders are removed whenever the public signal $s < \underline{s}$.

The probability that a leader of a given type is removed, therefore, is dictated by the chances Nature draws a sufficiently poor public signal. This probability is, in turn, a function of transparency.

Like individual incomes y_i, the public signal s is drawn probabilistically, where the probability of seeing any given value of s is determined by the leader's type. If the leader is a good type, who provides the public good, s is drawn from a normal distribution (bell curve) centered at $\gamma > 0$. If not, s is drawn from a curve centered at zero. As transparency increases (σ_s declines), these curves become more and more tightly centered around their respective means. Values of s far above or below the average value become less likely. This effect can be seen in Figure 5.4, which displays an opaque case on the top part of the graphic and a transparent case on the bottom.

Despite the similarity of appearance, Figure 5.4 differs in an important way from Figures 5.2 and 5.3. Figure 5.4 depicts the probability of witnessing a given *public signal s*, given the leader's type; whereas, previous figures focused on the probability of individual income level y_i. The shaded regions in this figure thus have a different interpretation. Recall that bad leaders are removed for any value of $s < \bar{s}$. This probability is given by the sum of the light-gray and dark-gray regions in Figure 5.4, and is equivalent to the expression $\Phi(\frac{\bar{s}}{\sigma_s})$. Good leaders are removed only if $s < \underline{s}$, a probability equivalent to the small dark-gray regions in Figure 5.4. Mathematically, this probability is given by the expression $\Phi(\frac{\underline{s}-\gamma}{\sigma_s})$.

Now, altering the level of transparency both changes the distribution from which the public signal s is drawn – as transparency rises these curves are more tightly distributed around their means – and shifts the thresholds $\bar{s}$ and $\underline{s}$. Figure 5.4 depicts these shifts for plausible parameter values. Intuitively, as transparency rises, a bad signal (low value s) grows more informative. It therefore takes a less extreme signal to induce all citizens to mobilize; $\underline{s}$ shifts to the right. Analogously, a strong public signal is more likely to indicate that the leader is a good type as transparency rises. So, the value of s such that all citizens choose to stay off the streets – $\bar{s}$ – also shifts to the right.[22]

Several intuitions become clear on the examination of Figure 5.4. First, consider the sizes of the light-gray and dark-gray regions in the top and the bottom parts of the graph: the light-gray region increases in size more rapidly than does the dark-gray region. These changes imply that as transparency increases, the probability of removing a bad leader rises relative to the probability of removing a good leader. With increasing transparency, the citizenry more effectively discriminates leader type. We define this tendency as the level of *discrimination* – which is expressed mathematically as $\Phi(\frac{\bar{s}}{\sigma_s}) - \Phi(\frac{\underline{s}-\gamma}{\sigma_s})$. While Figure 5.4 only depicts plausible parameter values in the model, we can demonstrate that discrimination rises in transparency for all parameter values, which we formally prove in the appendix at the end of the chapter.

Proposition 5.2. *Discrimination is strictly increasing in transparency (falling in* σ_s*).*

Bad leaders always attract higher levels of protest than good leaders do (recall Figure 5.3). We interpret this equilibrium effect as implying that autocratic leaders who experience poor economic outcomes are always more

---

[22] The direction of these shifts hold true for plausible parameter values – specifically for sufficiently small values of β relative to κ. Our formal proofs delineate which of our claims are more general.

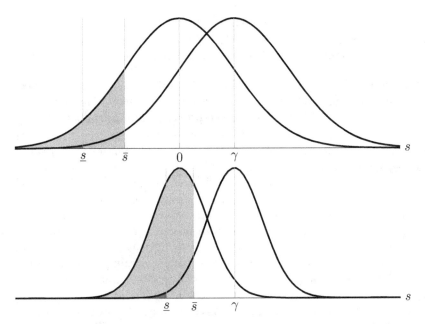

FIGURE 5.4. Marginal effect of increasing transparency under autocracy. The graph at the top depicts a low-transparency environment, and the graph at the bottom a high-transparency environment. $\bar{s}$ is the threshold in the public signal below which all bad types ($\theta = 0$) are removed. This outcome occurs with a probability indicated by the sum of the light-gray region and the small dark-gray region. $\underline{s}$ is the threshold in the public signal below which all good types ($\theta = 1$) are removed. This outcome occurs with a probability denoted by the small dark-gray region. Values of the public signal are drawn from the PDFs depicted, centered on zero when $\theta = 0$ and on γ when $\theta = 1$. When moving from the top to the bottom of the graph, the light-gray region increases more rapidly than the dark-gray region. So, as transparency increases, the probability that a bad leader is removed rises relative to the probability that a good leader is removed.

likely to be removed than those who experience good outcomes. Proposition 5.2 tells us that this difference rises with transparency.

We can take Proposition 5.2 a step further:

Corollary 5.1. *In equilibrium, poor economic performance is associated with autocratic removal; and poor economic performance in more transparent environments leads to even higher likelihood of autocratic collapse in equilibrium.*

We can also derive predictions about the unconditional relationship between transparency and leader survival. Compare again the top and bottom parts of Figure 5.4: the total shaded area rises as transparency increases. This pattern implies that the *ex ante* probability of leader removal – regardless of type – increases with transparency. However, this relationship holds only for certain parameter values of the model.

Proposition 5.3. *If* $-\frac{\sigma_y}{\gamma} ln(\frac{p\kappa}{(1-p)[\beta-\kappa]}) < \Phi^{-1}(T)$, *then there exists a level of* $\sigma_s \equiv \bar{\sigma}_s$ *such that the unconditional probability of leader removal is increasing for low levels of transparency (i.e., high levels of opacity:* $\sigma_s \geq \bar{\sigma}_s$).

Proposition 5.3 formally characterizes the sufficient (though not necessary) condition for transparency to have this effect. The condition $-\frac{\sigma_y}{\gamma} \ln(\frac{p\kappa}{(1-p)[\beta-\kappa]}) < \Phi^{-1}(T)$ is technical and proven in the appendix at the end of the chapter. Intuitively, however, this expression corresponds to the ease of mobilization and leader removal. Our results only hold if mobilization is not too easy – that is, if protesting is sufficiently costly for citizens to attempt.

To understand why this is the case, consider a citizen's mobilization decision. If the selective incentives for mobilization vastly outweigh the costs ($\beta \gg \kappa$), or if very few citizens are necessary to overthrow the government (T is small), then this individual would sensibly resort to protest even if highly uncertain of the type of government or the beliefs of other citizens (see Shadmehr and Bernhardt 2017). While this situation is allowable for certain parameter values of our model, it does not correspond to any real-world example of which we are aware. In reality, protesting against autocratic regimes is quite costly.

If mobilization is indeed costly, citizens require a great deal of reassurance regarding the likelihood of a protest's success before they are willing to join any of their fellows in the streets. Absent sufficient public information, any given citizen is unwilling to risk a failed mobilization, even if she believes the leadership to be pernicious. Because transparency may increase individuals' certainty that others are willing to engage in protest, mobilization becomes more likely. This corresponds to the shift of $\bar{s}$ and $\underline{s}$ to the right in Figure 5.4.

Remark 5.1 serves to clarify the requirement that mobilization is costly.

Remark 5.1. *As* $\beta \to \kappa$ *the probability of leader removal is rising in transparency for all* $\sigma_s \in \mathbb{R}_+$ *and for all* $T \in (0, 1)$.

Thus we conclude that under the typical costs and benefits of mass unrest, and the usually high threshold of participation to successfully unseat a regime, transparency is associated with an increase in the unconditional probability of mass unrest and of autocratic collapse.

5.2.5 Extending the Autocratic Model

In the real world, bad leaders go to great lengths to masquerade as good ones. What if, in our model, bad leaders have an incentive to hide their type by providing the public good γ just like a good leader would? In our baseline model, the leader's type $\theta \in \{0, 1\}$ is wholly determinative of his strategy to provide the public good (or not) in equilibrium. Theoretically, however, a bad leader might be willing to provide the public good if doing so reduces the chances of mass unrest, and thereby increasing his chances of surviving in power.

In this model extension, therefore, we relax the assumption that leaders act according to type and consider circumstances under which bad types have an incentive to pool with good, setting $G_1 = 1$. It turns out that the comparative statics regarding transparency from the above baseline model hold in a separating equilibrium in this model extension.[23] We characterize this equilibrium below and document the conditions under which such an equilibrium exists.

Consider an interaction identical to the baseline model, save only for the utility function of the leader L. Leaders still gain utility from acting true to type, but they also gain benefits directly from holding office (even if they do not take policy actions that match their type). We denote the rents from holding office as B. Define L's utility in each period t as:

$$u_{L,t}(G_t; \theta) = \begin{cases} 1+B & \text{if } G_t = \theta \text{ and in office} \\ B & \text{if } G_t \neq \theta \text{ and in office} \\ 0 & \text{otherwise} \end{cases}$$

$$u_L = \sum_{t=1}^{2} u_{L,t}(G_t; \theta), \text{ where } B > 0 \text{ denote the rents from office.}$$

L still has a primitive preference for matching his action G_t with his type θ. Yet, now L also prefers to retain office and gain access to the rents B. Thus, L may deviate from his preferred choice of G_1 if doing so increases his chance of remaining in office.

Given this new setup, we offer two propositions below. The intuition behind the first proposition (Proposition 5.4) is that as long as the benefits from holding office are not too high – relative to other parameters in the model – then a separating equilibrium exists with characteristics similar to the baseline game. The next proposition (Proposition 5.5) goes on to assert that for any value of the benefits of holding office, there exist corresponding values for other parameters in the model for which the separating equilibrium holds. In other words, all of the findings of the baseline model hold for this model extension, though for a restricted set of parameter values.

We characterize a separating equilibrium to this game in the following proposition.

Proposition 5.4. *If $\frac{1}{1+B} \geq \Phi(\frac{\bar{s}}{\sigma_s}) - \Phi(\frac{\bar{s}-\gamma}{\sigma_s})$ then the following strategies and beliefs constitute a separating PBE to the extended model.*

1. *For the leader, $G_t = \theta$ for $t = 1, 2$.*
2. *For the citizens, their mobilization strategies are $a_i = 1$ if $y_{i,1} \leq \bar{y}(s)$ and $a_i = 0$ otherwise, for all i.*

---

[23] Pooling equilibria may also exist in this extension of our model. We characterize a pooling equilibrium in the appendix at the end of the chapter.

3. Posterior beliefs (after both the private and public signals) are:

$$Pr(\theta = 0 | y_{i,1}, s) = \frac{\phi(\frac{y_{i,1}}{\sigma_y})\phi(\frac{s}{\sigma_s})(1-p)}{p\phi(\frac{y_{i,1}-\gamma}{\sigma_y})\phi(\frac{s-\gamma}{\sigma_s})+\phi(\frac{y_{i,1}}{\sigma_y})\phi(\frac{s}{\sigma_s})(1-p)} \text{ for all } i \text{ (Bayes' rule)},$$

where ϕ is the PDF of the standard normal and $\bar{y}(s)$, where $\bar{y}(s)$ is defined in Definition 5.2.

Strategies in the separating equilibrium to the extended model are analogous to those described in the baseline model. Good leaders set $G_t = 1$, as this both satisfies their primitive preference and maximizes their chance of retention. Bad types also play according to type, setting $G_t = 0$. In the second period, this constitutes a dominant strategy. In the first, any gain in the chances of retention from providing the public good are more than offset by the losses of playing against type. Given that L plays according to type, each citizen i is faced with exactly the informational difficulties described above. Each i thus chooses to turn to the streets if $y_{i,1} < \bar{y}(s)$.

This separating equilibrium only exists, however, for a subset of parameter values. More precisely, a separating equilibrium exists only for low levels of transparency relative to the value of holding office B. We define the requisite value of σ_s necessary for a separating equilibrium as $\tilde{\sigma}_s$.

Proposition 5.5. *For any finite $B \geq 0$, there exists a $\tilde{\sigma}_s$ such that $\frac{1}{1+B} \geq \Phi(\frac{\bar{s}}{\sigma_s}) - \Phi(\frac{s-\gamma}{\sigma_s})$ for all $\sigma_s \geq \tilde{\sigma}_s$, where $\bar{s}$ and $\underline{s}$ are as defined in Definition 5.3.*

Remark 5.2. *For any finite B, a separating equilibrium exists for $\sigma_s \geq \tilde{\sigma}_s$, and in any separating equilibrium, all comparative statics characterized for the baseline model hold.*

A separating equilibrium exists if transparency is sufficiently low (equivalently, opacity is sufficiently high: $\sigma_s \geq \tilde{\sigma}_s$). Our findings thus hold for a restricted range of the (B, σ_s) parameter space. The intuition is straightforward: In a low-transparency environment, citizens are less likely to discern whether L has provided the public good, so bad leaders can play the game true to type and still hope to avoid mass unrest. The game plays out as before.

In addition to the separating equilibrium of the model extension that we have characterized here, other equilibria also exist. In a high-transparency environment, for example, bad leaders who fail to provide the public good are likely to be discovered by a large fraction of the citizenry, so they are willing to masquerade as the good type and provide the public good – lest the citizens mobilize. A range of pooling equilibria, in which bad types set $G_1 = 1$ in the hope of securing power, thus exist for alternate parameter values in the extended model. We characterize such equilibria in the appendix at the end of the chapter. Our comparative statics do not hold in the pooling equilibrium. As is the case with many models with multiple equilibria, it becomes an empirical question as to which equilibria manifest more systematically in the real world. We note, however, that the assumption of low transparency, necessary for the separating equilibrium, holds for the real-world type of country we are interested in for this model: autocracies.

Empirically, autocratic governments tend to be opaque, as seen in Chapter 3. To the extent that transparency is indeed low, the conditions should hold for the separating equilibrium that we have presented here. We can, however, empirically examine the possibility that levels of transparency may rise to such levels that a separating equilibrium no longer exists by allowing for a nonmonotonic relationship between levels of transparency and the hazard of regime collapse due to unrest or democratization. As we show in the next chapter, we find no evidence for a nonmonotonic relationship. To anticipate our empirical findings, the hazard of autocratic regime collapse is monotonically increasing in transparency.

5.2.6 Conclusions for Autocracies

The theory of this section points toward two main empirical patterns for autocracies that we examine in the next chapter. First, we have an unconditional hypothesis that transparency increases the risks of mass unrest under autocracy and of the collapse of autocratic regimes. The second hypothesis is an interactive one: the effect of transparency is conditioned on economic performance. The worse the economy is performing, the stronger the effect of transparency on mass unrest and on the collapse of autocratic regimes. These hypotheses are not mutually exclusive. Even when the economy is strong, increasing transparency may increase the risks to autocratic regimes. But these risks are exacerbated by a poorly performing economy.

5.3 THE DEMOCRATIC MODEL

We now transform our citizens into voters. The following democratic model is identical to the baseline autocratic model, except that we introduce contested elections where the incumbent must win the votes of citizens in order to survive in power – otherwise, the leader is replaced. Citizens can still choose to participate in mass unrest in order to topple the political regime, but they can also oust the incumbent via the ballot box.

Electoral institutions also play an additional role in the model: *election results provide voters information about the public level of satisfaction with the current leadership.* Citizens continue to receive other information: private signals about government performance through their individual incomes y_i and a public signal through aggregate data s. They further observe the outcome of the election, which informs their higher-order beliefs about the society's "distribution of discontent" with the regime. The voting process serves to aggregate the private signals of all citizens, such that all citizens – after elections have concluded – are fully informed of the government's type, regardless of the level of transparency.

If a leader receives fewer votes than would have been anticipated given the public signal, he must be a bad type. Because voters only realize this *after* the election, however, good leaders can be rejected and bad ones retained through the electoral process. When bad leaders win reelection, voters take to the streets.

So, we can vary the level of transparency of the public signal (again captured by the variance of the public signal, σ_s) to see how it might impact political stability. In a democratic context, the level of transparency does not alter the voters' perception of the distribution of discontent – thanks to the informational role of elections. But transparency still informs citizens about the leader's type before they head to the polls. Therefore, the informational environment can impact the electoral process. Enhancing transparency increases the probability that bad leaders are voted out of office, while good ones achieve victory at the ballot box. One might say that transparency improves the functioning of the electoral process.

Far from incentivizing voters to protest, therefore, transparency improves elections. Transparency helps the electorate discriminate between good and bad leaders. So the need to remove leaders through extra-constitutional means drops as transparency rises. Transparency lowers the risk of mass unrest under democracy.

5.3.1 Democratic Model Primitives

The model we use to examine democracies is almost identical to that for autocracies, so the mathematical notation remains largely unchanged. As before, there is a continuum of voters $i \in [0, 1]$, each voter receives a private signal y_i and a public signal s of the leader's type $\theta \in \{0, 1\}$, and voters may engage mass anti-governmental action $a_i \in \{0, 1\}$.[24] For reasons of symmetry with the autocratic model above, we maintain our focus on mass mobilization and protest. However, one might also think of a_i as more generally reflecting citizens' satisfaction with the democratic order, their willingness to defend this order in response to actions by anti-democratic elites, or, indeed, their willingness to support elite-led anti-democratic movements. Our findings in this section thus speak to a broader set of threats to democratic stability than our claims regarding threats to autocratic stability, which explicitly focus on mass mobilization.

---

[24] While we recognize that such mobilization is unthinkable in many established democracies, the scope of our analysis includes both new and old democracies. We believe that democratic consolidation is a condition that should be derived from the equilibrium of the model – not a condition to be assumed by restricting the action space of voters. Thus, voters in all democracies have the ability to mobilize, even if some choose – in equilibrium – never to exercise this option. We thank John Freeman for clarifying this point.

We alter the model in only one respect: voters may cast a ballot to remove the leader, and they do so after receiving their signals but before choosing whether or not to mobilize. To capture this new option, let $v_i \in \{0, 1\}$ denote a given voter's ballot decision, where $v_i = 1$ denotes a vote against the incumbent. Let $V \equiv \int_0^1 v_i di$ denote the sum total of voters who cast their vote against the incumbent. To capture majoritarian elections,[25] the leader is removed if $V \geq \frac{1}{2}$, and replaced by a new L, whose type is drawn from an identical distribution as the incumbent.

The order of play is as follows:

1. Nature chooses L's type, $\theta \in \{0, 1\}$, with $Pr(\theta = 1) = p$. The value of θ is revealed to L, but not to any voter.
2. L chooses whether to provide the public good $G_1 \in \{0, 1\}$.
3. Nature chooses $\epsilon_{i,1} \ \forall \ i$ and ρ; $y_{i,1}$ is revealed to each voter i, but not to any other voter; s is revealed to all voters.
4. Each voter chooses $v_i \in \{0, 1\}$. $V = \int_0^1 v_i di$ is revealed to all voters. If $V \geq \frac{1}{2}$, L is removed and replaced by another government, whose type θ is chosen by Nature, where again, $Pr(\theta = 1) = p$.
5. If $V < \frac{1}{2}$, the incumbent, L, is retained in the election. Each voter chooses whether to engage in collective action $a_i \in \{0, 1\}$.
6. If $R(A) = 1$, L is removed and Nature draws a replacement L of type $\theta \in \{0, 1\}$, where again $Pr(\theta = 1) = p$.
7. The sitting L chooses the value of $G_2 \in \{0, 1\}$.
8. Nature chooses $\epsilon_{i,2} \ \forall \ i$; $y_{i,2}$ is revealed to each voter, and the game ends.

5.3.2 Democratic Equilibrium

The democratic game, like the autocratic one, gives rise to a multiplicity of perfect Bayesian equilibria (Fudenberg and Tirole 1991). With a continuum of citizens, voting decisions may be nonstrategic. Moreover, coordination problems in the mobilization stage of the game similarly give rise to multiple equilibria.

We narrow the set of equilibria by restricting our attention to the following player strategies. First, we assume that citizens vote sincerely; citizens vote against the incumbent if, and only if, they believe that any replacement is likely to be a better type. In math, this requirement holds that $v_i = 1$ if and only if $Pr(\theta = 1|y_{i,1}, s) \leq p$. Second, we assume that each citizen i only mobilizes to overthrow the sitting leader if she believes with some positive probability that the leader is a bad type. Citizens never rebel – and will hold democracy in high regard – if they believe, with certainty, that elections have returned a good incumbent to power. That is, we require that $a_i = 0$ if $Pr(\theta = 1|V, s) = 1$.

---

[25] See Schwartzberg (2014) for a discussion on the origin of majority and super-majority rule.

This restriction rules out perverse equilibria in which all citizens coordinate on removing a leader known – with certainty – to be the good type.

We focus on a monotone PBE (with the above properties), which, as in the autocratic game, relies on cut-points. Indeed, before we characterize our equilibrium of interest, we must define a new cut-point necessary in the democratic setting: the threshold that voters use in their voting decision.

Definition 5.4. *Define $\tilde{y}(s)$ as $\tilde{y}(s) \equiv \frac{\gamma}{2}(\frac{\sigma_y^2}{\sigma_s^2} + 1) - \frac{s\sigma_y^2}{\sigma_s^2}$, and define*

$$V(s; G_1) = \begin{cases} \Phi(\frac{\tilde{y}(s)}{\sigma_y}) & \text{if } G_1 = 0 \\ \Phi(\frac{\tilde{y}(s) - \gamma}{\sigma_y}) & \text{if } G_1 = 1 \end{cases}$$

where Φ is the CDF of the standard normal distribution.

We define $\tilde{y}(s)$ as a key point of indifference: if, after receiving the public signal s, a citizen receives a private signal of $y_i = \tilde{y}(s)$, then her updated conditional probability that L is the good type ($\theta = 1$) is equal to p (the unconditional probability that L is the good type): $Pr(\theta = 1|\tilde{y}(s), s) = p$. Thus $\tilde{y}(s)$ is the value of the private signal such that any individual having received that private signal $\tilde{y}(s)$ and public signal s is indifferent between reelecting and evicting the incumbent. Since s is the common public signal, this threshold cut-point is common to all individuals. To anticipate, voters whose private signals $y_{i,1}$ exceed $\tilde{y}(s)$ vote to reelect L, while voters with incomes $y_{i,1}$ less than $\tilde{y}(s)$ vote against L.

Our monotone perfect Bayesian equilibrium consists of the following: (1) An action pair for each voter (v_i, a_i) mapping their signals into actions: with regard to their voting decision, the relevant signals are y_i and s, $v : \mathbb{R}^2 \to \{0, 1\}$; with regard to mobilization the relevant signals are the s and the vote share of the incumbent V, $\mathbb{R} \times [0, 1] \to \{0, 1\}$. (2) A strategy for L from type-to action-space, $G_t : \{0, 1\} \to \{0, 1\}$. (3) Posterior beliefs $Pr(\theta = 1|y_{i,1}, s)$ and $Pr(\theta = 1|V, s)$.

Proposition 5.7 characterizes this equilibrium.

Proposition 5.7. *The following strategies and beliefs constitute a perfect Bayesian equilibrium.*

1. *For the leader, $G_t = \theta$ for $t = 1, 2$.*
2. *$v_i = \begin{cases} 1 & \text{if } y_{i,1} \leq \tilde{y}(s) \\ 0 & \text{otherwise.} \end{cases}$ and $a_i = \begin{cases} 1 & \text{if } V > V(s, 1) \\ 0 & \text{otherwise.} \end{cases}$*
3. *Posterior beliefs (after both the private and public signals but before the vote) are:*

$$Pr(\theta = 1|y_{i,1}, s) = \frac{p\phi(\frac{y_{i,1} - \gamma}{\sigma_y})\phi(\frac{s - \gamma}{\sigma_s})}{p\phi(\frac{y_{i,1} - \gamma}{\sigma_y})\phi(\frac{s - \gamma}{\sigma_s}) + (1 - p)\phi(\frac{y_{i,1}}{\sigma_y})\phi(\frac{s}{\sigma_s})}$$

   and after the vote, but before political action:

$$Pr(\theta = 1|V, s) = \begin{cases} 0 & \text{if } V > V(s, 1) \\ 1 & \text{otherwise.} \end{cases}$$

Proofs are in the appendix at the end of this chapter.

Along the equilibrium path, L of type $\theta = 1$ provides the public good; L of type $\theta = 0$ does not. Hence, bad types of L receive more negative votes; good types of L receive fewer negative votes: $V(s; 1) < V(s; 0)$ for all s. Voters cast their ballots based on their public and private signals, which are unbiased, and seek to oust the incumbent if, and only if, $y_i < \tilde{y}(s)$.

With a large number of voters, such unbiased signals and voting strategies produce stable and predictable election results in which bad incumbents receive fewer votes than good incumbents receive. Indeed, for a given value of the public signal, each type of incumbent receives a unique vote share: $\mathbb{R} \times \{0, 1\} \to \mathbb{R}$. In other words, for any given public signal s, there is a unique vote total for L of type $\theta = 0$ and a different unique vote total for L of type $\theta = 1$. Specifically, for any given draw of s, more voters choose to remove a bad leader than would choose to remove a good leader because the *average* individual incomes of voters are lower by the amount γ under the bad leader. Therefore, if a voter knows the vote total for a given leader and the public signal, she can invert this mapping to deduce the leader's type.

Now, for some draws of s, democracy functions well. Specifically, for $V(s; 1) < \frac{1}{2} < V(s; 0)$, good leaders are reelected, and bad leaders are removed from office via the electoral process. There is no post-election mobilization or political action, the democratic process has worked to solve the adverse selection problem.

For some draws of s, however, it is possible for the electorate to retain a bad leader or evict a good one. Although a bad leader receives fewer votes than a good leader for any given draw of s, the threshold to remove the bad leader from office (half of the votes or more) is not always breached. That is, it is possible that $V(s; 0) < \frac{1}{2}$.

This unfortunate outcome occurs when there is a high draw of s relative to the draws of the individual incomes of the citizens. Remember that under the bad leader (where $G_1 = 0$), $s \sim N(0, \sigma_s^2)$. So through pure luck, there could be a high draw of s. (As a hint to where the intuition is going, readers should realize that an extraordinarily high draw of s is more likely with low transparency, $\frac{1}{\sigma_s^2}$.) Observing a relatively high value of s, some voters must assume that L has provided the public good. But actual economic performance, as reflected in the incomes of the voters, still leads too few of them to vote for L for the voters to conclude – after they see the results of the election – that the public good was provided. In other words, the combination of bad economic performance (as reflected by the actual incomes of voters) and low transparency (which makes a high draw of s more likely), can lead to the retention of bad leaders – which then provokes the dissatisfaction of masses of citizens. Political action emerges when the democratic process fails to address the adverse selection problem.

It is also possible for the voters to errantly remove a good leader through the electoral process. Such a mistake occurs when $V(s; 1) > \frac{1}{2}$. This happens when a good leader is subject to an unlucky draw of s relative to the incomes of voters. Remember that under the good leader (where $G_1 = 1$), $s \sim N(\gamma, \sigma_s^2)$. Through bad luck, s can manifest as extremely low. (Hinting again toward the intuition, this potential outcome is more likely with low transparency, $\frac{1}{\sigma_s^2}$.) Observing a relatively low value of s, some voters simply assume that L has failed to provide the public good. But actual economic performance, as reflected in the incomes of the voters, leads too many of them to vote for L for the voters to conclude – after they see the results of the election – that L was the bad type. Nevertheless, there is no political action because the leader has been removed by the democratic process and replaced with another good leader with probability p. Indeed, the voters' expected income for the second round equals their expected income from the first round when the democratic game began.

In the following subsection, we show that under low transparency, the electorate is more likely to make a mistake because of a misleading public signal s. Thanks to the informational role of elections, voters realize their mistake. And when they errantly retain a bad leader, dissatisfaction with democracy jeopardizes the democratic regime.

5.3.3 Comparative Statics: Enhancing Transparency under Democracy

In the democratic model, voters engage in mobilization if and only if a bad incumbent is reelected. So we ask: Does transparency enhance the likelihood that bad types are removed via the electoral process? The answer is yes.

To prove this answer, we again define upper and lower values of the public signal s – this time such that all leaders are reelected above $\tilde{s}$ and no government is reelected below $\underline{s}$. Democracy may face collapse when the public signal is above $\tilde{s}$ because bad leaders can win reelection in this situation.[26]

Definition 5.5. *Define $\tilde{s}$ implicitly by* $\Phi(\frac{\bar{y}(\tilde{s})}{\sigma_y}) = \frac{1}{2}$ *and define $\underline{s}$ implicitly by* $\Phi(\frac{\bar{y}(\underline{s})-\gamma}{\sigma_y}) = \frac{1}{2}$.

We show in the appendix at the end of this chapter that $\tilde{s}$ and $\underline{s}$ are well defined. If $s \geq \tilde{s}$, governments of all types are reelected. If $s \leq \underline{s}$, governments of all types are voted out of office. If $s \in (\underline{s}, \tilde{s})$, then governments are voted out of office if and only if $\theta = 0$. Bad incumbents are voted out of office whenever $s < \tilde{s}$; good leaders suffer defeat at the polls only if $s < \underline{s}$.

We can thus define the probability that a government of type $\theta = 0$ is voted out of office as $\Phi(\frac{\tilde{s}}{\sigma_s})$. This probability is analogous to the sum of the light-gray and small dark-gray shaded regions in Figure 5.5. And we can define the probability that a government of type $\theta = 1$ is voted out of office as $\Phi(\frac{\underline{s}-\gamma}{\sigma_s})$. This

---

[26] To stress another hint behind this intuition, note that high values of s that fail to match the actual average income of the voters is more likely under low transparency (high σ).

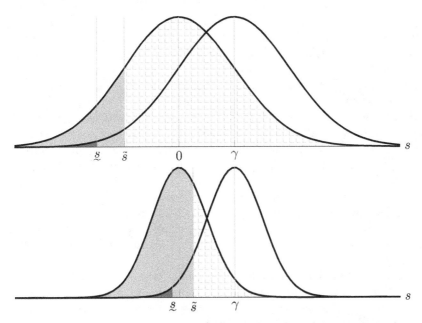

FIGURE 5.5. Marginal effect of increasing transparency under democracy. The graph at the top depicts a low transparency environment and the graph at the bottom a high transparency environment. $\tilde{s}$ is the threshold in the public signal below which all bad types $\theta = 0$ are *voted* out of office. This occurs with a probability indicated by the sum of the light-gray region and the small dark-gray region. If bad types are not voted out of office, they are removed via extraconstitutional means. This occurs with a probability given by the checked region. $\underline{s}$ is the threshold in the public signal below which all good types are removed. This occurs with a probability denoted by the small dark-gray region. Values of the public signal are drawn from the PDFs depicted, centered on zero when $\theta = 0$ and γ when $\theta = 1$.

probability is equivalent to the small dark-gray shaded regions in Figure 5.5. The extent to which electoral survival is conditioned on policy decisions or, equivalently, a government's type is thus $\Phi(\frac{\tilde{s}}{\sigma_s}) - \Phi(\frac{\tilde{s}-\gamma}{\sigma_s})$. We term this quantity the degree of *electoral discrimination*.

Proposition 5.8. *Electoral discrimination is strictly rising in transparency (falling in σ_s).*

Proposition 5.8 follows the form of Proposition 5.2 exactly. Only in this instance, underperforming democrats are more likely to be *voted* out of office as transparency rises, rather than ousted via mass unrest as in the autocratic case. Conversely, high-performing democrats are more likely to be reelected as transparency rises. As in the autocratic case, we take economic growth as a measure of leader performance. Leaders that inspire low growth are always more likely to lose elections (empirical evidence for such a claim can be found in such works as Hibbs 1982, 2000; Kayser and Peress 2012; Tucker 2006), and this difference is rising in levels of transparency.

However, Proposition 5.8 carries an additional implication in the democratic case: Because underperforming democratic leaders are more likely to be *voted* out of office when transparency is high, they are less likely to inspire the collapse of the regime. This effect is apparent in Figure 5.5. In this figure, where an opaque case is depicted above and a transparent below, the checked region corresponds to the probability of irregular (extra-judicial) leader removal. Notice that any increase in the light-gray region – the probability that underperforming leaders are voted out – corresponds to a reduction in this probability. Collapse takes place when, in reality, economic performance is poor ($G_1 = 0$), but the leader receives a sufficiently lucky public signal that he is reelected (s is relatively high). Since greater transparency ensures that the public signal corresponds more closely with reality, collapse is less likely to take place.

This result implies that regime collapse is always more likely when economic growth is low (that is, when the public good is not provided). But, the effect of economic growth on regime survival diminishes as transparency rises because bad types are more likely to be voted out of office, rather than ousted through extraconstitutional means.

Corollary 5.2 (elections). *In equilibrium, poor economic performance is associated with democratic leaders being voted out of office. Poor economic performance in a transparent environment leads to an even higher likelihood of electoral defeat.*

Corollary 5.3 (irregular removal). *Poor economic performance is associated with regime collapse in a democratic equilibrium. However, this relationship diminishes as transparency rises.*

As transparency rises, the probability that a government of type $\theta = 0$ is voted out of office rises; while the probability that a government of type $\theta = 1$ is voted out falls. The electoral process is better at solving the problem of adverse selection as transparency rises. Democratic legitimacy is enhanced when the public information influencing the reelection choice more reliably corresponds the policy choice of the leader.

In equilibrium, if a bad leader survives in office, the voters mobilize for his irregular removal. We use the shorthand "democratic collapse" to describe the instance where a leader is removed by means other than the electoral process. Since democratic collapse takes place when poor leaders are reelected, this probability is given by $(1 - p)[1 - \Phi(\frac{\bar{s}}{\sigma_s})]$, which is simply the *ex ante* probability that L is a type $\theta = 0$ multiplied by the probability that such a type survives the electoral process.

Increases in transparency – reductions in σ_s – make elections more effective in selecting good leaders, and make political action in the form of mass mobilization and democratic collapse less likely. When a bad leader wins reelection, the preferences of the masses become manifestly opposed to the results of democracy, and thus the public force aligns with the preferences of anti-democratic elites. Such elites may even lead a coup ahead of mass insurrection, knowing that the force is with them. Since the probability that a bad government is retained via an election is falling in transparency, so too is the risk of democratic collapse.

Proposition 5.9. *The probability of democratic collapse is strictly falling in transparency (rising in σ_s).*

Transparency improves the role of elections in addressing adverse selection problems in government. And, because protests and elections are substitute mechanisms for addressing such problems, the risk to democracy falls as elections grow more effective.

5.3.4 Extending the Democratic Model

In our main democratic model, as in the main autocratic model, the incumbent's type $\theta \in \{0, 1\}$ is wholly determinative of his strategy in equilibrium. Just as with the autocratic game, we can relax this restriction and all of our qualitative findings hold. In the appendix at the end of the chapter, we present this extension to the baseline model in which bad types of leaders have an incentive to mimic good types. While they still gain utility from acting according to type, leaders also attach value to holding office. We denote this value $B > 0$, such that the L's utility is identical to that in the extension to the autocratic model above. Because of this benefit, L may wish to deviate from his primitive policy preferences in order to retain power.

The extended model produces both pooling and separating equilibria. In a separating equilibrium, the incumbent sets G_1 in a manner consistent with her type. In a pooling equilibrium, bad types pool with good in setting $G_1 = 1$. In particular, we consider a separating equilibrium identical to that in the model above, in which citizens vote sincerely. We characterize such a separating equilibrium to this extension in the following proposition.

Proposition 5.10. *If $\Phi(\frac{\varsigma - \gamma}{\sigma_s}) \geq \frac{B}{1+B}$, then the following strategies and beliefs constitute a separating PBE to the extended model.*

1. *For the leader, $G_t = \theta$ for $t = 1, 2$.*
2. *For the citizens, their voting and mobilization strategies are*
$$v_i = \begin{cases} 1 & \text{if } y_{i,1} \leq \tilde{y}(s) \\ 0 & \text{otherwise} \end{cases} \quad \text{and} \quad a_i = \begin{cases} 1 & \text{if } V > V(s; 1) \\ 0 & \text{otherwise.} \end{cases}$$

3. *Posterior beliefs (after both the private and public signals but before the vote) are:*

$$Pr(\theta = 1 | y_{i,1}, s) = \frac{p\phi(\frac{y_{i,1}-\gamma}{\sigma_y})\phi(\frac{s-\gamma}{\sigma_s})}{p\phi(\frac{y_{i,1}-\gamma}{\sigma_y})\phi(\frac{s-\gamma}{\sigma_s})+(1-p)\phi(\frac{y_{i,1}}{\sigma_y})\phi(\frac{s}{\sigma_s})}$$

and after the vote, but before political action:

$$Pr(\theta = 1 | V, s) = \begin{cases} 0 & \text{if } V > V(s,1) \\ 1 & \text{otherwise.} \end{cases}$$

Strategies in this separating equilibrium are analogous to those described in the baseline model. Good incumbents set $G_t = 1$, as this both satisfies their primitive preference and maximizes their chance of retention. This is a dominant strategy. Bad types also play according to type, setting $G_t = 0$. In the second period, this also constitutes a dominant strategy. In the first, the incumbent could improve his chances of retention (from zero) by providing the public good. However, his risk of removal even after setting $G_1 = 1$, defined as $\Phi(\frac{s-\gamma}{\sigma_s})$, remains sufficiently high that he prefers to act according to type. Given that L plays according to type, each citizen is faced with exactly the same voting and mobilization decisions as described above. Each i thus chooses to vote against the incumbent if $y_i < \tilde{y}(s)$ and to mobilize against a reelected leader if $V > V(s; 1)$.

However, this separating equilibrium exists only for a subset of parameter values. More precisely, this separating equilibrium exists only if the level of transparency is sufficiently low (σ_s is sufficiently high) relative to the value of holding office B. For a sufficiently high value of holding office, this separating equilibrium will not exist for any value of transparency. We define the value of B below which a separating equilibrium exists as $\bar{B}$ and the requisite value of σ_s necessary for a separating equilibrium given $B \le \bar{B}$ as $\bar{\sigma}_s$. We characterize these values as follows.

Lemma 5.5. *For any finite $B \in [0, \bar{B}]$, there exists a $\bar{\sigma}_s$ such that $\Phi(\frac{\underline{s}-\gamma}{\sigma_s}) \ge \frac{B}{1+B}$ for all $\sigma_s \ge \bar{\sigma}_s$, where $\underline{s}$ is as defined in Definition 5.5.*

For alternative parameter values, the extended model gives rise to a pooling equilibrium in which bad types mirror the actions of good in time $t = 1$. In such an equilibrium, neither the public nor the private signal is informative as to the incumbent's type. All types of L adopt the same actions in equilibrium, hence all realizations of the signals y_i and s are equally likely for both types of leader. Voters cannot update their beliefs and are therefore indifferent between the incumbent and any challenger. Nonetheless, voters must continue to vote to remove incumbents if their signals (both public and private) are too low. Only by adopting such a strategy can the voters induce bad types of leaders to pool in the first period of play. We characterize such an equilibrium in which voters' behavior is unchanged relative to the above separating equilibrium in the following proposition.

Proposition 5.11. *If* $\Phi(\frac{\bar{s}-\gamma}{\sigma_s}) < \frac{B}{1+B}$*, then the following strategies and beliefs constitute a pooling PBE to the extended model.*

1. *For the leader* $G_1 = 1 \; \forall \; \theta$. $G_2 = 1$ *if* $\theta = 1$ *and* $G_2 = 0$ *if* $\theta = 0$.
2. *For the citizens, their voting and mobilization strategies are:*
$$v_i = \begin{cases} 1 & \text{if } y_{i,1} \leq \tilde{y}(s) \\ 0 & \text{otherwise} \end{cases} \quad \text{and} \quad a_i = \begin{cases} 1 & \text{if } V > V(s, 1) \\ 0 & \text{otherwise.} \end{cases}$$
3. *Posterior beliefs (after both the private and public signals but before the vote) are:* $Pr(\theta = 1 | y_{i,1}, s) = p$
and after the vote, but before political action:
$$Pr(\theta = 1 | V, s) = \begin{cases} 0 & \text{if } V > V(s, 1) \\ p & \text{otherwise.} \end{cases}$$

In this equilibrium, citizens continue to vote against the incumbent when the realization of their public and private signals is sufficiently poor – that is, when $y_{i,1} < \tilde{y}(s)$. Importantly, however, this is *not* because such signals are indicative of a bad type of leader. Both good and bad types of incumbent provide the public good in the first period, hence signals are uninformative of type. Voters are thus no longer behaving sincerely. Rather, they behave in this manner because of the economic damage a leader *might* cause off the equilibrium path. Voters must continue to vote according to their signals, despite the fact that these signals only reflect noise in equilibrium, because this is their only means of ensuring that leaders of all types have an incentive to behave well.

Analogously, citizens maintain their strategy of resorting to protest should the combination of vote totals and the public signal be sufficiently bad. However, since incumbents of all types set $G_1 = 1$, this combination is never realized in equilibrium. $V(s, G_t) = V(s, 1)$ for both bad and good incumbents and protest never takes place. The risk of autocratic reversion falls to zero in equilibrium – democracy becomes consolidated.

Proposition 5.12. *The probability of democratic collapse is weakly falling for all values of transparency (weakly rising in σ_s).*

Proposition 5.12 follows directly from the above. Lemma 5.5 establishes that the separating equilibrium described in Proposition 5.10 exists for sufficiently low levels of transparency (high values of σ_s). In this equilibrium, both citizen and incumbent strategies are identical to those in the baseline model, so the conclusions of Proposition 5.9 continue to hold. Within this separating equilibrium, the risk of democratic collapse strictly falls in transparency. For values of transparency greater than the threshold described in Lemma 5.5, the pooling equilibrium described in Proposition 5.11 exists. In this pooling equilibrium, democracy is consolidated. The risk of democratic collapse is constant and equal to zero for all levels of transparency above this value (all values of $\sigma_s < \bar{\sigma}_s$). The risk of democratic collapse is therefore weakly falling everywhere in transparency.

5.3.5 Conclusions for Democracies

Like many theories of the survival of democracy, ours is rooted in economic performance. Democracy is more likely to survive, and leaders more likely to win reelection, when the economy is performing strongly.[27] We introduce to this literature an important intervening variable: transparency.

We contend that, in general, transparency should be associated with the stabilization of democratic regimes. Furthermore, the impact of economic performance itself depends on transparency: when transparency is low and economic performance poor, democracies face a particularly high risk of collapse. But when transparency is high, democracy survives even under bad economic circumstances. This is because transparency increases the likelihood that good leaders win reelection while bad leaders are thrown out of office. In our model, a perception that elections fail to unseat incompetent leaders drives discontent with the democracy. Transparency enhances the effectiveness of elections – enabling the electorate en masse to better discriminate across good and bad leaders. Thus transparency reduces discontent and frustration with democratic political systems. In short, transparency helps make democracy work.

5.4 SUMMARY OF THE EMPIRICAL IMPLICATIONS OF THE TWO MODELS

The theory presented in this chapter has produced, using the logical rigor of mathematics, a number of hypotheses that we can test empirically in the next chapter. The theory is grounded in political economy and assumes that economic performance influences the fate of political regimes. We also find that the effects of economic performance interact with the effects of transparency. The conclusion is that transparency provokes unrest under autocracy while it stabilizes democracy.

More specifically, we have derived the following hypotheses:

Autocratic hypotheses

1. Transparency increases the risk of mass unrest (general strikes and mass demonstrations).
2. Transparency increases the risk of autocratic removal via mass revolt, leading either to democratization or to a new autocratic regime.
3. Poor economic performance increases the risk of autocratic removal via mass revolt and high levels of transparency exacerbate this risk.

---

[27] On the survival of democracy and economic performance, see Przeworski et al. (2000), Boix (2003), Boix and Stokes (2003), Epstein et al. (2006), and Gassebner, Lamla, and Vreeland (2013). For a contrasting view, see Acemoglu and Robinson (2006) and Acemoglu et al. (2008). On the reelection of leaders and economic performance, see Hibbs (1982, 2000).

Democratic hypotheses

1. Transparency decreases the risk of democratic collapse.
2. Transparency decreases the risk of irregular leader removal under democracy.
3. Economic growth makes democracy more likely to survive, but the effect is attenuated by transparency. If transparency is high, the effect of economic performance matters less for the survival of democracy.

The conclusions for autocracy contrast strikingly with the conclusions for democracy. Moreover, note that while the conclusions regarding autocracy point specifically to mass unrest, the conclusions for democracy point to a fuller range of threats. The democratic result is due to the enhanced informational environment under democracy – owing to the informative role that elections play. Elections reduce uncertainty about leaders types to such an extent that when a bad leader is retained it is obvious to all citizens that democracy is not working. In this case, there is no question that voters will mobilize to bring down the regime. Anticipating the certain collapse of democracy, all sorts of actors may intervene (Casper and Tyson 2014). A military coup or an elite-staged assassination may preclude the need for unrest and citizens – dissatisfied with the effectiveness of elections in removing bad leaders – are less likely to hold such efforts in check. In fact, if elites fail to take action, citizens simply take to the streets. One could say that low levels of transparency effectively cause the preferences of the masses of citizens to align with those of anti-democratic elites, so that opacity can cause both mass insurrection and elite-led coups under democracy.

We shall see in Chapter 10 that under autocracy, inner-circle elites have quite different motivations than the masses of citizens. We do not expect them to be encouraged by the dissatisfaction of the masses to overthrow the leadership. So, while the model in this chapter predicts an association between transparency and mass unrest for autocracies, we do not predict such an association with other types of threats, such as coups. In fact, Chapter 10 shows that elites may be protective of a leader threatened by unrest due to transparency, thus reducing the likelihood of elite-led coups under autocracy. For now, however, we turn to Chapters 6 and 7, where we empirically test the hypotheses generated thus far, focusing on mass unrest as a threat to autocratic rule and on regime collapse for democratic rule.

5.5 APPENDIX

5.5.1 Autocratic Appendix: Proofs of Theoretical Propositions of the Autocratic Model

Autocratic Baseline Model
Lemma 5.1. $\bar{y}^*(s)$ *is well-defined and monotone in s.*

Proof.   Definition 5.2 gives us $Pr(\theta = 0|\bar{y}^*(s), s)\beta = \kappa$. Substituting the posterior probability, conditional on signals s and $\bar{y}^*(s)$, generated by Bayes' rule, yields

$$\frac{\phi(\frac{\bar{y}^*(s)}{\sigma_y})\phi(\frac{s}{\sigma_s})(1-p)}{p\phi(\frac{\bar{y}^*(s)-g}{\sigma_y})\phi(\frac{s-g}{\sigma_s}) + \phi(\frac{\bar{y}^*(s)}{\sigma_y})\phi(\frac{s}{\sigma_s})(1-p)}\beta = \kappa$$

where ϕ is the PDF of the standard normal. Rearranging yields $\bar{y}^*(s) = \frac{s}{2}(1 + \frac{\sigma_y^2}{\sigma_s^2}) - \frac{s\sigma_y^2}{\sigma_s^2} - \frac{\sigma_y^2}{\gamma}\ln(\frac{p\kappa}{(1-p)[\beta-\kappa]})$ which is monotone in s. $\square$

PROOF OF AUTOCRATIC EQUILIBRIUM EXISTENCE

Proof of Proposition 5.1.   The leader has a dominant strategy to match his type. Since $u_{L,t}(G; \theta) = 1$ if $G_t = \theta$, zero otherwise, for $t \in \{1, 2\}$, it is always optimal to set $G_t = \theta$ in each period $t \in \{1, 2\}$ of the game. Following these equilibrium strategies, citizen i sets $a_i = 1$ if $y_{i,1} \le \bar{y}^*(s)$. Since there is a continuum of citizens, the proportion of citizens that mobilize, (that set $a_i = 1$) is either $Pr\{y_{i,1} \le \bar{y}^*(s)|\theta = 0\}$ or $Pr\{y_{i,1} \le \bar{y}^*(s)|\theta = 1\}$ depending on the type of leader. That is the proportion of citizens that protest is either $\Phi(\frac{\bar{y}^*(s)}{\sigma_y})$ or $\Phi(\frac{\bar{y}^*(s)-\gamma}{\sigma_y})$ where Φ is the CDF of the standard normal. If $\Phi(\frac{\bar{y}^*(s)}{\sigma_y}) \ge T > \Phi(\frac{\bar{y}^*(s)-\gamma}{\sigma_y})$, L is removed if and only if $\theta = 0$. Then for any citizen i, given the actions of other citizens and the leader, i will prefer to set $a_i = 1$ iff:

$$Pr(\theta = 1|y_{i,1}, s)\gamma$$
$$+ Pr(\theta = 0|y_{i,1}, s)[p\gamma + \beta] - \kappa \ge Pr(\theta = 1|y_{i,1}, s)\gamma + Pr(\theta = 0|y_{i,1}, s)p\gamma$$
$$Pr(\theta = 0|y_{i,1}, s)\beta \ge \kappa$$

The left hand side is the expected earnings to citizen i of protesting after receiving both her private and public signals. If the leader is a good type, in equilibrium he will survive the protest and implement policies that yield the citizen payoff γ in expectation in the second period (the first term). If, on the other hand, the leader is a bad type, he is removed for sure, and replaced with a good type with probability p that implements γ (a bad type would implement 0). There is also a benefit of β for participating in a successful protest (the second term). Of course political action incurs fixed costs κ. If the citizen does not protest, her payoffs are as on the right hand side. Since there is a continuum of citizens, no citizen is pivotal. Hence a good leader will survive the protest and implement γ in the second period; a poor leader will fall, and be replaced with a good leader with probability p who will institute good policy γ.

Therefore, when $\Phi(\frac{\bar{y}^*(s)}{\sigma_y}) \ge T > \Phi(\frac{\bar{y}^*(s)-\gamma}{\sigma_y})$, each citizen optimally protests (given the other citizens and the leader's actions) when $y_{i,1} \le \bar{y}^*(s)$. If, on the other hand, $\Phi(\frac{\bar{y}^*(s)}{\sigma_y}) < T$, and each citizen i is adopting a strategy of $a_i = 1$ if and only if $y_{i,1} \leq \bar{y}^*(s)$, then L would never be removed. Given that this is the case, the utility from setting $a_i = 1$ is $-\kappa < 0$, and so this cannot be a best response. Thus, $a_i = 0 \ \forall \ i$ if $\Phi(\frac{\bar{y}^*(s)}{\sigma_y}) < T$. We write this as $\bar{y}(s) = -\infty$ when $\Phi(\frac{\bar{y}^*(s)}{\sigma_y}) < T$.

Conversely, if $\Phi(\frac{\bar{y}^*(s)-\gamma}{\sigma_y}) \geq T$, and each citizen i is adopting a strategy of $a_i = 1$ if and only if $y_{i,1} \leq \bar{y}^*(s)$, then L would always be removed, regardless of type. Given that this is the case, the utility from setting $a_i = 1$ is $\beta - \kappa > 0$, the return from not participating. Hence $a_i = 1 \ \forall \ i$ if $\Phi(\frac{\bar{y}^*(s)-\gamma}{\sigma_y}) \geq T$ is a best response. We write this as $\bar{y}(s) = \infty$ when $\Phi(\frac{\bar{y}^*(s)-\gamma}{\sigma_y}) \geq T$.

Together these yield a best response for any citizen as $y_{i,1} \leq \bar{y}(s)$ where $\bar{y}(s)$ is as defined in Definition 5.2.

Finally, beliefs follow directly from Bayes' rule. $\qquad\qquad\square$

Lemma 5.2. *$\bar{s}$ and $\underline{s}$ are well-defined.*

Proof. Recall from Lemma 5.1 that $\bar{y}^*(s)$ is monotonic (and decreasing) in s. Further $\lim_{s \to \infty} \bar{y}^*(s) = -\infty$ and $\lim_{s \to -\infty} \bar{y}^*(s) = \infty$. Since $\Phi(\frac{\bar{y}^*(s)}{\sigma_y}) \ (\Phi(\frac{\bar{y}^*(s)-\gamma}{\sigma_y}))$ are monotonic and increasing in $\bar{y}^*(s)$ and limited below by zero and above by 1, it follows that there exist two values of s, which we define as $\bar{s}$ and $\underline{s}$, such that $T = \Phi(\frac{\bar{y}^*(\bar{s})-\gamma}{\sigma_y})$ and $T = \Phi(\frac{\bar{y}^*(\underline{s})}{\sigma_y})$. $\qquad\square$

TRANSPARENCY IMPROVES DISCRIMINATION UNDER AUTOCRACY

Proof of Proposition 5.2. Discrimination $= \Phi(\frac{\bar{s}}{\sigma_s}) - \Phi(\frac{\underline{s}-\gamma}{\sigma_s})$. Firstly, recall that $\Phi(\frac{\bar{y}^*(\bar{s})}{\sigma_y}) = T$. Substituting $\bar{y}^*(s)$ from Lemma 5.1 and solving we get $\bar{s} = \frac{\gamma}{2}(\frac{\sigma_s^2}{\sigma_y^2}+1) - \frac{\sigma_s^2}{\gamma}\ln(\frac{p\kappa}{(1-p)[\beta-\kappa]}) - \frac{\sigma_s^2}{\sigma_y}\Phi^{-1}(T)$. Similarly, since $\Phi(\frac{\bar{y}^*(\underline{s})-\gamma}{\sigma_y}) = T$, substituting and rearranging leads to $\underline{s} = \frac{\gamma}{2}(1 - \frac{\sigma_s^2}{\sigma_y^2}) - \frac{\sigma_s^2}{\gamma}\ln(\frac{p\kappa}{(1-p)[\beta-\kappa]}) - \frac{\sigma_s^2}{\sigma_y}\Phi^{-1}(T)$. Then $\frac{\partial}{\partial\sigma_s}(\frac{\bar{s}}{\sigma_s}) = \frac{\gamma}{2}(\frac{1}{\sigma_y^2} - \frac{1}{\sigma_s^2}) - \frac{1}{\gamma}\ln(\frac{p\kappa}{(1-p)[\beta-k]}) - \frac{1}{\sigma_y}\Phi^{-1}(T)$ and $\frac{\partial}{\partial\sigma_s}(\frac{\underline{s}-\gamma}{\sigma_s}) = \frac{\gamma}{2}(\frac{1}{\sigma_y^2} - \frac{1}{\sigma_s^2}) - \frac{1}{\gamma}\ln(\frac{p\kappa}{(1-p)[\beta-k]}) - \frac{1}{\sigma_y}\Phi^{-1}(T)$. To conserve on notation, we will label $Z \equiv \frac{1}{\gamma}\ln(\frac{p\kappa}{(1-p)[\beta-k]}) + \frac{1}{\sigma_y}\Phi^{-1}(T)$, and hence

$$\frac{\partial}{\partial\sigma_s}\left(\frac{\bar{s}}{\sigma_s}\right) = \frac{\gamma}{2}\left(\frac{1}{\sigma_y^2} - \frac{1}{\sigma_s^2}\right) - Z$$

$$\frac{\partial}{\partial\sigma_s}\left(\frac{\underline{s}-\gamma}{\sigma_s}\right) = \frac{\gamma}{2}\left(\frac{1}{\sigma_s^2} - \frac{1}{\sigma_y^2}\right) - Z$$

while $\frac{\gamma}{2}(\frac{1}{\sigma_s^2} - \frac{1}{\sigma_y^2}) > 0 > \frac{\gamma}{2}(\frac{1}{\sigma_y^2} - \frac{1}{\sigma_s^2})$, given that $\sigma_s < \sigma_y$. Notice too that

$$\frac{\gamma}{2}\left(\frac{1}{\sigma_s} + \frac{\sigma_s}{\sigma_y^2}\right) - \sigma_s Z = \frac{\bar{s}}{\sigma_s}$$

$$-\frac{\gamma}{2}\left(\frac{1}{\sigma_s} + \frac{\sigma_s}{\sigma_y^2}\right) - \sigma_s Z = \frac{s - \gamma}{\sigma_s}$$

Since $\phi(\cdot)$ is the PDF of a standard normal, we can also notice that

$$\phi\left(\frac{\bar{s}}{\sigma_s}\right) \gtreqless \phi\left(\frac{s - \gamma}{\sigma_s}\right) \Leftrightarrow Z \gtreqless 0. \tag{5.3}$$

Now consider a change in discrimination due to a change in σ_s:

$$\frac{\partial}{\partial \sigma_s}\left[\Phi\left(\frac{\bar{s}}{\sigma_s}\right) - \Phi\left(\frac{s - \gamma}{\sigma_s}\right)\right] < 0 \Leftrightarrow$$

$$\phi\left(\frac{\bar{s}}{\sigma_s}\right)\left[\frac{\partial}{\partial \sigma_s}\left(\frac{\bar{s}}{\sigma_s}\right)\right] < \phi\left(\frac{s - \gamma}{\sigma_s}\right)\left[\frac{\partial}{\partial \sigma_s}\left(\frac{s - \gamma}{\sigma_s}\right)\right] \tag{5.4}$$

Having defined these preliminaries, we can now evaluate condition 5.4. Let us first assume $\frac{\partial}{\partial \sigma_s}(\frac{\bar{s}}{\sigma_s}) > 0$. Notice that, since $\frac{\gamma}{2}(\frac{1}{\sigma_y^2} - \frac{1}{\sigma_s^2}) < 0$, this implies that $Z < 0$. Condition 5.4 can thus be expressed as:

$$\frac{\phi(\frac{\bar{s}}{\sigma_s})}{\phi(\frac{s-\gamma}{\sigma_s})} < \frac{\frac{\gamma}{2}(\frac{1}{\sigma_s^2} - \frac{1}{\sigma_y^2}) - Z}{\frac{\gamma}{2}(\frac{1}{\sigma_y^2} - \frac{1}{\sigma_s^2}) - Z}$$

Since $Z < 0$, we know from expression 5.3 that the left-hand side of this inequality is strictly less than one. We similarly know that the right-hand of this inequality must be strictly greater than one, given that $\sigma_s < \sigma_y$ and the denominator is positive. Thus, this inequality must hold.

Let us now consider the case where $\frac{\partial}{\partial \sigma_s}(\frac{\bar{s}}{\sigma_s}) < 0$. Then condition 5.4 can be rewritten as:

$$\frac{\phi(\frac{\bar{s}}{\sigma_s})}{\phi(\frac{s-\gamma}{\sigma_s})} > \frac{\frac{\gamma}{2}(\frac{1}{\sigma_s^2} - \frac{1}{\sigma_y^2}) - Z}{\frac{\gamma}{2}(\frac{1}{\sigma_y^2} - \frac{1}{\sigma_s^2}) - Z}$$

When $\frac{\partial}{\partial \sigma_s}(\frac{\bar{s}}{\sigma_s}) < 0$, $\frac{\partial}{\partial \sigma_s}(\frac{s-\gamma}{\sigma_s})$ may be either positive or negative. If it is positive, it is immediately apparent that this inequality must hold – the RHS will be strictly negative, while the LHS (by the definition of a PDF) is strictly positive.

Let us now consider the final possible case, in which $\frac{\partial}{\partial \sigma_s}(\frac{s-\gamma}{\sigma_s}) < 0$. Since $\frac{\gamma}{2}(\frac{1}{\sigma_s^2} - \frac{1}{\sigma_y^2}) > 0$, this implies that $Z > 0$ and $\frac{\frac{\gamma}{2}(\frac{1}{\sigma_s^2} - \frac{1}{\sigma_y^2}) - Z}{\frac{\gamma}{2}(\frac{1}{\sigma_y^2} - \frac{1}{\sigma_s^2}) - Z} \in (0, 1)$. $Z > 0$ implies that $\frac{\phi(\frac{\bar{s}}{\sigma_s})}{\phi(\frac{s-\gamma}{\sigma_s})} > 1$. Thus, the inequality holds.

Hence Condition 5.4 holds for all possible parameter values. Discrimination is therefore rising in transparency. $\square$

Corollary 5.1 follows directly from the strategies identified in the equilibrium in Proposition 5.1.

Proof of Proposition 5.3. The unconditional probability of autocratic removal is given by $(1 - p)\Phi(\frac{\bar{s}}{\sigma_s}) + p\Phi(\frac{s-\gamma}{\sigma_s})$. This probability is increasing in transparency if the quantity above is decreasing in σ_s. Thus, the unconditional probability of democratization is rising in transparency iff

$$(1 - p)\phi\left(\frac{\bar{s}}{\sigma_s}\right)\left[\frac{\partial}{\partial\sigma_s}\left(\frac{\bar{s}}{\sigma_s}\right)\right] + p\phi\left(\frac{s-\gamma}{\sigma_s}\right)\left[\frac{\partial}{\partial\sigma_s}\left(\frac{s-\gamma}{\sigma_s}\right)\right] < 0. \quad (5.5)$$

As we saw in the proof of Proposition 5.2, $\frac{\partial}{\partial\sigma_s}(\frac{s-\gamma}{\sigma_s}) > \frac{\partial}{\partial\sigma_s}(\frac{\bar{s}}{\sigma_s})$. Thus, a sufficient condition for condition 5.5 to hold is that $\frac{\partial}{\partial\sigma_s}(\frac{s-\gamma}{\sigma_s}) \leq 0$. Recall that

$$\frac{\partial}{\partial\sigma_s}\left(\frac{s-\gamma}{\sigma_s}\right) = \frac{\gamma}{2}\left(\frac{1}{\sigma_s^2} - \frac{1}{\sigma_y^2}\right) - Z$$

which is monotonic and decreasing in σ_s and converges to $-Z$ as $\sigma_s \to \sigma_y$. Thus, if $Z > 0$, there exists a value $\bar{\sigma}_s$ such that this expression is negative for all $\sigma_s \geq \bar{\sigma}_s$. Finally, $Z > 0$ implies that $\frac{1}{\gamma}\ln(\frac{p\kappa}{(1-p)[\beta-\kappa]}) + \frac{1}{\sigma_y}\Phi^{-1}(T) > 0$ or $\Phi^{-1}(T) > -\frac{\sigma_y}{\gamma}\ln(\frac{p\kappa}{(1-p)[\beta-\kappa]})$. $\quad\square$

Proof of Remark 5.1. From the proof of Proposition 5.3, a sufficient condition for the unconditional probability of autocratic removal to be rising in transparency (falling in σ_s) is $\frac{\partial}{\partial\sigma_s}(\frac{s-\gamma}{\sigma_s}) \leq 0$. Now $\frac{\partial}{\partial\sigma_s}(\frac{s-\gamma}{\sigma_s}) = \frac{\gamma}{2}(\frac{1}{\sigma_s^2} - \frac{1}{\sigma_y^2}) - Z$ and $Z = \frac{1}{\gamma}\ln(\frac{p\kappa}{(1-p)[\beta-\kappa]}) + \frac{1}{\sigma_y}\Phi^{-1}(T)$. Then $\lim_{\beta\to\kappa} Z = \infty \; \forall \, T > 0$ and hence $\lim_{\beta\to\kappa} \frac{\partial}{\partial\sigma_s}(\frac{s-\gamma}{\sigma_s}) < 0 \; \forall \sigma_s, T > 0$. $\quad\square$

PROOF OF THE EFFICIENCY OF THE CUT-POINT EQUILIBRIUM We consider the efficiency of the alternative equilibria from the perspective of public goods provision (i.e., the *ex ante* probability $G = 1$), ignoring the selective incentives for mobilization β. The expected utility of either "pooling" equilibrium, in which the public either always revolts or never revolts, is simply $2p\gamma$. By contrast, the expected utility of the "separating" equilibrium, depicted above, is given by $p[\gamma + Pr(s > \underline{s}|\theta = 1)\gamma + Pr(s \leq \underline{s}|\theta = 1)p\gamma] + (1 - p)[Pr(s \leq \bar{s}|\theta = 0)p\gamma]$. The latter expression dominates the former iff:

$$p\gamma + Pr(s > \underline{s}|\theta = 1)p\gamma + Pr(s \leq \underline{s}|\theta = 1)p^2\gamma$$
$$+ Pr(s \leq \bar{s}|\theta = 0)(1 - p)p\gamma \geq 2p\gamma$$
$$Pr(s \leq \bar{s}|\theta = 0) - Pr(s \leq \underline{s}|\theta = 1) \geq 0$$

substituting

$$\Phi\left(\frac{\bar{s}}{\sigma_s}\right) - \Phi\left(\frac{s-\gamma}{\sigma_s}\right) \geq 0$$

From the above, we have $\frac{\bar{s}}{\sigma_s} = \frac{\gamma}{2}(\frac{1}{\sigma_s} + \frac{\sigma_s}{\sigma_y^2}) - \sigma_s Z > \frac{s-\gamma}{\sigma_s} = -\frac{\gamma}{2}(\frac{1}{\sigma_s} + \frac{\sigma_s}{\sigma_y^2}) - \sigma_s Z$ implying that $\Phi(\frac{\bar{s}}{\sigma_s}) > \Phi(\frac{s-\gamma}{\sigma_s})$. Thus, the above equality must hold. $\square$

Autocratic Model Extension

AUTOCRATIC SEPARATING EQUILIBRIUM

Proof of Proposition 5.4. Taking the behavior of the leaders of each type as given, the citizens update in the same way as in the baseline game and their actions conditional on their beliefs are the same. Given the citizens' actions and beliefs, the probability of removal given $G_1 = 0$ is given by $\Phi(\frac{\bar{s}}{\sigma_s})$ while the probability of removal given $G_1 = 1$ is given by $\Phi(\frac{s-\gamma}{\sigma_s})$, where $\Phi(\cdot)$ is the CDF of the standard normal. Leaders of type $\theta = 1$ have a dominant strategy to set $G_t = 1 \ \forall \ t$. The return to leaders of type $\theta = 0$ when they separate, and set $G_1 = 0$ is larger than their return when they deviate, and set $G_1 = 1$ iff

$$1 + B + \left[1 - \Phi\left(\frac{\bar{s}}{\sigma_s}\right)\right](1+B) \geq B + \left[1 - \Phi\left(\frac{s-\gamma}{\sigma_s}\right)\right](1+B)$$

$$\frac{1}{1+B} \geq \Phi\left(\frac{\bar{s}}{\sigma_s}\right) - \Phi\left(\frac{s-\gamma}{\sigma_s}\right)$$

which is satisfied by the condition. Finally in all equilibria, leaders of type θ set $G_2 = \theta$. $\square$

Proof of Proposition 5.5. Given B, define $\bar{\sigma}_s$ such that $\frac{1}{1+B} = \Phi(\frac{\bar{s}}{\bar{\sigma}_s}) - \Phi(\frac{s-\gamma}{\bar{\sigma}_s})$. The definition of a CDF implies that $\Phi(\frac{\bar{s}}{\sigma_s}) - \Phi(\frac{s-\gamma}{\sigma_s})$ is bounded below by zero and above by one, since $\frac{\bar{s}}{\sigma_s} \geq \frac{s-\gamma}{\sigma_s}$. Proposition 5.2 establishes that this expression is monotonically decreasing in σ_s, it converges to zero as $\sigma_s \to \infty$. Then for any $\sigma_s \geq \bar{\sigma}_s$, $\frac{1}{1+B} \geq \Phi(\frac{\bar{s}}{\sigma_s}) - \Phi(\frac{s-\gamma}{\sigma_s})$. $\square$

AUTOCRATIC POOLING EQUILIBRIUM Since both types pool on providing the public good in the first period, the citizen learns nothing from the private signal $y_{i,1}$. While the citizen also cannot update on the type of leader by having observed the public signal (since both types take the same action), the posterior on the type of the leader does not change with the public signal either. However, the public signal can still be used as a coordination device such that whenever the signal lies below some threshold, say $\check{s}$, then all citizens protest; when the public signal is high enough, then they all stay home.

The threshold $\check{s}$ is not unique; there is a continuum of pooling equilibria.

Proposition 5.6. *For any $\check{s}$ such that $\frac{1}{1+B} < \Phi(\frac{\check{s}}{\sigma_s}) - \Phi(\frac{\check{s}-\gamma}{\sigma_s})$ then the following strategies and beliefs constitute a (pooling) PBE to the extended model.*

1. $G_1 = 1$ for $\theta = 0, 1$ and $G_2 = \theta$ for $\theta = 0, 1$.
2. $a_i = 1$ if $s \leq \check{s}$ and $a_i = 0$ otherwise, for all i.
3. $Pr(\theta = 0|y_{i,1}, s) = 1 - p$ for all i.

Proof. Leaders of type $\theta = 1$ will set $G_t = 1 \,\forall\, t$, for this is a dominant strategy. In a pooling equilibrium, leaders of type $\theta = 0$ set $G_1 = 1$. Such leaders always have a dominant strategy of setting $G_2 = 0$. Taking the behavior of the citizens, $Pr(remove|G_1 = 1) = \Phi(\frac{\check{s}-\gamma}{\sigma_s})$ where $\Phi(\cdot)$ is the CDF of the standard normal. If instead, the leader deviates and sets $G_1 = 0$, then the $Pr(remove|G_1 = 0) = \Phi(\frac{\check{s}}{\sigma_s})$. Then a type $\theta = 0$ pools with the strong leader iff

$$1 + B + [1 - Pr(remove|G_1 = 0)](1 + B) < B + [1 - Pr(remove|G_1 = 1)(1 + B)$$

$$\frac{1}{1+B} < \Phi\left(\frac{\check{s}}{\sigma_s}\right) - \Phi\left(\frac{\check{s}-\gamma}{\sigma_s}\right).$$

As for the citizens, if $s \leq \check{s}$, then everyone else is revolting and the leader will be removed; the best response is to revolt; if $s > \check{s}$, then no other citizen is revolting, and the best response is to set $a_i = 0$. $\qquad \square$

Remark 5.3. *Note that for $B \to \infty$, $\frac{1}{1+B} < \Phi(\frac{\check{s}}{\sigma_s}) - \Phi(\frac{\check{s}-\gamma}{\sigma_s})$ since $0 < \Phi(\frac{\check{s}}{\sigma_s}) - \Phi(\frac{\check{s}-\gamma}{\sigma_s})$ for all finite $\check{s}$ and σ_s by Proposition 5.2. Hence the parameter space for the pooling equilibrium is not empty.*

5.5.2 Democratic Appendix: Proofs of Theoretical Propositions of the Democratic Model

Lemma 5.3. $\tilde{y}(s) = \frac{\gamma}{2}(\frac{\sigma_y^2}{\sigma_s^2} + 1) - \frac{s\sigma_y^2}{\sigma_s^2}.$

Proof. Recall $Pr(\theta = 1|\tilde{y}(s), s) = p$. From Bayes' rule,

$$Pr(\theta = 1|\tilde{y}(s), s) = \frac{p\phi(\frac{\tilde{y}(s)-\gamma}{\sigma_y})\phi(\frac{s-\gamma}{\sigma_s})}{p\phi(\frac{\tilde{y}(s)-\gamma}{\sigma_y})\phi(\frac{s-\gamma}{\sigma_s}) + (1-p)\phi(\frac{\tilde{y}(s)}{\sigma_y})\phi(\frac{s}{\sigma_s})}.$$

Then $\tilde{y}(s) = \frac{\gamma}{2}(\frac{\sigma_y^2}{\sigma_s^2} + 1) - \frac{s\sigma_y^2}{\sigma_s^2}.$ $\qquad \square$

Proof of Democratic Equilibrium Existence
Proof of Proposition 5.7. The leader has a dominant strategy to match his type: L's best response is to set $G_t = \theta$ in $t \in \{1, 2\}$. In the voting stage, given the equilibrium strategies of the leader and the other voters, voter i votes against the incumbent (set $v_i = 1$) if and only if $Pr(\theta = 1|y_{i,1}, s) \leq p$. Substituting the equilibrium interim beliefs and simplifying yields the condition that $v_i = 1$ iff $y_{i,1} < \tilde{y}(s)$. So the voter is playing a best response which is consistent with beliefs. After the voting is complete, and given these strategies by the voters, the number of votes to remove L is given by $V(s; G_1)$, as defined in Definition 5.4. Notice that, for any value of s, $V(s; 1) < V(s; 0)$ the vote share of the incumbent is strictly lower if he fails to provide the public good than if

he provides the public good. This then implies that – given the public signal – each citizen i can deduce L's type with certainty based on his vote share. More precisely, each citizen i's posterior beliefs will be given by:

$$Pr(\theta = 1 | V, s) = \begin{cases} 0 & \text{if } V > V(s; 1) \\ 1 & \text{otherwise.} \end{cases}$$

Given these posterior beliefs, it is an equilibrium response if all voters mobilize if the actual vote count is larger than the expected vote count in the instance that the leader is good, that is, if $V > V(s; 1)$. If all other voters are mobilizing it is optimal for the i'th voter to mobilize too in order to benefit from participating in a successful uprising; if the other voters are not mobilizing (which happens when $V \leq V(s; 1)$), then there is no benefit to protesting. Hence for voter i a best response is $a_i = 1$ if $V > V(s; 1)$ and 0 otherwise. Finally both interim and posterior beliefs follow Bayes' rule. □

Democratic Discrimination and Transparency
Lemma 5.4. *$\tilde{s}$ and $\underline{s}$ are well-defined.*

Proof. $\Phi(\frac{\tilde{y}(\tilde{s})}{\sigma_y}) = \frac{1}{2}$ and $\tilde{y}(s) = \frac{\gamma}{2}(\frac{\sigma_y^2}{\sigma_s^2} + 1) - \frac{s\sigma_y^2}{\sigma_s^2}$ from Lemma 5.3. Substituting and solving yields $\frac{\gamma}{2}(1 + \frac{\sigma_s^2}{\sigma_y^2}) = \tilde{s}$. Similarly, $\Phi(\frac{\tilde{y}(\underline{s}) - \gamma}{\sigma_y}) = \frac{1}{2}$. Substituting and solving yields $\frac{\gamma}{2}(1 - \frac{\sigma_s^2}{\sigma_y^2}) = \underline{s}$. □

Democratic Discrimination Rises with Transparency
Proof of Proposition 5.8. Electoral discrimination $= \Phi(\frac{\tilde{s}}{\sigma_s}) - \Phi(\frac{\tilde{s} - \gamma}{\sigma_s})$. $\frac{\partial}{\partial \sigma_s}[\Phi(\frac{\tilde{s}}{\sigma_s}) - \Phi(\frac{\tilde{s} - \gamma}{\sigma_s})] = \phi(\frac{\tilde{s}}{\sigma_s})\frac{\partial}{\partial \sigma_s}[\frac{\tilde{s}}{\sigma_s}] - \phi(\frac{\tilde{s} - \gamma}{\sigma_s})\frac{\partial}{\partial \sigma_s}[\frac{\tilde{s} - \gamma}{\sigma_s}]$. Now the first term $\phi(\frac{\tilde{s}}{\sigma_s})\frac{\partial}{\partial \sigma_s}[\frac{\tilde{s}}{\sigma_s}] = \phi(\frac{\tilde{s}}{\sigma_s})\frac{\gamma}{2}(\frac{1}{\sigma_y^2} - \frac{1}{\sigma_s^2}) < 0$ since $\sigma_s < \sigma_y$. The second term $\phi(\frac{\tilde{s} - \gamma}{\sigma_s})\frac{\partial}{\partial \sigma_s}[\frac{\tilde{s} - \gamma}{\sigma_s}] = \phi(\frac{\tilde{s} - \gamma}{\sigma_s})\frac{\gamma}{2}(\frac{1}{\sigma_s^2} - \frac{1}{\sigma_y^2}) > 0$ again since $\sigma_s < \sigma_y$. Hence $\frac{\partial}{\partial \sigma_s}[\Phi(\frac{\tilde{s}}{\sigma_s}) - \Phi(\frac{\tilde{s} - \gamma}{\sigma_s})] < 0$. □

Unrest Falls with Transparency under Democracy
Proof of Proposition 5.9. Mass unrest takes place in equilibrium if and only if an incumbent of type $\theta = 0$ survives the electoral stage of the game. From the proof of Proposition 5.8, this probability is $1 - \Phi(\frac{\tilde{s}}{\sigma_s})$. Then $\frac{\partial}{\partial \sigma_s}[1 - \Phi(\frac{\tilde{s}}{\sigma_s})] = -\phi(\frac{\tilde{s}}{\sigma_s})[\frac{\partial}{\partial s}\frac{\tilde{s}}{\sigma_s}]$. From the proof of Proposition 5.8, $\frac{\partial}{\partial s}\frac{\tilde{s}}{\sigma_s} < 0$. Since ϕ is the PDF of the standard normal (and hence positive), $\frac{\partial}{\partial \sigma_s}[1 - \Phi(\frac{\tilde{s}}{\sigma_s})] > 0$. The probability of unrest under democracy is falling in transparency. □

5.5.3 Democratic Model Extension

Proof of Existence of a Separating Equilibrium
Proof of Proposition 5.10. When $\theta = 1$, L has a dominant strategy of setting $G_t = 1 \ \forall \ t$. For this to be a separating equilibrium, when $\theta = 0$ L must set $G_t = 0 \ \forall \ t$. When L sets $G_1 = 0$, he is removed from office with certainty – either via elections or following unrest. When L sets $G_1 = 1$ he is removed with probability $\Phi(\frac{\underset{\sim}{s}-\gamma}{\sigma_s})$. Hence, types $\theta = 0$ prefer to set $G_1 = 0$ iff:

$$1 + B \geq B + \left[1 - \Phi\left(\frac{\underset{\sim}{s} - \gamma}{\sigma_s}\right) \right] (1 + B)$$

$$\Phi\left(\frac{\underset{\sim}{s} - \gamma}{\sigma_s}\right) \geq \frac{B}{1 + B}.$$

Given $\Phi(\frac{\underset{\sim}{s}-\gamma}{\sigma_s}) \geq \frac{B}{1+B}$, L's strategy of $G_t(\theta) = \theta \ \forall \ t$, and the equilibrium strategies of all other voters, voter i votes against the incumbent if and only if $Pr(\theta = 1|y_{i,1}, s) \leq p$. Hence, $v_i = 1$ iff $y_{i,1} \leq \tilde{y}(s)$, where $\tilde{y}(s)$ is as defined in Definition 5.4. Given this strategy by each voter i, the number of voters voting to remove L is as given by $V(s; G_1)$, again as defined in Definition 5.4. As in the baseline model, for any realization of s, a strictly greater number of citizens vote to remove when $G_1 = 0$ than when $G_1 = 1$. Hence, each citizen i's beliefs at the conclusion of the voting stage will be given by:

$$Pr(\theta = 1|V, s) = \begin{cases} 0 & \text{if } V > V(s; 1) \\ 1 & \text{otherwise.} \end{cases}$$

Given these posterior beliefs, is an equilibrium response for all voters to mobilize iff $V > V(s; 1)$. $\qquad \square$

Proof of Equilibrium Threshold in Transparency and Benefits to Office
Proof of Lemma 5.5. The threshold $\bar{\sigma}_s$ is defined such that for all $\sigma_s \geq \bar{\sigma}_s$, $\Phi(\frac{\underset{\sim}{s}-\gamma}{\sigma_s}) \geq \frac{B}{1+B}$. To prove the existence of $\bar{\sigma}_s$, note that:

$$\underset{\sim}{s} = \frac{\gamma}{2}\left(1 - \frac{\sigma_s^2}{\sigma_y^2}\right)$$

$$\Leftrightarrow \frac{\underset{\sim}{s} - \gamma}{\sigma_s} = -\frac{\gamma}{2\sigma_s} - \frac{\gamma \sigma_s}{\sigma_y}$$

Taking the limits:

$$\lim_{\sigma_s \to \sigma_y} \Phi\left(\frac{\underset{\sim}{s} - \gamma}{\sigma_s}\right) = \Phi\left(-\frac{\gamma}{\sigma_y}\right)$$

$$\lim_{\sigma_s \to 0} \Phi\left(\frac{\underset{\sim}{s} - \gamma}{\sigma_s}\right) = 0$$

Moreover, as established in Proposition 5.8, $\Phi(\frac{s-\gamma}{\sigma_s})$ is monotonic and increasing in σ_s.

$\frac{B}{1+B}$ is similarly monotonic and increasing in B, with $\lim_{B\to 0} \frac{B}{1+B} = 0$ and $\lim_{B\to\infty} \frac{B}{1+B} = 1$. Hence, for any γ, σ_y, we can define a value of $B \equiv \bar{B}$ s.t. $\frac{\bar{B}}{1+\bar{B}} = \Phi(-\frac{\gamma}{\sigma_y})$.

Given the monotonicity of $\Phi(\frac{s-\gamma}{\sigma_s})$, and the limits described above, for any $B < \bar{B}$ there must exist a corresponding $\bar{\sigma}_s$ s.t. for all $\sigma_s \geq \bar{\sigma}_s$, $\Phi(\frac{s-\gamma}{\sigma_s}) \geq \frac{B}{1+B}$.   □

Proof of Existence of a Pooling Equilibrium
Proof of Proposition 5.11.   When $\theta = 1$, L has a dominant strategy of setting $G_t = 1 \ \forall \ t$. When $\theta = 0$, L has a dominant strategy of setting $G_2 = 0$. For this to be a pooling equilibrium, L must prefer to set $G_1 = 1$ when $\theta = 0$, which is possible if and only if the gains in the probability of survival are sufficiently high.

In a pooling equilibrium, all types of L set $G_1 = 1$, hence all realizations of $y_{i,1}$ and s are equally likely regardless of type. $Pr(\theta = 1|y_{i,1}, s) = p \ \forall \ y_{i,1}, s$. Voters are thus indifferent between setting $v_i = 0$ and $v_i = 1$. It thus remains a best response for all i to set $v_i = 1$ iff $y_{i,1} \leq \tilde{y}(s)$, where $\tilde{y}(s)$ is as defined in Definition 5.4. Given this voting strategy, vote returns will always be given by $V(s; 1)$ as defined in Definition 5.4, and voter posterior beliefs are given by $Pr(\theta = 1|V, s) = p \ \forall \ s$. Posterior beliefs for $V > V(s; 1)$ are not defined by Bayes' rule, and may be set such that $Pr(\theta = 1|V > V(s; 1), s) = 0 \ \forall \ s$. Given these beliefs, it is a best response for all i to set $a_i = 1$ iff $V > V(s; 1)$ and to set $a_i = 0$ otherwise.

Given these equilibrium strategies by all citizens i, L faces certain removal should he deviate and set $G_1 = 0$ and will be retained with probability $\Phi(\frac{s-\gamma}{\sigma_s})$ if he sets $G_1 = 1$. Hence, types $\theta = 0$ strictly prefer to set $G_1 = 1$ iff:

$$1 + B < B + \left[1 - \Phi\left(\frac{s-\gamma}{\sigma_s}\right)\right](1+B)$$

$$\Phi\left(\frac{s-\gamma}{\sigma_s}\right) < \frac{B}{1+B}.$$

Thus, if $\Phi(\frac{s-\gamma}{\sigma_s}) < \frac{B}{1+B}$, the above strategies and beliefs constitute a pooling PBE to the game.   □

Comparative Statics to the Extended Democratic Model
Proof of Proposition 5.12.   The strategies of all players in the separating equilibrium to the extended model are identical to those of the baseline model. Hence, for any $B \leq \bar{B}$ and $\sigma_s \geq \bar{\sigma}_s$, the conclusion of Proposition 5.9 still holds. The probability of collapse is strictly falling in transparency (rising in σ_s).

For any $B > \bar{B}$ or $\sigma_s < \bar{\sigma}_s$, the pooling equilibrium holds. Along the equilibrium path, $V = V(s; 1)$ regardless of L's type, hence $a_i = 0 \; \forall \; i$. The probability of collapse is invariant and equal to zero for all values of transparency.

Taken together, these results indicate that the probability of democratic collapse is weakly falling for all values of transparency (weakly rising for all values of σ_s). □

6

The Evidence

Examples and Descriptive Data

Collapsing political regimes bring down with them a hail of uncertainty and can wreak havoc on the lives of citizens, not to mention financial markets. Accordingly, the field of comparative politics has devoted much attention to studying regime transitions.[1] With such an abundance of scholarship apportioned to the topic, debates rage about nearly every aspect of the phenomenon: the causes of autocratic failure, the emergence of democracy, the survival and breakdown of democracy, even the very categories of political regime and how to define a regime transition.

This chapter focuses on the empirical effect of transparency on political stability. We seek to test the specific hypotheses generated by our autocratic and democratic models of Chapter 5. Fully engaging all of the debates surrounding political stability lies beyond the purview of our project. Instead, we accommodate, to an extent, alternative perspectives by testing our theory in different empirical contexts, thus avoiding the need to take sides. This chapter shows that when we control for factors prominent in the scholarly literature, our conclusions about the effects of transparency on political stability hold.

The HRV index proxies as an empirical measure of the concept of transparency in our theoretical models. Recall that in Chapter 5, transparency enters our models as the inverse of the standard deviation of the publicly observable signal of government performance witnessed by all citizens, σ_s. Our concept of transparency thus pertains to information that is (1) publicly observable – and known to be publicly observable by all actors – and (2) allows citizens to

---

[1] Some examples from the copious literature, which spans more than half a century, include Lipset (1959); Moore (1966); Rustow (1970); Linz (1978); Huntington (1991); O'Donnell (1979); O'Donnell and Schmitter (1986); Putnam (1993); Olson (1993); Haggard and Kaufman (1995); Linz and Stepan (1996); Schedler (1998); Diamond (1999); Rosendorff (2001); McFaul (2005); Diskin, Diskin, and Hazan (2005); Slater (2010); Bohlken (2016).

draw accurate inferences regarding government performance. The HRV index, based on the reporting/non-reporting of information to the World Bank's World Development Indicators (WDI) data series, mirrors our criteria. The disclosure of economic information to the World Bank reflects the public dissemination of credible data.

Of course, we do not expect many members of the public to seek access to such data directly from the World Bank. Instead, the public more likely obtains such information straight from the government or through domestic news reports informed by government disclosures. What then is the advantage of World Bank data? We use the World Bank as a means of verifying the *credibility* of publicly disclosed data. Information that fails to meet World Bank standards is omitted from the WDI dataset. The World Bank and other international organizations weed out sub-par data reported by national governments using rigorous standards referenced previously (recall the DQAF and the GDDS). If the World Bank rejects data reported by a national government, it is likely that other organizations and individuals similarly recognize government reports as dubious. Citizens likely adjust their expectations to account for false government information – either by disregarding reports that always claim performance to be good, regardless of reality, or by adjusting their expectations of what constitutes good performance in the face of repeated exaggerations.

Only *credible* data allow citizens to make more nuanced inferences about government performance. As additional credible data on aggregate economic performance become available, citizens can better discern the performance of the overall economy beyond the experiences of a given circle of friends, family, and acquaintances. Citizens can then assess the distributional consequences of economic policy and assess the government's role relative to that of cyclical fluctuations. While these inferences are imperfect ($\sigma_s > 0$), increases in the dissemination of accurate aggregate economic data help to improve these inferences in ways that are common knowledge across the citizenry.

The key theoretical insight of Chapter 5 is that the relationship between data disclosure and political stability depends on political institutions. Under autocracy, higher levels of data transparency inform the higher-order beliefs of citizens: Citizens not only learn about the economic consequences of government policy, they also become informed of what other citizens know. This knowledge across the citizenry facilitates collective action. Under democracy, elections serve the role of informing higher-order beliefs, and data transparency simply makes the electoral process more efficient at rooting out incompetent or corrupt leaders. So, while transparency causes mass unrest under autocracy, it stabilizes democratic rule. This chapter tests these empirical implications.

In order to test our hypotheses about the effects of transparency, we do need to make some specific ontological decisions about how to measure our dependent variables. Some of these decisions are controversial. Scholars disagree about which measures best capture the various features of political instability – where alternative measures are available, we select those that best fit our theory. In other cases, limited availability of alternative measures constrains our choice of dependent variable.

The chapter is thus organized as follows: first, we discuss the nature and measurement of political (in)stability. Having established how to measure the empirical phenomena we seek to explore, we then use our measure of transparency – the HRV index – to test our hypotheses. We begin by presenting fitting examples from Africa, Asia, Europe, and Latin America. Of course, one can almost always find some cases that appear to confirm a theory. Recall that the HRV index covers 125 countries for the 1980–2010 period; there are many relevant examples. We therefore also consider systematic patterns, presenting the bivariate relationships between the HRV index and various forms of political stability.

We intend this initial empirical exploration to provide intuitive evidence supporting our hypotheses. To address concerns about alternative mechanisms and reverse causality, we rigorously test our hypotheses using statistical techniques to analyze comprehensive datasets in Chapter 7. We conclude Part II with a summary of the empirical evidence, which shows that transparency stabilizes democracies while in autocracies it causes mass unrest that can topple these regimes.

6.1 MEASURES OF POLITICAL (IN)STABILITY

What is the nature of political instability and how should it be measured? The theoretical models presented in Chapter 5 indicate a number of specific forms of political instability that transparency should predict. Our hypotheses pertaining to autocratic instability call for measures of (1) transitions to democracy, (2) the ouster of autocratic governments, and (3) specific forms of mass unrest. Our hypotheses about democratic stability call for measures of (1) the survival of democracy and (2) regular versus irregular removal of democratically elected leaders.

The theoretical mechanisms identified in Chapter 5 also imply that transparency predicts only specific forms of political instability – not others. Under autocracy, transparency is predictive of political threats such as mass anti-government protests and general strikes, which involve the higher-order beliefs of masses of citizens. Transparency is not predicted to increase the likelihood of coups or assassinations, which involve elite-groups with clear leadership and shared information. Under democracy, a lack of transparency causes the preferences of the masses to align with anti-democratic elites, so the risk of all threats to democratic stability increase with opacity.

With various forms of political instability at stake, this section discusses several distinct indicators, exploring how to best measure the empirical nature of these phenomena.

6.1.1 The Emergence and Survival of Democracy

Schumpeter (1942: 269) argues that the hallmark of modern-day democracy is electoral contestation: "the democratic method is that institutional arrangement for arriving at political decisions in which individuals acquire the power to decide by means of a competitive struggle for the people's vote." Przeworski et al. (2000) operationalize this view of democracy, providing a dichotomous measure that follows Schumpeter's idea: democracy is the political system in which key government offices are filled through contested elections.[2] Importantly, they code regimes as democratic only if incumbents have lost elections and complied with the results – turning the reigns of power over to opposition parties. The coding rules raise the bar far above the electoral charades that many autocratic governments conduct; the definition of democracy is not "just elections." Rather, democracy involves true contests for executive and legislative power through electoral means.

This minimalist measurement of democracy – which Cheibub, Gandhi, and Vreeland (2010) have christened "DD" (for democracy-dictatorship) – confers three specific advantages to our study. First, the measurement is "clean": the coding rules make no reference to levels of transparency or to the informational environment. Other commonly used measures of democracy (such as the Polity and Freedom House measures) explicitly employ the term "transparent" in their codebooks. So any correlation between transparency and these measures of democracy could represent a tautology.

Second, the coding of the Przeworski et al. (2000) measure matches exactly with the theoretical models presented in Chapter 5. Recall that the only difference between Chapter 5's autocratic and democratic models is that the incumbent leader must win election in order to retain office in the democratic model. Elections determining the fate of incumbents is also the defining feature of the Przeworski et al. (2000) measure.

Finally, and perhaps most importantly for this chapter, Przeworski et al. (2000) developed their measure to capture *transitions* precisely. The dichotomous nature of the measure is tailored to this purpose. When a country goes from 0 to 1, we know that during that year, elections begin to determine the fate of incumbent politicians. When a country goes from 1 to 0, we know that elections cease to fill the leader's (or legislature's) position. When a country continues to be coded 1, we know that democracy has survived another year.

Many have taken issue with Schumpeter's minimalist view of democracy. Perhaps the most famous critic is Dahl (1971), who contends that electoral

---

[2] The definition has two parts: "key government offices," which the authors define as the executive and the legislature; and "contested," which implies that more than one party has some probability of winning office through election. Because "probability" is not directly observable, the authors stipulate further criteria to establish true contestation: (1) elections must have *ex ante* uncertainty, (2) electoral results must be irreversible *ex post*, and (3) there must be some alternation in power under consistent electoral rules.

contestation alone fails to define democracy. He proposes that several guarantees are necessary for democracy, including alternative sources of credible
information (Dahl 1971: 4). Note, however, that requiring alternative sources of
information as part of the definition of democracy would preclude the growing
literature on democracy and transparency. If we define democracy as requiring
a rich informational environment, we can simply categorize all states lacking
in transparency as undemocratic and cease further exploration into this relationship (see Manin 1997; Przeworski, Stokes, and Manin 1999; Schwartzberg
2014).

If researchers do wish to go beyond minimalist criteria, they should take
care in selecting which additional features they seek to include in their definition of democracy. Polity and Freedom House both reference transparency in
their coding rules. Moreover, they fail to provide a substantive definition of stability versus transition. Take, for example, the commonly used Polity measure
of political regime (see Marshall and Jaggers 2013). This variable combines
five different measures of various aspects of political systems to arrive at an
overall index spanning from -10 to $+1021$ gradations of political regime. The
demarcation of a crisp dividing line between democracies and autocracies – a
feature necessary to define regime-type transitions – is not obvious in a 21 point
scale. The Polity codebook thus offers a nonsubstantive definition of a regime
transition based on arbitrary cut-points.[3] The lack of a reference to substance
in this definition is necessary because different political changes across the five
components of the measure can result in the same cardinal shifts.

The Przeworski et al. (2000) measure thus better suits our purposes than the
Polity measure.[4] The clear and substantive definition of a regime transition –
grounded in consequential electoral contestation – neatly fits with our theory.
We can use the DD variable both to measure transitions from autocracy to
democracy and to measure the survival of democracy.

6.1.2 Autocrat Removal

Changes in an autocratic regime do not always result in a transition to
democracy. Sometimes mass unrest unseats autocracies, but the government
is replaced by a new autocracy – with no transition to democracy. In other

---

[3] A "major democratic transition" is defined as a "six points or greater increase in [the] POLITY
score over a period of three years or less including a shift from an autocratic POLITY value $(-10$
to 0) to a partial democratic POLITY value $(+1$ to $+6)$ or full democratic POLITY value $(+7$ to
$+10)$ or a shift from a partial democratic value to a full democratic value" (Marshall and Jaggers
2005: 34).

[4] We stress that the Polity project codes a wealth of useful information and includes a rigorous
codebook. Other measures of political regime, which do not have such a rigorous codebook
available publicly, can also be used for research purposes. For example, Freedom House is fruitful
for the study of how advocacy organizations make their regime coding decisions. For an excellent
example of such work, see Roberts and Tellez (2017).

instances, transitions may occur through processes not involving mass unrest (see, for example, Ansell and Samuels 2010; Lizzeri and Persico 2004; Llavador and Oxoby 2005). So, while the Przeworski et al. (2000) measure offers us the opportunity to test part of our theory – the transition to democracy – it may miss important changes across different dictatorships, which are coded as continuations of autocratic rule by Przeworski and his colleagues.

We therefore require an additional, more nuanced measure of autocratic regime transition. We cannot, however, simply consider a change in the titular leader of an autocratic regime. Some regimes prove quite durable beyond the initial leadership, handing power down to designated successors. Moreover, even when one autocracy replaces another, the change is not always due to mass unrest. Some autocracies fall to coups or assassinations that do not involve masses of citizens, and thus do not fit with the type of instability designated by our theoretical model. So we require a measure of a real change in an autocratic regime that also indicates the circumstances surrounding that change.

Svolik (2012) defines an instance of authoritarian collapse as the removal of an autocratic leader by an alternative leader or coalition not politically affiliated with the sitting clique. This empirical definition fits our theoretical model. Furthermore, the dataset of Svolik (2012) documents with great precision the manner through which autocratic regimes fall from power. We consider the collapse of autocratic regimes that result from either democratization or mass revolt – excluding alternative forms of collapse, such as those brought about via coups.

Svolik's dataset on the duration of authoritarian regimes codes democratization conservatively – he identifies fewer transitions than the Cheibub, Gandhi, and Vreeland (2010) dataset. His dataset has an additional advantage because it also includes removal of autocratic leadership through mass revolt, which is exactly the form of unrest identified by our model. Our theoretical mechanism operates via mass unrest, and thus focusing particularly on instances of leader removal brought about by democratization in particular or mass revolt in general is well suited to our theory. We group Svolik's observations of democratization and removal via mass revolt because separate analyses of each separately produce similar results (although with fewer degrees of freedom, statistical confidence is lower in the separate analyses). We view Svolik's dependent variable as an uncontroversial extension beyond the test of democratic transitions. Indeed, the specific coding of autocrat removal via unrest makes this dependent variable a stronger test of our theory.

6.1.3 Threats to Autocratic Rule

Beyond the analysis of regime stability at the macro level, we can also examine the political activities of masses and elites. By narrowing our empirical analysis, we can distinguish across different types of threats to autocratic regimes.

We predict that transparency under autocracy makes mass unrest more likely. This theoretical prediction follows from the view that an enhanced informational environment helps individual citizens to form higher-order beliefs about other citizens' views of the sitting leadership. These higher-order beliefs are vital for the mobilization of masses of citizens, who may never make face-to-face contact, and must make an educated guess as to whether other citizens will turn out on the streets to protest. The decision is an important one for citizens. While an individual citizen may hope to participate in a mobilization effort to overthrow a political regime, she does not want to go forward alone. Our model thus speaks directly to the probability of anti-government demonstrations and general strikes against government policy. The model makes no prediction about other forms of instability under autocracy that do not draw on large masses for support, such as revolutions, coups, or assassinations.

Revolutions, coups, and assassinations usually involve explicit coordination across the conspirators. Revolutions, for example, involve organized forces. Coups require clandestine collaborators – as do assassination attempts. While accomplices meet in secret and may not always be honest with one another, revolutionaries, coup collaborators, and the plotters of assassinations share information directly.[5] They face coordination problems of a qualitatively different nature than those faced by masses of citizens, whose primary concerns involve the higher-order beliefs of other citizens whom they do not know personally. Our theoretical model, grounded in the coordination of masses of citizens in an informationally imperfect environment, predicts that transparency encourages mass unrest but should have no such similar effect on other forms of instability under autocracy. (Indeed, Chapter 10 shows that it can have the opposite effect in some cases.)

Thus we seek further refined measures of the threats faced by autocratic regimes. We draw our measures of mass mobilization and unrest from the Cross National Time Series Archive (Banks 1979), as made available by Bueno de Mesquita et al. (2003). This dataset includes annual observations for the individual countries covered by the HRV index. To gauge collective dissatisfaction with the government, we use the "anti-government demonstrations" variable. Banks (1979) defines anti-government demonstrations as "Any peaceful public gathering of at least 100 people for the primary purpose of displaying or voicing their opposition to government policies or authority, excluding demonstrations of a distinctly anti-foreign nature." To gauge collective dissatisfaction with the economy, we use the "general strikes" variable. Banks (1979) defines general strikes as "Any strike of 1,000 or more industrial or service workers that involves more than one employer and that is aimed at national government policies or authority."[6] Both of these variables code unrest

---

[5] Though, the informational problems facing coup plotters and the masses may be interrelated, see Casper and Tyson (2014).

[6] The definitions of anti-government demonstrations and general strikes, respectively, are available through www.cntsdata.com/#!domconflict/c1svs, accessed April 1, 2016.

undertaken by a mass of citizens specifically targeting the government and governmental policies.

The Cross National Time Series Archive also includes other measures of domestic conflict, about which our theory does not make predictions. These variables prove useful as counterfactual phenomena that we can evaluate. By showing that transparency predicts the forms of instability identified by our theoretical model, but that transparency does *not* predict other forms of instability, we increase our confidence in our model's causal mechanism.

Riots, for example, are a form of mass mobilization, that need not target the government. The Banks (1979) dataset defines "riots" as "Any violent demonstration or clash of more than 100 citizens involving the use of physical force."[7] Often such riots involve clashes between communities and ethnic groups (Scacco 2008). Consequently, we do not consider rioting to be a manifestation of the type of unrest documented in our model.

Guerrilla movements, revolutions, assassinations, and coups involve varying degrees of collective action, but transparency impacts the conspirators in ways distinct from how it influences the participants in the forms of mass unrest predicted by our autocratic model. Guerrilla movements are defined as "Any armed activity, sabotage, or bombings carried on by independent bands of citizens or irregular forces and aimed at the overthrow of the present regime." Revolutions are defined as "Any illegal or forced change in the top government elite, any attempt at such a change, or any successful or unsuccessful armed rebellion whose aim is independence from the central government." Assassinations are defined as "Any politically motivated murder or attempted murder of a high government official or politician." Coups are defined as "The number of extraconstitutional or forced changes in the top government elite and/or its effective control of the nation's power structure in a given year."[8]

Guerrilla movements and revolutions involve organized bands of citizens. Their organizational structure enables members to coordinate directly, thus obviating the problem of higher-order beliefs. Successful coups and assassinations usually involve careful planning by a tightknit group of elites. Again, the higher-order beliefs about the beliefs of collaborators are not a problem because these actions involve direct coordination by participants – and these participants are typically government actors with privileged access to information withheld from the general public. Riots are spontaneous and do involve higher-order beliefs, but they may not be directed toward the government.

Anti-government demonstrations and general strikes stand in contrast to these other threats. They involve masses of citizens who oppose government policies but have no face-to-face contact with each other. Their taking to the

---

[7] The definition is available through www.cntsdata.com/#!domconflict/c1svs, accessed April 1, 2016.

[8] See www.cntsdata.com/#!political-data-definitions/c8i1 (accessed April 1, 2016) for the definition of a coup. See www.cntsdata.com/#!domconflict/c1svs (accessed April 1, 2016) for definitions of guerrilla movements, revolutions, and assassinations.

streets involve risks – if the group is too small, participants may face violence, imprisonment, or worse. Higher-order beliefs loom large in the minds of individuals who would participate in these activities and thus economic transparency should facilitate them under autocracy. The theory developed in Chapter 5 leads us to predict that anti-government demonstrations and strikes grow more frequent under autocracy – it offers no expectations about the alternative forms of unrest.

The Banks (1979) dataset is widely used, but like all datasets, it has weaknesses.[9] The data are coded based on reporting found in the *New York Times* archives. This approach to coding enables data collectors to offer broad temporal and cross-country coverage. Yet Schedler (2012) documents that this methodology tends to undercount instances of unrest.

A general tendency to undercount unrest would bias against our hypothesis – unless the measurement error is systematically correlated with our measure of transparency. If governments that disclose more information to the World Bank are also more open to *New York Times* reporters, perhaps instances of unrest are more severely undercounted in opaque countries than in transparent ones. If this is the case, our results would be biased in favor of our hypotheses.

The fact that we expect transparency to predict specific forms of domestic conflict, but not others, somewhat insulates us from this concern. There is little reason to expect that biases affect the reporting of mass demonstrations and general strikes, but not guerrilla movements, riots, coups, or assassinations. The biases should run in the same direction for all of the Banks (1979) variables. The fact that we have different hypotheses about the effects of transparency on these dependent variables allow for a distinctive test of our theory.

To further mitigate potential bias, we include a robustness check that incorporates a control for freedom of the press as suggested by Schedler (2012). Specifically, we include a control for an indicator variable which takes the value of 1 if the press is coded as "Not Free" by Freedom House's Freedom of the Press index.[10]

6.1.4 The Regular and Irregular Removal of Democratically Elected Leaders

Shifting our attention to democracies, our theory makes rather different predictions about the effect of transparency. Because elections provide information about the distribution of support for the government across the citizenry, transparency reveals nothing to the masses that would encourage unrest. Instead, the dissemination of reliable economic data simply makes the electoral process more effective and thus legitimates the survival of democratic rule.

---

[9] As evidence of the wide use of this dataset, *Google Scholar* numbers the citations to it in the thousands.

[10] See www.freedomhouse.org/report-types/freedom-press, accessed January 6, 2016.

The democratic model thus requires measures of political stability under electoral rule. We have already introduced one measure of the survival of democracy – this phenomenon complements the emergence of democracy, discussed above. We continue to rely on the Przeworski et al. (2000) DD measure, which defines democracy as the political system in which incumbents lose power through contested elections (see also Przeworski 1991). Democracy survives when truly contested elections continue to fill the offices of the legislature and the executive.[11]

We narrow our analysis of democratic stability by considering a measure of the removal of incumbent leaders under democracy. We consider the regular versus irregular removal of democratic leaders, using the Archigos dataset (Goemans 2006; Goemans, Gleditsch, and Chiozza 2009). This dataset codes leadership exit as *regular* "when the leader is removed in accordance with explicit rules or established conventions of his or her particular country" (Goemans, Gleditsch, and Chiozza 2009: 2). The dataset codes extraconstitutional methods of removal as *irregular* when the leader is removed "in contravention of explicit rules and established conventions," which includes instances of "coups, (popular) revolts and assassinations" (Goemans, Gleditsch, and Chiozza 2009: 2–3). The authors of the dataset stress that "most irregular removals from office are done by domestic forces" (Goemans, Gleditsch, and Chiozza 2009: 3). Importantly, however, the dataset separately codes removal from office by or with the help of foreign interventions. The dataset also flags leaders who leave office due to natural causes or suicide. Thus Archigos covers the full spectrum of possible departures from office, which permits us to focus on the two key categories specified by our theory, where *domestic* forces remove leaders (either democratically or undemocratically).

The Archigos dataset enables us to pursue a more micro-level analysis because of its focus on leaders as opposed to regimes. So, our tests of democratic stability begin with an analysis of the survival of democratic regimes and then move to an examination of the removal of democratic leaders.

6.1.5 Summary of Dependent Variables

Our dependent variables range from broad to specific, fitting ever more closely with Chapter 5's exact hypotheses about the interaction of citizens and leaders under different levels of transparency. To test our autocracy hypotheses, we

---

[11] Our concern with democratic survival is analogous to that of a literature on democratic consolidation, if one adopts a narrow definition of the latter term (Schedler 1998). We do not, however, relate our theory to more expansive definitions of democratic consolidation, which might include the extension of civil rights or the institutionalization of democracy (O'Donnell 1996). Our focus on democratic survival is shared by many other works, including Linz (1978); Linz and Stepan (1996); Diamond (1994, 1999); Przeworski et al. (2000, 2005); Svolik (2013c); Wright (2008b).

first consider transitions to democracy, followed by the removal of autocratic leaders through mass unrest, and finally the precise forms of instability under autocracy. To test our democracy hypotheses, we begin with the survival of democratic regimes and then examine the specific manner by which democratic leaders are removed from office.

6.2 EXAMPLES AND DESCRIPTIVE DATA

We begin our empirical work with concrete examples from history. Our illustrations of the relationship between transparency and (in)stability draw on the characteristic experiences of South Korea, Mexico, the Philippines, Côte d'Ivoire, Bulgaria, Bangladesh, Central African Republic, Guinea-Bissau, and Uganda.

We also present an overview of patterns in the data. The descriptive patterns we present in this section are bivariate and intended only to be suggestive. We pair each dependent variable with our measure of transparency so that we can consider whether any descriptive pattern exists. We do not consider this initial exploration of the data to stand as a rigorous test of our theory – we reserve further analysis of the data for the next chapter. There, we consider alternative hypotheses by explicitly including a host of control variables, accounting for duration dependence, and pursuing a number of robustness checks.

For now, we seek merely to get some intuitions about how the history of data dissemination and political stability have unfolded in some key countries as well as in our overall sample of 125 countries for the period of 1980 to 2010.

6.2.1 Autocratic Instability

Our initial empirical analysis of instability under autocracy starts with three examples: (1) South Korea, (2) Mexico, and (3) the Philippines. We then present descriptive patterns in the data looking at the relationship between the HRV index and transitions to democracy using the DD data. We next present the example of Côte d'Ivoire as a case of one autocracy replacing another, and then present the broader relationship between the HRV index and the replacement of one autocratic regime by a new regime using the data of Svolik (2012). Finally, we examine the example of Bulgaria and look at the association between transparency and measures of mass unrest using the data of Banks (1979).

The Emergence of Democracy in South Korea
Consider the case of South Korea, depicted in Figure 6.1. The shaded region in this figure refers to a period of autocratic rule ending in 1987. The figure shows that in 1980, the country's HRV score was 1.74. This transparency score jumped up to 2.93 in 1981 and continued to rise from 1982 through 1986, settling at a score of 4.14 in 1987. During this period, the government provided data on a host of new economic measures that were not reported before 1981,

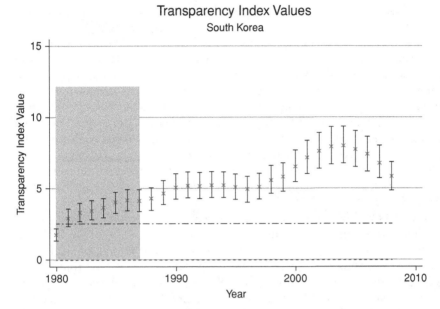

FIGURE 6.1. South Korea pre- and post-transition. HRV values are plotted on the y-axis, while the x-axis measures time in years. Cross-marks correspond to mean HRV scores, while whiskers are 95 percent credible intervals. The shaded region marks years in which South Korea was an autocracy, the unshaded years are democratic. The two dashed lines correspond to the mean HRV scores among autocracies (−0.003, the lower line), and democracies (2.54, the upper line).

including detailed unemployment rates (50 percent of the unemployed in 1987 were workers with secondary education), the turnover ratio of the domestic share of stocks traded (which exploded during the 1980s, going from 50 percent in 1980 to 110 percent in 1987), the market capitalization of domestic companies listed on the stock market (which also exploded from 6 percent of GDP in 1981 to 22 percent in 1987 and 47 percent in 1988), and rates of immunization against diphtheria, pertussis, and tetanus (which dropped from a high of 76 percent in the mid-1980s to 57 percent in 1987) (World Bank, n.d.).

As data dissemination increased, so did unrest in the streets, which eventually led to a transition to democracy. The climax of protests for democracy occurred during the summer of 1987 when the June Democratic Uprising broke out in South Korea. Did our causal mechanism – that data dissemination facilitated collective action – play a role?

Adesnik and Kim (2008: 2) argue that the four main constituencies of the protest movement – students, labor unions, churches, and parliamentary opposition parties – achieved a high level of political unity during this period, which helped drive the democracy movement. Indeed, Im (1995) contends that this exceptional level of unity – absent in previous efforts to bring forward democracy – was the crucial factor in the success of the opposition.

The successful efforts of the increasingly united opposition to unseat authoritarian rule is reflected in the data. While the Cross National Time Series Archive reports an average of fewer than seven anti-government demonstrations per year from 1980 to 1986, there were 24 anti-government demonstrations in 1987, according to the Banks (1979) reckoning from the *New York Times*. Katsiaficas (2012: 278–279) suggests a much higher level of protest, detailing that for 19 consecutive days in June hundreds of thousands of people protested in the streets of every major city in South Korea – demanding democracy. The police reported an average of more than one hundred demonstrations per day and a total of 3,362 total anti-government demonstrations (Katsiaficas 2012: 278–279).

To understand how the rising level of transparency may have played a role in helping protestors coordinate, consider a comparison of what unfolded in South Korea during 1987 to a previous period of political upheaval in 1979.

Protests also took place in 1979 – but ultimately they failed to bring about a democratic transition, arguably because protestors did not coordinate as well as they would in the 1980s (Adesnik and Kim 2008; Im 1995). Perhaps lower levels of transparency hindered such coordination back in 1979.

Note that while the HRV score was 4.14 in 1987, it was only 1.74 in 1980. Fitting with our theory, Adesnik and Kim (2008: 2,12) and Im (1995) explain that the pro-democratic coalition, or *chaeya*, was less united in 1979 than in 1987. The 1979 protests – taking place under conditions of lower levels of data transparency – were unsuccessful in overturning autocratic rule. Instead, the ruling elite took matters into its own hands. The autocratic leader, President Park Chung Hee, was assassinated by someone within his clique (his own intelligence chief) (Adesnik and Kim 2008: 1). The political elite then entrenched itself under the rule of Park's protégé, General Chun Doo Hwan.

The unified protest movement of 1987, operating under higher levels of transparency, achieved quite a different outcome. Enjoying a flourishing economy but facing a highly united protest movement, Chun "surrendered to the protesters' demand for free and fair elections" (Adesnik and Kim 2008: 1). Elections were held in December of 1987 and in 1988 the HRV index reached 4.30 as more credible information on the economy became publicly available, including data on tariffs, high-technology exports, and military expenditures (World Bank, n.d.). Democracy has survived in South Korea ever since.

Interestingly, the economic expansion and emergence of democracy in South Korea has been cited one of the "dream cases of a modernization theorist" (Przeworski and Limongi 1997), where modernization theory refers to a set of claims that transition from autocracy to democracy grows more likely as the economy becomes more developed, individuals become more educated, and a middle class demands greater rights (for canonical treatments, see Lipset 1959; Moore 1966). Alternative explanations of the emergence of democracy in

South Korea, however, raise doubts about the application of modernization theory to this case (Im 1995). Modernization theory offers no explanation, for example, as to why the political crisis in 1979 resulted in a coup and a new dictator, while the crisis in 1987 resulted in a transition to democracy – other than the notion that Korea had not yet reached the nebulous economic prerequisites in 1979.

To explain political (in)stability in South Korea, Im (1995) stresses, instead, the respective levels of organizational unity within the authoritarian power bloc, on the one hand, and within the democratic opposition, on the other. He observes that in both 1979 and 1987, the authoritarian power bloc was split. In 1979, however, the democratic opposition was loosely organized, while in 1987, the opposition achieved a high degree of unity. The organization of the opposition movement explains the differing outcomes of a coup in 1979 and a democratic transition in 1987.

Why, then, was there greater unity among protestors in 1987 than in 1979? We suggest that the increasing levels of data transparency facilitated this unity. This increased transparency helped to facilitate collective action by informing the higher-order beliefs of the masses of citizenry. In 1979, protestors had less of an idea of just how widespread was the discontent with the regime. In this particular case, they did not know the extent of economic expansion and the degree of expanding trade in the face of growing levels of inequality. As data on a full range of these economic variables became available, the opposition was better able to coordinate. Mass demonstrations increased in frequency and attracted increasing numbers of protestors. Thus, in response to the disparate opposition under lower levels of transparency of 1979, hardliners staged a coup (Im 1995: 136). But in 1987, a unified opposition under higher levels of transparency achieved a transition to democracy.

The Emergence of Democracy in Mexico

Mexico represents another interesting example where rising transparency corresponds to democratization. Consider Figure 6.2 where the shaded region represents a period of autocratic rule ending in the year 2000. Again, we observe an association between rising transparency and a transition to democracy.

Mexico experienced one-party autocratic rule from 1929 until 2000, under the Partido Revolucionario Institucional (PRI).[12] Near the end of the twentieth century, the government began to disseminate increasing amounts of economic data. From 1980 until 1987, the HRV score averaged less than 1.00. But in 1988, under the administration of President Carlos Salinas, transparency increased to 1.34, and it averaged 2.40 through 1994. However, Figure 6.2

---

[12] The party was known as the Partido Nacional Revolucionario from 1929 until 1938 and the Partido de la Revolución Mexicana from 1938 until 1946 (Meyer 2007: 279).

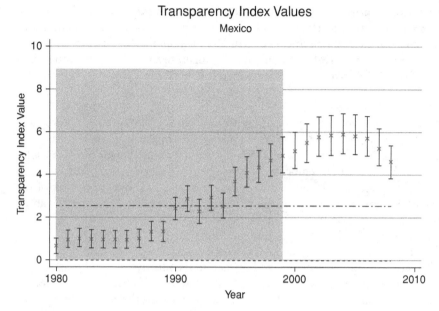

FIGURE 6.2. Mexico pre- and post-transition. HRV values are plotted on the y-axis, while the x-axis measures time in years. Cross-marks correspond to mean HRV scores, while whiskers are 95 percent credible intervals. The shaded region marks years in which Mexico was an autocracy, the unshaded years are democratic. The two dashed lines correspond to the mean HRV scores among autocracies (−0.003, the lower line), and democracies (2.54, the upper line).

reveals varying levels of transparency under Salinas. After an initial improvement, the Salinas government put the brakes on increasing transparency (for a discursive exposition, see Tutino 2011).

When President Ernesto Zedillo assumed office in 1994, the government dramatically increased transparency to 3.68 in 1995 and 4.11 in 1996. Zedillo's presidency showed a real commitment to data dissemination. The HRV score reached 4.91 in 1999 and 5.11 in 2000. By the late 1990s, the government was reporting data that had been unavailable in the 1980s – on variables such as education expenditures, levels of education among the labor force, school enrollment rates, health care expenditures (public and private), unemployment rates, and tariff rates (World Bank, n.d.).

Interestingly, the Salinas administration made data on tariffs available in 1991 but then apparently changed policy as data were not available in 1992–1994. The tariff data then became available every year of Zedillo's presidency (World Bank, n.d.). This pattern is consistent with historical accounts of these administrations. As Meyer (2007: 277) describes, Salinas "returned to traditional regime practices, even while official discourse abused the term 'modern politics.'" Still, the Salinas administration advanced the liberal agenda by negotiating the North American Free Trade Agreement, and subsequently the Zedillo administration championed economic reform.

As our theoretical model suggests, making economic data available may have encouraged unrest. Just as transparency was increasing in Mexico, so too was the number of anti-government demonstrations. The Cross National Time Series Archive reports zero such demonstrations in the early 1980s, but four in the late 1980s, seven in the early 1990s, and 16 in the late 1990s – with both 1995 and 1998 experiencing five demonstrations each, the highest for a single year recorded for Mexico (Banks 1979). As Meyer (2007: 277) relates, "a real opposition grew, consolidated itself on both the left and the right, and gathered demands for political democracy." Also during the mid-1990s, a revolutionary movement broke out in the state of Chiapas, although that movement never spread beyond southern Mexico (Reina, Servín, and Tutino 2007: 17).

General dissatisfaction with the one-party rule of the PRI also led to a shift in legislative voting patterns. In 1997, for the first time under the PRI, control of the legislature gave way to new majorities in both chambers, and Zedillo confronted divided government.[13] Nevertheless, President Zedillo's administration continued to make more data available and the PRI finally lost power during the 2000 elections. The incumbent party lost the executive election and Vicente Fox of the Partido Acción Nacional took office as the first president of Mexico elected through contested elections (Meyer 2007: 277–278).

Following our theoretical model, the Salinas administration may have been crafty when it reversed the trend of becoming more transparent. Putting the brakes on transparency may have hindered the organizational efforts of opposition groups. By contrast, the data-rich environment that the Zedillo administration cultivated may have facilitated the higher levels of coordination across the political spectrum that led to the transition to democracy in 2000. Zedillo is indeed credited with ushering democracy into Mexico.[14]

The Emergence of Democracy in the Philippines

The Philippines also experienced a rise in economic transparency followed by a transition to democracy via mass revolt in 1986 – see Figure 6.3. The toppled autocratic regime had come to power in 1965, when Ferdinand E. Marcos won election to office before quickly turning to violence to maintain power, ruling as an autocrat until 1986. The shaded region in Figure 6.3 refers to the end of this period of autocratic rule (Slater 2010: 104, 115, 127).

The HRV data begin in 1980, when the score for the Philippines was 0.91. The government thereafter made increasing amounts of data available each

---

[13] For a thorough examination of executive-legislative relations in Mexico and the change in 1997, see Casar (2002).

[14] Knight (2007); Semo (2007); Servín (2007); Haber et al. (2008); and Tutino (2018) address Zedillo's role in ushering democracy with different emphases.

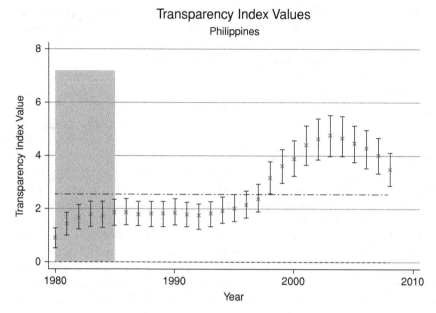

FIGURE 6.3. The Philippines pre- and post-People Power. HRV values are plotted on the y-axis, while the x-axis measures time in years. Cross-marks correspond to mean HRV scores, while whiskers are 95 percent credible intervals. The shaded region marks years under the Marcos regime, the unshaded years correspond to years in which that regime was not in power. The two dashed lines correspond to the mean HRV scores among autocracies (−0.003, the lower line), and democracies (2.54, the upper line).

year, and the HRV score reached 1.78 in 1983, 1.84 in 1985, and 1.87 in 1986. During this time, data on politically sensitive issues became available, including data on levels of education and unemployment as well as income distribution data (World Bank, n.d.).

Also during this time, mass protests flared. The Philippines democracy movement, known as the "People Power" revolution and the "middle class" revolution, consisted of a series of popular protests beginning in 1983 and ending with the establishment of democratic rule in 1986 (Hutchcroft and Rocamora 2003; Thompson 2004; Slater 2010; Rivera 2002, 2011).[15] According to the Cross National Time Series Archive, the number of anti-government demonstrations increased from two in 1980 to five in each of 1981 and 1982, and reached 13 in 1983 (Banks 1979). That year, a leading figure in the opposition

---

[15] The movement is also called the Epifanio de los Santos Avenue (EDSA) revolution, named for Manila's massive thoroughfare, which was the focal point of the final showdown between the forces of Marcos and some one million protestors (Slater 2010: 202–203). See also Chapter 1 of Thompson (2004).

movement against the Marcos regime, Senator Benigno Aquino Jr., was assassinated (Rivera 2011: 238). Protests continued in 1984: Banks (1979) reports 12 protests in 1984 and an additional 12 protests during 1985 and 1986.

In 1986, Marcos held presidential elections and declared himself the winner, though the results were considered fraudulent. Throngs took to the streets – perhaps even a million people – during the final showdown in 1986 (Slater 2010: 202–203).[16] Amid these massive demonstrations in the streets, Marcos fled the country and Corazón Aquino, who was recognized as the legitimate winner of the election, assumed the presidency under democratic rule (Slater 2010: 201–202).

Interestingly, the trend of increasing data transparency reversed and then stagnated from 1986 until 1994. Perhaps correspondingly, the Aquino administration (1986–1992) was plagued by seven attempted coups (Rivera 2011: 238). We return to the effect of low levels of transparency on democratic instability below.

Transparency and Transitions to Democracy: The Bivariate Relationship

The stylized stories we tell of South Korea, Mexico, and the Philippines reflect a broader pattern in the data. Autocracies are substantially and significantly more transparent during periods leading up to a democratic transition than during other periods. Figure 6.4 plots the average transparency score in a five year window leading up to transition across all such transitions in our data (labeled "Within Five Years of Democratization" in the figure). We compare this average to transparency scores in all other years under autocratic rule (labeled "All Other Years" in the figure).

In the five years leading up to a transition, the average HRV index score is 0.52 – while during all other years the average score is −0.02. This difference is substantively quite large. Across all autocratic regimes (both those that transition and those that do not) HRV index scores average 0.03 with a standard deviation of 1.52. The difference is also statistically significant.

We further find that following periods of stable democratic transition, countries continue to increase their levels of disclosure. We return to this point below when discussing the stability of democracy. For now, we emphasize that historical examples and descriptive data confirm a correspondence between high levels of transparency and transitions from autocracy to democracy.

Autocrat Replacement in Côte d'Ivoire

Not all autocratic governments that collapse experience a democratic transition – they may also be replaced by a new autocracy. Consider the example of Côte d'Ivoire, where autocrat Henri Konan Bédié is replaced by another

---

[16] See also Haggard and Kaufman (1995); McCoy (1999); Rivera (2002).

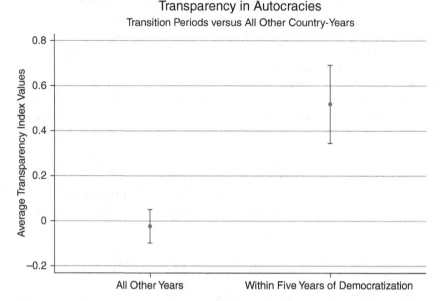

FIGURE 6.4. Transparency during periods of democratization. A comparison of transparency levels in autocracies on the eve democratization to those that are not. The y-axis depicts average transparency scores in each group of autocracies. The x-axis groups autocracy years based on whether they fall within a 5-year period prior to an episode of democratization, or do not fall into such a window. (All years in which democratization takes place are excluded.) Dots depict the average HRV index score in each group, whiskers depict 95 percent confidence intervals around this average.

autocrat, Robert Guéï, who is, in turn, replaced by yet another autocrat, Laurent Gbagbo. In Figure 6.5, the shaded region refers to the period under the Guéï regime, which is both brought to power and then subsequently unseated by mass protest. In this case, rising transparency corresponds with mass protest leading to the ousting of one autocratic government by another. Interestingly, the new government sustains the increased levels of transparency and, in turn, is quickly ousted by yet another autocracy (led by Gbagbo). Finally, this new autocracy changes course and survives. Only when transparency declines after 2000 do we observe renewed autocratic stability.

Côte d'Ivoire was ruled by one party under President Houphouët-Boigny from independence in 1959 until his death in 1993, when Henri Konan Bédié assumed the presidency, after a brief but relatively peaceful power struggle among him, Laurent Gbagbo, and Alassane Ouattara (Vidal 2003: 48). Throughout Houphouët-Boigny's rule, transparency was low. After a stunted rise in the HRV score from 0.07 in 1980 to 0.50 in 1982, the HRV score dropped to 0.03 in 1991 and remained relatively low until 1995. With Bédié in power, transparency jumped up to 0.62.

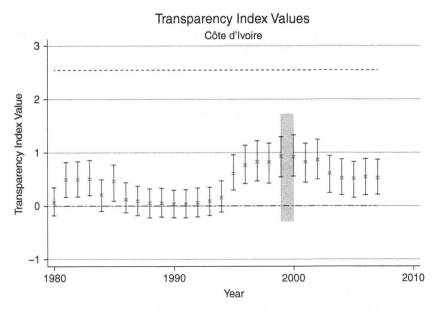

FIGURE 6.5. Côte d'Ivoire pre- and post-mass unrest. HRV values are plotted on the x-axis, while the y-axis measures time in years. Cross-marks correspond to mean HRV scores, while whiskers are 95 percent credible intervals. The shaded region marks years under the Guéï regime, the unshaded years correspond to years in which that regime was not in power. The two dashed lines correspond to the mean HRV scores among autocracies (−0.003, the lower line), and democracies (2.54, the upper line).

Transparency increased throughout the late 1990s under Bédié and the HRV index reached 0.93 in 1999. During this period, data on a host of variables became available, including data on education enrollment rates and government education expenditures, public and private health expenditures and health outcomes (such as tuberculosis treatment success rate), unemployment rates, and importing and exporting figures as well as financial flows such as transfers of income between Ivoirians and the rest of the world – data surprisingly reveal hundreds of millions of dollars in *outflows* (World Bank, n.d.). As fitting with our model, this increase in transparency under autocracy corresponds to increased levels of mass unrest. In 1999, an anti-government demonstration broke out, leading to the ousting of Bédié by the military (Banks 1979).

General Robert Guéï then took power. The new government continued to release data at the highest levels ever for Côte d'Ivoire. In accordance with our theory, popular protests broke out again. In 2000, mass unrest across rival political factions resulted in the death of approximately 180 people – killed in the streets (Al Jazeera 2011). This disorder led to the downfall of Guéï, who was then replaced by Laurent Gbagbo.

Gbagbo soon established autocratic rule as civil unrest broke out throughout the country (Piccolino 2014: 54–55). Under his regime, transparency finally *declined*. The HRV index fell to 0.82 in 2001, 0.61 in 2003, and 0.51 in 2005. The government stopped reporting much of the education and some of the health data that had been released under Bédié. With lowered levels of transparency, Gbagbo maintained power for more than a decade. Indeed, he was never removed from office by purely democratic forces. Gbagbo was only ousted in 2011, when – following internal strife brought on by falsified election results – he was arrested by international forces and brought before the International Criminal Court for crimes against humanity conducted during the civil war (Lynch and Branigin 2011; BBC 2011).

Following our theory, the increase of transparency under the autocratic rule of Bédié made him vulnerable to removal by mass protests. In this case, he was replaced by the new autocratic rule of putschist General Guëï – who continued to increase transparency. With transparency still on the rise, mass protests led to a failed transition to democracy, as Gbagbo assumed power through elections but soon turned to violence to maintain power. He then reversed the trend of increasing transparency, and, as is fitting with our theory, survived in power for a decade. Domestic forces never removed his nontransparent regime from power and instead the international community intervened.

Transparency and Autocrat Removal by the Masses: The Bivariate Relationship

To see that the experience of Côte d'Ivoire is part of a pattern, we turn to the Svolik (2012) data on autocratic collapse resulting from mass unrest. Recall that Svolik's coding of autocratic collapse is more conservative than that of Cheibub, Gandhi, and Vreeland (2010). Slovik's data include 32 collapses of autocracy via democratization or mass revolt.

The average HRV score for autocracies in this sample is 0.13. The year before a transition to democracy, the HRV is substantively higher than the average for the autocratic sample as a whole: 0.42. Once again, we see higher levels of transparency associated with autocratic instability due to mass unrest.

Moreover, we observe that average transparency trends slightly upward starting three years before the collapse of an autocratic regime. Figure 6.6 depicts the average HRV score for autocracies before a collapse. As the figure shows, the average HRV score is 0.12 five years before a collapse, roughly 0.21 three and four years before, 0.26 two years before, and 0.42 the year before a collapse. We have another descriptive pattern: increasing transparency is associated with autocratic collapse.

Instability and Unrest under Autocracy

Our theory of transparency identifies a specific threat to autocratic rule: mass unrest. We thus consider anti-government protests as measured by the Cross National Time Series Archive (Banks 1979). Recall from the examples of

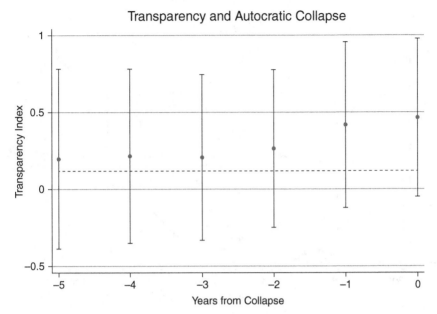

FIGURE 6.6. Transparency and autocratic collapse. Trends in HRV index scores in autocratic regimes prior to their collapse as defined by Svolik (2012). The HRV index score is plotted on the y-axis, the number of years until an instance of collapse (via mass revolt or democratization) is plotted on the x-axis. Dots depict mean transparency scores, by year. Whiskers denote 95 percent confidence intervals around this mean. The dotted line depicts the mean HRV index score of autocratic regime-years not proximate to a collapse.

South Korea, Mexico, Philippines, and Côte d'Ivoire the coincidence of increasing transparency and anti-government demonstrations. Consider, further, the example of Bulgaria. Transparency is notably low in Bulgaria in the 1980s, averaging −0.08 from 1980 to 1988. The HRV index jumps to −0.01 in 1989, a year with three anti-government demonstrations (Banks 1979). The HRV index jumps up further to 0.10 in 1990, a year with three more anti-government demonstrations (Banks 1979). The autocratic regime also collapsed that year and democracy emerged (see Figure 6.7).

Figure 6.8 presents descriptive evidence that these examples are part of a broader pattern. The figure shows the average number of protests for increasing levels of transparency, broken down by quartile.

The frequency of protest is roughly constant across the first three quartiles of transparency, at about 0.5 per year. When transparency rises above the 75th percentile in the sample, however, the number of protests increases: Autocratic regime-years with this high level of transparency experience, on average, 1.25 anti-government demonstrations per year.

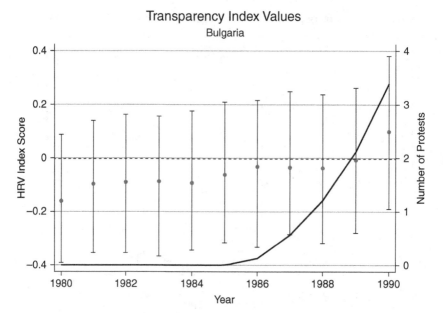

FIGURE 6.7. Transparency in Bulgaria. Protest trends upward with transparency in
Bulgaria. HRV index scores are plotted on the left y-axis, while the number of anti-
government demonstrations are plotted on the right y-axis. The year is plotted on the
x-axis. Dots depict mean HRV index scores, while whiskers denote 95 percent credible
intervals. The solid line plots the number of anti-government demonstrations (using a
lowess smoother). The dashed line depicts the mean level of transparency in autocracies
in the sample.

Summary of the Autocratic Instability Evidence

Summarizing this initial examination of empirical evidence of transparency and
political instability under autocracy, we find evidence supportive of our theory
looking at (1) democratization, (2) autocrat removal via mass unrest, and (3)
a direct measure of mass unrest. Indeed, the data on anti-government demonstrations confirms our theory that transparency causes mass unrest under autocracy. The descriptive evidence presented so far supports the autocratic theoretical model.

6.2.2 Democratic Stability

Turning to the empirical predictions of our democratic model, we expect outcomes opposite of those under autocracy. As democracies become more transparent, we predict consolidation. Democracies with low levels of transparency
face risks of collapse and the irregular removal of leaders. We begin our exploration of these hypotheses by presenting the cases of democratic collapse under
low levels of transparency, highlighting the example of Bangladesh. We then

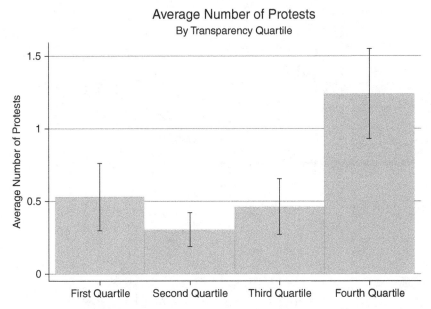

FIGURE 6.8. Protest by transparency quartile. The average frequency of anti-government protests, by quartile of transparency across autocracies. The respective bins on the x-axis depict, among autocratic regime-years, the quartile into which a given autocratic regime-year falls. The y-axis plots the average level anti-government demonstrations among all autocratic regime-years that fall in a given transparency bin. Whiskers depict 95 percent confidence intervals around these averages.

present contrasting patterns in the data on transparency for cases of transitions to democracy that survive and for those that eventually revert back to autocracy, using the DD data. Next we examine the regular and irregular removal of democratically elected leaders using the Archigos dataset, highlighting examples from Central African Republic, Guinea-Bissau, and Uganda.

The Survival of Democracy

Consider first some key examples where low levels of transparency under democracy coincide with the collapse of democratic rule. Figure 6.9 presents 18 cases in the data where rising transparency under autocracy gives way to democratic rule, but transparency does not rise enough to stabilize the democratic regime.

At the top of Figure 6.9, we see the example of Bangladesh, where democracy emerged in the mid-1980s. General Hussain Muhammad Ershad, who had taken power through a coup in 1982, won contested presidential elections in 1986 with 84 percent of the vote, and alternation in power subsequently occurred in 1991 when the opposition Bangladesh Nationalist Party

Transparency Index Values

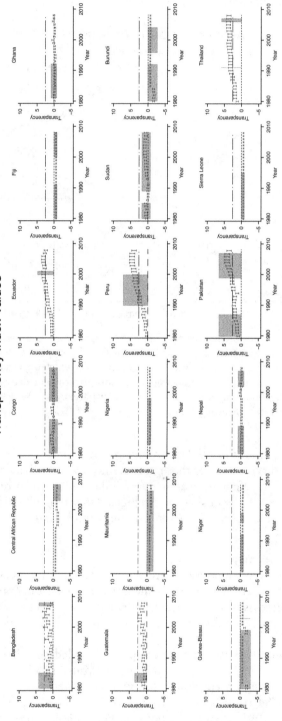

FIGURE 6.9. Countries experiencing multiple transitions. Time periods shaded in gray represent autocratic rule. Unshaded (white) time periods represent democratic rule. For the graph of each country, the upper dashed line represents the mean HRV score for all democracies (2.54), and the lower dashed line represents the mean HRV score for all autocracies (−0.003). Most of these multiple-transition cases appear to maintain HRV scores in a "danger zone." They are either unusually transparent autocracies or unusually opaque democracies.

took power under the leadership of Khaleda Zia (Heitzman 1989: 169; http://rulers.org/rulb1.html#bangladesh).[17]

This emergence of democracy in Bangladesh somewhat fits the pattern suggested by our autocratic model: in 1982, the HRV index is 0.56. Then transparency increases to 0.88 in 1983 and to 1.58 in 1984. Following our theory, anti-government demonstrations broke out during those years (see Banks 1979). The demonstrations continued in 1985 and 1986. During this period, a total of five anti-government demonstrations erupted, and the autocratic regime gave way to democracy in 1986.[18]

Transparency rose and autocracy transitioned to democracy – except that the incumbent autocrat was not removed but rather became a democrat. After the transition to democracy, however, the trend of the Bangladeshi government supplying increasing levels of data did not continue. Accordingly, the democratic regime eventually descended into chaos in January 2007 (Siddiqi 2009: 22).

Note that the HRV index jumps up and down throughout the 1990s and the 2000s. So, rather than the typical trend of increasing transparency coinciding with the consolidation of democracy, we see irregular and spotty reporting of data – followed by the collapse of democracy. The HRV index reaches as high as 2.59 in 2005, but the government does not sustain this level of data dissemination and transparency drops to 1.47 in 2006 and to 1.15 in 2007 – the year that democracy finally collapses.

In 2007, the opposition parties boycotted the Bangladesh electoral process amid violent protests and deaths in the streets (see Rahman 2007; *The Economist* 2007). A caretaker government, required by the constitution to oversee elections, ceded power to the military (Ahsan and Banavar 2009: 86).

The experience of Bangladesh exemplifies a broader pattern seen in the 18 examples depicted in Figure 6.9. They constitute all of the countries that experience multiple transitions in our sample. Throughout their histories, nearly all these cases can be categorized as either unusually transparent autocracies or unusually opaque democracies. Note that in Figure 6.9, for each country we include two dashed lines. The upper dashed line represents the mean HRV score for all democracies (2.54), and the lower dashed line represents the mean HRV score for all autocracies (−0.003).

Figure 6.9 shows that when these countries experience autocratic rule, their level of transparency is above average for autocracies, and, following our theory, transition to democracy is likely. Under democratic rule, however, their level

---

[17] On the military finally having to take a backseat to democratic politics, see Riaz and Fair (2009) and Islam (2009).

[18] The coding of Bangladesh requires a tough judgment call. Polity codes the transition in 1991 and, even at this point, Polity codes the legislature as substantially limiting the executive but not as having parity in power. Polity also codes political competition as "factional" as opposed to "competitive." Still, the executive wins elections in 1986 and then the opposition wins in 1991, which is why Cheibub, Gandhi, and Vreeland (2010) code the transition in 1986. See also Mohsin and Guhathakurta (2007) and Flores and Nooruddin (2016: note 1).

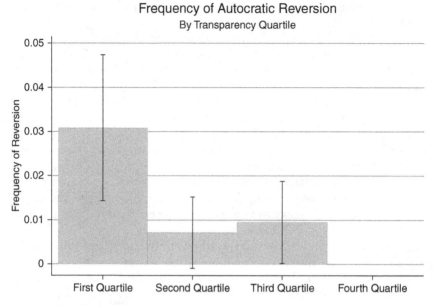

FIGURE 6.10. Transparency and autocratic reversion. The frequency of autocratic reversions, by quartile of transparency across democracies. The respective bins on the x-axis depicts, among democratic regime-years, the transparency quartile into which a given democratic regime-year falls. The y-axis plots the frequency of democratic collapse/autocratic reversion among all democratic regime-years that fall in a given transparency bin. Whiskers depict 95 percent confidence intervals around this frequency.

of transparency is below average and, again following our theory, democratic collapse is likely. Taken all together, the data seem to suggest that countries with a middling level of transparency – between autocratic average of −0.003 and the democratic average of 2.54 – reside in a transparency "danger zone" (see Loggins, Moroder, and Whitlock 1986).[19]

Figure 6.10 depicts an alternative view of the relationship between transparency and democratic collapse. It examines the frequency of autocratic reversions (democratic to autocratic transitions) among all democratic regime-years in our sample. Figure 6.10 divides the democracy-years by their level of transparency – those with scores in the 24th percentile or below are grouped together into the first quartile, those with scores from the 25th to the 49th percentiles in the second quartile, and so on. The frequency of autocratic reversions falls sharply as transparency levels rise. Roughly three percent of democracy-years in the first quartile experience a reversion. This frequency falls to less than one percent in the second and third quartiles. No democracy-years with

---

[19] We acknowledge Sterling Archer for this reference.

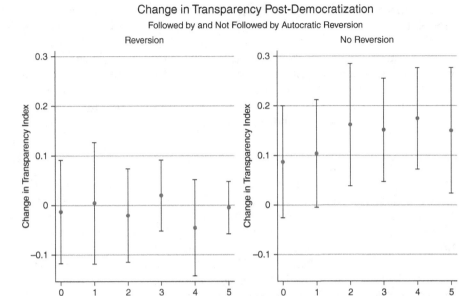

FIGURE 6.11. Transparency, democratization, and autocratic reversions. The average change in HRV index scores following an episode of democratization. The change in the HRV index is presented on the y-axis, while the number of years from an episode of democratization is presented on the x-axis. The graph to the left depicts episodes of democratization which are followed, at some point in our sample, by a reversion to autocracy. The graph to the right depicts instances of democratization which, in our sample, remain democratic. Dots depict the average level of change in HRV scores, across countries, for each year post-democratization. Whiskers depict 95 percent confidence intervals around these averages.

transparency scores above the 75th percentile experience a reversion during our sample period.

Putting together the data presented in Figure 6.10 and the transparency "danger zone" discussed above demonstrates a further empirical regularity: it is possible to predict which episodes of democratization survive and which end in a reversion to autocracy, based on patterns of data disclosure. On average, stable transitions to democracy are followed by substantial increases in disclosure. Transitions which lead to a subsequent reversion to autocracy, by contrast, typically see transparency stagnate at the levels implemented under the previous autocratic regime.

Figure 6.11 depicts this relationship. It compares the change in transparency scores in the five years following a democratic-to-autocratic transition in countries where (1) there is a subsequent autocratic reversion (left panel) and (2) democracy survives throughout our sample (right panel). Transitions followed by a reversion see practically no change in transparency on average in the five years following transition. Stable transitions, on average, see increases in their HRV score in each year following democratization, a pattern that is statistically significant from years 2 through 5. The difference in the rate of change of transparency between unstable and stable democracies is statistically significant at the 10 percent level or above in two of the five years, if examined individually, and significant at above the 1 percent level if one considers all observations in the six-year post-transition window.

The Removal of Democratic Leaders

We can further examine the predictions of our democratic model using the Archigos data on "regular" and "irregular" removal of democratic leaders (Goemans 2006; Goemans, Gleditsch, and Chiozza 2009). Recall that the regular removal of democratic leaders includes losing elections, facing term limits, or retiring – all in accordance with the rules and conventions of the country (Goemans, Gleditsch, and Chiozza 2009: 2). The irregular removal of democratic leaders includes domestically driven coups, revolts, and assassinations – in contravention of the rules and conventions of the country (Goemans, Gleditsch, and Chiozza 2009: 2–3). (Also recall that Archigos categorizes the removal of leaders through foreign intervention separately.)

Figure 6.12 splits our democratic sample by quartile of transparency (the 24th percentile and below, the 25th–49th percentiles, the 50th–74th percentiles, and the 75th percentile and above). As can be seen in the figure, irregular removals are more frequent in the low-transparency democracy-years than in high-transparency democracy-years. At the lowest category of transparency, irregular leader removal occurs in more than 4 percent of years. As transparency rises, the frequency of such removals falls sharply to around 2 percent of years in the second quartile and about 1.75 percent in the third. No irregular removals of democratically elected leaders take place in the most transparent democracy-years.

Some examples of democratically elected leaders ousted through irregular means stand out in the Archigos dataset. Consider Central African Republic, which experienced democratic rule under President Ange-Félix Patassé from 1993 until 2003. Democracy limped along during this period under low levels of transparency – with an abysmal average HRV score of −1.08.

Fitting with our theory, Patassé faced mutinies by the country's armed forces amid armed opposition movements in 1996–1997 (Bradshaw 1997). Despite widespread opposition, however, Patassé enjoyed support from a diverse set of large ethnic groups, thanks to his mixed heritage and marital ties (Bradshaw 1997). The Bangui Agreements of 1997 restored some order (see Mbadinga 2001). So, even though Patassé's political party lost parliamentary elections in 1998, he won the presidential election in 1999 – despite strong opposition

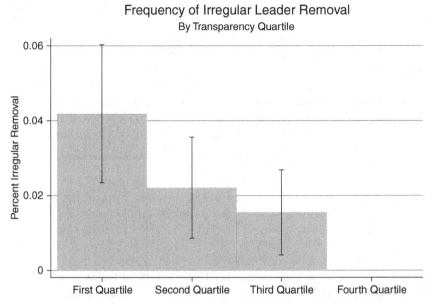

FIGURE 6.12. Transparency and irregular leader removal by transparency quartile among democracies. The respective bins on the x-axis depicts, among democratic regime-years, the transparency quartile into which a given democratic regime-year falls. The y-axis plots the frequency of irregular leader-removals among all democratic regime-years that fall in a given transparency bin. Whiskers depict 95 percent confidence intervals around this frequency. Irregular leader removal is less likely under high levels of transparency.

(Kalck 2004: 113). Patassé survived a coup attempt in 2001, but was not so lucky in 2003, when he was ousted by General François Bozizé, who then established a military dictatorship (Kalck 2004: 154–156). In the end, this nontransparent democracy fell.

The story of Guinea-Bissau is similar. The country experienced a brief period of democratic rule when Kumba Ialá won the 1999/2000 presidential elections, thanks to support from the Balante ethnic group (Ferreira 2004a: 47). Yet, the country suffered from profoundly low levels of data dissemination – the HRV score in 2000 was −1.26. The government made efforts to improve, but only brought the HRV score up to an average of −0.67 for the 2001–2003 period.

In accordance with our predictions about low transparency under democracy, Ialá faced protests, strikes, and an alleged coup attempt (Ferreira 2004b). In 2003, Ialá dissolved parliament, after receiving a vote of no confidence, and then repeatedly delayed new legislative elections (IRIN 2003). In September of that year, he was finally ousted in a bloodless military coup. The military cited the "incapacity" of Ialá's government to resolve Guinea-Bissau's economic problems and ongoing political crises as the reason for their intervention (IRIN 2003).[20]

We see the pattern again under President Milton Obote in Uganda. Following the end of the brutal rule of President Idi Amin in 1979, succession was messy, but eventually elections were held. Two provisional presidencies (respectively led by Yusufu K. Lule and Godfrey L. Binaisa) were replaced by a military commission (led by Paulo Muwanga), which, in turn, was replaced by a presidential commission.[21] The commission held multiparty elections in December 1980, which may have been flawed (Holman 2005), but finally brought about multiparty civilian rule under the presidency of Obote (Kasfir 2006: 53).

During Obote's time in office, transparency was low, averaging −0.70. Correspondingly, the democratic regime functioned exceedingly poorly. Obote's presidency was marred by horrendous violence and the birth of the National Resistance Army (NRA), which struggled against Obote's rule (Doom and Vlassenroot 1999: 9). The leader of the NRA, Yoweri Museveni opposed the multiparty political system, which he saw as the cause of ethnic tensions (Doom and Vlassenroot 1999: 9). Over 300,000 people were massacred during Obote's "Operation Bonanza" in 1983 (Ofcansky 1996; Doom and Vlassenroot 1999: 9). Obote was eventually deposed in 1985 by his own military commanders, and then Museveni's NRA took power in 1986, abolishing multiparty politics (Kasfir 2006). Museveni has ruled Uganda ever since (see Tangri and Mwenda 2010).

Our model suggests that in countries like these – with low levels of data transparency – democracy cannot function as a means to oust leaders who fail to deliver strong economic performance. In a low-data environment, voters have no way of knowing whether they should attribute economic outcomes to government policies or to the broader economic environment. Moreover, they do not know if their personal economic situation is reflective of the broader pattern in society. In this setting, citizens cannot trust one another to cast economically informed votes that will enhance overall social welfare. Elections serve to put into power politicians whose power base has little to do with their ability to deliver strong economic performance.

Indeed, in the cases of Central African Republic, Guinea-Bissau, and Uganda, citizens often vote along ethnic lines, instead of voting according to the economic performance of the country.[22] How can they possibly choose leaders

---

[20] See also the interview of Henrique Rosa, Ialá's successor, in appendix 7 of Cogley (2013: 249).

[21] See http://rulers.org.

[22] In Uganda, Museveni acted to explicitly prevent voters from even coordinating along ethnic lines by abolishing political parties (Kasfir 2006). For research on ethnic voting under democracy see Chandra (2004, 2005, 2006). For research showing where economic voting models fail to predict electoral outcomes, see Campello and Zucco (2016). Note that while economic voting models perform strongly in economically advanced democracy, this should not imply that ethnic politics cease to matter – see, for recent examples, Abrajano and Hajnal (2015) and Parker and Barreto (2014).

according to aggregate economic indicators in such an information-poor environment? Democracy cannot be justified to the masses of citizens as enhancing the overall material welfare of society, and the political system may thus (justifiably) suffer from a lack of legitimacy across different social groups. General dissatisfaction with the regime persists across society, which opens the door to mass unrest, coups, assassinations, and all sorts of threats to political stability. Political will to resist such threats is low. Under low levels of transparency, democracy is less likely to survive.

6.3 SUMMARY OF THE EXAMPLES AND DESCRIPTIVE DATA

Our initial foray into empirical evidence confirms the hypotheses of Chapter 5. This chapter discusses examples from around the world, including South Korea, Mexico, the Philippines, Côte d'Ivoire, Bulgaria, Bangladesh, Central African Republic, Guinea-Bissau, and Uganda. We highlight these examples because they illustrate the various theoretical expectations about the effects of transparency laid out in Chapter 5. The cases do not appear to be idiosyncratic but rather stand as archetypical cases fitting into broader patterns in the data.

Indeed, in addition to the examples, this chapter presents the bivariate relationships between transparency and a number of different approaches to measuring political stability: (1) the emergence of democracy, (2) autocrat removal, (3) the number of anti-government demonstrations, (4) the survival of democracy, and (5) the regular versus irregular removal of democratically elected leaders. Summary statistics of descriptive data confirm our main hypotheses that transparency causes mass unrest under autocracy while it stabilizes democracy. Put another way, opacity reduces the risk that autocracies lose power due to mass unrest, while opaque democracies struggle to survive.

Still, we have yet to explore competing hypotheses. The descriptive relationships between transparency and (in)stability revealed in this chapter may actually be driven by other factors. Examples of such factors include (1) level of economic development, (2) a general correspondence between political stability and liberalization, (3) the effects of specific political institutions, (4) trends in the data, and (5) country-specific factors. In short, we need controls. In the next chapter, we put our data to more rigorous testing that enables us to examine our hypotheses about transparency alongside alternative explanations for the patterns we have so far observed.

7

The Evidence

Regression Analyses

Readers may rightly wonder if other factors explain the patterns thus far revealed. We contend, for example, that data dissemination can cause democratization. We have seen that under high levels of data-transparency, autocracies transition to democracies, and we have also seen that democratic rule survives when transparency is high. Yet these processes of democratization correlate with economic development too, and recall from Part I that data dissemination is also correlated with economic development. Modernization theorists might therefore reasonably argue that increasing economic development could explain democratization as well as the general tendency toward data transparency (see, for example, Epstein et al. 2006). Indeed, an empirical connection between GDP per capita and democratic stability has been thoroughly established (Lipset 1959; Przeworski and Limongi 1997; Przeworski et al. 2000; Benhabib, Corvalan, and Spiegel 2011). Perhaps, then, the connection between transparency and democratization is spurious – driven instead by economic development, which causes both phenomena.

Economic liberalization stands as another potential explanation for the patterns we have revealed so far. Maybe data transparency is simply one facet of liberalization and democratization is another. If so, the direction of causality could be reversed or some other overarching cause of the general tendency to liberalize may cause both transparency and democratization.

Alternatively, some readers might simply suggest that time trends explain the patterns. Over time, data dissemination has increased due to rising demand for data and better technology to collect and organize it. Coincident with this trend, autocracy has collapsed around the world, giving rise to more and more stable democracies. Simply because these phenomena trend together over time does not imply a causal connection. The connections of the HRV index to democratization, autocratic instability, mass unrest, and the removal of democratic leaders through regular means may result from historical coincidence.

Other readers may simply wonder if idiosyncratic heterogeneity across individual countries might better explain their experiences of transparency and stability. The experiences of the countries discussed above – South Korea, Mexico, the Philippines, Côte d'Ivoire, Bulgaria, Bangladesh, Central African Republic, Guinea-Bissau, and Uganda – may each be better explained with reference to the countries' individual histories, rather than as part of a broader systematic pattern.

We welcome all of this skepticism and invite readers to examine patterns in the data more rigorously in this section. We introduce a host of techniques to analyze the data, which enable us to put our theory up against competing hypotheses. We revisit each of the measures of stability presented above, using various methods of regression where we introduce control variables, such as GDP per capita as a proxy for economic development and openness to trade as a proxy for liberalization. We also account for duration dependence to correct for trends over time in the data and adjust standard errors to account for patterns of serial correlation and country-specific idiosyncrasies.

To anticipate our empirical results regarding autocratic instability, we find support for our main theoretical prediction: transparency is associated with an increased risk of autocrat removal via mass revolt or democratization. Transparency is *not* associated with other forms of instability under autocracy, such as assassinations or guerrilla movements. In fact, transparency is associated with a *reduced* risk of a coup, a finding that we revisit in Chapter 10.

Regarding democratic stability, we find that transparency is associated with the survival of democratic regimes and with the regular removal of democratic leaders. Increased transparency is negatively associated with the irregular removal of democratic leaders.

All of these findings are associational – they do not demonstrate that transparency causes increased protests under autocracy or causes democratic consolidation. Given the relative infrequency of such events and the cross-national nature of these data, proof of causality is extraordinarily difficult. Moreover, this set of results cannot fully insulate our findings from the threat of endogeneity. Indeed, we acknowledge that endogeneity persists – our estimates are likely to be biased. As we show, however, our tests suggest that such biases are unlikely to be large. Importantly, plausible alternative explanations for any one result cannot systematically explain *all* of our empirical findings. We conclude that the evidence convincingly supports our theory.

We present our analysis of each measure of (in)stability in turn – in the same order that we discussed them in the previous chapter. We begin with autocratic instability, looking at (1) the transition to democracy, (2) the collapse of autocratic regimes through mass movements, and (3) incidents of unrest and other threats to autocratic rule. We then turn to democratic stability, analyzing (1) the survival of democracy and (2) regular versus irregular removal of democratic leaders. So, as in Chapter 6, we begin with the broader dependent variables and then consider narrower dependent variables so as to test more specifically the causal mechanism that explains transparency's dual effects of instability under autocracy and stability under democracy.

7.1 ANALYSIS OF AUTOCRATIC INSTABILITY

This subsection empirically demonstrates that: (1) transparency is associated with an increased likelihood of transition to democracy. (2) Transparency is associated more broadly with an increased risk of regime removal via mass unrest or via a transition to democracy. (3) Transparency is associated with increased frequency of anti-government demonstrations and general strikes directed at the government. Additionally, the section shows that transparency is not associated with other forms of autocratic instability, such as assassinations or guerrilla movements, and it is associated with a reduced risk of a coup. These supplementary findings serve to strengthen our confidence in the causal mechanism we describe. Data dissemination informs the high-order beliefs of citizens and facilitates the coordination necessary for successful mass protest movements.

Following our theoretical model, we estimate the effect of transparency conditional on economic performance. We do so by including the variables *Transparency* (measured as the HRV index), *Growth* (measured as the percentage change in real GDP per capita), and their interaction (*Transparency* × *Growth*). *Transparency* gives empirical form to the parameter $1/\sigma_s^2$ in the autocratic model in Chapter 5. *Growth* maps onto the parameter G_t (or, equivalently, onto the leader's type θ) in the model. In equilibrium, leaders who perform more poorly in office are more likely to be removed – poor growth should predict regime collapse. Proposition 5.2 establishes that this relationship between growth and collapse should grow stronger as transparency rises. And Proposition 5.3 establishes that transparency should have a direct effect on increasing the risk of regime removal.

In our empirical tests of these theoretical propositions, we take a number of steps to control for alternative mechanisms that may drive the relationship between transparency and mass unrest. For example, we analyze a plethora of dependent variables that enable us to test the causal mechanism with increasing precision. If our theoretical model is correct, transparency should cause some threats to autocratic rule (those involving mass movements against the government) but not others (those involving tightknit groups). We also account for potential trends over time and for idiosyncrasies of particular periods of autocratic rule.

The danger of reverse causality – that some states choose to liberalize (disclose more information) in response to popular discontent – stands as a particularly acute concern. This danger is somewhat mitigated by the nature of our measure of transparency, which varies far more across autocratic regimes than over time. (The average longitudinal standard deviation in transparency across countries is 25 percent of the overall standard deviation.) Moreover, any such reverse causality would tend to bias against our findings. If autocratic leaders disclose more information in response to public pressure, one would expect that transparency would have the effect of dissipating unrest. (To the extent that such efforts are undertaken, our results at least indicate that they are unsuccessful.)

We additionally include a variety of control variables to adjust for other forms of liberalization which might be undertaken in response to public pressure. The control variables for liberalization include both political and economic factors.

As for political liberalization, we draw two variables pertaining to autocratic political institutions from the Democracy and Development (DD) dataset (Cheibub, Gandhi, and Vreeland 2010). We control for an indicator variable *Party* $\in \{0, 1\}$, equal to one if multiple parties hold positions in the legislature.[1] We include this control to adjust for the possibility that autocratic leaders co-opt nascent opposition groups by giving them a place in regime decision-making (Gandhi 2008; Gandhi and Przeworski 2006, 2007; Svolik 2012). If co-optation takes place, and this type of political liberalization is also correlated with data disclosure (a question we revisit in Chapter 10), then our findings may be biased absent this control variable. We also control for *Military* $\in \{0, 1\}$, equal to one if the head of government is a representative of the military. We include this variable because autocracies headed by the military exhibit differential behaviors from those controlled by civilians (Cheibub 2007; Davenport 2007; Wright 2008a; Svolik 2012).

In our analysis of the Banks (1979) dataset – which looks at specific threats to autocratic rule – we also include a control for fuel exports, drawn from Easterly and Sewadeh (2001). This control is included given the political form of the "resource curse" hypothesis, which finds that fuel exports are correlated with autocratic longevity (Ross 1999; Jensen and Wantchekon 2004).[2]

To account for economic liberalization, we include a standard measure of economic openness: $\left(\frac{Exports + Imports}{GDP}\right)$. This control variable is important because of the potential linkages between economic and political liberalization. We seek to distinguish the effect of transparency from other forms of liberalization. This *Ec. Openness* variable further serves as a valuable control because economies open to high levels of trade face a certain vulnerability to global shocks to economic performance, and thus economic growth may be a less valuable signal of government competence to voters in these countries (Duch and Stevenson

---

[1] This variable is a recoding of an analogous trichotomous indicator $\{0, 1, 2\}$ that appears in the DD dataset.

[2] We do not include this control variable when analyzing the Cheibub, Gandhi, and Vreeland (2010) or Svolik (2012) datasets because this term does not vary over time and takes the value of 1 for less than 16 percent of our sample. Including this term in our analyses does not substantively affect these results and it never has statistically significant effects. For a recent study of natural resource wealth and transparency, see Vadlamannati and De Soysa (2015).

2008). In related work, we substitute for the $\frac{Exports + Imports}{GDP}$ measure using other measures of economic openness: (1) the economic restrictions component of the KOF Index of Globalization (Dreher 2006) and (2) an updated variant of the Sachs-Warner measure of economic openness (Sachs and Warner 1995) composed by Wacziarg and Welch (2008). Our qualitative findings presented below are unchanged when we use these alternative controls for economic liberalization (see the appendix to Hollyer, Rosendorff, and Vreeland 2015).

Importantly, we also control for GDP per capita, measured in thousands of purchasing power parity 2005 US dollars. This measure is included to account for modernization theory – the role of economic development in facilitating democratization (Burkhart and Lewis-Beck 1994). It is also crucial to control for the level of economic development because of the possibility that a state's capacity to collect and disseminate data may increase with economic development.

These economic measures are all drawn from the Penn World Table (PWT) version 6.3 (Heston, Summers, and Aten 2009). The PWT offers several advantages as a measure of economic performance for this study. First, the PWT data are adjusted and interpolated by external researchers with no affiliation to reporting governments (though, the underlying data are still based on national accounts). Specifically, the PWT relies on both national accounts subcomponents from benchmark countries and information collected by the United Nations International Comparisons Program (ICP) and the US State Department.[3] The PWT measure of *Growth* can thus be seen as a proxy for true economic performance (G_t or – equivalently – the incumbent's type θ in our model) rather than as a realization of the government's public announcement of economic performance (s in our model).

Second, country-time series included in the PWT are uninterrupted. This is important when employing a measure of data missingness as an explanatory variable. Were missing data present in the PWT, it would be likely that missing values would correlate with transparency levels. Listwise deletion would therefore censor variation in a key explanatory variable, potentially inflating standard errors and understating measures of model fit (King et al. 2001). The profound confound that missing data would entail limits the control variables that we can include, but, fortunately, all of the variables we list above provide complete coverage for our sample of autocracies.

7.1.1 Analysis of the Emergence of Democracy

We begin our analysis of autocratic instability by looking at the emergence of democracy, following the definition developed by Przeworski et al. (2000) and updated by Cheibub, Gandhi, and Vreeland (2010). This definition enables us

---

[3] For details, see Summers and Heston (1991).

to explore the relationship between transparency and the duration of continued autocratic rule. Autocratic collapse, in this instance, is defined as democratization; time is defined as the number of years of continuous autocratic rule.

We use a Cox proportional hazards model, which estimates the probability that a spell of autocratic rule ends in year t conditional on not already having done so. We prefer the Cox specification over alternatives for two reasons. First, the Cox model readily incorporates censoring. Many autocratic regimes are still in place at the end of the time period covered by our data, and we need a method that can address the fact that they have not (yet) collapsed. Second, the Cox specification deals with time dependence in a flexible manner. Over time, autocratic rule may become more durable, due to consolidation of the ruling elite or habituation of the population – or autocratic rule may become more fragile over time due to the build up of grievances – or perhaps the effect of duration is nonmonotonic. Our theoretical model does not speak to the question of whether autocratic rule becomes more consolidated, more vulnerable, whether risks systematically oscillate over time – but we do not wish to ignore the possibility that time matters. The Cox model allows us to control for any effect that longevity might have on the risk of autocratic collapse – positive, negative, or nonmonotonic.[4]

Our analysis is complicated by the presence of autocratic regimes that have experienced prior instances of instability in the data. Past instability may influence current stability. Our preferred approach to dealing with this issue is to employ conditional gap time models, in which the baseline hazard is estimated separately for autocratic regimes in states that experienced prior autocratic collapses and in states that have not (Box-Steffensmeier and Zorn 2002). In so doing, we allow both the level and the shape of the baseline hazard to vary depending on past experiences of instability.[5]

Hence, in one set of models, we estimate the baseline hazard conditional on whether there has been a prior autocratic collapse (labeled as "Cond. Prior Transition" in Table 7.1). In another, we estimate separate baseline hazards based on the number of instances of collapse (labeled as "Cond. Num. Transitions" in Table 7.1), which range between 0 and 3 in our sample. In a final set of specifications, we estimate the model dropping all countries that have experienced a prior transition from the dataset (labeled as "No Prior Transition" in Table 7.1). We cluster all errors by autocratic spell.

Our Cox model takes the following form:

$$h_i(t, p_i) = h_0(t, p_i)exp(\delta Transparency_{i,t-1} + \gamma Growth_{i,t-1}$$
$$+ \mu Transparency_{i,t-1} \times Growth_{i,t-1} + X_{i,t-1}\beta) \qquad (7.1)$$

---

[4] To understand how the Cox model does this, see Beck, Katz, and Tucker (1998). See also Box-Steffensmeier, Reiter, and Zorn (2003).

[5] For an empirical application of conditional gap time models in a different context, see Tiernay (2011).

where i denotes country, t denotes time, and $h_0(t, p_i)$ is the baseline hazard function, which captures the risk of a transition to democracy for country-years when all explanatory variables in the model are set to 0, and p_i is the measure of the number of prior transitions.[6] Time, in this instance, is defined as the number of years of consecutive autocratic rule in a country.

As discussed above, the variables *Transparency*, *Growth*, and *Transparency* × *Growth* correspond directly to our theoretical model. *Transparency* maps onto $1/\sigma_s^2$ in our theoretical model, while *Growth* gives empirical form to the parameter G_t (or, equivalently, the leader's type θ). We estimate the coefficients δ, γ, and μ to give us their marginal effects.

The model also includes $\mathbf{X}_{1,t}\beta$, which represents the product of a data vector of control variables and a corresponding vector of estimated coefficients. The control variables, explained above, include *GDP per capita*, *Ec. Openness*, *Party*, and *Military*. We include the interaction of the *Party* variable and *Time*, measured as the number of years of autocratic rule, because tests of the Schoenfeld residuals indicate that the *Party* variable alone violates the proportional hazards assumption.[7] We follow the guidance of Box-Steffensmeier and Jones (2004) in this instance – the marginal effect of multiple legislative parties varies depending on the duration of the autocratic regime.

Results of our analysis of the emergence of democracy specified in Equation 7.1 are presented in Table 7.1. The table reports coefficient values – not hazard ratios. So, a positive coefficient indicates that a given covariate increases the risk of autocratic collapse, while a negative coefficient indicates the reverse. For each set of models – Cond. Prior Transition, Cond. Num. Transitions, No Prior Transition – we first include the control variables when estimating the effects of transparency and economic growth and then we re-estimate these effects without the control variables.

Table 7.1 shows that the direct effect of transparency on autocratic transitions is positive, statistically significant, and robust across model specifications: transparency increases the hazard of democratization. In the specifications that include the control variables, the p-values on *Transparency* (not reported in Table 7.1) range from 0.014 to 0.024; in the specifications without control variables, the p-values range from 0.018 to 0.052. Our point estimates suggest that a one standard deviation increase in the level of transparency increases the hazard of autocratic collapse by between 38 and 61 percent.

---

[6] We test the assumption that covariates alter the level, but not the shape, of the baseline hazard. Where these tests indicate violations of the proportional hazards assumption, we adjust the model according to the recommendations of Box-Steffensmeier and Jones (2004) and Keele (2010).

[7] The Schoenfeld residuals test checks for independence between residuals and time, and thus the assumption of the proportional hazard. Box-Steffensmeier and Jones (2004) suggest interacting variables that violate this assumption with time to allow the effect of the variable to vary with duration. See Schoenfeld (1982).

TABLE 7.1. Cox model of democratic transitions, DD definitions.

	Cond. Prior Transition		Cond. Num. Transitions		No Prior Transition	
Transparency	0.231	0.214	0.284	0.255	0.317	0.237
	[0.030, 0.431]	[0.035, 0.394]	[0.057, 0.511]	[0.044, 0.466]	[0.059, 0.575]	[−0.002, 0.476]
Growth	−0.039	−0.034	−0.038	−0.035	−0.039	−0.034
	[−0.079, 0.000]	[−0.068, −0.001]	[−0.079, 0.003]	[−0.070, −0.000]	[−0.084, 0.007]	[−0.070, 0.003]
Transparency × Growth	−0.014	−0.013	−0.014	−0.015	−0.019	−0.019
	[−0.033, 0.005]	[−0.032, 0.005]	[−0.034, 0.007]	[−0.036, 0.007]	[−0.035, −0.003]	[−0.036, −0.002]
GDP per capita	−0.260		−0.252		−0.350	
	[−0.776, 0.257]		[−0.755, 0.252]		[−0.956, 0.255]	
Ec. Openness	−0.008		−0.010		−0.013	
	[−0.017, −0.000]		[−0.018, −0.001]		[−0.024, −0.003]	
Party	1.253		1.392		2.323	
	[0.134, 2.372]		[0.179, 2.604]		[0.050, 4.595]	
Party × Time	−0.038		−0.044		−0.069	
	[−0.075, −0.002]		[−0.081, −0.006]		[−0.134, −0.005]	
Military	0.276		0.237		0.474	
	[−0.389, 0.942]		[−0.459, 0.933]		[−0.288, 1.236]	
# of Subjects	106	106	106	106	80	80
# of Failures	52	52	52	52	34	34

Cox proportional hazards regressions of the hazard of transition to democracy, where democracy and autocracy are defined by the *Democracy and Development* dataset (Cheibub, Gandhi, and Vreeland 2010). Models in the first two columns report a conditional gap time model wherein the baseline hazard is separately estimated for regimes that experience a prior regime failure and for those that did not. Those in the next two columns estimate separate baseline hazards based on a categorical measure that reflects the number of prior collapses. Those in the final two columns simply drop all observations with prior transitions. Ninety-five percent confidence intervals are presented in brackets. All standard errors are clustered by autocratic spell.

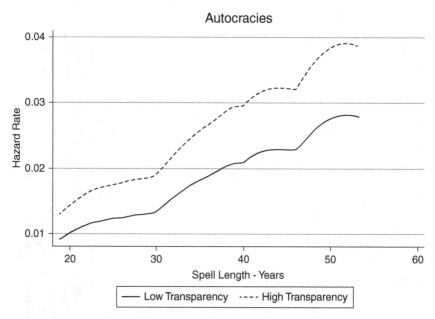

FIGURE 7.1. The effect of transparency on autocratic survival, holding constant growth. Plots of the smoothed estimates of the hazard rate, based on estimates from the fifth column of Table 7.1 (the first column with No Prior Transitions). The hazard rate is presented on the y-axis, while regime duration (measured in years) is presented on the x-axis. The solid line depicts estimates when transparency is at the sample mean, the dashed line when transparency is one standard deviation above the sample mean. Both the *Party* and *Party* × *t* terms are held at zero, while all other variables are held at their sample means. The graph suggests that in year 20 of an autocratic regime spell, a one standard deviation increase in transparency is associated with a 50 percent rise in the hazard rate, from roughly 1 to 1.5 percent.

To better grasp the substantive meaning of this difference, assume that an autocratic regime faced a constant hazard rate of 1 percent in every year it is in office. (Figure 7.1 demonstrates that this is not the case, hazard rates are rising over time – this example is for illustrative purposes only.) That hypothetical regime would be expected to survive for 100 years, on average. Now consider an analogous regime that faces a 1.5 percent hazard rate in each year of its existence. This regime would be expected to survive for 67 years. This marginal impact of a 50 percent increase in the (low) hazard rate is substantively meaningful.[8]

---

[8] It is important to emphasize that transitions to democracy are rare and hard to predict (an issue to which we return in the concluding chapter of the book). Considering just how rare democratic transitions are, and how few factors are reliably associated with them, the effect we estimate is substantial. In their extreme bound analysis of the predictors of democratic transitions,

Transparency also has a substantively large conditioning role on the relationship between *Growth* and democratization: economic growth is more important to survival when transparency is high, as predicted by our theoretical model. The coefficient on this interaction term is, however, not statistically significant except in the specifications for countries with no history of prior transition. The direct effect of growth is negative and statistically significant at the 10 percent level (or stronger) throughout the models: poor economic performance increases the risk of transition.

Due to the nonlinearity of our model and the presence of the interaction term between *Transparency* and *Growth*, the interpretation of the coefficients is not straightforward. The functional form of the Cox model implies an interactive effect of transparency and growth. Even without the interactive term, the functional form of our model assumes that the relationship between growth and regime removal is conditional on transparency in the manner expected theoretically (for a discussion, see Berry, DeMeritt, and Esarey 2010; Ai and Norton 2003; Greene 2010; Nagler 1991).

Figure 7.2 presents these estimates graphically. It plots smoothed estimates of the baseline hazard (on the y-axis) against the duration of autocratic rule (on the x-axis). The graph to the left (labeled Low Transparency) depicts estimates with transparency fixed at the 10th percentile in the sample. The graph to the right (labeled High Transparency) depicts analogous estimates with transparency fixed at the 90th percentile in the sample. The dashed lines in each graph depict the hazard rate when economic growth is at its 90th percentile and solid lines when it is at its 10th percentile.

Taken together, the graphs indicate that when growth is high, transparency has only a small effect on the hazard of regime transition. Note that the dashed lines have similar shapes and values across the left-hand and right-hand graphs in Figure 7.2. However, when growth is low, an increase in transparency substantially increases the risk of transition. Note how much higher the solid line is in the right-hand graph (where transparency is high) compared to the solid line in the left-hand graph (where transparency is low).

The graphics in Figure 7.2 suggest that economic growth matters more when transparency is high; autocracies face their highest risk of a transition to democracy when, jointly, growth is low and transparency is high.[9] According to our theory, the risk increases in this situation because high transparency informs higher-order beliefs. Not only do citizens experience low growth, they also

---

Gassebner, Lamla, and Vreeland (2013) conclude that out of 59 variables discussed in the literature, only three reliably predict democratic transitions: GDP growth (negatively), past transitions (positively), and OECD membership (positively).

[9] For clarity of presentation, we present results from the fifth column of Table 7.1 because a single hazard rate is estimated in the "No Prior Transition" model. In the "Cond. Prior Transition" and "Cond. Num. Transitions" models presented in Table 7.1, there are multiple baseline hazards corresponding to different past experiences of democratic collapse.

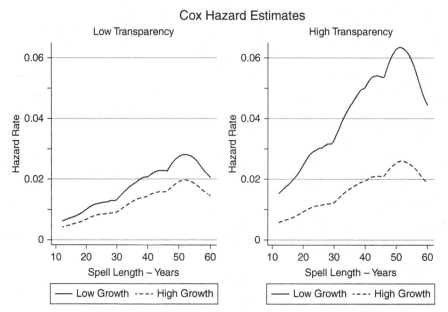

FIGURE 7.2. Transparency, growth, and the hazard of democratization. Plots of the smoothed estimates of the hazard rate, based on estimates from the fifth column of Table 7.1 (the first column with No Prior Transitions). The hazard rate is presented on the y-axis, while regime duration (measured in years) is presented on the x-axis. The graph to the left depicts estimates when transparency is at its 10th percentile in the sample, the graph to the right when transparency is at its 90th percentile. The solid lines depict estimates when growth is at its 10th percentile in the sample, the dashed lines when growth is at its 90th percentile. Both the *Party* and *Party* × *t* terms are held at zero, while all other variables are held at their sample mean. The graphs suggest that economic growth matters more when transparency is high; the risk of transition to democracy is highest when growth is low and transparency is high.

know that others do as well (and they know that the others know, etc.). The failure of the government to deliver strong economic performance becomes common knowledge (see Aumann 1995; Chwe 2013).

As for the control variables, *GDP per capita* has a negative but statistically insignificant effect on transitions to democracy. The finding stands in contrast to the prediction of a cornerstone of the literature on democratization, modernization theory, which expects that as autocracies develop economically, society becomes too complex for autocratic rule. An emergent middle class begins to demand political freedoms and autocracies become increasingly likely to transition to democracy. The negative effect that we estimate is consistent with the results of several other empirical studies (see, for example, Przeworski et al. 2000; Gassebner, Lamla, and Vreeland 2013). The negative effect of *GDP per capita* is also consistent with the view that economic development correlates with state capacity: highly capable autocratic states are more likely to survive threats. Still, we do not want to read too much into the negative effect of *GDP per capita*, as it is estimated imprecisely. Rather, we stress the result for those who suspect that a correlation between state capacity to collect data and democratic transitions drives the correlation between transparency and democratic transitions. Even after controlling for the level of economic development (our proxy for state capacity), the effect of transparency holds.

Ec. openness, interestingly, reduces the risk of transition. This result counters the view that our transparency result is simply part of a larger effect of liberalization. While the dissemination of economic data increases the risk of autocratic collapse, increasing economic openness reduces the risk. So our main result of interest does not appear to be part of a broader pattern of liberalization. The effect of economic openness is statistically significant at the 5 percent level and robust across all specifications in Table 7.1.

As for political institutions under autocracy, the presence of multiple political parties (*Party*) increases the risk of transition, though this effect diminishes over the time an autocratic regime is in power (dropping to zero after about 30 years); autocracies led by a representative of the military (*Military*) face an increased risk of transition, although the effect is not statistically significant in any of our models.

The upshot of this empirical analysis is that we find statistically significant evidence that poor economic growth predicts autocratic transitions to democracy and – consistent with Proposition 5.2 – this relationship between growth and collapse becomes stronger as transparency rises. The latter effect is estimated imprecisely and does not achieve statistical significant in all of our models. Proposition 5.3 – which establishes that transparency should have a direct effect on increasing the risk of regime removal – receives unambiguous support. Transparency increases the risk of the collapse of autocracy via democratization.

7.1.2 Analysis of Autocrat Removal

Using the data of Svolik (2012), we test our claim that transparency is associated with an increased probability of the collapse of autocratic leaders through mass unrest – resulting in either democratization or a new autocratic regime. The unit of observation here is the autocratic regime-year, where autocratic regimes are defined in accordance with Svolik (2012). Svolik's definition of what constitutes an autocracy is similar to that of Cheibub, Gandhi, and Vreeland (2010) – however, it does not require an alternation of political parties in power for a country to be considered democratic and all cases of "no authority" in the data are dropped from Svolik's sample.[10] Because of these two

[10] See: http://campuspress.yale.edu/svolik/the-politics-of-authoritarian-rule/, accessed March 3, 2016.

requirements, Svolik codes somewhat fewer autocratic-to-democratic transitions than do Cheibub, Gandhi, and Vreeland. Some observations are dropped from the sample while others fail to meet the stringent requirements of the DD dataset initially, but subsequently transition to democracy; while Svolik's laxer requirements treat these observations as democratic throughout.

The empirical model used here is similar to the one we employ above, except that we rely on a Cox *competing* hazards model of regime removal.[11] Autocratic regimes can collapse through multiple channels – uprisings, coups, assassinations, foreign intervention, and so on. Our interest is in *mass mobilization*. The theoretical model presented in Chapter 5 does not speak to the threats that autocratic leaders face from coups or military interventions, nor does it speak to the risks of intervention by foreign powers or those resulting from civil wars. Our model estimates the probability that the ruling clique is unseated by a mass revolt or a transition to democracy in year t conditional on surviving until year t. Alternative mechanisms of regime collapse act as competing risks. We estimate our model on all autocratic regimes in Svolik's (2012) dataset, but those regimes that exit via other methods are treated as censored.[12]

As before, our analysis is complicated by the presence of autocratic regimes that have experienced prior instances of instability in the data. We again use conditional gap time models, which allow both the level and the shape of the baseline hazard to vary depending on past experiences of instability. In one set of models, we separately estimate the baseline hazard conditional on whether there has been a prior regime collapse (labeled as "Cond. Past Collapse" in Table 7.2). In another, we estimate separate baseline hazards based on the number of instances of collapse (labeled as "Cond. Hist. Instability" in Table 7.2).[13] In a final set of specifications (labeled as "Control Past Collapse" in Table 7.2), we simply control for whether there has been a prior collapse with the indicator variable *Ever Collapse*. In all models, we cluster the errors by autocratic regime to account for autocorrelation of the error process.

Following the previous analysis, we test the effects of *Transparency*, *Growth*, and their interaction term *Transparency* × *Growth*. First we estimate these effects along with the same set of control variables as before: *GDP per capita*, *Ec. Openness*, *Party*, and *Military*. We introduce controls for higher-order

---

[11] Again, we prefer the Cox specification for the reasons noted above. The ability of the Cox model to address censoring is even more of an issue here where we analyze the survival of ruling cliques that may be removed through means not covered by our theoretical model in Chapter 5.

[12] For an empirical application and discussion of the competing hazards model see Goemans (2008). This model assumes that hazard of one form of removal is conditionally independent of other forms of removal, an assumption analogous to the independence of irrelevant alternatives (IIA) assumption in multinomial logit specifications (Gordon 2002).

[13] Given the substantial variation in the history of instability in our sample, we again code the number of past regime removals as a categorical variable. This variable takes the value 1 if there has never been a prior collapse, 2 if there has been one collapse, 3 if there have been between two and four collapses, and 4 if there have been more than four collapses.

polynomials of economic openness ($\frac{Ec.\ Openness^2}{100}$, $\frac{Ec.\ Openness^3}{10,000}$) to adjust for violations of the proportional hazards assumption, in keeping with the recommendations of Keele (2010).[14] We then present specifications that drop the *Ec. Openness* variables. Finally, we present specifications that include only our variables of interest, *Transparency*, *Growth*, and their interaction.

Thus, the model takes on almost the identical form as the one presented above, except that autocratic country i is replaced by regime l because of our focus on specific autocratic regimes:

$$h_l(t, p_l) = h_0(t, p_l)exp(\delta Transparency_{l,t-1} + \gamma Growth_{l,t-1}$$
$$+ \mu Transparency_{l,t-1} \times Growth_{l,t-1} + X_{l,t-1}\beta) \qquad (7.2)$$

Results from the model specified in Equation 7.2 are presented in Table 7.2, which reports coefficient values – not hazard ratios. A positive coefficient indicates that a given covariate increases the risk of autocratic collapse (via mass revolt or democratization); a negative coefficient indicates the reverse.

The results of the analysis suggest that transparency increases the risk of the removal of autocratic regimes. *Transparency* has a positive effect that is statistically significant at the 10 percent level or higher in all models, except when we include all control variables. These controls themselves, however, do not have statistically significant effects, and the coefficient on transparency is stable across all specifications – suggesting that our models do not suffer from omitted variable bias when they are dropped. We therefore expect that the inclusion of the controls in this case leads to inefficiency, while their exclusion does not appear to cause bias.

All estimates of the effect of *Transparency* place the bulk of the posterior probability mass above zero – p-values (not reported in Table 7.2) range from a high of 0.17 to a low of 0.05 across all specifications. Our point estimates suggest that a one standard deviation increase in the level of *Transparency* increases the hazard of autocratic collapse by 40 to 50 percent.

The coefficient on economic growth is negative and statistically significant in all but one model. In keeping with theoretical expectations, autocratic governments that inspire economic growth are at lower risk of collapse than those that do not achieve economic success. A one standard deviation increase in the growth rate is associated with a reduction in the risk of revolt of between 30 and 50 percent.

Our theoretical expectations further contend that the relationship between growth and the hazard of regime collapse should be conditional on the level of

---

[14] Keele (2010) points out that conventional tests of the proportional hazard assumption are, in fact, tests of model misspecification. Instances in which a given covariate should enter the Cox link function in a nonlinear manner appear as violations of the proportional hazards assumption. When a (roughly) continuous covariate violates proportional hazards, he suggests that researchers fit models including more flexible functional forms – e.g., higher order polynomials – of this term.

TABLE 7.2. *Cox models, autocrat removal from below.*

	Cond. Past Collapse			Cond. Hist. Instability			Control Past Collapse		
Transparency	0.234 [-0.076, 0.543]	0.278 [-0.025, 0.581]	0.259 [0.005, 0.513]	0.245 [-0.056, 0.545]	0.245 [-0.045, 0.534]	0.239 [-0.040, 0.517]	0.221 [-0.087, 0.530]	0.265 [-0.041, 0.572]	0.262 [-0.008, 0.531]
Growth	-0.034 [-0.069, 0.001]	-0.033 [-0.068, 0.002]	-0.028 [-0.061, 0.005]	-0.050 [-0.099, -0.002]	-0.049 [-0.096, -0.002]	-0.042 [-0.086, 0.002]	-0.036 [-0.075, 0.003]	-0.034 [-0.073, 0.005]	-0.029 [-0.065, 0.007]
Transparency × Growth	-0.004 [-0.041, 0.033]	-0.006 [-0.043, 0.030]	-0.006 [-0.036, 0.025]	-0.002 [-0.047, 0.043]	-0.005 [-0.051, 0.041]	-0.007 [-0.042, 0.028]	-0.002 [-0.043, 0.038]	-0.005 [-0.046, 0.035]	-0.005 [-0.040, 0.030]
GDP per capita	0.195 [-0.325, 0.715]			0.090 [-0.476, 0.655]			0.145 [-0.282, 0.571]		
Ec. Openness	-0.033 [-0.077, 0.011]			-0.031 [-0.074, 0.013]			-0.043 [-0.090, 0.003]		
Ec. Openness^2	0.026 [-0.013, 0.065]			0.022 [-0.016, 0.061]			0.034 [-0.009, 0.077]		
Ec. Openness^3	-0.005 [-0.014, 0.003]			-0.004 [-0.012, 0.004]			-0.007 [-0.017, 0.002]		
Party	-0.004 [-0.915, 0.906]	-0.105 [-1.010, 0.800]		-0.216 [-1.245, 0.813]	-0.282 [-1.272, 0.708]		0.112 [-0.816, 1.039]	-0.002 [-0.940, 0.935]	
Military	0.703 [-0.116, 1.523]	0.616 [-0.164, 1.397]		0.521 [-0.293, 1.335]	0.500 [-0.262, 1.262]		0.683 [-0.134, 1.501]	0.593 [-0.174, 1.361]	
Ever Collapse							0.614 [-0.387, 1.616]	0.562 [-0.424, 1.547]	0.723 [-0.213, 1.658]
# of Subjects	137	137	143	137	137	143	137	137	143
# of Failures	30	30	31	30	30	31	30	30	31

Cox competing hazards regressions of the hazard of autocrat removal via revolt or democratization. The models depicted in the first three columns, the middle three columns, and the last three columns differ in the manner in which they deal with countries that experienced multiple autocratic failures. Those in the first three columns report a conditional gap time model wherein the baseline hazard is separately estimated for regimes that experience a prior regime failure and for those that did not. Those in the next two columns estimate separate baseline hazards based on a categorical measure that reflects the number of prior collapses. Those in the final three columns simply control for prior collapses, rather than stratifying the baseline hazard. Ninety-five percent confidence intervals are presented in brackets. All standard errors are clustered by autocratic regime.

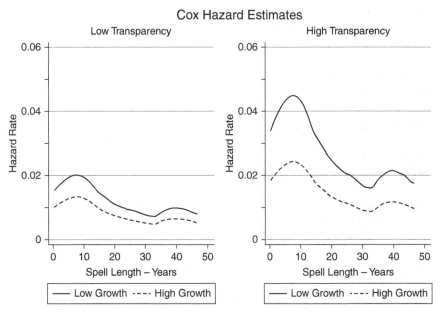

FIGURE 7.3. Hazard rates as a function of transparency and growth. Plots of smoothed estimates of the hazard rate based on the eighth column of Table 7.2. The graph to the left depicts the change in the hazard rate when growth moves from the 10th percentile to the 90th percentile in the sample when the transparency score is at the 10th percentile observed in the sample. The graph to the right depicts the change in the hazard rate when growth changes from the 10th to the 90th percentile when transparency is at the 90th percentile. The *Party* and *Military* variables are held at 0, and the *Ever Collapse* variable is held at 1. This figure suggests that the differential effects of low/high growth on autocratic survival are greater when transparency is high.

transparency. We thus include interactions of growth and transparency in all models. This estimate is negative in all nine models estimated and is substantively meaningful.

To better grasp the relationship between transparency, growth, and autocratic collapse, we plot smoothed estimates of the hazard function – based on the results in the eighth column in Table 7.2 – for different values of growth and transparency in Figure 7.3. (For this exercise, we set the control variables *Party* and *Military* equal to 0 and *Ever Collapse* to 1.) Figure 7.3 leads to three conclusions. First, the risk of autocrat removal is higher when growth is low. Second, the risk of autocrat removal rises when transparency is high. Third, the effect of changing the level of economic growth is stronger when transparency is high.

As for the control variables, their effects are not precisely estimated in any of the specifications presented in Table 7.2. The estimated coefficients for *GDP per capita* are all positive, which is the opposite of what Table 7.1

reports; for *Ec. Openness* (and its polynomials) the coefficients are negative; for *Party* all but one are negative; and for *Military* they are positive. These last results fit with those presented in Table 7.1. The effect of *Ever Collapse* is estimated to be positive in all models where it is included, suggesting that instability in the past also predicts it in the future. Again, however, these coefficients are not reliably estimated as the standard errors are all relatively high.

We conduct two further tests using the Svolik (2012) data to help better identify our causal mechanism. Recall that Table 7.2 estimates the effect of transparency on autocrat removal *from below* – via mass unrest or democratization. The estimation does not consider autocrat removal through coups, which do not involve masses of citizens and usually come from within the ruling clique. Indeed, our theory does not pertain to coups, which do not require the same updating of higher-order beliefs among the masses that data dissemination facilitates. Svolik (2012) records instances of such coups, however. So, in Table 7.3, we estimate the effect of transparency on all forms of autocrat removal. That is, we pool all forms of removal to test whether transparency has an effect.

Here we find no significant effect of *Transparency*. Coefficients on *Transparency*, *Growth*, and their interaction are never statistically significant. Moreover, the point estimate of the coefficient on transparency is consistently small – approximately equal to zero – and switches signs across the various specifications. So, transparency is associated with increased autocratic instability via threats from below, but its relationship to the threat of coups emerging from within the regime appears to follow a different pattern.

To push this analysis further, we look more carefully at the risk of autocratic regime collapse exclusively from coups. Surprisingly, given our previous results, Table 7.4 demonstrates that transparency is associated with a *reduced* threat of coups! The coefficient on transparency is negative and large in all specifications, and significant at the 90 percent level or above in all specifications that do not control for GDP per capita and economic openness. Furthermore, the coefficient on growth (and its interaction with transparency) is consistently positive in all specifications.

Compared with instability as brought about via unrest, transparency has the opposite association with instability as brought about via coups. This puzzling contrast calls for further investigation into the effect of transparency on other forms of autocratic instability beyond mass unrest. We thus return to this puzzle later in this chapter and then more fully explore it in Chapter 10. For now, we take the contrasting results as confirmation of the causal mechanism posited by the autocratic theoretical model from Chapter 5.

Transparency, as measured by data dissemination, is not associated with autocratic instability in general, but only with collapse resulting from forms of unrest that require masses of citizens to update their higher-order beliefs about the distribution of discontent with the ruling regime. We can assert with

TABLE 7.3. *Cox models, autocrat removal via all methods.*

	Cond. Past Collapse			Cond. Hist. Instability			Control Past Collapse		
Transparency	0.014 [-0.159, 0.187]	0.000 [-0.181, 0.181]	0.040 [-0.117, 0.197]	0.010 [-0.171, 0.190]	-0.029 [-0.218, 0.160]	-0.009 [-0.184, 0.167]	0.012 [-0.170, 0.194]	0.001 [-0.192, 0.193]	0.042 [-0.125, 0.209]
Growth	-0.005 [-0.030, 0.020]	-0.006 [-0.030, 0.018]	-0.009 [-0.034, 0.015]	-0.006 [-0.039, 0.027]	-0.007 [-0.038, 0.024]	-0.012 [-0.042, 0.018]	-0.008 [-0.034, 0.019]	-0.008 [-0.033, 0.017]	-0.011 [-0.036, 0.015]
Transparency × Growth	0.015 [-0.011, 0.042]	0.012 [-0.014, 0.037]	0.006 [-0.010, 0.022]	0.013 [-0.019, 0.045]	0.011 [-0.020, 0.042]	0.007 [-0.013, 0.026]	0.017 [-0.011, 0.045]	0.012 [-0.016, 0.040]	0.006 [-0.011, 0.022]
GDP per capita	-0.265 [-0.705, 0.174]			-0.330 [-0.796, 0.135]			-0.274 [-0.709, 0.161]		
Ec. Openness	-0.040 [-0.066, -0.014]			-0.031 [-0.057, -0.006]			-0.046 [-0.071, -0.021]		
Ec. Openness^2	0.034 [0.009, 0.059]			0.027 [0.003, 0.050]			0.038 [0.015, 0.062]		
Ec. Openness^3	-0.008 [-0.015, -0.002]			-0.006 [-0.012, -0.001]			-0.009 [-0.015, -0.003]		
Party	0.392 [-0.101, 0.884]	0.364 [-0.122, 0.850]		0.272 [-0.239, 0.784]	0.262 [-0.225, 0.748]		0.414 [-0.095, 0.923]	0.371 [-0.125, 0.867]	
Military	0.060 [-0.406, 0.525]	0.094 [-0.360, 0.548]		0.026 [-0.426, 0.478]	0.076 [-0.363, 0.516]		0.071 [-0.397, 0.540]	0.098 [-0.360, 0.556]	
Ever Collapse							0.283 [-0.227, 0.793]	0.288 [-0.237, 0.813]	0.356 [-0.144, 0.856]
# of Subjects	137	137	143	137	137	143	137	137	143
# of Failures	87	87	93	87	87	93	87	87	93

Cox regressions of the hazard of autocrat removal via any method. The models depicted in the first three columns, the middle three columns, and the last three columns differ in the manner in which they deal with countries that experienced multiple autocratic failures. Those in the first three columns report a conditional gap time model wherein the baseline hazard is separately estimated for regimes that experience a prior regime failure and for those that did not. Those in the next two columns estimate separate baseline hazards based on a categorical measure that reflects the number of prior collapses. Those in the final three columns simply control for the number of prior collapses, rather than stratifying the baseline hazard. Ninety-five percent confidence intervals are presented in brackets. All standard errors are clustered by autocratic regime.

TABLE 7.4. Cox models, autocrat removal via coup.

	Cond. Past Collapse			Cond. Hist. Instability			Control Past Collapse		
Transparency	-0.163	-0.293	-0.239	-0.243	-0.320	-0.315	-0.200	-0.294	-0.240
	[-0.477, 0.151]	[-0.586, 0.000]	[-0.451, -0.028]	[-0.765, 0.280]	[-0.691, 0.050]	[-0.676, 0.046]	[-0.523, 0.122]	[-0.579, -0.009]	[-0.443, -0.037]
Growth	0.042	0.041	0.041	0.068	0.056	0.057	0.029	0.034	0.035
	[-0.020, 0.105]	[-0.016, 0.097]	[-0.011, 0.094]	[-0.009, 0.146]	[-0.004, 0.116]	[-0.003, 0.116]	[-0.025, 0.082]	[-0.020, 0.089]	[-0.014, 0.085]
Transparency	-0.001	0.014	0.015	0.021	0.028	0.024	0.001	0.009	0.013
× Growth	[-0.044, 0.042]	[-0.028, 0.055]	[-0.007, 0.037]	[-0.049, 0.090]	[-0.024, 0.080]	[-0.021, 0.068]	[-0.040, 0.042]	[-0.030, 0.048]	[-0.007, 0.034]
GDP per capita	-1.411			-1.421			-1.324		
	[-3.083, 0.262]			[-3.131, 0.288]			[-3.010, 0.362]		
Ec. Openness	0.034			0.039			0.023		
	[-0.030, 0.098]			[-0.022, 0.101]			[-0.038, 0.083]		
Ec. Openness^2	-0.011			-0.013			-0.004		
	[-0.062, 0.040]			[-0.061, 0.034]			[-0.057, 0.048]		
Ec. Openness^3	0.001			0.001			-0.001		
	[-0.010, 0.012]			[-0.008, 0.011]			[-0.012, 0.011]		
Parry	-0.140			-0.406	0.045		-0.185	-0.005	
	[-1.230, 0.950]			[-1.529, 0.717]	[-1.010, 1.100]		[-1.375, 1.005]	[-1.226, 1.216]	
Military	0.389			0.362	0.660		0.398	0.680	
	[-0.581, 1.359]			[-0.531, 1.256]	[-0.266, 1.585]		[-0.628, 1.423]	[-0.364, 1.725]	
Ever Collapse							0.482	0.318	0.470
							[-0.551, 1.516]	[-0.679, 1.316]	[-0.553, 1.493]
# of Subjects	137	137	143	137	137	143	137	137	143
# of Failures	16	16	18	16	16	18	16	16	18

Cox competing hazards regressions of the hazard of autocrat removal via coup. The models depicted in the first three columns, the middle three columns, and the last three columns differ in the manner in which they deal with countries that experienced multiple autocratic failures. Those in the first three columns report a conditional gap time model wherein the baseline hazard is separately estimated for regimes that experience a prior regime failure and for those that did not. Those in the next two columns estimate separate baseline hazards based on a categorical measure that reflects the number of prior collapses. Those in the final three columns simply control for prior collapses, rather than stratifying the baseline hazard. Ninety-five percent confidence intervals are presented in brackets. All standard errors are clustered by autocratic regime.

confidence that transparency is associated with autocratic instability from below: mass unrest and democratization.

7.1.3 Analysis of Unrest and Other Threats

We have established that more transparent autocracies are more likely to experience regime failures through mass unrest and democratization than less transparent autocracies. We also have established suggestive evidence that the magnitude of such risks is greater under low levels of economic growth and that the effect of growth increases with transparency. These findings are consistent with our theoretical predictions. But, because they rely on the ultimate outcome variable – autocratic collapse – they constitute indirect evidence that transparency causes mass unrest under autocracy.

We now bring our analysis one step closer to the microfoundations supporting our model. Rather than looking at regime change, we instead look directly at the manifestation of specific threats to autocratic rule. As we have emphasized, our theory pertains to the higher-order beliefs of masses of citizens. Under autocracy, transparency should lead to threats involving mass movements against the government – such as anti-government protests and general strikes directed at government policies. We do not necessarily predict transparency to be associated with other forms of mass unrest, such as riots, which may not be directed at the government. And we certainly do not expect the dissemination of data to facilitate assassinations, coups, guerrilla warfare, or revolutions, which are led by tightknit groups who can share information face-to-face.

Thus we turn to the Cross National Time Series Archive (Banks 1979), as made available by Bueno de Mesquita et al. (2003). This dataset includes counts (at the country-year level) of various forms of instability, including the annual numbers of (1) anti-government demonstrations, (2) general strikes, (3) riots, (4) guerrilla movements, (5) revolutions, (6) assassinations, and (7) coups. We expect transparency to increase the frequency of anti-government demonstrations and general strikes. We do not expect transparency to increase assassinations, coups, guerrilla warfare, or revolutions, which tend to be executed by a small elite or counter-elite. We also examine riots, which do involve mass mobilization, but often do not target the government. Contrasting the effects of transparency on these various threats to autocratic rule can increase our confidence in the causal mechanism posited by our theoretical model.

It is also important to examine the full range of threats to autocracy to rule out various forms of selection bias. For example, one could imagine a competing theoretical account, which holds that weak autocracies give in to demands for transparency and are also inherently susceptible to all sorts of threats. In this story, autocratic weakness leads both to transparency and to instability. Relatively weak autocracies capitulate to demands for transparency in exchange for greater citizen support; and weak autocracies are also more prone to collapse. So, our results presented above could be driven by omitted variable bias (Heckman 1979).

The analysis in this section speaks to this concern in two ways. First, if weak governments capitulate to citizen demands by granting transparency, the relationship between mass mobilization and transparency should be biased downward. If governments increased levels of transparency to drive down the risk of unrest, they would presumably cease such reform efforts if they proved systematically ineffective. So, if we find a positive relationship between transparency and mass unrest, one must conclude that any such bias is relatively small.

Second, weak autocrats are prone to several forms of instability, not just to protests and strikes. If we do not observe a relationship between transparency and other forms of unrest – assassinations, coups, guerrilla warfare, and revolutions – we can say with increased confidence that the relationship between transparency and autocrat removal is mediated by mass mobilization.

To test the relationship between transparency and unrest, we examine seven measures of threats to autocratic rule from the Banks (1979) dataset. For our modeling approach, we rely on country fixed-effects negative binomial regressions. We employ a negative binomial because the Banks data are measured as count variables, and because the data are likely to be over-dispersed due to the large number of zero-valued observations.[15]

Our fixed-effects negative binomial (*FENegBin*) model is thus:

$$Unrest_{c,t} = FENegBin(\rho Unrest_{c,t-1} + \eta Transparency_{c,t-1} + \zeta Growth_{c,t-1}$$
$$+ \xi Transparency_{c,t-1} \times Growth_{c,t-1} + \mathbf{X}_{c,t-1}\nu + \mathbf{T}\iota) \quad (7.3)$$

where *Unrest* represents one of the seven measures of instability, *c* denotes country, *t* year, **T** a cubic polynomial of time, and ι is a vector of associated coefficients. We again use $\mathbf{X}_{c,t-1}$ to denote a vector of control variables, and ν is a vector of associated coefficients. We include a cubic polynomial of time to control for the potential confounding effects of time trends using a general functional form. We include a lagged dependent variable in all specifications to adjust for the dynamics of the data generating process (Beck and Katz 2011). As before, we interact *Transparency* with *Growth*.

Results from the model specified in Equation 7.3 are reported in Table 7.5. To ensure our results are robust to possible overfitting, we also present models dropping the control variables in Table 7.6.

As seen in Table 7.5, increased levels of transparency are associated with more frequent general strikes and demonstrations. They are also associated with more frequent riots, though, as we demonstrate below, this result is not robust to controlling for media freedom. The direct association between

---

[15] A fixed-effects negative binomial regression allows the value of the over-dispersion parameter of the negative binomial to vary across panels. Note that this type of "fixed-effects" model differs from typical settings.

TABLE 7.5. *Fixed-effects negative binomial models, unrest.*

	General Strikes	Riots	Demonstrations	Revolutions	Guerrilla	Coups	Assassinations
Lag Unrest	0.215	0.084	0.097	0.182	0.558	-0.156	0.030
	[-0.001, 0.430]	[0.039, 0.128]	[0.063, 0.131]	[0.103, 0.260]	[0.359, 0.756]	[-1.034, 0.721]	[-0.050, 0.110]
Transparency	0.650	0.193	0.332	0.023	0.015	-0.185	0.064
	[0.170, 1.130]	[0.010, 0.376]	[0.167, 0.497]	[-0.086, 0.133]	[-0.106, 0.137]	[-0.647, 0.277]	[-0.154, 0.282]
Growth	-0.030	0.003	-0.011	0.001	0.005	-0.047	-0.041
	[-0.061, 0.000]	[-0.018, 0.025]	[-0.029, 0.006]	[-0.012, 0.014]	[-0.009, 0.020]	[-0.095, 0.001]	[-0.065, -0.018]
Transparency × Growth	-0.017	-0.006	0.002	0.002	0.002	-0.019	-0.012
	[-0.044, 0.010]	[-0.018, 0.006]	[-0.010, 0.013]	[-0.004, 0.008]	[-0.005, 0.009]	[-0.037, -0.002]	[-0.023, 0.000]
GDP per capita	0.480	0.519	0.316	1.007	0.245	-5.611	0.883
	[-1.228, 2.188]	[-0.328, 1.367]	[-0.432, 1.064]	[-0.014, 2.027]	[-1.030, 1.519]	[-17.015, 5.794]	[-0.121, 1.886]
Ec. Openness	0.001	-0.008	-0.001	-0.005	-0.003	0.003	-0.008
	[-0.018, 0.020]	[-0.016, 0.001]	[-0.008, 0.006]	[-0.010, -0.000]	[-0.008, 0.003]	[-0.014, 0.019]	[-0.019, 0.003]
Parry	0.799	-0.007	-0.114	-0.012	0.216	1.157	0.765
	[-0.020, 1.619]	[-0.447, 0.434]	[-0.511, 0.284]	[-0.334, 0.310]	[-0.220, 0.653]	[0.384, 1.930]	[0.214, 1.315]
Military	0.343	-0.215	-0.131	-0.345	-0.503	-0.270	0.035
	[-0.529, 1.215]	[-0.707, 0.277]	[-0.586, 0.324]	[-0.743, 0.052]	[-1.064, 0.059]	[-1.175, 0.635]	[-0.654, 0.724]
Fuel Exports	-1.509	0.468	-0.323	2.751	0.659	1.488	-0.807
	[-3.983, 0.966]	[-0.698, 1.633]	[-1.235, 0.590]	[-1632.841, 1638.343]	[-378.747, 380.064]	[-673.296, 676.273]	[-2.053, 0.439]
Constant	-2.868	-0.640	-0.723	16.280	11.352	7.892	0.102
	[-5.159, -0.578]	[-1.801, 0.522]	[-1.774, 0.328]	[-1577.942, 1610.503]	[-88.470, 111.175]	[-87.565, 103.348]	[-1.699, 1.903]
Cubic Time Polynomial	✓	✓	✓	✓	✓	✓	✓
#Obs	590	986	1014	1002	671	514	635
#Countries	42	66	70	65	43	33	41

Fixed-effects negative binomial regressions of levels of unrest as a function of transparency and growth. Measures of unrest are drawn from (Banks 1979). All models include a lagged dependent variable, the coefficient on which is reported in the first row of the table. Ninety-five percent confidence intervals are presented in brackets.

TABLE 7.6. *Fixed-effects negative binomial models, unrest (no control variables).*

	General Strikes	Riots	Demonstrations	Revolutions	Guerrilla	Coups	Assassinations
Lag Unrest	0.302	0.087	0.085	0.216	0.548	−0.196	0.065
	[0.102, 0.502]	[0.043, 0.130]	[0.053, 0.116]	[0.139, 0.292]	[0.359, 0.736]	[−1.009, 0.618]	[−0.010, 0.139]
Transparency	0.610	0.176	0.359	−0.031	−0.019	−0.179	0.085
	[0.204, 1.016]	[0.007, 0.346]	[0.210, 0.508]	[−0.137, 0.075]	[−0.127, 0.089]	[−0.606, 0.248]	[−0.106, 0.275]
Growth	−0.029	0.002	−0.010	0.005	0.003	−0.063	−0.037
	[−0.058, 0.000]	[−0.019, 0.024]	[−0.028, 0.008]	[−0.008, 0.018]	[−0.011, 0.017]	[−0.110, −0.017]	[−0.062, −0.013]
Transparency × Growth	−0.012	−0.006	0.004	0.004	0.001	−0.022	−0.009
	[−0.038, 0.014]	[−0.018, 0.006]	[−0.008, 0.016]	[−0.002, 0.009]	[−0.005, 0.007]	[−0.039, −0.006]	[−0.023, 0.005]
Constant	−1.097	−1.244	−1.261	2.841	14.148	11.207	−0.985
	[−1.782, −0.412]	[−1.568, −0.920]	[−1.550, −0.973]	[0.036, 5.646]	[−429.290, 457.587]	[−781.071, 803.486]	[−1.430, −0.540]
#Obs	590	986	1014	1002	671	514	635
#Countries	42	66	70	65	43	33	41

Fixed-effects negative binomial regressions of levels of unrest as a function of transparency and growth. Measures of unrest are drawn from (Banks 1979). All models include a lagged dependent variable, the coefficient on which is reported in the first row of the table. Ninety-five percent confidence intervals are presented in brackets.

transparency and the frequency of revolutions, guerrilla movements, coups, and assassinations is not significantly different from zero.

As noted above, the interpretation of transparency's role in conditioning the effect of growth on unrest is not straightforward in nonlinear models. More precisely, when the estimated coefficient on the *Transparency* term is large and positive, the functional form of the model dictates that the marginal effect of a change in *Growth* will rise as values of *Transparency* increase. Estimates indicate that transparency plays a substantial – but not statistically significant – conditioning role in the relationship between growth and general strikes. It does not play either a significant or a substantial conditional role with regard to the relationship between growth and demonstrations – or between growth and riots. And there is no conditioning nor direct relationship between transparency and assassinations, guerrilla movements, or revolutions.

These results face a particular risk, given the reliance of the Cross-National Time Series dataset on the *New York Times* to code political threats. Schedler (2012) documents that this approach undercounts political threats. The fact that we make predictions with regard to specific forms of unrest – anti-government demonstrations and strikes – and not other threats to autocratic rule, somewhat insulates our results from this concern. There is little reason to expect that media biases affect the reporting of anti-government demonstrations and strikes but not riots or coups, for example.

Still, we pursue a robustness check that incorporates a control for freedom of the press, as suggested by Schedler (2012). Specifically, we include a control for an indicator variable set to 1 if the press is coded as "Not Free" by Freedom House's Freedom of the Press index (and set to 0 otherwise).[16] The inclusion of this control somewhat truncates our time-series – observations are only available from 1982.[17] We include an indicator for "Not Free" country-years, rather than using the full range of the Freedom House index – "Free," "Partially Free," and "Not Free" – given that only 5 percent of country-year observations in our sample of autocracies are coded as Free. The central distinction in this sample of the data is between Partially Free and Not Free observations.

We report our findings using the *Not Free* control variable in Table 7.7 (which also includes our other control variables), and in Table 7.8 (which only includes the *Not Free* control variable). In keeping with the dangers of biased reporting noted by Schedler (2012), the coefficient on the *Not Free* indicator is consistently negative (excepting for counts of guerrilla movements) and is

---

[16] www.freedomhouse.org/report-types/freedom-press, accessed January 6, 2016

[17] The Freedom House data begin their coverage in 1979. Temporal coverage is not consistent from one year to the next, however, and all of 1981 and most of 1982 is collapsed into a single observation. We thus only consider observations post-1982, when reporting becomes consistent. Prior to 1988, the index separately codes the print and broadcast media. We only use the print measure in these instances, given that our concern is specifically with *New York Times* reporting.

TABLE 7.7. *Fixed-effects negative binomial models of unrest, including Freedom House control.*

	General Strikes	Riots	Demonstrations	Revolutions	Guerrilla	Coups	Assassinations
Lag Unrest	0.175 [−0.052, 0.403] (0.131)	0.076 [0.027, 0.124] (0.002)	0.083 [0.046, 0.121] (0.000)	0.179 [0.099, 0.259] (0.000)	0.557 [0.346, 0.769] (0.000)	−0.070 [−0.997, 0.858] (0.883)	0.099 [−0.002, 0.199] (0.055)
Transparency	0.596 [0.104, 1.088] (0.018)	0.077 [−0.123, 0.278] (0.450)	0.212 [0.046, 0.379] (0.013)	−0.006 [−0.120, 0.109] (0.922)	0.005 [−0.123, 0.134] (0.935)	−0.187 [−0.668, 0.294] (0.445)	0.047 [−0.169, 0.262] (0.672)
Growth	−0.030 [−0.062, 0.002] (0.066)	0.004 [−0.021, 0.028] (0.773)	−0.008 [−0.028, 0.012] (0.412)	0.001 [−0.013, 0.015] (0.885)	0.010 [−0.005, 0.025] (0.207)	−0.040 [−0.089, 0.008] (0.106)	−0.036 [−0.060, −0.012] (0.003)
Transparency × Growth	−0.018 [−0.046, 0.010] (0.218)	−0.007 [−0.022, 0.008] (0.355)	0.001 [−0.010, 0.013] (0.851)	0.003 [−0.003, 0.009] (0.311)	0.004 [−0.004, 0.011] (0.328)	−0.017 [−0.035, −0.000] (0.048)	−0.008 [−0.020, 0.004] (0.188)
GDP per capita	−0.059 [−1.957, 1.839] (0.952)	0.523 [−0.733, 1.780] (0.414)	0.467 [−0.399, 1.333] (0.291)	1.634 [0.225, 3.044] (0.023)	0.233 [−1.127, 1.593] (0.737)	−11.099 [−22.757, 0.560] (0.062)	1.100 [−0.220, 2.421] (0.102)
Ec. Openness	0.006 [−0.015, 0.027] (0.559)	−0.011 [−0.020, −0.002] (0.021)	−0.004 [−0.011, 0.004] (0.310)	−0.006 [−0.011, −0.001] (0.026)	−0.002 [−0.008, 0.003] (0.435)	−0.003 [−0.020, 0.014] (0.770)	−0.012 [−0.027, 0.002] (0.103)
Party	0.800 [−0.077, 1.678] (0.074)	−0.351 [−0.864, 0.162] (0.179)	−0.248 [−0.707, 0.211] (0.289)	−0.006 [−0.362, 0.350] (0.974)	0.331 [−0.168, 0.831] (0.194)	0.774 [−0.128, 1.677] (0.093)	0.423 [−0.205, 1.051] (0.186)
Military	0.493 [−0.492, 1.478] (0.327)	−0.019 [−0.571, 0.534] (0.947)	0.120 [−0.387, 0.627] (0.643)	−0.281 [−0.708, 0.146] (0.197)	−0.570 [−1.186, 0.046] (0.070)	0.242 [−0.790, 1.274] (0.646)	−0.299 [−1.087, 0.488] (0.456)
Fuel Exports	−1.933 [−4.455, 0.589] (0.133)	0.237 [−0.924, 1.397] (0.689)	−0.190 [−1.256, 0.875] (0.726)	0.135 [−188.909, 189.178] (0.999)	−0.435 [−294.428, 293.559] (0.998)	5.305 [−89.719, 100.329] (0.913)	−0.177 [−1.839, 1.485] (0.835)
Not Free	−0.642 [−1.296, 0.013] (0.055)	−0.699 [−1.138, −0.259] (0.002)	−0.357 [−0.742, 0.028] (0.069)	−0.259 [−0.618, 0.101] (0.158)	0.388 [−0.146, 0.922] (0.154)	−0.595 [−1.527, 0.336] (0.210)	−0.384 [−0.931, 0.163] (0.169)
Constant	−3.415 [−5.701, −1.128] (0.003)	−1.609 [−2.907, −0.312] (0.015)	−2.998 [−4.240, −1.756] (0.000)	9.939 [−106.368, 126.247] (0.867)	11.006 [−100.054, 122.066] (0.846)	2.053 [−2.802, 6.909] (0.407)	−2.797 [−4.764, −0.830] (0.005)
Cubic Time Polynomial	✓	✓	✓	✓	✓	✓	✓
#Obs	511	808	846	791	566	423	522
#Countries	40	62	65	56	40	30	37

Fixed-effects negative binomial regressions of levels of unrest as a function of transparency and growth. Measures of unrest are drawn from (Banks 1979). All models include a lagged dependent variable, the coefficient on which is reported in the first row of the table. Ninety-five percent confidence intervals are presented in brackets, while p-values are

TABLE 7.8. *Fixed-effects negative binomial models of unrest, including Freedom House control (other controls dropped).*

	General Strikes	Riots	Demonstrations	Revolutions	Guerrilla	Coups	Assassinations
Lag Unrest	0.258	0.077	0.077	0.192	0.543	-0.029	0.161
	[0.047, 0.469]	[0.031, 0.123]	[0.042, 0.111]	[0.113, 0.272]	[0.342, 0.744]	[-0.912, 0.854]	[0.063, 0.260]
	(0.017)	(0.001)	(0.000)	(0.000)	(0.000)	(0.949)	(0.001)
Transparency	0.523	0.055	0.269	-0.038	-0.029	-0.191	0.032
	[0.103, 0.943]	[-0.125, 0.235]	[0.109, 0.428]	[-0.149, 0.074]	[-0.145, 0.086]	[-0.639, 0.257]	[-0.159, 0.224]
	(0.015)	(0.551)	(0.001)	(0.508)	(0.619)	(0.403)	(0.739)
Growth	-0.027	0.005	-0.005	0.005	0.006	-0.059	-0.026
	[-0.057, 0.003]	[-0.019, 0.028]	[-0.025, 0.014]	[-0.008, 0.018]	[-0.008, 0.021]	[-0.106, -0.012]	[-0.049, -0.002]
	(0.082)	(0.692)	(0.595)	(0.426)	(0.383)	(0.014)	(0.033)
Transparency × Growth	-0.008	-0.007	0.004	0.004	0.002	-0.021	-0.004
	[-0.034, 0.018]	[-0.021, 0.008]	[-0.008, 0.017]	[-0.001, 0.010]	[-0.005, 0.008]	[-0.038, -0.005]	[-0.017, 0.008]
	(0.530)	(0.383)	(0.493)	(0.136)	(0.570)	(0.011)	(0.507)
Not Free	-0.572	-0.615	-0.307	-0.261	0.205	-0.742	-0.438
	[-1.218, 0.074]	[-1.036, -0.193]	[-0.676, 0.062]	[-0.645, 0.123]	[-0.300, 0.711]	[-1.575, 0.092]	[-0.979, 0.103]
	(0.082)	(0.004)	(0.103)	(0.183)	(0.426)	(0.081)	(0.113)
Constant	-0.849	-0.917	-1.083	3.537	10.903	10.426	-0.535
	[-1.614, -0.084]	[-1.319, -0.515]	[-1.449, -0.717]	[-2.069, 9.142]	[-92.673, 114.478]	[-683.356, 704.208]	[-1.094, 0.024]
	(0.030)	(0.000)	(0.000)	(0.216)	(0.837)	(0.977)	(0.061)
#Obs	511	808	846	791	566	423	522
#Countries	40	62	65	56	40	30	37

Fixed-effects negative binomial regressions of levels of unrest as a function of transparency and growth. Measures of unrest are drawn from (Banks 1979). All models include a lagged dependent variable, the coefficient on which is reported in the first row of the table. Ninety-five percent confidence intervals are presented in brackets, while p-values are presented in parentheses.

sometimes statistically significant at the ten percent level for strikes, demonstrations, and coups. The negative effect of *Not Free* on riots is more precisely estimated, statistically significant at the one percent level. The set of results suggests that the *New York Times* might be less likely to report political instability in countries that do not enjoy a free press and that the effect on riots is particularly strong. Accordingly, when we include the *Not Free* indicator in the regression exploring the frequency of riots, the indicator is statistically significant while the coefficient on transparency is smaller than previously estimated and is not significant. Importantly, however, our finding that transparency is associated with an increased frequency of strikes and anti-government demonstrations – but not with other forms of unrest – is unaffected by the inclusion of this control.

Autocracies face many threats to their rule. Our theory indicates that transparency should increase only the risk of *mass unrest* directed toward the government. Our analysis here finds exactly this: transparency is associated with an increase in the risks of anti-government demonstrations and general strikes directed at autocratic governments.

7.2 ANALYSIS OF DEMOCRATIC STABILITY

We now turn to testing our predictions about the effect of transparency on democratic stability. We demonstrate in this subsection that: (1) transparency is associated with an increased likelihood of the survival of democracy, and (2) transparency is associated with a decreased risk of the irregular removal of democratically elected leaders. That is, in democracies with high levels of data transparency, leaders face lower risks of coups, popular revolts, and assassinations.

As with the tests of the autocratic model, we estimate the effect of transparency conditional on economic performance by including the variables *Transparency* (measured as the HRV index), *Growth* (measured as the percentage change in real GDP per capita), and their interaction (*Transparency* × *Growth*). Our theoretical model of democracy includes the parameter $1/\sigma_s^2$, which maps onto the *Transparency* variable in our empirical tests, and the parameter G_t (or θ), which maps onto *Growth*.

Proposition 5.9 contends that transparency should be associated with the stabilization of democratic regimes. Our model predicts that instability under democracy is driven by the perception that electoral rules fail to unseat rent-seeking or incompetent politicians. Enhancing the effectiveness of elections – by increasing transparency – serves to decrease the likelihood of unrest. Transparent democracies should face a lower hazard of collapse than opaque democracies. Leaders elected in opaque democracies, by contrast, face higher risks of irregular removal from office.

As with the regressions focusing on autocratic stability, we draw all economic controls from the Penn World Table, which has the advantages of (1) involving the input of external researchers and (2) being free of missing values. Because of (1), we interpret the growth variable provided by the PWT as representing the true state of the economy, or G_t in our theoretical models – rather than the public signal of the economy s. Hence, when growth is low, democracy is more likely to collapse. This effect should be conditioned by transparency – which corresponds to the inverse of the variance of s, $\frac{1}{\sigma_s^2}$ in our theoretical model. As transparency rises, the marginal effect of G_t on survival should fall, as underperforming leaders are voted out of office, rather than removed through extraconstitutional means, with greater frequency.

Thus, this section addresses three dependent variables. We first explore the survival of democracy (as measured by the DD dataset). We then compare the effects of transparency on irregular versus regular leader removal (as measured by the Archigos dataset). Note that unlike in the previous section, we do not distinguish across various types of threats – demonstrations, strikes, coups, assassinations, and so on. Recall that the causal mechanism leading to the breakdown of a political regime in our democracy model is quite distinct from the one in the autocracy model. In the latter, the key involves the higher-order beliefs of citizens, whose decision to protest depends on the decisions of other citizens to protest. In the democracy model, citizens' higher-order beliefs are informed by the electoral process itself. Democracy breaks down as a result of a lack of legitimacy in the electoral process when citizens are unable to base their voting decisions on credible economic data. Under these circumstances, countries may experience first the temporary suspension of democracy and, often, the accession of leaders or movements with anti-democratic aspirations. As argued by Linz (1978), popular mobilization against leaders may also open the door to coups. Indeed, we contend elsewhere in this book, when democracy loses popular legitimacy, the masses' regime-type preference aligns with the preference of anti-democratic elites.

So, while we predict (1) the survival of democracy under high levels of transparency, and (2) the irregular removal of democratically elected leaders under low levels of transparency, we make no prediction here about the specific manner by which the leader is removed, whether due to mass demonstration in the streets, a coup led by tightknit conspirators, or a combination of the two.

Alternative explanations loom large. So we take several steps to control for alternative causal mechanisms. Perhaps the most well-known predictor of the survival of democracy is level of economic development (Cheibub and Vreeland 2011). Empirical models of democratic survival that fail to include this variable likely suffer from omitted variable bias. This variable is even more important to include in our study because of its connection to the capacity of states to collect data.

We additionally include controls for a variety of other economic factors – as in the regression specifications for autocracies above. As in the previous section, all such measures are drawn from the PWT version 6.3.

Beyond economic factors, we also control for political institutions. A much contested literature points to differences in the stability of parliamentary and presidential regimes (for example, Cheibub 2007; Lijphart 1992). We therefore control for a binary indicator of whether the country has a parliamentary system, and another indicator equal to one if the country has a mixed parliamentary/presidential style system. The omitted (residual) category is presidentialism.

Following the sections above, we employ conditional gap time models in all specifications, which flexibly control for past experiences of regime transition (Box-Steffensmeier and Zorn 2002). Controlling for past transitions is critically important given that the frequency of past autocratic reversions is among the most robust predictors of democratic collapse identified in the literature (see, for instance, Przeworski et al. 2000; Gassebner, Lamla, and Vreeland 2013). Time matters and it is important to address potential trends in the data. We continue to control for duration dependence using Cox specifications. We also take care to address country- and leader-specific idiosyncrasies. In the models of democratic survival, we cluster unobserved factors on spells of continuous democratic rule. In the models of leader removal, we cluster such error terms on leaders.

7.2.1 Analysis of the Survival of Democracy

Our outcome of interest here is thus a democratic-to-autocratic transition, which we define using the DD dataset (Cheibub, Gandhi, and Vreeland 2010). The unit of observation is the democratic spell-year, where a democratic spell is defined as one or more continuous years of democratic rule.

We test the relationship between transparency and such transitions using Cox proportional hazards regressions in conditional gap time models. We estimate models where we stratify the baseline hazard rate based on an indicator for whether there has been a prior transition, or, alternatively, an ordered variable based on the number of prior transitions. As a final robustness test, we drop all cases that have experienced a prior democratic collapse from the model.

Our empirical hypothesis holds that the hazard of democratic collapse should fall in transparency. To test this hypothesis, we estimate models of the following form:

$$h_d(t, p_d) = h_0(t, p_d)exp(\delta Transparency_{d,t-1} + \gamma Growth_{d,t-1}$$
$$+ \mu Transparency_{d,t-1} \times Growth_{d,t-1} + \mathbf{X}_{d,t-1}\beta) \qquad (7.4)$$

where d denotes democratic-spell, t denotes time (measured in years) of continuous democratic rule, p_d is a measure of past instances of democratic collapse. The baseline hazard rate, $h_0(t, p_d)$, is estimated separately in each strata based on the history of past democratic collapses. *Transparency* (measured as the HRV index), *Growth* (measured as the percentage change in real GDP per capita), and their interaction (*Transparency* × *Growth*) directly correspond to the democratic model from Chapter 5. We estimate the coefficients δ, γ, and μ to give us the marginal effects of these variables. The model also includes $X_{d,t}\beta$, which represents the product of a data vector of control variables and a corresponding vector of estimated coefficients. As control variables in $X_{d,t}$, we include *GDP per capita*, which famously predicts the survival of democracy (Przeworski et al. 2000), *Ec. Openness*, to control for economic liberalization, and the dichotomous indicators *Parliamentary* and *Mixed System* to account for type of political system, following Cheibub (2007).

Results from these regressions are presented in Table 7.9. The first two columns present coefficient estimates from a conditional gap time model in which the baseline hazard rate is stratified by whether there was a prior transition (Cond. Prior Transition), the next two present similar models stratified based on the number of prior transitions (Cond. Num. Transitions), and the final two present estimates from a model run on democracies that did not experience a prior transition to autocracy between 1870 and 2008 (No Prior Transition). As throughout the chapter, we present estimates of coefficient values, not hazard ratios.

As can be seen from Table 7.9, the coefficient on transparency is consistently negative and large. The 95 percent confidence intervals are bounded away from zero in all but one specification – the p-value in the exceptional case is 0.052. When economic growth is at its mean level in the sample, the point estimates of the effect of transparency suggest that a one standard deviation increase in transparency serves to reduce the hazard of democratic collapse by between roughly 45 to 85 percent.

Figure 7.4 presents estimates of the smoothed hazard function from the model in the fifth column of Table 7.9. The graph on the left of Figure 7.4 presents estimates from when transparency is at its 10th percentile in the sample; while, the graph on the right presents the smoothed hazard when transparency is at its 90th percentile. Solid lines depict the estimated hazard when growth is at its 10th percentile; dashed lines depict the same when growth is at its 90th percentile.

As is apparent in Figure 7.4, an increase in transparency is associated with a marked decline in the estimated hazard rate. Comparison of the left and right graphs in Figure 7.4 is stark. Moreover, the effect of economic growth is small in highly transparent democracies; growth matters more for the survival of democracy when transparency is low. These results support Corollary 5.3: economic growth matters more for democratic survival in opaque, as opposed to transparent, democracies. The results also offer support for Proposition 5.9: as levels of transparency rise, the risk of democratic collapse sharply declines. Transparency reinforces democracy.

Also consistent with our theory, economic growth is negatively associated with the hazard of autocratic reversion. This result is significant at the 95 percent level in all specifications that include all observations in the sample.

TABLE 7.9. *Transparency and the hazard of democratic collapse.*

	Cond. Prior Transition		Cond. Num. Transitions		No Prior Transition	
Transparency	−0.491	−0.528	−0.413	−0.478	−1.162	−1.135
	[−0.939, −0.042]	[−0.848, −0.209]	[−0.830, 0.003]	[−0.773, −0.182]	[−1.953, −0.371]	[−1.838, −0.431]
Growth	−0.158	−0.130	−0.162	−0.135	−0.082	−0.077
	[−0.234, −0.082]	[−0.191, −0.069]	[−0.237, −0.087]	[−0.196, −0.074]	[−0.183, 0.019]	[−0.167, 0.014]
Transparency × Growth	0.023	0.027	0.045	0.040	0.127	0.131
	[−0.036, 0.081]	[−0.045, 0.098]	[0.011, 0.078]	[0.002, 0.079]	[0.020, 0.234]	[0.023, 0.238]
GDP per capita	−2.062		−1.558		−0.962	
	[−4.291, 0.168]		[−3.959, 0.844]		[−7.763, 5.838]	
Ec. Openness	−0.001		−0.004		−0.022	
	[−0.021, 0.019]		[−0.025, 0.016]		[−0.076, 0.032]	
Parliamentary	2.112		1.970		0.955	
	[0.841, 3.383]		[0.854, 3.086]		[−0.194, 2.104]	
Mixed System	0.690		0.626		0.115	
	[−0.586, 1.967]		[−0.699, 1.951]		[−1.369, 1.598]	
# of Subjects	88	88	88	88	53	53
# of Failures	19	19	19	19	8	8

Cox proportional hazards regressions of the hazard of democratic collapse. The models depicted in the first two columns, the middle two columns, and the last two columns differ in the manner in which they deal with countries that experience prior autocratic spells. Those in the first two columns report a conditional gap time model wherein the baseline hazard is separately estimated for regimes that experience a prior transition and for those that did not. Those in the next two columns estimate separate baseline hazards based on the number of prior transitions. Those in the final two columns examine only autocratic spells that did not experience a prior transition. We present estimates of coefficient values, not hazard ratios, with 95 percent confidence intervals are presented in brackets. All standard errors are clustered by democratic spell.

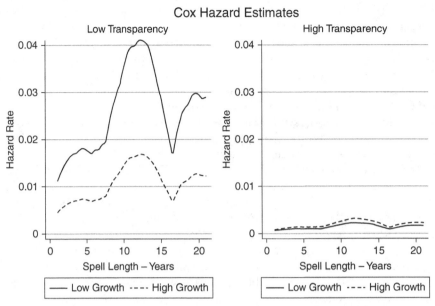

FIGURE 7.4. Democracy hazard rates as a function of transparency and growth. Plots of smoothed estimates of the hazard rate based on the fifth column of Table 7.9. The graph to the left depicts the change in the hazard rate when growth moves from the 10th percentile to the 90th percentile in the sample when the transparency score is at the 10th percentile. The graph to the right depicts the change in the hazard rate when growth changes from the 10th to the 90th percentile when transparency is at the 90th percentile. All other covariates are held at their mean values – save the *Parliamentary* and *Parliamentary* × *t* variables, which are held at 0.

Coefficients on the interaction between transparency and economic growth are consistently positive, indicating that variations in growth rates have a diminished impact on the survival of highly transparent regimes. These coefficients are imprecisely estimated, however, and never rise to levels of statistical significance.

As for the control variables, recall that GDP per capita stands out as the most robust predictor of democratic survival, according to the rich literature on the subject. Interestingly, however, the coefficients on *GDP per capita* are imprecisely estimated in our regressions. In the first model in Table 7.9, which returns the largest coefficient on this term, a one standard deviation shift in GDP per capita is estimated to lead to an approximately 50 percent decline in the hazard rate, but the effect is statistically significant only at the 10 percent level. In the models presented in the third and fifth columns of Table 7.9, the estimated coefficients are small and not statistically significant. These results stand in contrast to a highly cited literature on the effect of economic development sustaining democracy.

We attribute these new results to the inclusion of our transparency variable, which is correlated with GDP per capita. We stress that the statistical significance of the HRV index in this context suggests that transparency is part of the mechanism underlying existing findings that high-income democracies are less susceptible to collapse (Boix 2003; Boix and Stokes 2003; Przeworski and Limongi 1997; Przeworski et al. 2000). Because the HRV index and GDP per capita are positively correlated, we do not suggest that the existing development-democracy literature is misguided. Rather, our work speaks to a new causal mechanism that explain the connection between development and democracy: data disclosure sustains democracy.

As for the other control variables, the effect of *Ec. Openness* is not estimated to be statistically significant, nor is the effect of the *Mixed System* variable. In two of three models we have a surprising result: *Parliamentary* democracies are more likely to collapse than *Presidential* (recall that the *Presidential* variable is the residual category) systems.

The parliamentary result stands in contrast to a deep literature, dating at least back to Linz (1978), but is not inconsistent with theoretical arguments of the more recent work of Cheibub (2007).[18] We double-checked that parliamentary democracies are, *ceteris paribus*, at greater risk of autocratic reversion (and, as seen below, of irregular leader removal) than are presidential democracies. The finding is surprising given that so many studies have noted the stability of parliamentary democracies. We suspect that our new findings are driven (1) in part by the sample and (2) in part by the argument of Cheibub (2007).

If we use a simple Cox model to analyze our sample of states, including only indicators for *Parliamentary* and *Mixed Systems* (leaving *Presidential* systems as the residual category), and not adjusting the baseline hazard for past transitions, there is no statistically significant difference in the likelihood of autocratic reversion among the three types of democracy. The point estimate on *Parliamentary* is slightly positive, indicating increased risk of collapse, but is small and far from statistical significance. So, it seems this result is a product of the post-1980 sample – earlier findings are likely driven by past historical patterns (or by countries excluded from our 125 state sample).

As soon as one stratifies the baseline hazard by past experiences of transition, the coefficient on *Parliamentary* rises in size (by roughly 50 percent) and becomes statistically significant. So, as Cheibub (2007) suggests, parliamentary regimes only appear more stable because they are located in countries that have a history of stable rule. When we add controls for GDP per capita and transparency, the coefficient on *Parliamentary* rises still further. We conclude from this finding that parliamentary regimes have been found to be stable in the past in part because they are richer and more transparent than most presidential

---

[18] See also Shugart and Carey (1992); Power and Gasiorowski (1997); Mainwaring and Shugart (1997); Bernhard, Nordstrom, and Reenock (2001); Foweraker and Landman (2002); and Cheibub, Elkins, and Ginsburg (2011).

systems. All else equal, parliamentary regimes are not more stable than presidential ones – to the contrary, we estimate them to be less stable.

As for our central finding that transparency reduces the risk of democratic collapse, we conduct a series of additional robustness checks of our Table 7.9 baseline specifications in related work: Hollyer, Rosendorff, and Vreeland (2018). In addition to other robustness checks, the results are robust to relaxing the "type 2" restriction that the DD coding applies to the definition of democracy. Cheibub, Gandhi, and Vreeland (2010) (following Alvarez et al. 1996) treat all country-years under regimes that have yet experience a peaceful transfer of power as nondemocracies, regardless of the presence of electoral institutions. If a transfer of power takes place, country-years are retroactively coded as democratic. If we also include as democracies countries that appear to have democratic electoral institutions but have not yet experienced alternation in power (for example, Botswana), our results are substantively unchanged.

Our results are also robust to the exclusion of the interaction term between transparency and economic growth from the specification. They are also substantively unchanged by the inclusion of a quadratic term of transparency and the coefficient on the quadratic term itself is small and imprecisely estimated. Finally, our results are substantively unchanged – though, in some instances, slightly less precisely estimated – if alternative definitions of economic openness are used in place of the $\frac{Exports+Imports}{GDP}$ measure.

7.2.2 Analysis of the Regular and Irregular Removal of Democratic Leaders

Our theory in Chapter 5 contends that democracies are less likely to collapse as transparency rises – an effect brought about through low levels of public willingness to oust leaders through undemocratic methods when transparency is high. Some ousters may not appear as autocratic reversions in the analysis above, since – following a nondemocratic usurpation – new elections may be held before the year's end. So rather than focus on democratic *regimes*, we now examine the removal of democratic *leaders*.

To do this, we rely on the Archigos dataset, which codes leaders' times in office and the manner of their removal (Goemans 2006). This dataset codes leader exit as regular (leader voted out of office, subject to term limits, or retired), irregular (leader ousted via extraconstitutional methods), due to death (by natural causes or suicide), or due to foreign interventions. We are particularly interested in regular versus irregular leader exit.

Our unit of observation is the democratic leader-year, where democracy is coded based on the DD dataset used in the regressions above, and our sample runs from 1980 to 2004. Our theory indicates that transparency should be negatively correlated with the hazard of irregular removal and – insofar as "bad" leaders are more likely to be voted out of office when transparency is high – positively correlated with the hazard of regular removal.

We assess these claims through Cox competing hazards regressions, using specifications identical to those employed to assess the hazard of democratic collapse above. We use competing hazards models to assess the risk a leader faces from a *specific* form of removal (here regular or irregular removal), when these leaders also face a variety of other risks (natural death, suicide, and foreign intervention). Our models estimate the probability that a given leader is ousted by either regular or irregular methods in year t, given that they have yet to be removed via any method.

We present results from the competing hazards regressions on irregular and regular democratic leader removal in Tables 7.10 and 7.11, respectively. Consistent with our theory, transparency is associated with a fall in the hazard of irregular removal and a rise in the hazard of regular removal. Point estimates indicate that a one standard deviation increase in transparency is associated with a reduction in the hazard democratic leaders face of irregular removal of between 50 and 82 percent, when economic growth is at its mean level in the sample. This result is statistically significant at the 90 percent level or above in every specification.

Leaders in transparent democracies are less likely to be removed via extra-constitutional means, and, correspondingly, they face a higher risk of being replaced by constitutional procedures – either by losing election, facing a term limit, or choosing to retire.[19] This translates into a marginally increased hazard of regular removal in each year of their tenure – point estimates indicate that a one standard deviation increase in transparency boosts the hazard of regular removal by between 4 and 13 percent when economic growth is at its mean level in the sample. This effect is statistically significant at the 90 percent level or above in three of six specifications.

Our theory further contends that, in opaque democracies, underperforming leaders are likely to be ousted through nondemocratic means; while in transparent democracies, these leaders are ousted via the ballot box. Treating economic growth as a proxy for leader performance, our empirical results offer suggestive support for this contention. The coefficient on economic growth is negative and statistically significant in all specifications examining the hazard of irregular removal, except those specifications that drop democracies with a history of autocratic reversions from the sample. However, interpreting this coefficient requires attention to the interaction with transparency, whose

---

[19] The finding contrasts with Nolan and Nolan (2008: 29) – who contend that a democratic leader must "either die a hero or ... live long enough to ... become the villain," referring to Caesar's suspension of democracy around 44 BCE. Our results suggest that more typically, when democracy functions well, democratic leaders simply leave office through constitutional means, not necessarily dying as heroes and certainly not suspending democratic rule. Of course, in their extended story, the public official's obfuscation contributes to a collapse of the local democratic order, which is broadly consistent with our theory and findings (see Nolan and Nolan 2012).

TABLE 7.10. *Transparency and irregular leader removal.*

	Cond. Prior Transition		Cond. Num. Transitions		No Prior Transition	
Transparency	−0.407	−0.666	−0.404	−0.654	−0.833	−0.900
	[−0.815, 0.001]	[−0.997, −0.336]	[−0.846, 0.038]	[−1.011, −0.297]	[−1.377, −0.288]	[−1.382, −0.417]
Growth	−0.069	−0.064	−0.064	−0.058	−0.013	−0.030
	[−0.121, −0.016]	[−0.119, −0.008]	[−0.123, −0.006]	[−0.121, 0.006]	[−0.091, 0.066]	[−0.114, 0.054]
Transparency × Growth	0.045	0.051	0.042	0.049	0.047	0.051
	[−0.019, 0.109]	[−0.009, 0.112]	[−0.029, 0.113]	[−0.018, 0.117]	[−0.003, 0.097]	[0.015, 0.088]
GDP per capita	−0.133		−0.115		−0.042	
	[−0.271, 0.006]		[−0.246, 0.015]		[−0.127, 0.043]	
Ec. Openness	−0.003		−0.005		−0.009	
	[−0.012, 0.007]		[−0.016, 0.006]		[−0.026, 0.009]	
Parliamentary	1.244		1.174		0.070	
	[0.252, 2.235]		[0.201, 2.148]		[−1.369, 1.509]	
Mixed System	0.610		0.732		0.111	
	[−0.455, 1.675]		[−0.417, 1.881]		[−1.369, 1.591]	
# of Subjects	442	442	442	442	295	295
# of Failures	27	27	27	27	13	13

Cox competing hazards regressions of the hazard of irregular leader removal in democratic regimes. The models depicted in the first two columns, the middle two columns, and the last two columns differ in the manner in which they deal with countries that experience prior autocratic spells. Those in the first two columns report a conditional gap time model wherein the baseline hazard is separately estimated for regimes that experience a prior transition and for those that did not. Those in the next two columns estimate separate baseline hazards based on the number of prior transitions. Those in the final two columns examine only autocratic spells that did not experience a prior transition. We present estimates of coefficient values, not hazard ratios, with 95 percent confidence intervals presented in brackets. All standard errors are clustered by leader.

TABLE 7.11. *Transparency and regular leader removal.*

	Cond. Prior Transition		Cond. Num. Transitions		No Prior Transition	
Transparency	0.073	0.068	0.064	0.066	0.037	0.053
	[−0.004, 0.151]	[0.007, 0.129]	[−0.015, 0.143]	[0.004, 0.127]	[−0.055, 0.129]	[−0.018, 0.124]
Growth	−0.004	−0.002	−0.007	−0.004	0.010	0.011
	[−0.031, 0.024]	[−0.031, 0.026]	[−0.035, 0.021]	[−0.032, 0.025]	[−0.033, 0.053]	[−0.032, 0.054]
Transparency × Growth	−0.008	−0.009	−0.005	−0.007	−0.013	−0.015
	[−0.022, 0.005]	[−0.022, 0.004]	[−0.019, 0.008]	[−0.020, 0.006]	[−0.032, 0.007]	[−0.033, 0.003]
GDP per capita		−0.005	−0.003		0.002	
		[−0.021, 0.010]	[−0.019, 0.012]		[−0.014, 0.018]	
Ec. Openness		−0.003	−0.005		−0.004	
		[−0.006, −0.000]	[−0.008, −0.001]		[−0.008, 0.000]	
Parliamentary		0.186	0.184		−0.028	
		[−0.095, 0.467]	[−0.099, 0.468]		[−0.325, 0.269]	
Mixed System		−0.285	−0.278		−0.349	
		[−0.691, 0.121]	[−0.689, 0.133]		[−0.770, 0.072]	
# of Subjects	442	442	442	442	295	295
# of Failures	322	322	322	322	223	223

Cox competing hazards regressions of the hazard of regular leader removal in democratic regimes. The models depicted in the first two columns, the middle two columns, and the last two columns differ in the manner in which they deal with countries that experience prior autocratic spells. Those in the first two columns report a conditional gap time model wherein the baseline hazard is separately estimated for regimes that experience a prior transition and for those that did not. Those in the next two columns estimate separate baseline hazards based on the number of prior transitions. Those in the final two columns examine only autocratic spells that did not experience a prior transition. We present estimates of coefficient values, not hazard ratios, with 95 percent confidence intervals are presented in brackets. All standard errors are clustered by leader.

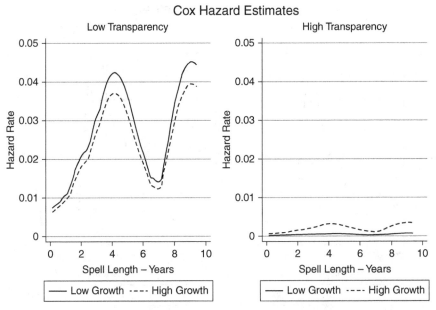

FIGURE 7.5. Transparency, growth, and the hazard of irregular leader removal. Plots of smoothed estimates of the hazard rate of irregular leader removal based on the sixth column of Table 7.10. The graph to the left depicts estimates when transparency is one standard deviation below its sample mean, while the graph to the right depicts estimates when transparency is one standard deviation above its sample mean. Solid lines depict the hazard rate when growth is one standard deviation below its sample mean, and dashed lines when growth is one standard deviation above its sample mean. Leaders face the highest risk of irregular removal when transparency and growth are both low. When transparency is high, the risk of irregular leader removal is substantially lower, regardless of the level of economic growth.

coefficient is positively signed and of similar magnitude to the coefficient on growth in all specifications.

When this interaction is taken into account (see Figures 7.5 and 7.6), the model indicates that in opaque democracies, low growth is associated with an increased hazard of irregular removal. High transparency attenuates this effect, such that growth is not associated with irregular removal in democracies with transparency scores at or above the sample mean. Monte Carlo simulations indicate that these differences in the marginal effect of growth are present in every specification, if somewhat imprecisely estimated. They are statistically significant at conventional levels in two of six specifications.

Compared to the irregular leader-removal results, the results on regular leader removal are somewhat less suited to test this aspect of our theory. We contend that leader performance should be more strongly correlated with electoral returns in transparent than opaque democracies – and thus that

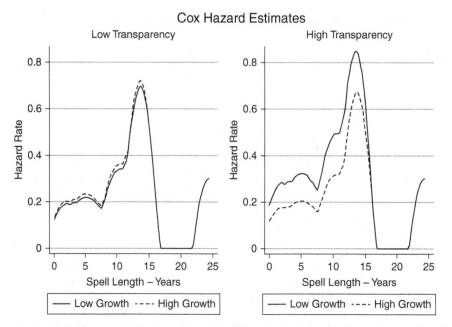

FIGURE 7.6. Transparency, growth, and the hazard of regular leader removal. Plots of smoothed estimates of the hazard rate of regular leader removal based on the sixth column of Table 7.11. The graph to the left depicts estimates when transparency is one standard deviation below its sample mean, while the graph to the right depicts estimates when transparency is one standard deviation above its sample mean. Solid lines depict the hazard rate when growth is one standard deviation below its sample mean, and dashed lines when growth is one standard deviation above its sample mean. When transparency is low, economic growth plays almost no role in the risk of regular leader removal, presumably because voters cannot accurately discern the aggregate state of the economy. When transparency is high, economic growth plays a bigger role, and lower growth increases the risk of regular leader removal.

underperforming leaders are more likely to be voted out of office in transparent democracies. However, our measure of regular leader removal encompasses instances in which leaders retire or face term limits, in addition to instances when leaders are voted out of office. This imprecision in our measure tends to bias against the discovery of any relationship. Nonetheless, the point estimates in Table 7.11 are consistent with our theory. Our results consistently indicate that the marginal effect of growth on the hazard of regular leader removal is roughly twice as large in transparent as opposed to opaque democracies. These differences in the marginal effect of growth in transparent and opaque democracies are not, however, significant at conventional levels – Monte Carlo simulations find that the difference in the marginal effect of growth has a t-statistic ranging from -0.82 to -1.58 across the six specifications.

Table 7.12 presents the estimated marginal effects of a one standard deviation shift in the growth rate in both transparent and nontransparent

TABLE 7.12. *Estimates of marginal effects of a one standard deviation increase in growth.*

	Transparent	Not Transparent	Difference
Irregular Removal	0.09	−0.41	0.49
	(0.12)	(0.08)	(0.15)
Regular Removal	−0.25	0.17	−0.27
	(0.14)	(0.07)	(0.18)

Estimated marginal effects of a one standard deviation increase in the growth rate, reported as percentage changes in the hazard (divided by 100). Estimates are based on Monte Carlo simulations from the models in the second columns of Table 7.10 and 7.11, respectively. Transparency levels are set at the 90th percentile in the sample and the 10th percentile in the sample. Growth rates are set at their mean and one standard deviation plus the mean to assess the marginal effect. Standard errors from simulations are reported in parentheses.

democracies on the hazards of both regular and irregular removal. In transparent democracies, changes in economic growth have little impact on the risk of irregular removal. Increasing economic growth, however, significantly reduces the risk of regular removal. Put another way, when growth is high, incumbents win elections, and when growth is low, incumbents lose elections (see Hibbs 1982, 2000).

In nontransparent democracies, we observe the reverse: changes in economic growth have little impact on the risk of regular removal. Presumably, the low-transparency environment prevents voters from making economically informed decisions at the ballot box. Economic growth does influence the risk of irregular removal. If economic performance is strong, those risks are reduced; if not, those risks are increased.

Table 7.10 further indicates that GDP per capita is negatively associated with the risk of irregular leadership transitions in democracies; while Table 7.11 indicates that this result is absent when considering regular forms of removal. These results are consistent with the literature that finds high-income democracies are less prone to autocratic reversion (Boix and Stokes 2003; Przeworski and Limongi 1997; Gassebner, Lamla, and Vreeland 2013). Income is negatively associated with extraconstitutional attempts to unseat leaders. Interestingly, parliamentary systems are associated with an increased hazard of irregular removal; whereas, parliamentary, presidential and mixed systems seem to experience similar rates of regular removal. Finally, *Ec. Openness* is associated with a reduction in the hazard of leader removal via regular methods, perhaps owing to the welfare consequences of trade in democracies (Mansfield, Milner, and Rosendorff 2000; Hollyer and Rosendorff 2012).

7.3 CONCLUSION

This chapter presents a multitude of empirical findings that confirm the hypotheses from the pair of theoretical models of Chapter 5. We find that transparency predicts: (1) autocratic-to-democratic transitions; (2) the ouster of autocratic regimes via mass unrest or democratization; (3) the increased frequency of anti-government demonstrations and strikes under autocracy; (4) the stabilization of democratic regimes; (5) the reduced frequency of irregular removals of democratic leaders; and (6) the (slightly) increased frequency of regular removals of (underperforming) democratic leaders. All six of these findings fit with the predictions developed in the autocratic and democratic theoretical models in Chapter 5.

We further demonstrate that, while transparency is associated with the types of threats to autocrats predicted by our theory (mass unrest and democratization), it is not positively associated with other forms of instability (assassinations, coups, guerrilla warfare, revolutions, or riots). Challenges to the regime that do not require the masses updating their higher-order beliefs on the distribution of discontent with the regime do not correlate with transparency. Indeed, transparency is associated with a *reduced* risk of autocratic collapse brought on by coups.

This chapter and the previous methodically present evidence in favor of our theory. First, illustrative examples from around the world – Africa, Asia, Europe, and Latin America – provide historical details fitting with the logic of our theoretical models. We then further build our case with bivariate comparisons of the HRV index and various measures of (in)stability. These comparisons reveal that the patterns presented in our stylized examples persist throughout a longitudinal, global perspective. Finally, this chapter's regression analyses show that our causal story remains plausible when considered alongside alternative explanations. Alternative theories may account for some subset of these findings, and we are limited in our ability to make causal claims from observational data (particularly data on infrequent events such as regime transitions). Nonetheless, the patterns we find across a wide array of outcome variables constitute substantial support for our theoretical claims. One would be hard-pressed to come up with a single alternative mechanism that would account for all of the results presented in these chapters.

Our findings speak to a long-standing concern in political science with democratization and the forces that stabilize democracy. They bear a more than passing semblance to the claims of modernization theory – which posits that democracy is most likely to emerge and survive when certain prerequisites, pertaining particularly to economic development, are satisfied. Whereas modernization theory contends the same about a rather vague notion of economic development, we contend that a specific factor, economic transparency, both facilitates democratization and stabilizes existing democracies. Unlike traditional variants of modernization theory, our claims are based on micro-founded models of individual choice and political actions, rather than on structural arguments that abstract away from political decision-making.

Our empirical results also cast light on a staple finding of both modernization theorists and their critics: that economic development is robustly associated with the survival of democratic regimes. In our results, GDP per capita is driven to statistical insignificance when we include economic transparency in regression specifications. While one should be careful not to make too much of these results – transparency and development are highly correlated, implying that including both terms may give rise to issues of co-linearity – our results suggest that transparency may be *part* of the reason why economically developed democracies are overwhelmingly secure from the threat of autocratic reversion.

Armed with rigorous theory and an assemblage of empirical evidence, we can confidently assert that economic transparency stabilizes democratic rule while it destabilizes autocratic rule through the specific threat of mass unrest.

A puzzle remains – given the dangers posed by transparency, why would autocratic leaders ever choose to disclose credible economic information? We have established that transparency renders such leaders more vulnerable to threats from below – being ousted as a result of mass protest or democratization. What then do such leaders gain from disclosure? Are benefits purely economic? Or are there political benefits for democratic and autocratic leaders to disclose data? We address these questions in Part III.

PART III

WHY DISCLOSE

> A lack of transparency results in distrust and a deep sense of insecurity.
>
> Dalai Lama, *The Telegraph* (May 13, 2012)

The journey of this inquiry now turns to a question that has been with us from the beginning: why do some governments disclose data while others do not? We have assumed throughout this project that governments have a natural inclination toward opacity. They may better accomplish their priorities in office when not subject to the insistent glare of the population. There may also be financial gains from governing under obscurity. The bright light of transparency makes all sorts of corrupt practices more difficult – bribery, extortion, gombeenism, patronage, graft, embezzlement, and so on. What economic and political benefits might transparency hold for leaders to sacrifice governing in the shadows?

For democratic regimes, Part II reveals benefits of transparency in terms of stability. But do these benefits translate into electoral gains that outweigh the potential for rent-seeking under opacity? Will democratic leaders choose transparency when tempted by the financial gains to be had when the population is left in the dark about the economy?

Turning to autocracies, we have a real puzzle: transparency can lead to unrest. So why would an autocrat ever gamble by disclosing more data? What political benefits does transparency hold for autocrats?

Part III addresses these questions in three steps. Chapter 8 examines the economic benefits of transparency focusing narrowly on investment – both domestic and foreign. The next two chapters address the political rationale to disclose – first for democratically elected leaders (Chapter 9) and then for autocratic leaders (Chapter 10).

In Chapter 8, we argue that transparency brings economic returns in the form of increased investment. Even an autocrat fearing mass unrest may be lured by the sirens of the material gain promised by transparency. As Chapter 8 demonstrates, however, these economic returns are systematically lower for autocrats than for democrats, even as Chapter 9 contends that autocratic leaders care less about these economic gains than do democratic leaders. We conclude that economic benefits may only constitute part of the story of why autocrats would disseminate data.

Chapter 9 then presents a simple political model where the political leader can obtain individual financial benefits under opacity, while society as a whole benefits economically from transparency. We show that under these simple assumptions, autocrats should not disclose. Only when we introduce democratic elections – the outcomes of which are (at least partially) determined by the overall economic performance of society – do we see an incentive for governments to disclose. When elections determine the fate of incumbents and voters choose on the basis of economic performance, the government chooses transparency.

Testing the model empirically, we revisit – now with more empirical rigor – the correlation between democracy and transparency previously presented in Chapter 4. Chapter 9 concludes that democracies in fact disclose more data than autocracies – a finding that holds for all levels of economic development.

The puzzle remains: why do autocrats ever disclose? Survival in power as the objective of leaders has pervaded this book. So Chapter 10 shifts focus from the economic benefits of transparency to autocrats' *political* calculus. We present a logic that is both serpentine and perfidious.

Chapter 10 recognizes that mass unrest is just one side of a treacherous coin confronting autocratic leaders. The flip side presents a threat from the elite inner circle, whose continued support is vital for the leader to remain in power. This elite controls the military, the police, and the economy. Without them, the leader cannot control the masses. Of course, when the masses revolt, they threaten to overturn not just the leader, but the entire regime, including inner-circle elites. When the masses stand at the gate, the loyalty of the inner circle to their leader increases.

So the logic offered in Chapter 10 for why autocrats disclose introduces an ironic twist. Precisely because transparency increases the threat autocracies face from the masses, it frees dictators from accountability to elite members of the regime. Transparency increases the threat from the masses in a manner dictators can use to cow rival members of the elite. So we can recast the question of autocratic transparency as a decision to trade off the threats of mass and elite revolt. It turns out that an autocracy sustains itself only by balancing threats from the masses and the elites off of one another – a house of cards.

8

Transparency and Investment

Investment requires a guess about the future. The investor sacrifices consumption today to create wealth tomorrow. Information about what the future might hold is necessary to make a rational decision about the trade-off between present and future consumption. Transparency informs this decision. Indeed, throughout this book, we underscore the importance of our notion of transparency – the public disclosure of aggregated information pertaining to citizen welfare – by advancing a simple premise: such disclosure matters for economic decision-makers.

We recognize that data dissemination impacts a state's economic development. Business people – charged with choosing to expand or contract production, hiring or firing employees, and deciding how to allocate portfolios – perform their tasks with a close eye on the performance of the broader economy. They rely on the government to provide data. Public goods problems inhibit the private production of aggregate economic data, so when the government fails to make such information available, it leaves economic decision-makers blind.

A reader might rightly wonder why, out of all potential economic aggregates, we choose to begin with investment. Our theoretical models focus on the overall performance of the economy, so one might consider looking at the effect of data dissemination on economic growth. As Roodman (2007a) explains, however, growth fluctuates for idiosyncratic reasons and may not represent a good starting point (see also Dreher et al. 2013). We thus take a straightforward approach and break down economic growth into its components: technological change, capital stock growth, and labor force growth. It may not be obvious how data dissemination would directly affect labor force growth, but transparency does matter for technological change and, perhaps most importantly, for growth in capital.

Investment, both foreign and domestic, is critical to economic performance. The rate of investment, in the short term, dictates the growth rate of the economy and, in the long term, the equilibrium level of production (Solow 1957). Certain investment from abroad (foreign direct investment) may additionally involve transfers of technology and skills between countries, with positive spillovers that increase the rate of growth for the economy as a whole (Grossman and Helpman 2001; Jensen 2006).

Investment is thus critical for economic performance, and theory connects it directly to the dissemination of aggregate data: investment decisions hinge on the informational environment (see Shen and Sliwinski 2015; Clore and McGrath 2015). Investors must be able to forecast future economic trends – changes in demand, rates of inflation, interest, and unemployment, for example.

Such forecasting becomes viable only where extensive information on past and current economic performance is available. If this information is lacking in a given country, potential investors may choose to place their resources elsewhere. They may choose to devote funds for consumption rather than investment or they may simply choose to hoard resources in the form of cash or commodities.

Transparency may influence investment still further. An improved informational environment does not merely increase the *level* of investment, it also reduces its *volatility*. Casual observation reveals that investment is subject to booms and busts – subject to what Keynes referred to as the "animal spirits" of investors (Keynes 2011: 66). This tendency toward volatility arises, in part, because the value of many investments hinges on the willingness of others to invest. Transparency both helps investors to anticipate changes in government policy and constrains the range of policy changes a government can make.

If transparency encourages investment and market stability, we may have a clue as to why governments disclose data. Democrats may enjoy higher reelection rates if the economy performs better. Autocrats may enjoy greater rents from public office as the economy expands – and these expanded benefits may make the risks of mass unrest worthwhile to some autocrats.

Rather than simply assume that transparency matters for economic performance, this chapter presents concrete evidence. We seek to demonstrate that transparency matters for economic outcomes. We theorize that countries in which the informational environment is rich – with high levels of transparency – enjoy significantly higher levels of fixed investment, both domestic and foreign. Additionally we claim that countries in which large volumes of economic information are made publicly available are less prone to capital flow volatility than opaque states.

We also suggest that the relationship between transparency and investment may vary across regime-types – between democracies and autocracies. Empirically, we find that domestic investment is more responsive to publicly disclosed information in democracies than in autocracies. We argue that this discrepancy across regimes arises because of differences in the composition of investors in democratic and autocratic states.

In autocracies, a larger proportion of domestic investors are closely linked with the ruling clique. These links may be formalized – in the case of state owned enterprises (SOEs), for instance – or may be informal. Autocratic governments tend to incorporate large economic interests into the "winning coalition" of the regime (Gehlbach and Keefer 2011, 2012). Such regime insiders likely have access to information collected by the government, regardless of whether it is disclosed to the broader public.

By contrast, in democracies, investors may be somewhat removed from the political elite. Hence, these investors lack privileged access to information and are reliant on disclosures made to the general public. We anticipate that domestic investors rely on and are responsive to transparency in democratic regimes.

We do not expect the same differences across regime type for foreign direct investment. Foreign investors are – almost by definition – excluded from the ruling clique of a country. We therefore anticipate that foreign direct investment (FDI) responds to transparency in both democracies and autocracies. The chapter presents evidence that this is the case. Foreign investors – as outsiders – have no particularly privileged access to autocratic over democratic governments.[1] Thus, foreign investment responds to changes in the informational environment in similar ways across regime type.

This chapter thus makes three contributions: (1) we find that transparency increases investment, both foreign and domestic; (2) transparency reduces the volatility of investment; and (3) the effect of transparency on domestic investment is somewhat muted in autocracies but strong in democracies.

In what follows, we first elaborate the relationship between investment and information. We then discuss the moderating role of institutions. Finally, we present a series of statistical findings on the relationship between transparency and investment. These results paint a consistent picture: Investment increases in transparency, particularly under democratic rule.

---

[1] This is not to say that foreign firms never have privileged access to certain governments. Their position may be improved by international agreements (see, for example, Büthe and Milner 2008; Tobin and Busch 2010; Tobin and Rose-Ackerman 2011). Moreover, scholarship in international relations has established that strategically important developing countries often have special economic relationships with powerful countries, such that firms in these developed countries have privileged access to information (see, for example, Berger et al. 2013). On a related point, see Dube and Vargas (2013). For an argument that FDI may have special status and effects distinct from domestic investment, see Rudra and Joshi (2011). We do not expect such relationships to vary systematically by regime-type. Still further research should explore exceptions. When one country has strong influence over another, the public disclosure of data may matter less because the special relationship between the countries leads to insider information obviating the need for public disclosure.

8.1 INVESTMENT AND INFORMATION

Investment, especially in industrial plant and equipment, is sensitive to the informational environment because it constitutes a gamble over the future. Investors incur expenses today in order to gain access to anticipated returns tomorrow, but estimates of these future payoffs (and their volatility) depend on the availability of reliable, credible facts about government practices and policies.

We emphasize, in this chapter, the role transparency plays in influencing capital formation and we offer three findings. First, transparency increases direct investment, both domestic and foreign. Second, evidence suggests that the effect of transparency on domestic investment is driven more by democracies than by autocracies. Finally, we find that transparency lowers investment volatility (across both regime types).

Direct investment usually means an investment in which the investor plays some some sort of role in the management of the company.[2] While information is undoubtedly an important factor in portfolio investment decisions (investment in more liquid, usually financial assets, such as equity or debt), we leave these considerations for future exploration and focus here on fixed investments.

In deciding whether to invest in a productive entity (at home or abroad), a potential investor considers two factors: (1) her expected return and (2) the uncertainty surrounding this expectation. An investor's expected return refers to the level of profit she would make averaged across a range of possible different economic scenarios, with each scenario weighted according to probability the investor attaches to its realization. The expected return is – appropriately – the profit the investor expects to make, on average.

The rational investor also pays attention to risk. Consider, for instance, an investment that guarantees a small, but positive, profit across a wide range of different possible economic scenarios. Now, consider an alternative that offers some probability of a massive profit and also the possibility of a total loss. The second investment may offer a similar expected return to the first – say both return slightly positive profits on average, across different possible scenarios. But, the second investment is riskier than the first and is less likely to be undertaken by a risk averse investor.

Transparency, we argue, reduces investor uncertainty. It does so by increasing the precision with which individuals can forecast economic scenarios. Investors seeking entry into a given market might be concerned with, for example, future changes in interest or exchange rates. Movements in these rates are likely to be a function of the current stage of the business cycle, recent movements in price levels, fiscal and monetary policies, and changes in the balance of trade. The

---

[2] The UN Conference on Trade and Development treats the acquisition of a 10 percent or greater stake in a foreign firm as an example of FDI, as opposed to portfolio investment. See http://unctadstat.unctad.org/wds/TableViewer/summary.aspx?ReportId=96740, accessed August 9, 2017.

more information investors have about these aggregates – that is, the greater the level of transparency – the more accurately they can forecast movements in economic fundamentals. Where such information is absent, investors remain more uncertain about the future.

Greater transparency, therefore, translates into reduced risk. Since investors are risk averse, they are more willing to invest, all else being equal, when transparency is high. Foreign investors are more willing to invest in a transparent country than an opaque one. Domestic investors may be more willing to invest at home, rather than abroad, or to make investments rather than consuming their resources or simply hoarding cash as transparency rises.

Of course, investors may take steps to reduce uncertainty on their own, even in environments where transparency is lacking. Multinational corporations, for instance, regularly hire risk consultants or purchase political risk insurance to help reduce the uncertainty surrounding investing in new markets. These, of course, are costly. Moreover, the private procurement of such information is subject to the public goods problem discussed in Part I (Rodrik 1995). If one firm privately determined which markets were worth entering – and if it were generally known that this firm was acquiring such information – that firm's competitors would simply piggy-back on its efforts. They would wait for it to reach an investment decision and then ape its behavior. Since acquiring investment information is costly, the danger of free-riding causes underinvestment in the procurement of information.

The claim that transparency reduces uncertainty, and thus enhances investment, echoes several studies in political science and economics (see, for example, Canes-Wrone and Park 2012; Almeida, Grant, and Phene 2002). Uncertainty over the direction of public policy and economic fundamentals has previously been linked to recessions (Baker, Bloom, and Davis 2016; Bloom 2009), currency attacks, and financial crises (Carlsson and Van Damme 1993; Leblang and Satyanath 2006; Morris and Shin 1998), longer economic crises (Shambaugh and Shen 2017), a lack of international investment (Rodrik 1991, 1995), and lower levels of international trade (Mansfield and Reinhardt 2008).

In addition to reducing risk, transparency may also raise the expected returns of potential projects. This prospect may make new projects desirable where previously the expected returns were too low to justify the investment. Projects that faced political risk (regulatory capture, expropriation, discriminatory taxation, for instance) may be made more attractive if governments can credibly commit to refrain from such infringements on property rights. Governments may use increases in transparency to indicate that they have a favorable attitude toward business, that they will not attempt to expropriate investors' assets, and that they are generally pursuing sound economic policies.[3]

---

[3] On the threat posed by government hostility toward investors and the value of credible guarantees of fair or favorable treatment, see, for instance, Acemoglu, Johnson, and Robinson (2001); Gehlbach and Keefer (2011, 2012); Jensen (2006); North and Weingast (1989); Stasavage (2003a, 2011).

Increases in disclosure may prove an effective signal of governments' good intent because disclosure is costly. This is true in a very literal sense. The gathering of aggregate economic data requires the staffing of statistical offices with knowledgeable professionals; surveys of prices and employment – like most surveys – are costly to administer; censuses sometimes require staffs of enumerators numbering in the hundreds of thousands, or even millions.[4] Perhaps more importantly, data disclosure is costly in a political sense. Governments have a natural taste for opacity. Greater disclosure implies increased accountability and reduced opportunities for rent-seeking, slacking, or blame shifting.

Transparency is costly, hence not just any government is willing to disclose. To the extent that governments vary in their desire to attract investment, only those governments that value investment most heavily are willing to bear these costs. Alternatively, to the extent that governments vary in the level of their rent-seeking or tendency to expropriate (which may be revealed by greater transparency), only those governments with the least to hide choose to disclose. Disclosure may act as a *credible* signal to investors of the government's pro-investment policy tendencies (for a related argument, see Chen and Xu 2015).

The effects of transparency on reducing uncertainty and on raising expected returns reinforce one another. Both causal mechanisms suggest that greater transparency should be associated with greater investment. Disentangling these two effects would be a difficult undertaking – one we do not attempt here. Rather, we pursue a more modest goal in this chapter and simply seek to shed light on an overarching theme of this book. Investigating the aggregate of these two effects, we ask: Is transparency associated with greater levels of investment?

We further contend that transparency reduces investment *volatility*. Scholars have linked a poor informational environment to currency attacks and financial crises due to the herd-like behavior of international financiers (Carlsson and Van Damme 1993; Leblang and Satyanath 2006; Morris and Shin 1998). These dynamics are most clear with regard to portfolio investment. Herd-like behavior may also influence some forms of direct investment, though, here, the strategic complementarities underlying this behavior are less clear-cut.

Nonetheless, we argue that the volatility of fixed investment (both foreign and domestic) is likely to decline as transparency rises. Fixed investors – purchasers of plant and equipment – face risks associated with potential taxation and expropriation, potential confiscatory regulatory action, as well as monetary and exchange rate uncertainty. Transparency alters these risks in two ways. First, greater transparency enables investors to better anticipate changes in government policy. Second, transparency likely constrains the range of policies and procedures that a government may adopt.

---

[4] For instance, the most recent Indian census required 2.7 million workers, who often had to travel enormous distances, to complete the enumeration. See "Heads Up: A National Head Count Should Show Dramatic Changes." *The Economist*, February 24, 2011, www.economist .com/node/18233732?story_id=18233732, accessed July 11, 2017.

In an opaque regulatory environment, rules, regulations, policies, and procedures may be changed without due process, advisory periods, requests for consultations, and so on. Transparency reflects the willingness of government bodies to provide information regarding their decision-making processes (Keefer and Stasavage 2003) and improves the precision with which the public observes the outcome of government decisions or the government's policy choice (Besley 2006). Consequently, in a transparent environment, regulatory and policy changes may be anticipated well in advance. Investors may thus smooth any responses to such changes over time, rather than engaging in "fire sales" when the government adopts adverse policies. Investors may also be able to alter their production process to respond to the policy environment in a manner that does not require liquidation of an enterprise (Jensen 2007).

Transparency also has a political effect: governments are more likely to face political consequences from antimarket policies or violating property rights when transparency is high. Policy is thus likely to be constrained as transparency rises and constrained in a pro-investor direction. By contrast, in opaque polities, governments are unconstrained. Some may choose to, nonetheless, adopt investor-friendly policies, but others will not. Some may alternate between pro- and anti-investor policies depending on prevailing economic conditions.

Adserà, Boix, and Payne (2003), for instance, examine the effect of information on government corruption, bureaucratic quality, and the rule of law. Democracies, they find, perform significantly better than autocracies in all four measures and the role of democracy is accentuated when information (proxied by the level of circulation of daily newspapers) flows freely. Hollyer, Rosendorff, and Vreeland (2014) establish that data dissemination is associated with the measures of bureaucratic quality, law and order, and corruption. In transparent polities, policies are constrained and constrained to be "good." By contrast, in relatively unconstrained polities, governance outcomes are typically worse on average – but, they also display high levels of variance. Autocracies, for instance, vary more than democracies in their ability to bring about economic growth and attract investment (Besley and Persson 2007; Przeworski et al. 2000).

The range of politically feasible policies is constrained in transparent, relative to opaque, environments, so the variance in investment will be lower in the former and higher in the latter. Transparency reduces the volatility of fixed investment.

8.2 THE IMPACT OF REGIME TYPE

Our argument, so far, is an economic one: transparency increases investment and lowers its volatility. In this section, we introduce political nuance. We suggest that political institutions moderate transparency's economic effects. We expect a stronger effect of transparency on investment in democracies than in autocracies – at least when we confine attention to investment undertaken by domestic actors.

In our account above, investors are autonomous from the government, reliant on the government's *public* disclosures for information on economic trends. This account resembles investors' reality under democratic rule, but not under autocratic rule.

Autocratic regimes consist not only of leaders with limited accountability to the broad polity, but also of coalitions of elites on whom the leader relies for support. These elites control many of the resources available for investment in autocratic economies. Economic and political elites often (but not necessarily always) consist of largely the same individuals. Dictators retain the support of their "winning coalition" of elites by steering private goods – cash, control over economic resources, or personal services (including providing insider information) – to the elite (Bueno de Mesquita et al. 2003). Political elites thus gain riches by virtue of their political positions, which they can, in turn, funnel toward new investments. Members of society outside of the elite are less likely to have access to the economic engines of an economy, or to the government fiscus, and therefore tend to lack the resources to invest.

Control over resources also buys access to the political elite. Autocratic governments have incentives to co-opt powerful social actors, such as successful businesspeople, by granting these actors a place within the ruling circle (Gandhi 2008; Gandhi and Przeworski 2006). Their place in the ruling coalition serves as a credible commitment to elites that they will continue to benefit from the ruling regime's policies, reducing the incentive to devote their substantial resources to securing the regime's ouster (Acemoglu 2008; Gehlbach and Keefer 2012).[5] So, under autocracy, existing investors are likely to be incorporated into the ruling elite, and their position in the ruling elite tends to reinforce their control over investment resources.

One need consider only a few examples to see the link between politically elite status and economic control under autocracy. Under the Suharto regime in Indonesia, firms that sought to participate in the country's lucrative natural resource sectors were typically forced to give substantial stakes to individuals affiliated with the regime, sometimes to Suharto's own family members.[6] Through such methods, Suharto's family was able to accumulate an estimated $35 billion in holdings over the course of his rule.[7] In Tunisia, the ruling Ben Ali family owned firms that accounted for 21 percent of all private sector profits

---

[5] On this point, and related arguments concerning credible commitments to regime elites, see Myerson (2008) and Stasavage (2003a).

[6] See, for example, Pepinsky (2013: 856); Tajima (2014: 46); and, more generally, Pepinsky (2009).

[7] See "How Did Suharto Steal $35 Billion?" by Brendan Koerner, *Slate*, March 26, 2004, www.slate.com/articles/news_and_politics/explainer/2004/03/how_did_suharto_steal_35_billion .html, accessed January 25, 2016.

in the country.[8] In other instances, the links between political power and economic control are more direct. For instance, estimates of the Egyptian military's financial holdings under the Mubarak regime indicate that it controlled 30 percent of the country's economy.[9] In China, state-controlled enterprises exercise an enormous economic role, particularly within the financial sector, which is dominated by three large state-owned banks.[10]

Because of their elite status, investors under autocracy possess access to information likely unavailable to less politically connected individuals. These elites benefit from information collected by the government that is *not* disclosed to the broader public. Under autocracy, the people with resources to invest need not rely on transparency when making their investment decisions. They can use their private sources of information. To be clear, investors under autocracy still rely on government-collected information. As discussed in Chapter 4, many autocratic governments have the capacity to aggregate economic data, and seemingly do collect it for use by the regime, but fail to disclose it to the public. When they do disclose data, however, we expect little impact on the decision-making of domestic investors because those investors already had access to the necessary information, whether it was made public or not.

In democracies, by contrast, political and economic power are less tightly linked and investors are less likely to have privileged access to information. We do not contend that economic power never buys political influence under democracy – there is considerable evidence to the contrary (for influential accounts, see Bartels 2008; Gilens and Page 2014).[11] Rather, we argue that electoral institutions and the existence of checks and balances on power limit the ability of political elites to leverage information to their economic advantage (Acemoglu, Johnson, and Robinson 2001; Jensen 2006; North and Weingast 1989). Under democracy, investors are more likely to rely on *public* information. In other words, transparency and domestic investment should be more strongly linked under democracy than under autocracy.

---

[8] See "Widespread Graft Benefited Tunisian Leader's Family, Studies Say," by Carlotta Gall, *New York Times*, June 25, 2015, www.nytimes.com/2015/06/25/world/africa/widespread-graft-expanded-after-tunisan-revolt-study-says.html, accessed January 25, 2016. On the corporate-authoritarian order under Ben Ali, see King (2003).

[9] See "Inside the Egyptian Military's Brutal Hold on Power," by Charles M. Sennot, *PBS Frontline,* January 24, 2012, www.pbs.org/wgbh/frontline/article/inside-the-egyptian-militarys-brutal-hold-on-power, accessed January 25, 2016. See also Brown and Hamzawy (2010). On the formidable political and economic position of the military in Egypt, see Masoud (2011: 24–26).

[10] On state-owned banks and state-owned enterprises, see Wei and Wang (1997) and Cull and Xu (2003). To understand how the Chinese Communist Party maintains tight control of China despite a politically decentralized system, see Landry (2008) and Birney (2014). See also Truex (2016). On the political preferences of private sector actors, see K. Tsai (2007).

[11] Indeed, the links between money and power are part of the reason that Dahl (1971) contends all extant regimes fall short of the democratic ideal, and he instead classifies modern democracies as "polyarchies."

We argue that this discrepancy across regime types in the effect of transparency on investment should not exist for *foreign* direct investment. Foreign investors may seek to gain privileged access to the inner workings of government by partnering with members of the political elite.[12] But they seek such privileges from democracies and autocracies, and, in either case, such alliances are costly. Absent such elite connections, foreign investors depend on publicly released information. Transparency therefore promotes FDI under both autocracy and democracy (Rosendorff and Shin 2012, 2015).[13]

As we turn to the data, we seek to test the following hypotheses. First, we expect investment to rise with transparency. For domestic investment, we expect a stronger effect of transparency for democracies than for autocracies. For foreign investment, we expect a positive effect of transparency regardless of regime type. Finally, we expect the volatility of investment to decline with rising transparency; the effect should hold across types of investment and across regimes.

8.3 EMPIRICS

In this section, we confront the ideas presented above with data. After introducing our measures of investment, we present descriptive data, showing the bivariate relationship of transparency and investment and, respectively, investment volatility. We then move to more rigorous analysis, controlling for alternative explanations in a regression analysis framework.

8.3.1 Measuring Investment and Volatility

We consider four measures of investment – two domestic and two foreign. As one domestic measure, we use *Gross Fixed Capital Formation* – which includes purchases of new equipment or industrial plant, land improvements, and investment in infrastructure. We also use the more inclusive *Gross Capital Formation* – which consists of gross fixed capital formation *plus* changes in business inventories. In both cases, we are concerned with long-run investments. These types of investments involve the intense use of data to make forecasts and investors must also rely on credible commitments from the government to maintain property rights. These capital formation measures (especially the fixed capital formation measure) contrast with portfolio investment, which can be easily liquidated. Both of these domestic dependent variables are

---

[12] For example, Securities and Exchange Commission (SEC) investigators allege that JP Morgan systematically hired the children of elite officials in China. See "JPMorgan Hiring Put China's Elite on an Easy Track," by Jessica Silver-Greenberg and Ben Protess, *New York Times*, August 29, 2013, https://dealbook.nytimes.com/2013/08/29/jpmorgan-hiring-put-chinas-elite-on-an-easy-track/, accessed, June 5, 2014.

[13] On the political role of FDI under autocracy, see Arias, Hollyer, and Rosendorff (forthcoming).

measured as a percentage of gross domestic product (GDP) and are made available in the World Development Indicators.

To measure foreign investment, we restrict our attention to net foreign direct investment (FDI), measured first in terms of net inflows and second as a percentage of GDP (the various measures are debated; see Li 2009; Choi 2009; Li and Resnick 2003). We focus on net FDI because of its particular sensitivity to the long-run health of the economy. Our hypotheses relate to investor use of data to make long-run forecasts and to investor reliance on government commitments to property rights (see Kerner and Lawrence 2014). FDI involves a firm in one country building or taking possession of a fixed asset – such as a plant or factory – in another country. As with the above measures, this form of investment stands as distinct from portfolio investment, which is more easily liquidated and does not require the active management of a firm on the part of investors (Jensen 2006). FDI requires investors to make a commitment.

As outsiders, foreign investors rely heavily on credible information about various features of the country's economy. Because they commit their resources in ways that prevent quick escapes, they look for credible commitments of the safety of their investments from governments. FDI thus goes to countries with governments that can credibly commit to respect the rights of business people to profit from their investments – maintaining a consistent regulatory environment, keeping taxation rates relatively low and consistent, and avoiding expropriation at all costs (Jensen 2003, 2006, 2007).[14]

The two ways we measure FDI include (1) aggregate amounts, measured as net *FDI Inflows in Billions of US Dollars* and (2) proportions of the overall recipient country economy, as net *FDI Inflows as a Percentage of GDP*. These data are made available by the United Nations Conference on Trade and Development (UNCTAD).[15]

In addition to analyzing investment *levels*, we also study investment *volatility*. We construct three measures of volatility from the measures of investment levels discussed above: *Gross Capital Formation, Gross Fixed Capital*

---

[14] Scholars have divided the activities of multinational firms engaged in FDI along two dimensions: vertical and horizontal (Jensen 2006: 43). Vertical integration involves the chain of production – seeking primary resources from some countries, low-technology assembly in other countries, and high-technology production and design in still others (Helpman 1984). For this kind of investment, firms may require data on the composition of the overall economy across primary products, low-level manufacturing, and high-skilled activities, as well as data on basic infrastructural features and the demographics of the labor force of the country. Horizontal integration involves firms performing the same activity across different countries, often marketing the same goods and services in different cultures (Markusen 1984). These ventures require data on consumption patterns and rates of inflation and economic growth. Both forms of investment require confidence in currency exchange rates, which entails data on interest rates, current and capital account pressures, as well as government taxing and spending patterns. Both forms of investment also require confidence in property rights as well, which entails political accountability – see North (1990).

[15] See http://unctad.org/en/Pages/Home.aspx, accessed August 12, 2016.

Formation, and *FDI Inflows as a Percentage of GDP*. To measure volatility, we take the standard deviation of each measure during rolling five-year windows for each country. Thus, for a given country, our measure of volatility in 1984 is the standard deviation of investment from 1980 to 1984, inclusive; our measure of volatility in 1985 is the standard deviation from 1981 to 1985, and so on.

The standard deviation captures the extent to which investment in a given five-year window varies relative to its average value – hence it is a measure of volatility. The standard deviation roughly captures the extent to which investment differs from its average value, averaged across all observations in the five-year window.

We should note that all our measures of investment contain some missing values. Since data missingness is correlated with transparency, list-wise deletion tends to increase the noise in our results. (This is particularly problematic for the *Gross Fixed Capital Formation* and *Gross Capital Formation* variables because they come from the WDI.) If countries that do disclose investment data, despite low transparency scores, systematically differ from low-transparency countries that do not disclose these data, our results are biased. Such bias, if it exists, probably runs against our main hypothesis, that transparency leads to investment. Most likely, governments that choose to report these data despite a generally closed informational environment do so because investment figures are surprisingly strong, which would bias the marginal effect of transparency on investment toward zero. With such a potential bias in mind, we turn to a preliminary look at the data.

8.3.2 Descriptive Data

The general relationship that we anticipate, that transparency is positively correlated with both domestic and foreign investment, is readily visible in a simple bivariate setting. Figures 8.1, 8.2, and 8.3 depict this relationship graphically for *Gross Capital Formation*, *Gross Fixed Capital Formation*, and *FDI Inflows as a Percentage of GDP*, respectively.[16] These graphs depict the average level of investment at various quartiles of transparency, as measured by the HRV index. That is, we plot the average level of investment for all country-years with transparency at the 24th percentile or below, the 25th–49th percentile, the 50th–74th percentiles, or the 75th percentile and above in our respective samples. In each figure, we first present the data for all country-years and then present the data for democracies only and autocracies only, respectively.

Across all three measures, investment is greatest when transparency is higher. When looking at all country-years, both *Gross Capital Formation*, and *Gross Fixed Capital Formation*, rise steadily as levels of transparency increase,

---

[16] We omit the descriptive figure for *FDI Inflows in Billions of US Dollars* because it would basically repeat what is seen in the *FDI Inflows as a Percentage of GDP* figure.

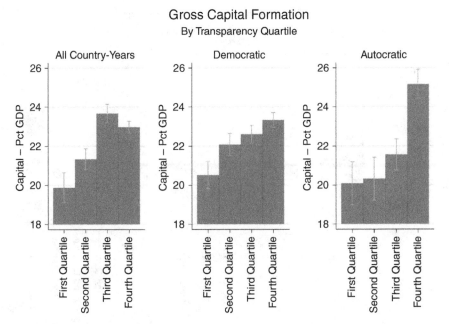

FIGURE 8.1. Gross capital formation, as a percent of GDP, versus transparency. Average gross capital formation values (as a percent of GDP) by transparency quartile. Gross capital formation values are depicted on the y-axis. The x-axis depicts transparency quartiles, where quartiles are calculated separately for each sample (respectively, all country-years, democratic country-years, and autocratic country-years, as coded by the DD dataset). The height of each bar denotes the average investment level, whiskers denote 95 percent confidence intervals around this mean. The y-axis is constrained to be of identical scale across all three graphs. Investment, as measured by *Gross Capital Formation*, tends to rise with transparency.

with some evidence of a plateau effect at the highest levels of transparency. Net FDI inflows are highest in the top quartile of transparency, but differences in investment at lower quartiles are imprecisely estimated. Oddly, levels of FDI inflows appear to fall slightly as one moves from the first to second quartile of transparency.

Evidence for our secondary claims – that domestic investment is more sensitive to transparency under democratic rule, but foreign investment is no more sensitive – is less visible in these graphs. In democracies, domestic investment appears to increase more or less linearly as transparency rises. Moving from one quartile in the transparency index to the next produces a fairly steady, large, and typically statistically significant jump in investment levels. In autocracies, investment also rises in transparency. But, movements from the first through third quartiles of transparency are associated with relatively small, and imprecisely estimated, changes in domestic investment. Investment then jumps dramatically in the highest quartile of autocratic transparency. The most

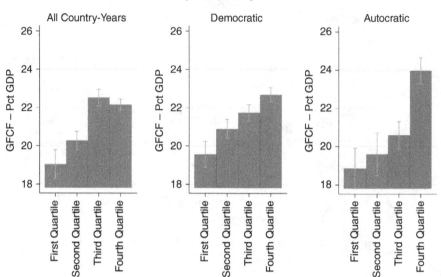

FIGURE 8.2. Gross fixed capital formation, as a percent of GDP, versus transparency. Average gross fixed capital formation values (as a percent of GDP), by transparency quartile. Gross fixed capital formation values are depicted on the y-axis. The x-axis depicts transparency quartiles, where quartiles are calculated separately for each sample (respectively, all country-years, democratic country-years, and autocratic country-years, as coded by the DD dataset). The height of each bar denotes the average investment level, whiskers denote 95 percent confidence intervals around this mean. The y-axis is constrained to be of identical scale across all three graphs. Investment, as measured by *Gross Fixed Capital Formation*, tends to rise with transparency.

transparent autocracies appear qualitatively different from their counterparts. It is important to caveat these comparisons though. Transparency scores are higher and more variable among democracies than autocracies, so a change from one quartile to the next in the democratic graphs is not directly comparable to a change from one quartile to the next in the autocratic graphs.

Turning our attention to FDI, net inflows are greatest among the most transparent country-years. However, differences between the least transparent states and those with middling levels of transparency are less marked, both for democracies and autocracies. Indeed, there is some evidence of a nonmonotonic relationship between transparency and FDI at the low end of the transparency scale. We revisit this pattern in our regression analyses below.

As for our claims regarding the relationship between transparency and investment volatility, in both democracies and autocracies, we expect volatility to decline as transparency rises. Figures 8.4, 8.5, and 8.6 graphically depict this relationship.

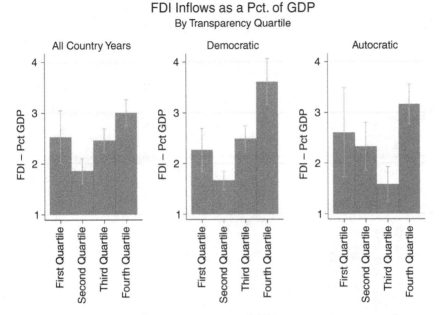

FIGURE 8.3. Net FDI inflows, as a percent of GDP, versus transparency. Average net FDI inflows (as a percent of GDP), by transparency quartile. Net FDI inflow values are depicted on the y-axis. The x-axis depicts transparency quartiles, where quartiles are calculated separately for each sample (respectively, all country-years, democratic country-years, and autocratic country-years, as coded by the DD dataset). The height of each bar denotes the average investment level, whiskers denote 95 percent confidence intervals around this mean. The y-axis is constrained to be of identical scale across all three graphs. FDI is highest among the most transparency country-years.

Figures 8.4 and 8.5 clearly demonstrate the predicted relationship. In democracies and autocracies – as well as the full sample – the volatility of both capital formation and gross fixed capital formation falls steadily in transparency. The declines in volatility from one transparency quartile to the next are typically large and statistically significant. Interestingly, domestic investment volatility is also consistently higher in autocracies than in democracies. This pattern is consistent with extant work showing that autocracies tend to have more volatile growth rates than democracies (Besley and Kudamatsu 2007; Przeworski et al. 2000) – and is broadly consistent with work that suggests that unconstrained governments have difficultly in making long-term credible commitments to protect investor rights (Gehlbach and Keefer 2011, 2012; Jensen 2003, 2006; North and Weingast 1989).

Figure 8.6 depicts FDI volatility as a function of transparency. The bivariate relationship is consistent with theoretical expectations in the full country-year sample and in the autocracy sample. Volatility declines in transparency, though there is some evidence that the relationship between these terms is

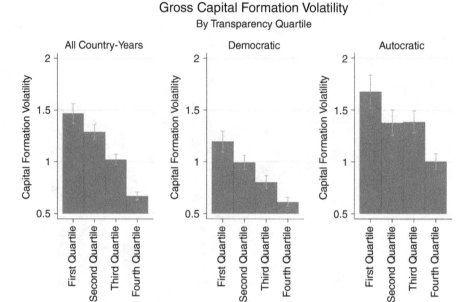

FIGURE 8.4. Gross capital formation volatility versus transparency. Average gross capital formation volatility by transparency quartile. Average gross capital volatility is calculated as the standard deviation of gross capital formation rates, measured as a percentage of GDP, within rolling 5-year windows for a given country. The height of the bars depicts mean volatility levels within each transparency quartile, while whiskers depict 95 percent confidence intervals around this mean. The y-axis is constrained to be of identical scale across all three of the graphs. Investment volatility, as measured by *Gross Capital Formation*, declines as transparency rises.

convex – transparency is subject to diminishing marginal returns in terms of reduced volatility. Interestingly, the bivariate relationship between transparency and FDI volatility is largely flat in democracies – and even *increases* in the highest quartile of transparency. Though, we should emphasize here that the weak relationship between FDI volatility and transparency appears only when we fail to include controls in our specifications. In a more rigorous analysis (see below), FDI volatility declines in transparency for democratic states. It is likely that failing to control for FDI levels obscures the relationship between volatility and transparency in this instance – volatility tends to increase as investment levels rise and, as we saw in Figure 8.3, FDI inflows are substantially higher in the most transparent democracies than in their more opaque counterparts.

This evidence – that investment (both foreign and domestic) appears greatest among the most transparent states, and that this relationship differs somewhat between democracies and autocracies – however, is only suggestive. Transparency correlates strongly with other characteristics, such as GDP per capita

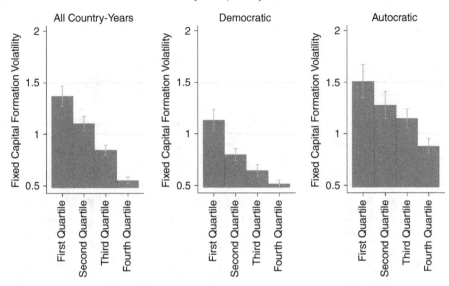

FIGURE 8.5. Gross fixed capital formation volatility versus transparency. Average gross fixed capital formation volatility by transparency quartile. Average gross fixed capital volatility is calculated as the standard deviation of gross fixed capital formation rates, measured as a percentage of GDP, within rolling 5-year windows for a given country. The height of the bars depicts mean volatility levels within each transparency quartile, while whiskers depict 95 percent confidence intervals around this mean. The y-axis is constrained to be of identical scale across all three of the graphs. Investment volatility, as measured by *Gross Fixed Capital Formation*, declines as transparency rises.

and economic openness, that may confound its relationship with all forms of investment. Specific countries may, for idiosyncratic reasons, score highly on our transparency index and attract high levels of investment. We therefore now turn to a systematic investigation of the relationship between transparency and investment, using regression techniques that allow us to adjust for these confounds.

8.3.3 Model Specifications

We now more rigorously estimate the relationship between investment and transparency. In all of our regressions, our measure of transparency is the HRV index, as described in Part I. Since this index does not have a natural interpretation as to scale, we standardize values for our respective samples by subtracting the mean sample value and dividing by the standard deviation. Regression coefficients on this term thus reflect the marginal effect

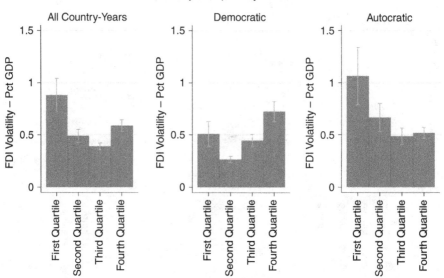

FIGURE 8.6. Foreign direct investment volatility versus transparency. Average foreign direct investment (FDI) volatility, by transparency quartile. Average FDI volatility is calculated as the standard deviation of FDI inflows, measured as a percentage of GDP, within rolling 5-year windows for a given country. The height of the bars depicts mean volatility levels within each transparency quartile, while whiskers depict 95 percent confidence intervals around this mean. The y-axis is constrained to be of identical scale across all three of the graphs. The bivariate relationship between FDI volatility and transparency is negative for the All Country and Autocratic samples. The bivariate relationship in the Democratic sample is largely flat because, we suspect, omitted control variables bias the depicted result.

of a one standard deviation shift in transparency on the relevant investment variable.

To account for alternative explanations and to attenuate potential omitted variable bias, we control for a variety of economic and political factors that may influence levels of investment. The economic factors include GDP and GDP per capita, both measured in constant 2005 PPP US dollars, where the former is measured in units of one hundred million and the latter in units of one thousand. The former control is included because larger economies may make for more attractive markets, attracting higher levels of (particularly foreign) investment. The latter control is included given that standard models of economic growth posit that investment, as a share of output, declines as per capita income rises and the economy reaches a steady state (Solow 1957). We additionally include controls for economic growth, since rapidly growing markets may attract greater investment, and for economic openness ($\frac{Exports+Imports}{GDP}$), since more open economies may tend to attract greater foreign investment. All these measures are drawn from the Penn World Table version 7.1 (Heston, Summers, and Aten 2012). We lag all such measures and additionally include a control for the lagged value of our investment outcome variable, to adjust for the dynamic nature of the data generating process, given that investment time-series are slow-moving (Beck and Katz 2011).

To control for the influence of political institutions on investment, we employ a variety of controls from the Democracy and Development Revisited (DD) dataset (Cheibub, Gandhi, and Vreeland 2010). Most importantly, this dataset provides our definition of democracy. This variable serves both to define our unit of observation – the regime-spell year, where a regime-spell is defined as one or more years of continuous autocratic or democratic rule – and acts as a control variable in our pooled specification. This control is included given extant arguments that the checks on arbitrary government behavior entailed by democracy serve to promote investment, both foreign and domestic (North and Weingast 1989; Jensen 2003, 2006). We subsequently divide our sample between democracies and autocracies, to examine our hypothesis regarding the differential effects of transparency in each.

In addition to the democracy variable, we control for a variety of additional institutional features, as measured by the DD dataset. These include an indicator equal to one if a meaningful legislature is present (this variable is equal to one for all democracies, but only a subset of autocracies); an indicator equal to one if the head of state is a member of the military; and indicators for, respectively, parliamentary and semi-presidential (mixed) democracies. We include the legislature and military head measures because a literature suggests that such institutions influence investment under autocratic rule (Gehlbach and Keefer 2011, 2012; Jensen, Malesky, and Weymouth 2014). We include the various indicators for democratic institutions because of evidence that economic policies and political behavior differ systematically across different types of democracy (Persson, Roland, and Tabellini 1997, 2000; Samuels and Shugart 2010; Tsebelis 2002).

We assess the relationship between these various forms of investment and transparency using a series of varying-intercepts hierarchical models, all of the form:

$$investment_{i,t} \sim N(\mu_{i,t}, \sigma_I^2)$$

where

$$\mu_{i,t} = \alpha_i + \rho \; investment_{i,t-1} + X_{i,t-1}\beta$$
$$\alpha_i \sim N(Z_i\gamma, \sigma_\alpha^2) \tag{8.1}$$

Here i denotes regime-spell; t denotes year; $X_{i,t-1}\beta$ is a vector of time-varying controls and associated coefficients; $Z_i\gamma$ is a vector of time-invariant controls and associated coefficients; and σ_I^2 and σ_α^2 capture the variance of the regression and of the varying intercepts term, respectively. To be clear, $X_{i,t-1}$ includes our measure of transparency. It also includes the following time-varying control variables: *Lag investment*, *GDP per capita*, *Growth*, *Ec. Openness*, and *GDP*. The time-invariant controls are *Democracy*, *Legislature*, *Mixed*, and *Mil. Head*. Technically, these political institutions – other than democracy – may vary within a regime-spell year, though they do so very rarely. If fundamental constitutional reforms are launched or a given regime is toppled and replaced by another of the same autocratic/democratic type, these terms may change. However, given the infrequency of these changes, we treat these terms as invariant over time and take the median value of the institutional measures within a given regime-spell as our measures of political institutions.

The varying-intercepts hierarchical modeling approach that we employ represents an efficient means of estimating relationships where observations are clustered into groups (in our case, regime-spells) and in which characteristics of interest (political institutions) vary little or not at all over time (Gelman and Hill 2006; Jusko and Shively 2005).[17]

We first investigate our hypotheses that (1) transparency should be positively associated with investment and (2) this relationship should be stronger in democracies than autocracies for domestic investment. We assess the first hypothesis using a sample of all regime-spell years in our data, using a regression of the form of Equation 8.1. This approach has the advantage of maximizing the degrees of freedom for our analysis – our estimates are less noisy if we make use of all available data.

In our analysis of the second hypothesis, we split our sample between democracies and autocracies, and estimate regressions of the form of Equation 8.1 in each sample. This approach allows for maximal flexibility of our empirical specifications – all model parameters are free to vary by regime-type.

We also use varying-intercepts hierarchical models to assess the relationship between transparency and volatility. All are analogous to the models presented in Equation 8.1, with volatility substituted for investment. In addition to the controls discussed above, all such specifications include a control for investment in levels. Volatility tends to increase as investment levels rise, ensuring that our results would be biased toward zero if this control were not included.

As with the investment results in levels, we estimate our models of volatility both for the full sample of country-years and in separate democratic and autocratic samples. We do not have strong expectations about how the relationship between transparency and volatility varies across regime types. However, since we expect the relationship between investment (in levels) and transparency to vary across regimes, we can avoid potential confounding by splitting the sample and allowing the coefficients on control terms to vary across the two samples.

---

[17] We estimate these models via MCMC, using JAGS 3.3.0, as run from R.3.0.2. For a discussion of an alternative modeling approach, see Plümper and Troeger (2007).

TABLE 8.1. *Investment and transparency: all regime-years.*

	Gross Capital Formation	Gross Fixed Capital Formation	FDI Inflows (Billions USD)	FDI Inflows (Pct. GDP)
Transparency	0.24	0.18	0.48	0.332
	[0.034, 0.43]	[0.002, 0.346]	[0.039, 0.876]	[0.102, 0.549]
Lag Investment	0.821	0.845	0.773	0.455
	[0.789, 0.852]	[0.82, 0.87]	[0.742, 0.805]	[0.419, 0.489]
GDP per capita	−0.018	−0.012	0.033	−0.008
	[−0.039, 0.002]	[−0.029, 0.004]	[−0.006, 0.068]	[−0.032, 0.014]
Growth	0.055	0.062	0.011	0.058
	[0.034, 0.077]	[0.043, 0.082]	[−0.025, 0.046]	[0.04, 0.078]
Ec. Openness	0.007	0.006	0.012	0.018
	[0.004, 0.012]	[0.003, 0.01]	[0.004, 0.02]	[0.013, 0.022]
GDP	0.018	0.016	0.367	−0.002
	[−0.001, 0.037]	[0.001, 0.032]	[0.312, 0.424]	[−0.025, 0.02]
Democracy	−0.113	−0.185	−0.387	−0.057
	[−0.564, 0.392]	[−0.743, 0.202]	[−1.24, 0.57]	[−0.601, 0.56]
Legislature	0.424	0.336	−0.464	−0.448
	[−0.46, 1.34]	[−0.305, 1.099]	[−2.258, 1.316]	[−1.606, 0.531]
Parliamentary	0.384	0.359	0.119	0.051
	[−0.19, 0.887]	[−0.04, 0.767]	[−0.937, 1.121]	[−0.644, 0.652]
Mixed	0.238	0.276	0.059	0.149
	[−0.373, 0.907]	[−0.211, 0.783]	[−1.213, 1.335]	[−0.653, 0.984]
Mil. Head	−0.373	−0.339	0.045	−0.146
	[−0.817, 0.061]	[−0.672, 0.003]	[−0.839, 0.893]	[−0.699, 0.354]
σ	3.732	3.383	8.1	3.96
	[3.629, 3.824]	[3.299, 3.472]	[7.905, 8.295]	[3.861, 4.051]
N	3213	3160	3354	3354

Results of a regression of investment on transparency. Different measures of investment are noted at the top of the table. Gross capital formation and gross fixed capital formation are measured as a percentage of GDP. Coefficients on time-varying covariates are presented in the upper panel and those on time-invariant (regime-level) covariates in the lower panel. Ninety-five percent credible intervals are presented in brackets.

More generally, this approach allows for greater flexibility and avoids bias if the relationship between any of our control terms and volatility varies with regime-type.

8.3.4 Regression Results

Results depicting the relationship between transparency and investment from the full sample are presented in Table 8.1. Estimates of time-varying parameters are presented in the upper panel of Table 8.1, while estimates of time-invariant parameters are presented in the next panel down.

In all specifications, the coefficient on transparency is positive and precisely estimated. The 95 percent credible intervals are all bounded away from zero,

TABLE 8.2. *Investment and transparency: democracy versus autocracy.*

	Gross Capital Formation		Gross Fixed Capital Formation		FDI Inflows (Billions USD)		FDI Inflows (Pct. GDP)	
	Dems	Auts	Dems	Auts	Dems	Auts	Dems	Auts
Transparency	0.253	0.06	0.147	0.035	0.404	0.096	0.248	0.046
	[0.042, 0.485]	[−0.189, 0.345]	[−0.05, 0.326]	[−0.199, 0.281]	[−0.338, 1.176]	[0.014, 0.183]	[0.07, 0.428]	[−0.281, 0.377]
Lag Investment	0.754	0.834	0.792	0.843	0.753	0.98	0.651	0.395
	[0.709, 0.812]	[0.794, 0.873]	[0.747, 0.841]	[0.807, 0.872]	[0.707, 0.799]	[0.95, 1.014]	[0.604, 0.7]	[0.347, 0.445]
GDP per capita	−0.017	−0.011	−0.007	−0.013	0.069	0.004	−0.006	−0.021
	[−0.045, 0.012]	[−0.047, 0.026]	[−0.031, 0.017]	[−0.046, 0.019]	[−0.007, 0.152]	[−0.007, 0.013]	[−0.024, 0.014]	[−0.064, 0.022]
Growth	0.121	0.033	0.131	0.039	0.049	0.002	0.041	0.063
	[0.086, 0.156]	[0.006, 0.064]	[0.104, 0.162]	[0.011, 0.067]	[−0.076, 0.194]	[−0.007, 0.011]	[0.013, 0.07]	[0.036, 0.088]
Ec. Openness	0.015	0.005	0.01	0.006	0.035	0.001	0.018	0.016
	[0.008, 0.022]	[−0.001, 0.011]	[0.004, 0.017]	[0, 0.011]	[0.011, 0.056]	[−0.001, 0.003]	[0.013, 0.024]	[0.01, 0.024]
GDP	0.013	0.063	0.01	0.056	0.388	0.197	0.001	0.006
	[−0.007, 0.037]	[0.007, 0.125]	[−0.008, 0.028]	[0.003, 0.109]	[0.301, 0.479]	[0.155, 0.238]	[−0.015, 0.015]	[−0.071, 0.073]
Parliamentary	0.568		0.458		−0.23		−0.009	
	[−0.06, 1.175]		[−0.075, 0.936]		[−1.765, 1.327]		[−0.394, 0.402]	
Mixed	0.247		0.273		−0.121		0.071	
	[−0.414, 0.952]		[−0.297, 0.849]		[−2.045, 1.74]		[−0.391, 0.531]	
Legislature		0.411		0.341		−0.025		−0.389
		[−0.632, 1.449]		[−0.575, 1.204]		[−0.343, 0.293]		[−1.585, 1.063]
Mil. Head		−0.467		−0.431		−0.023		−0.274
		[−1.106, 0.118]		[−0.985, 0.073]		[−0.22, 0.162]		[−1.024, 0.515]
σ	2.754	4.501	2.364	4.142	11.412	1.707	2.448	4.949
	[2.647, 2.856]	[4.342, 4.672]	[2.261, 2.456]	[3.994, 4.304]	[11.049, 11.822]	[1.649, 1.762]	[2.364, 2.534]	[4.767, 5.109]
N	1633	1580	1618	1542	1640	1714	1640	1714

Results of a regression of investment on transparency. Different measures of investment are noted at the top of the table. Gross capital formation and gross fixed capital formation are measured as a percentage of GDP. Estimates for the democratic sample (Dems) and those for the autocratic sample (Auts) are presented side by side. Coefficients on time-varying covariates are presented in the upper panel and those on one time-invariant (regime-level) covariates in the lower panel. Ninety-five percent credible intervals are presented in brackets.

implying that we can be quite certain that these results are not simply the product of statistical noise. A one standard deviation rise in transparency is associated with an increase of between 0.03 and 0.43 percentage points (of GDP) in gross capital formation and an increase of between 0.002 and 0.35 percentage points in gross fixed capital formation.

The positive relationship also holds for net FDI inflows, and appears to be stronger. A one standard deviation increase in transparency is associated with an increase in FDI as a percentage of GDP of between 0.1 and 0.55 percentage points, with a point estimate of 0.33. Where FDI is measured in absolute flows (rather than as a percentage of GDP), this increase is between $39 million and $871 million per annum, with a point estimate of $480 million.

These estimates represent contemporaneous effects. Because we include the lagged value of investment in all regressions, the long-term impact of a one standard deviation increase in transparency can be calculated by multiplying the above by $\frac{1}{1-\rho}$, where ρ is the coefficient on the lagged investment term. In other words, the long-term effects of transparency are between 6.5 times (in the case of gross fixed capital formation) and 1.8 times (in the case of FDI measured as a percent of GDP) greater than the contemporaneous effects.

Turning to the effects of our control variables, we find mainly anticipated results. Economic growth is consistently associated with increased investment flows, as is economic openness. GDP also is typically associated with increased investment – particularly, as one might anticipate, where FDI is measured in dollar terms rather than as a percent of GDP. Interestingly, estimates on GDP per capita are consistently estimated imprecisely and are close to zero. Estimates on the political controls do not rise to levels of conventional significance.

Table 8.2 presents our results when we split our sample between democracies and autocracies. We place results side-by-side for democracies and autocracies. Recall that we should expect the marginal effect of transparency to be greater in democracies than autocracies, particularly with regard to domestic investment (gross capital formation and gross fixed capital formation). As before, we place time-varying controls in the top panel of Table 8.2 and time-invariant controls in the next panel down.

The results in Table 8.2 indicate that transparency is positively associated with investment in democracies. Coefficients are positive in all specifications, and 95 percent credible intervals are bounded away from zero when we examine gross capital formation and FDI as a percent of GDP. Results when examining gross fixed capital formation border on significance at conventional levels (the lower bound of the 95 percent credible interval is -0.05). Estimates when FDI is measured in dollars are sufficiently noisy that they remain far from conventional levels of significance.

Point estimates for autocracies, while consistently positive, are smaller and less precisely estimated than those for democracies. Indeed, transparency is only significantly associated with FDI (measured in dollars) under autocratic rule. In part, the discrepancies between the FDI measures may be explained by model

TABLE 8.3. *Differences between democracies and autocracies in contemporaneous marginal effect of one standard deviation increase in transparency.*

Gross Capital Formation	0.084
	[−0.207, 0.378]
Gross Fixed Capital Formation	0.048
	[−0.237, 0.294]
FDI (Billions USD)	0.134
	[−0.314, 0.552]
FDI (pct. GDP)	0.095
	[−0.229, 0.446]

Estimated difference in the contemporaneous marginal effect of shift in transparency (one autocratic standard deviation) between democracies and autocracies. Positive values indicate a larger effect in democracies, negative coefficients indicate the reverse. Ninety-five percent credible intervals presented in brackets.

fit. Notice that the standard error of the regression is far lower under autocracy than under democracy when inflows are measured in dollar terms, and far lower under democracy than under autocracy when FDI is measured as a percent of GDP.

While the coefficient estimates for autocracies are consistently smaller than for democracies in Table 8.2, in line with our expectations from our second hypothesis, these values should not be directly compared. This is because the coefficients reflect the marginal effect of a one standard deviation shift in transparency, *in the sample under consideration.* HRV scores vary more among democracies than autocracies, hence a one standard deviation shift in the democratic sample represents a larger change than in the autocratic sample. Moreover, when considering the long-run effects of transparency, one must also account for discrepancies in the coefficient on the lagged investment term across the democratic and autocratic specifications.

We address these issues in Tables 8.3 and 8.4, which present the estimated difference in the marginal effect of transparency under democracy and autocracy, along with measures of the certainty of this difference.[18]

---

[18] To construct these estimates, we transform 2,000 draws from the posterior density on the transparency coefficient from the regressions in the democratic sample. We do this by multiplying these values by the ratio of the standard deviation of transparency among autocracies to the standard deviation of transparency among democracies. This step ensures that the coefficient from the democratic sample is in the same unit of measure as the coefficient from the autocratic sample. We then subtract 2,000 draws of the coefficient from the autocratic sample from the 2,000 draws of the (transformed) coefficient from the democratic sample. Table 8.3 presents the mean value of these differences, across the 2,000 draws, and 95 percent credible intervals around this mean.

TABLE 8.4. *Differences between democracies and autocracies in long-run marginal effect of one standard deviation increase in transparency.*

Gross Capital Formation	0.233
	[−1.35, 2.037]
Gross Fixed Capital Formation	0.184
	[−1.474, 1.859]
FDI (Billions USD)	−90.574
	[−43.613, 46.506]
FDI (pct. GDP)	0.329
	[−0.284, 0.922]

Estimated difference in the long-run marginal effect of shift in transparency (one autocratic standard deviation) between democracies and autocracies. Positive values indicate a larger effect in democracies, negative coefficients indicate the reverse. Differences reflect long-run equilibrium marginal effects, constructed by multiplying the coefficient value on transparency by $\frac{1}{1-\rho}$ where ρ is the coefficient on the lagged dependent variable. Ninety-five percent credible intervals presented in brackets.

Table 8.3 reveals that, even after adjusting for the greater variation in transparency scores under democracy than under autocracy, the marginal effect of transparency on investment is consistently larger in democracies. This finding is in line with our second hypothesis. However, this evidence is, at most, suggestive. While these differences in marginal effects are present in all regressions, and are substantively large, they are not precisely estimated. The 95 percent credible intervals include zero in all cases. Moreover, we do not see a discrepancy in these contemporaneous effects between FDI and domestic investment – all the differences presented in Table 8.3 are positive.

Table 8.4 presents differences in the estimated *long-run* equilibrium marginal effects of an (equal) shift in HRV scores in democracies and autocracies. Here, again, we see that transparency is more strongly associated with domestic investment under democracy – though, again, these results are only suggestive. With regard to foreign investment, we see a discrepancy depending on whether FDI is measured in dollars or as a percent of GDP. When measured in dollars, the long-run effect of a shift in transparency is greater in autocracies – though this difference is not statistically significant. When measured as a percentage of GDP, we see the reverse, though again the difference is not statistically significant. In sum, these results present some suggestive evidence in favor of the theoretical mechanisms we discuss. But, this evidence is only suggestive – our estimates are too noisy to point to definitively indicate systematic differences in investors' response to transparency across regime-types.

We conclude that while there is suggestive evidence of a stronger effect of transparency on domestic investment in democracies, we have greater

TABLE 8.5. *Investment volatility and transparency: all regime-years.*

	Gross Capital Formation	Gross Fixed Capital Formation	FDI Inflows (Pct. GDP)
Transparency	−0.066	−0.064	−0.017
	[−0.093, −0.039]	[−0.09, −0.039]	[−0.05, 0.013]
Lag Volatility	0.801	0.809	0.845
	[0.778, 0.823]	[0.781, 0.835]	[0.821, 0.87]
GDP per capita	−0.001	−0.001	0.002
	[−0.003, 0.002]	[−0.004, 0.001]	[−0.001, 0.006]
Growth	−0.005	−0.005	0.003
	[−0.009, −0.002]	[−0.008, −0.002]	[0.001, 0.005]
Ec. Openness	0	0	0
	[0, 0.001]	[0, 0.001]	[0, 0.001]
GDP	−0.002	−0.001	−0.001
	[−0.004, 0.001]	[−0.004, 0.001]	[−0.004, 0.002]
Investment	0.076	0.078	0.063
	[0.057, 0.098]	[0.058, 0.1]	[0.043, 0.086]
Democracy	0.014	0.022	−0.061
	[−0.037, 0.062]	[−0.03, 0.082]	[−0.141, 0.024]
Legislature	0.051	0.058	−0.014
	[−0.077, 0.186]	[−0.074, 0.201]	[−0.18, 0.129]
Parliamentary	−0.033	−0.026	0.032
	[−0.094, 0.034]	[−0.09, 0.042]	[−0.063, 0.125]
Mixed	0.032	0.034	0.084
	[−0.034, 0.112]	[−0.04, 0.113]	[−0.02, 0.206]
Mil. Head	0.033	0.02	−0.007
	[−0.016, 0.082]	[−0.034, 0.08]	[−0.082, 0.076]
σ	0.487	0.453	0.498
	[0.475, 0.501]	[0.44, 0.466]	[0.486, 0.511]
N	2710	2652	3192

Results of a regression of investment volatility on transparency and covariates. Outcome variables are noted above each column. These include the standard deviation over a rolling five-year window of gross capital formation (Capital Volatility), gross fixed capital formation (GFCF Volatility), and net FDI inflows (FDI Volatility) all measured as a percentage of GDP. Ninety-five percent credible intervals are presented in brackets. Coefficients on time-varying covariates are presented in the upper panel and on time-invariant (regime-level) covariates in the lower panel.

confidence in the overall finding that rising transparency leads to increased investment, both domestic and foreign, regardless of regime type.

Finally, we turn to investment volatility. Table 8.5 presents estimates from the full sample. As in the previous tables, we place time-varying controls in the top panel of the table and time-invariant controls in the next panel down.

As can be seen in Table 8.5, a one standard deviation increase in transparency is associated with a 0.066 decline in gross capital volatility and a 0.064 decline in gross fixed capital volatility. However, as before, this is a contemporaneous association. The long-run equilibrium decline in volatility levels in terms of standard deviations is 0.33 as implied by the coefficient on the lagged dependent variable. In both instances, the 95 percent credible intervals are bounded away from zero.

The relationship between transparency and volatility in FDI is somewhat weaker and less precisely estimated. A one standard deviation is associated with a contemporaneous decline in FDI volatility of 0.017 standard deviations, and a long-run decline of 0.11 standard deviations. The 95 percent credible intervals on this term overlap zero, suggesting lower confidence in the FDI results.

Table 8.6 presents results from models estimated separately on both democratic and autocratic samples. Here transparency is robustly associated with a decline in volatility across all forms of investment. Estimates for the relationship between transparency and volatility in gross capital and gross fixed capital formation are much as in the above. FDI volatility is also negatively associated with transparency – a result that (unlike in the above) is precisely estimated at the 95 percent level for democracies and somewhat less so (at the 90 percent level) for autocracies. In democracies, a one standard deviation increase in transparency is associated with a roughly 0.02 standard deviation decline in FDI volatility contemporaneously, and a 0.1 standard deviation decline in the long-run. In autocracies, the analogous figures are a 0.03 and 0.4 standard deviation decline, respectively.

It seems that both the relationship between FDI volatility and FDI in levels, and the relationship between current and past volatility, varies systematically across democracies and autocracies, obscuring the relationship with transparency in the full sample. Taken altogether, our analysis suggests that transparency reduces the volatility of both domestic and foreign investment.

8.4 CONCLUSION

Transparency is robustly associated with increased levels of investment. Across a variety of different measures, which capture the activities of both domestic and foreign investors, a richer informational environment leads to higher investment levels. This finding fits with the theory developed in this chapter: greater availability of public information reduces investor uncertainty, which encourages capital formation.

The chapter also provides some evidence for one mechanism that may drive the relationship between transparency and investment. More transparency is robustly associated with declines in investment volatility. In environments where investors are less susceptible to unforeseen policy shifts and the vagaries of unpredictable governmental regulation, investment flows are less prone to volatility.

Finally, the chapter suggests that the relationship between transparency and investment depends to some extent on regime type. Our empirical analysis

TABLE 8.6. *Investment volatility and transparency: democracies versus autocracies.*

	Capital Volatility (Dem)	Capital Volatility (Aut)	GFCF Volatility (Dem)	GFCF Volatility (Aut)	FDI Volatility (Dem)	FDI Volatility (Aut)
Transparency	-0.06 [-0.095, -0.028]	-0.067 [-0.101, -0.025]	-0.061 [-0.091, -0.029]	-0.06 [-0.095, -0.024]	-0.023 [-0.046, 0]	-0.033 [-0.069, 0.006]
Lag Volatility	0.78 [0.74, 0.82]	0.783 [0.748, 0.815]	0.784 [0.748, 0.826]	0.797 [0.763, 0.831]	0.764 [0.74, 0.789]	0.91 [0.86, 0.954]
GDP per capita	-0.003 [-0.007, 0]	0.001 [-0.004, 0.007]	-0.003 [-0.007, 0]	0 [-0.005, 0.005]	0.005 [0.002, 0.007]	-0.002 [-0.006, 0.003]
Growth	-0.013 [-0.017, -0.008]	-0.002 [-0.007, 0.002]	-0.011 [-0.015, -0.007]	-0.002 [-0.007, 0.002]	-0.003 [-0.008, 0.001]	0.004 [0.001, 0.007]
Ec. Openness	0.001 [0, 0.002]	0 [-0.001, 0.001]	0.001 [0, 0.002]	0 [-0.001, 0.001]	0.001 [0, 0.001]	0 [-0.001, 0.001]
GDP	0 [-0.003, 0.003]	-0.006 [-0.014, 0.002]	0 [-0.002, 0.003]	-0.006 [-0.013, 0.001]	-0.001 [-0.003, 0]	-0.001 [-0.009, 0.007]
Investment	0.06 [0.036, 0.084]	0.108 [0.069, 0.152]	0.068 [0.044, 0.092]	0.105 [0.068, 0.147]	0.105 [0.082, 0.129]	0.043 [0.007, 0.08]
Parliamentary	-0.029 [-0.106, 0.041]		-0.039 [-0.126, 0.031]		-0.004 [-0.05, 0.035]	
Mixed	0.049 [-0.035, 0.133]		0.04 [-0.047, 0.124]		0.046 [-0.011, 0.097]	
Legislature		0.065 [-0.132, 0.256]		0.053 [-0.107, 0.209]		-0.015 [-0.178, 0.132]
Mil. Head		0.014 [-0.063, 0.094]		-0.009 [-0.09, 0.069]		-0.022 [-0.103, 0.065]
σ	0.359 [0.345, 0.374]	0.598 [0.573, 0.62]	0.328 [0.315, 0.341]	0.562 [0.54, 0.585]	0.372 [0.359, 0.384]	0.604 [0.58, 0.625]
N	1461	1246	1446	1206	1583	1609

Results of a regression of investment volatility on transparency and covariates. Outcome variables for democracies (Dems) and autocracies (Auts) are noted above each column. These include the standard deviation over a rolling five-year window of gross capital formation (Capital Volatility), gross fixed capital formation (GFCF Volatility), and net FDI inflows (FDI Volatility) all measured as a percentage of GDP. Ninety-five percent credible intervals are presented in brackets. Coefficients on time-varying covariates are presented in the upper panel, and on time-invariant (regime-level) covariates in the lower panel.

provides point estimates consistent with the claim that *domestic* investment responds more to information under democracy than autocracy. While we cannot reject the claim that these discrepancies are merely chance findings and not systematic, the general positive association across transparency, economic performance, and democracy appears particularly strong.

Still, our statistical tests do not conclusively indicate that splitting the sample by regime-type is the appropriate approach. Transparency clearly predicts investment when we consider all countries. When we split the sample, this relationship remains for democracies, and coefficients are smaller and less precisely estimated for autocracies. But, the differences between democracies and autocracies are not themselves, typically, statistically significant.

Our evidence thus indicates that transparency is associated with increased investment in all settings, though the evidence for this association is somewhat weaker (with regard to domestic investment) in autocracies. The results of this chapter therefore address the puzzle left to us by the previous chapter. Why do autocrats ever disclose data? Chapter 5 shows that doing so increases all sorts of risks for autocrats. Enhancing the informational environment enhances the ability of citizens to coordinate in their protests against autocratic regimes. Mass unrest leading to democratization or the replacement of the autocratic regime by another becomes more likely. But this chapter suggests that the economic benefits may outweigh the risks: autocratic rents may also increase with transparency. If investors – especially foreign investors – are more likely to put their resources into a country where transparency is high, autocrats have an incentive to disclose data. Doing so may lead to an expansion in economic activity, which lines the pockets of the ruling clique. Moreover, autocracies are known to extract rents directly from investment activity. These economic incentives offset the political risks of disclosing data.

Some readers may not, however, find this economic answer satisfying. First, the domestic investment results for autocracies are imprecisely estimated. Second, the strongest investment result for autocracies pertains to *foreign* investment, and many scholars of international relations and political economy believe that domestic factors reign paramount in the calculus of governments when conducting economic policy.[19] Autocrats may care more about domestic investors because they are connected to the ruling clique, and transparency may not be required to incentivize the participation of domestic elites in the economy.

In raising these doubts, we do not mean to dismiss the importance of the findings of this chapter for autocracies. We do have evidence that transparency

[19] Examples of research promoting this view include Bueno de Mesquita et al. (2003); Gehlbach and Keefer (2011, 2012); Gilligan (1997); Grossman and Helpman (1994); Hollyer and Rosendorff (2012); Mansfield, Milner, and Rosendorff (2000, 2002); Milner (2006b); Milner and Tingley (2015). For somewhat contrasting views on the manner in which international economic policy shapes domestic politics, see Gourevitch (1978); Hollyer (2010); Malesky (2008).

increases investment for *all* regime-types, and the statistical justification for splitting the sample is not strong enough for us to disregard this overarching finding. Rather, we raise doubts about the economic argument about why autocrats may disclose data to force ourselves to consider political explanations for why autocrats disclose.

In the next chapters we more fully explore the effect of transparency on the decisions of democrats and autocrats, respectively, to disclose. Armed with the finding that transparency enhances investment, we first explore the incentives of democracies more so than autocracies to choose transparency (Chapter 9). Then we turn to the puzzle of disclosure under autocracy (Chapter 10). The economic benefits may influence democratic leaders more than they influence their autocratic counterparts because they face different logics of political survival. In particular, we contrast the risks that autocrats face from the masses to those risks that autocrats face from within their ruling cliques. Just as transparency may destabilize from without, it may consolidate from within: As transparency encourages masses of citizens to take to the streets, the loyalties of the inner circle to their leader may become stalwart.

9

Why Democracies Disseminate More Data
than Autocracies

Are democracies more transparent than autocracies? Some would seek to answer this question by definition. The current secretary general of the OECD, Angel Gurría, identifies transparency as a key ingredient "necessary for the functioning of democracies."[1] Many people agree: transparency has become synonymous with democracy. As Shapiro (2003: 200) suggests, "democratic leaders can never be entirely free from a commitment to truth-telling." One could argue that if a country lacks transparency, it is simply not a democracy.

But should we assume, by definition, that democracies inherently seek to disseminate more data than autocracies? Doing so would preclude important questions, such as whether electoral competition leads governments to provide honest assessments of the economy or whether it causes governments to hide the truth.

Indeed, their vulnerability to public disapproval through elections may make democratic officials *more* inclined to obfuscate or withhold information concerning the performance of their policies than their autocratic counterparts – who need worry less about public perceptions. Political scientists and economists, in fact, have offered theories and evidence that the policymaking of democratic governments is shaped by issues of information revelation. Importantly, democratic governments have incentives to obfuscate (see, for example, Beitz 1989; Busch 2000; Stasavage 2004; Kono 2006; Rejali 2007; Mani and Mukand 2007; Culpepper 2010; Harding and Stasavage 2014; Jacobs and King 2016).

Still, governments that survive by winning elections also have incentives to disclose economic data. The previous chapter reveals an association between

[1] See www.oecd.org/fr/etatsunis/opennessandtransparency-pillarsfordemocracytrustandprogress.htm, accessed August 11, 2016.

transparency and investment. If investment improves economic welfare, which, in turn, influences elections, democratic governments may do well to provide transparency. In fact, Chapter 8 shows that the association between transparency and domestic investment appears stronger for democracies than for autocracies. This chapter builds on these results, investigating whether the economic advantages of transparency hold more value for democrats than for autocrats. We examine whether electoral contestation provides incentives for governments to disseminate data.

Note that this inquiry requires distinct conceptions of democracy and transparency, where one term is not directly defined by the other. As discussed in Part I, many definitions of transparency include explicit references to democracy, and vice versa. Any empirical relationship between such variables would, at least partly, constitute a tautology. In studying the empirical relationship between transparency and democracy, we use the HRV index of transparency, which relies exclusively on the reporting of economic data, and the DD index of democracy, which uses a minimalist approach to code regimes based on the contestation of elections to fill government offices. Neither in theory nor in empirics do we assume a relationship between transparency and democracy. Rather, we seek to explore a possible causal connection between two distinct variables.

What we find may reassure democratic theorists. When the fate of the incumbent government depends on the outcome of contested elections, governments do have incentives to be more transparent – at least with respect to the dissemination of data. In this chapter, we build a theoretical argument that depicts the conditions under which governments prefer to make information available to their citizens about the aggregate outcomes of policy. This information allows citizens to make informed decisions – particularly economic decisions – raising social-material welfare. In electoral systems where the survival of the government depends more strongly on the overall welfare of its citizens – that is, in democracies, where the votes of citizens determine the fate of the government – the ruling elite prove more willing to disclose data. By so doing, the government helps promote the welfare of voters and thus ensures its continued survival in office.[2]

---

[2] Our claims here resemble those advanced by Bueno de Mesquita et al. (2003). They argue that regimes with larger "winning coalitions" – in other words, democracies – are more likely to disclose information than regimes with small winning coalitions. Our measure of transparency takes its inspiration from their work. To test their claim, they examine governments' reporting of data on tax revenues and national income (using binary indicators for each). The selectorate model used by Bueno de Mesquita and colleagues is a complete information game, however, and it is difficult to discern the meaning or purpose of transparency in such a model. Unlike Bueno de Mesquita and his colleagues, we explicitly consider government transparency in a model of incomplete information. We also rely on our more nuanced (continuous) measure of transparency based on the missing values from a broad array of variables, rather than relying on binary indicators of reporting on a couple of variables.

In what follows, we present some relevant background on transparency and democracy. We then proceed to show theoretically the incentives of democratically elected leaders to disclose data. Next, we subject the hypothesis that democracies are more transparent than autocracies to several empirical tests, controlling for factors such as the capacity to collect data, participation in international surveillance programs, and time dependence. We conclude with a discussion of the methodological implications from our findings for studies of democracies.

9.1 DEMOCRACY AND TRANSPARENCY

In *The Moral Foundations of Politics*, Shapiro (2003) asserts that democracies are more likely than nondemocracies to converge on the truth, but the argument offers neither theory nor evidence. Elsewhere, democracies are simply assumed to be more transparent or democracy is used explicitly as a proxy for transparency (for example, Broz 2002). This conceptualization introduces an analytical tension into the inquiries of the relationship between democracy and transparency.

Consider the work of Mani and Mukand (2007), Harding and Stasavage (2014), Kono (2006), Busch (2000), Stasavage (2004), Rejali (2007), and Conrad, Hill, and Moore (2014), which suggests that democratic governments benefit from opacity in varied contexts. For example, Mani and Mukand (2007) argue that democratic governments, more so than authoritarian ones, have incentives to allocate resources to public goods that are highly visible, ignoring issues that are less visible.[3] They consider the issues of famine and malnutrition in India and China. Mani and Mukand concede the point of Sen (1999: 43) that India has not suffered from famine since the emergence of democracy, while famines persist in authoritarian China, but they point out that malnutrition persists at high levels in India, while China has seen malnutrition levels drop. They argue that persistently high levels of malnutrition actually hurt social welfare more than intermittent famines, but famines catch headlines – and thus public attention. More so than malnutrition, therefore, famines draw the attention of democratically elected governments. The upshot is that contested elections provide perverse incentives to democratic governments to address highly visible issues while ignoring more opaque ones. Harding and Stasavage (2014) find a similar effect with regard to schooling in Africa. Democratic governments are likely to abolish highly visible primary school fees, but show no concomitant greater willingness to invest in educational infrastructure and quality as compared to autocratic regimes.

While Mani and Mukand (2007) and Harding and Stasavage (2014) show that democracies devote more attention to more transparent issues at the

---

[3] See also Bueno de Mesquita et al. (2003); Bueno de Mesquita (2007); Lake and Baum (2001); and Saint-Paul and Verdier (1993).

expense of attention to less transparent ones, Kono's (2006) work shows that political regime-type can also influence the very visibility of certain issues. He argues that democratic governments actively promote the transparency of trade policy areas where they can take actions that please voters, while they seek to obscure policy areas where government action goes against the will of the majority. He thus contends that democracy does not necessarily improve citizens' knowledge of all government policies even while recognizing that the legal environment of democracy may require disclosure. Indeed, he presents quantitative evidence that political regime does shape policy precisely because democracy-induced transparency causes governments to adopt complex and opaque trade policies. Busch (2000) shows that obfuscation at the level of international negotiations can help democracies achieve better trade dispute settlement outcomes. Stasavage (2004) makes a similar point more broadly for international negotiations.

Rejali (2007), with respect to human rights, argues that political regime influences the *type* of torture techniques that governments employ – but not *whether* they engage in torture. If democracies have laws against torture, he contends, governments can adopt practices that leave no marks, such as waterboarding, lest government officials be held accountable. Democratic governments opt for "clean" techniques that leave no visible trace *ex post*, thereby obfuscating their activities. Conrad, Hill, and Moore (2014) argue that the majoritarian nature of electoral institutions actually does *not* provide incentives for governments to hide torture because they tend to use the practice on minorities; rather it is the strength of the judiciary that leads governments to engage in "stealth torture."

Despite the fact that theorists often assume an association between democracy and transparency, the relationship is complex and may depend on the policy context. Our question in this chapter focuses on a general question: Do contested elections increase or decrease a government's incentive to provide aggregate economic data? Given that all governments enjoy some degree of obfuscation, do democratic governments rely more or less on opacity because they face the possibility of eviction from office through the will of the majority?

9.2 THE EFFECT OF DEMOCRACY ON TRANSPARENCY

To highlight the incentives of governments to disclose, we develop a simple demonstrative model. Democracy is defined as the degree to which the will of the voters is reflected in whether incumbents are reelected. This theoretical construct represents a continuous Schumpeterian conception of democracy. It follows the Przeworski et al. (2000) binary conception, but allows for gradations (see Vreeland 2003a).

We assign all leaders (democratic and autocratic alike) the same preference over transparency: they always prefer less to more. In this way, we do not make transparency an assumed feature of democratic polities or the preferences of democratic leaders; the extent of transparency rather emerges in equilibrium.

To anticipate the game theoretic model presented below, aggregate economic performance and hence social welfare increases in transparency, and the inclination of the voters to reelect the incumbent increases with social welfare. Transparency, therefore, affects reelection probabilities.

In polities where the will of the voters is irrelevant for the survival of governments, elections have no effect on the government's choice of the level of transparency. Transparency would hinder these autocrats from engaging in graft, embezzlement, fraud, favoritism, bribery, extortion, and state capture of rents (for an overview of forms corruption, see Morris 2011). In polities where the will of the voters is determinative, the welfare-enhancing effect of more precise information outweighs the disutility from a more open government for the regime leaders. Hence democratic governments, subject to greater electoral accountability, choose to offer more precise public signals about aggregate economic outcomes.

In our model, citizens condition their votes on their material well-being. Voters may be sociotropic, or not – there is little distinction here between the welfare of the voter and that of society as a whole (as in the work of Bartels 2008). We are agnostic, here, as to whether voters reward or punish their executives for past performance (as in retrospective voting models; Fiorina 1981; Ferejohn 1986), or instead, use the performance of the economy (and their welfare) as a signal of the competence and/or preferences of the executive (as in prospective voting models; Lewis-Beck 1988). In either case, current economic conditions, as indicated by the current welfare, determine the share of the population who vote for the incumbent. Voting is therefore largely "economic" (Lewis-Beck and Stegmaier 2009; Hibbs 1982).

To present our theory more precisely, we introduce some mathematics. We could just rely on intuition, of course. But scholars have made intuitive arguments both that democracies are more transparent and that democracies are less transparent than autocracies. Using a mathematical approach forces us to lay bare our assumptions and allows us to test our logic with rigor. While readers unfamiliar with game theory might wish to skip ahead to the empirical tests of the theory, we encourage readers to give this section a try. We put the most technical materials in the appendix to this chapter and rely on the bare-bones of the model and its logic here in the main text.

To summarize the simple game, consider a polity with a continuum of citizens indexed by i on the unit interval $[0, 1]$. In this one-shot game, the government moves first by determining the degree of transparency (in a manner explained below). The government's action is not observed by the citizens. Citizens only receive a public signal, which may give them a more or less accurate picture of the economy, depending on the level of transparency. Then the citizens engage in economic activity, which determines social welfare. The game ends when an election is held – although the election may or may not be binding. The voting decisions of citizens depend on their economic welfare. And the extent to which votes actually matter for the fate of the government depends on the (exogenous) level of democracy.

When the citizens engage in economic activity, they each choose an action a_i. Let a denote a profile of actions for all citizens. The goal of each citizen is to match her economic action to the policy environment, which we denote g.

The utility of each citizen i (in this case, a loss function) is $u_i(a, g) = -(a_i - g)^2$. It is straightforward to see that citizens maximize their utility by setting a_i exactly to g. We can think of g as some policy-relevant variable and the voters must take an action to accommodate this policy.

For example, workers have incentives to provide labor until the point that the real wage is equal to the marginal disutility of effort. The real wage, of course, is determined by (among other factors) the inflation rate, a variable over which there may be more or less available information. As another example, a firm must choose its level of inputs (and hence output) based on its expectations about the price level or aggregate demand and the government may choose to provide more or less information about its spending behavior. Or, a portfolio investor must match the mix of assets to a well-diversified portfolio, which depends on the expected returns on a variety of risky assets. To take a particularly prickly political issue, exporters as well as import-competing firms must invest according to fluctuations in exchange rates, tariffs, quotas, and a growing number of various forms of health, safety, and labeling regulations. In all these instances, citizens have incentives to take actions that match the state of the policy environment.

The problem is that no one has perfect information about all factors that influence the economy. In terms of our model, no citizen knows exactly her optimal a_i because her estimate of g is, at best, an educated guess, which we define as y below. Thus, citizens have a preference for more information about the value of g.[4] Governments can help people make a better guess by making more information available, which can make y resemble g more closely. The government is the only entity potentially capable of collecting and disseminating aggregate data on the myriad factors that influence the economic lives of individuals.

Here is the central problem for the citizen: she is imperfectly informed about the state of this environment and the government chooses the degree to which this information is available. Each citizen receives the same public signal y, about the state of the policy environment, g, with $y = g + \eta$ where η is distributed symmetrically around mean zero with variance σ^2. It is useful to denote the "precision" of the signal as $\alpha = \frac{1}{\sigma^2}$. In this model, therefore, the level of precision, α, is the measure of transparency and it is set by the government.

It may at first seem odd that we model uncertainty as symmetrically distributed with mean zero, given that governments' efforts at obfuscation nearly always reflect some form of bias. However, so long as the government's

---

[4] We take this policy environment variable g to be exogenous; ultimately, the policy is chosen by the government and voters may be able to estimate its value from information other than received via the public signal (such as past policy choices). We consider here only a one-shot game where these concerns do not apply.

incentive to dissemble is known, the public – in equilibrium – can account for such bias in policy pronouncements. In most models of information transmission (for example, Crawford and Sobel 1982; Johns 2007), higher levels of bias on the part of the sender translate into greater uncertainty on the part of the receiver. They do not lead to biased beliefs on the part of the receiver. Rather than burdening our model with undue complexity by fully modeling this interaction, we rely on the assumption that uncertainty is symmetrically distributed with mean zero as a reduced form.

What this modeling assumption means intuitively is that if we were to play this game over and over, the public signal would be on target when averaged across all the possible draws. But for any given game, citizens may guess too high or too low. To continue with the examples above, laborers may work too much or too little because they do not have a clear enough picture of where inflation is headed; firms may invest too much or too little because they do not have a clear enough picture of where demand is headed; investors may diversify their portfolios too much or too little because they do not have a clear enough picture of where asset values are headed; exporting and importing-competing firms may invest too much or too little to deal with their competition abroad because they do not have a clear enough picture of where the exchange rate is headed or which trade regulations will be in effect. If a given draw of the public signal is way off target, individuals make suboptimal economic choices. Aggregated across all citizens, the economy will perform below its optimal level if the government is opaque.

In the model, social welfare is the average utility of all individuals.[5] Hence we have $W(a, g) = -\int_0^1 (a_i - g)^2 di$. This equation averages the utility of all citizens of a country – and every time a citizen makes a wrong guess about the policy-environment, g, by setting a_i too high or too low, societal welfare is not as large as it could be.

The government, however, is not necessarily interested in maximizing social welfare. We assume that governments primarily wish to hold onto office. Social welfare only impacts the government's utility by altering the probability with which it retains office. We model, quite simply, the outcome of the election as increasing in social welfare: $Pr\{reelection\} = P(W(a, g))$ with higher social welfare translating into a greater probability of winning reelection, although with diminishing marginal returns ($P' > 0$ and $P'' < 0$). We assume that all governments hold elections at the end of the period – but not all of those elections are meaningful (autocracies govern some countries, so elections are virtually meaningless for leadership tenure).[6]

The degree to which the "will of the people" is reflected in who actually holds is our measure of political regime (treated as exogenous to the model). Following Mansfield, Milner, and Rosendorff (2002), we characterize each

---

[5] Since we are integrating over all individuals, who are indexed over the [0,1] interval, the average and the sum are equivalent.

[6] Although, see Gandhi and Lust-Okar (2009).

polity by a scalar $\Delta \in [0, 1]$ which captures the degree to which elections are binding on the executive. This notion follows closely the Przeworski et al. (2000) notion of "contested" elections.

The government's payoff is modeled, therefore, as: $G(a, \alpha, g) = \Delta P(W(a, g)) + (1 - \Delta) - \frac{1}{2}\alpha^2$. If the will of the voters is always honored, we have $\Delta = 1$, such that elections completely determine the survival of the government; a pure autocracy has $\Delta = 0$ because the votes do not matter at all. In this theoretical model, we permit a continuous measure of the degree to which the executive is bound by elections and the typical government's welfare is a convex combination of the returns to a pure democracy, and a pure autocracy.[7]

In a pure democracy, social welfare has the largest weight in the government's objective function, since the will of the electorate is determinative. Pure democracy implies $\Delta = 1$, so the government seeks to maximize: $G(a, \alpha, g) = P(W(a, g)) - \frac{1}{2}\alpha^2$. The democratic government loses some utility by providing transparent economic data (that is, by increasing α): $-\frac{1}{2}\alpha^2$. But the government makes up these loses because increasing α also helps individuals make optimal economic decisions, thereby increasing social welfare, $W(a, g)$ and thus the probability of winning reelection.

On the other hand, when social welfare has no impact on the likelihood that the executive retains office, the government's concerns over transparency (or a lack thereof) become determinative – the pure autocracy case. Pure autocracy implies $\Delta = 0$, so the government seeks to maximize: $G(a, \alpha, g) = 1 - \frac{1}{2}\alpha^2$. Here, the government can only lose by providing transparent economic data (that is, by increasing α). Increasing transparency simply limits the innumerable forms of rent-seeking in which the autocrat can engage.

Thus the last term in the government's objective function $(-\frac{1}{2}\alpha^2)$ reflects the disutility all leaders face from transparency, α. The government has a natural tendency toward obfuscation – this permits questionable policies to be blamed on others; rent redistributions to be only weakly observed or not at all; and even outright corruption that flies under the radar. All regimes have this tendency, and we do not assume that it varies with regime type. Ferejohn (1986) argues that elected officials have a significant informational advantage over the voters that permits the officials to engage in opportunistic behaviors, behaviors that can be mitigated by enhancing accountability. Ferejohn (1999) offers a related model in which the degree of monitoring that the voters can undertake is endogenously determined and chosen optimally by the policymaker. Note that in our model, democrats gain from engaging in corruption; they are simply constrained by their desire to win election – a constraint that autocrats do not face.

---

[7] One could also solve the game using a binary indicator (which is how we measure democracy in the empirical work below).

A subgame perfect equilibrium to this game is a pair (a, α) such that each actor is playing a best response (Fudenberg and Tirole 1991). We solve the game by backward induction. We start with the decisions of citizens to set a_i. Once we know what they will do, we move back to see what level of transparency, α, the government chooses to set.

Given any α, each voter must choose a_i in order to maximize her expected utility given the signal y. Then

$$E(u_i(a, g)|y) = -a_i^2 + 2a_iE(g|y) - E(g^2|y). \tag{9.1}$$

Taking the derivative of this expected utility with respect to a_i and setting that derivative equal to zero (the first order condition for a maximum) yields $a_i = E(g|y) = y$. Citizens would be best off, of course, setting $a_i = g$, but they do not observe g directly. The best they can do is go with the public signal, setting $a_i = y$.

Conditional on any policy environment g therefore, we can compute social welfare. Recall that $W(a, g) = -\int_0^1 (a_i - g)^2 di = -(y - g)^2$. Substituting $y = g + \eta$, we have $W(a, g) = -\eta^2$. The average value of η may be 0, but any random draw could be high or low, and the further away from zero, the worse for society. Since increasing α decreases the variance of η, it lowers the chances of a bad draw. Thus, increasing α increases social welfare.

Conditional on the fact that citizens set $a_i = y$, we can now consider the government's problem. It must solve

$$\max_{\alpha} EG(a, \alpha, g) \text{ subject to } a_i = y. \tag{9.2}$$

To obtain closed-form solutions, we make two functional form assumptions at this point. We first assume that the electoral probability follows an exponential distribution: $P(x; \beta) = \beta e^{-\beta x}$ for any $x > 0$. We then assume that η has a normal distribution (with mean 0 and variance $\frac{1}{\alpha}$). To ensure the satisfaction of the second order condition for a maximum (that the second derivative is negative), we also assume that $\alpha > 2\beta$. That is, the variance of the signal is always bounded above by (half of) the mean of the electoral probability distribution.[8] We prove in the appendix to this chapter that for any arbitrarily large scalar $C \gg 0$,[9] the following proposition holds:

Proposition 9.1. *The equilibrium* (a^*, α^*) *is* $\left(y, \beta\left(1 + \sqrt{1 + \left(\Delta\beta e^{-\beta C}\right)^{\frac{2}{3}}}\right)\right).$

[8] We make these assumptions for purposes of tractability. However, any function $P(\cdot)$ that satisfies the properties $P' > 0, P'' < 0, P \in [0, 1]$ $\forall$ $W(a, \alpha)$ and any distribution of η that is symmetric and centered around zero yields similar comparative static results.

[9] One can think of C as the baseline probability of winning reelection. The scalar literally corresponds to the probability of retention for an infinitely transparent leader. From a mathematical perspective, C here is just a normalizing factor for the exponential distribution. Because social welfare is technically negative, we need to include a constant so that the probability of reelection is greater than 0.

We can now consider the comparative statics on the equilibrium level of precision as a function of the degree of electoral accountability. We prove in the appendix that this proposition holds as well:

Proposition 9.2. *The equilibrium level of precision rises with electoral accountability,* $\frac{\partial \alpha^*}{\partial \Delta} \geq 0$.

As the degree of electoral accountability rises, the weight of social welfare in the government's objective function also rises. Social welfare here is a function of transparency because greater transparency allows voters to more precisely match their behaviors to the policy environment. Because survival in office depends more on social welfare when a government is more democratic (as Δ rises), the more democratic government is more willing to disseminate policy-relevant information. Notice that the increased precision is provided to placate the voters, who are more important in determining whether the executive retains office. All governments are assumed to suffer an equivalent cost of transparency, but the marginal benefits to data dissemination rise with the level of democracy.

9.3 EVIDENCE

Proposition 9.2 holds that the government's optimal level of transparency increases with the level of electoral accountability: $\frac{\partial \alpha^*}{\partial \Delta} > 0$. As the level of electoral accountability rises, so too does the government's interest in ensuring that economic agents – for example, investors – make optimal investment and consumption decisions. Therefore, a greater responsiveness to the interests of the voters induces governments to disclose more relevant economic data. We explore this hypothesis by first considering descriptive data and presenting some examples. We then turn to regression analysis to test the hypothesis more rigorously.

9.3.1 Examples and Descriptive Data

We measure the government's willingness to disclose economic data using the HRV index. This measure relates closely to the theoretical conception of transparency used in our model. In our model we treat transparency as reducing the variance of the public's perception of the policy environment. One may think of the public as holding prior beliefs regarding the policy environment – credible policy pronouncements by the government cause members of the public to update these beliefs to form more confident (precise) posteriors. In the absence of any credible data dissemination, no updating takes place and beliefs remain diffuse. Thus, the missingness of credible data from the WDI reasonably proxies for the imprecision of the public's beliefs regarding a given country's policy environment.

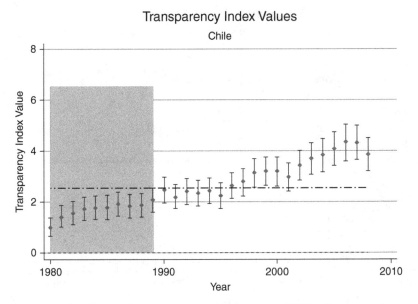

FIGURE 9.1. Chile under autocracy and democracy. HRV values are plotted on the y-axis, while the x-axis measures time in years. Diamonds correspond to mean HRV scores, while whiskers are 95 percent credible intervals. The shaded region marks years in which Chile was an autocracy, the unshaded years are democratic. The two dashed lines correspond to the mean HRV scores among autocracies (−0.003, the lower line), and democracies (2.54, the upper line).

Consider Chile as an illustrative example. From 1980 through 1989, the HRV index averaged 1.7 under the brutal and repressive rule of Augusto Pinochet.[10] In 1990, after the transition to democracy, the HRV index jumped from 2.1 to 2.5. The HRV score continued to climb, averaging 2.6 during the 1990s and 3.7 during the 2000s. Figure 9.1 presents the HRV scores for each year during the autocratic and democratic periods of our sample.

We see a similar pattern in Paraguay, where the HRV index averaged 0.9 from 1980 to 1988, under the extraordinarily harsh rule of Alfredo Stroessner Matiauda (for a discussion of the transition to democracy, see Horst 2003). After the emergence of democracy in 1989, we observe transparency jump up from 1.1 to 1.3. The upward trajectory is sustained under democracy, with an

---

[10] On economic transparency, Fairfield (2010: 44, 66) reports that the Pinochet regime actually enacted strict banking secrecy laws in 1986 – which were not fully loosened until 2009 when Chile was pressured to do so to secure membership in the Organization of Economic Co-operation and Development (OECD). On labor relations and the repressive Pinochet regime, see Carnes (2014: 112–115). For an overview of the transition to democracy, see Constable and Valenzuela (1991).

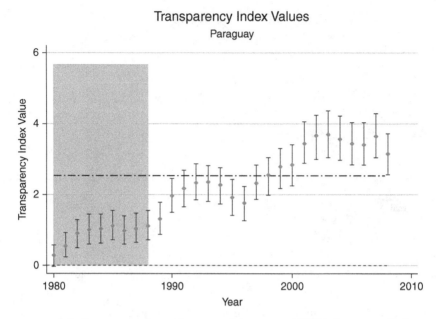

FIGURE 9.2. Paraguay under autocracy and democracy. HRV index scores for Paraguay over time. HRV values are plotted on the y-axis, while the x-axis measures time in years. Diamonds correspond to mean HRV scores, while whiskers are 95 percent credible intervals. The shaded region marks years in which Paraguay was an autocracy, the unshaded years are democratic. The two dashed lines correspond to the mean HRV scores among autocracies (−0.003, the lower line), and democracies (2.54, the upper line).

average of 2.3 in the 1990s and 3.3 in the 2000s (for year-by-year data, see Figure 9.2).

Or consider capacity-constrained Nepal, presented in Figure 9.3.[11] Under autocratic rule until 1989, democracy emerged with the "people's revolt" (the *"jana andolan"*) movement in 1990 (Nepal, Bohara, and Gawande 2011: 888) – only to collapse in 2002. Transparency was low throughout. Even in this country, however, where the weakness of the government's capacity to collect and disseminate data is apparent, we see a pattern of more data under democracy and less data under autocracy. From 1980 through 1989, the HRV index averaged −0.3 under autocracy. It increased to an average of −0.1 under democratic rule from 1990 to 2001. Then transparency dropped again – after democracy collapsed – to an average of −0.2 from 2002 to 2007. The democratic period was far from perfect (for a discussion, see Riaz and Basu 2007: 13–15).

---

[11] For an excellent presentation of the political history of Nepal, see Hoftun, Raeper, and Whelpton (1999). On the violence during the 1996–2003 period, see Nepal, Bohara, and Gawande (2011). On the failure of democratization, see Ganguly and Shoup (2005).

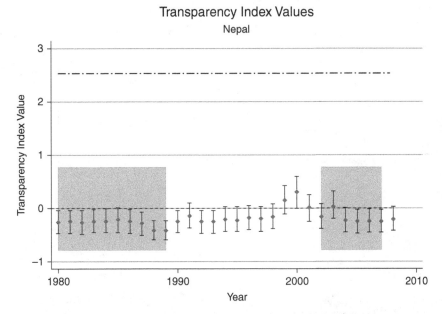

FIGURE 9.3. Nepal under autocracy and democracy. HRV values are plotted on the y-axis, while the x-axis measures time in years. Diamonds correspond to mean HRV scores, while whiskers are 95 percent credible intervals. The shaded region marks years in which Nepal was an autocracy, the unshaded years are democratic. The two dashed lines correspond to the mean HRV scores among autocracies (−0.003, the lower line), and democracies (2.54, the upper line).

The democracy suffered from severe factionalism, which led to an extremely violent civil war. But unlike the periods prior and after, political parties were legal and contested elections – and the government made more of an effort to supply and disclose aggregate economic data.

The examples of Chile, Paraguay, and Nepal fit with an overall pattern in the data. Figure 9.4 shows the average HRV transparency score by political regime, and the variability of these scores within each class of regime. Scores average only −0.003 for autocracies, while they average 2.54 for democracies. In contrast to previous graphs, the whiskers in Figure 9.4 depict the inter-quartile range within each regime category. That is, they plot the 25th and 75th percentiles, by transparency score, among autocracies and democracies. Hence, Figure 9.4 indicates that an autocracy that is more transparent than 75 percent of similar regimes receives an HRV score that is roughly equal to that of a democracy that is *less* transparent than roughly 75 percent of elected governments. The descriptive data show a clear tendency for democracies to report more data than autocracies.

Of course this simple analysis does not account for other factors, notably level of economic development. As is well known, democracies have higher

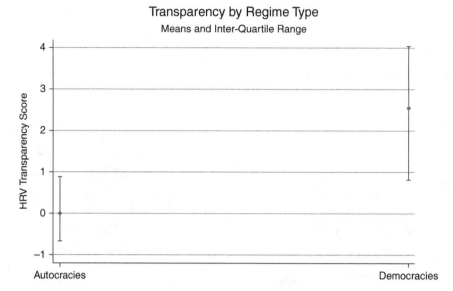

FIGURE 9.4. Average HRV transparency score by political regime. HRV transparency averages −0.003 for autocracies and 2.54 for democracies. The whiskers represent inter-quartile ranges. The descriptive data show a clear tendency for democracies to report more data than autocracies.

average levels of GDP per capita, and GDP per capita is correlated with data dissemination. The latter relationship may be driven by state capacity. The governments of the poorest countries may simply lack the resources necessary to collect the massive amounts of information required to put together aggregate economic data.

Consider, however, Figure 9.5, which presents average HRV transparency scores for democracies and autocracies according to the level of economic development. The figure splits the sample at the median level of GDP per capita for the entire sample. The pattern of disclosure by regime type persists. In countries below the median GDP per capita of $3,900 (in 2005 constant USD), HRV transparency averages −0.24 for autocracies and 0.73 for democracies. In countries above the median GDP per capita, HRV transparency averages 0.51 for autocracies and 3.29 for democracies. In both economic categories, democracies disseminate more data. In fact, low-income democracies, on average, report more data than high-income autocracies report.

Still, the distribution of cases presented in Figure 9.5 is skewed so that autocracies remain poorer than democracies in both categories, so reasonable doubt may remain. Yet recall Figure 4.5 from Chapter 4, which suggests that for every level of economic development, democracies have higher HRV transparency scores than autocracies have. Taken altogether, the descriptive data begins to look convincing.

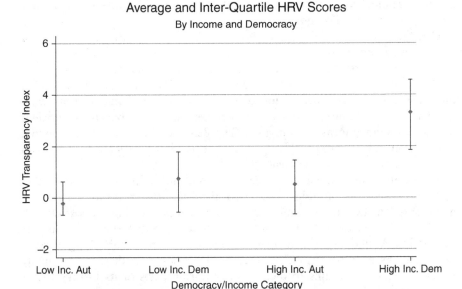

FIGURE 9.5. Average HRV transparency score below and above median GDP per capita by political regime. In countries below the median GDP per capita of $3,900, HRV transparency averages −0.24 for autocracies and 0.73 for democracies. In countries above the median GDP per capita, HRV transparency averages 0.51 for autocracies and 3.29 for democracies. In both economic categories, democracies disseminate more data. In fact, low-income democracies report more data, on average, than high-income autocracies report. The whiskers represent inter-quartile ranges. After correcting for level of economic development, the descriptive pattern persists: Democracies report more data than autocracies.

9.3.2 Control Variables

We now take the analysis further, introducing more rigor into how we account for GDP per capita as well as other factors. To assess whether elections increase the willingness of governments to report economic data, we regress our HRV transparency index on the DD measure of political regime. We restrict attention to this institutional – minimalist – conception of democracy. Our theoretical concept, Δ is best captured using minimalist definition of democracy – one where the contestability of elections is primary.[12]

In our multiple regression specifications, we employ a parsimonious set of controls precisely because our dependent variable measures the degree of data availability. As our set of controls grows more extensive, we are increasingly likely to censor observations of our outcome variable. Such censoring tends to

---

[12] Similar results hold when we use the Polity IV index (see Hollyer, Rosendorff, and Vreeland 2011).

eliminate country-years that report a small fraction of WDI variables from our dataset, potentially biasing results.

Our first control is *GDP per capita*, measured as the natural logarithm of thousands of PPP weighted constant dollars, drawn from the Penn World Table version 6.3 (Heston, Summers, and Aten 2009). Note that GDP per capita is likely to relate to the ability of governments to collect and disseminate high quality statistical data. Since democracies have, on average, higher incomes than nondemocracies, failure to control for GDP per capita may bias the coefficient on our democracy measures upwards. The Penn World Table has no missing observations for our sample. Thus, the use of this control variable does not lead to censoring in our outcome measure.

We additionally control for *Under IMF*, and indicator of participation in IMF programs. This variable accounts for the international scrutiny a government faces. The IMF often requires that governments receiving support publish relevant economic data. A pillar of the IMF Fiscal Transparency Guidelines is the "Public Availability of Information," particularly the "publishing of comprehensive fiscal information."[13] Since the IMF has been disproportionately likely to extend programs to dictatorships during parts of its history (Vreeland 2003b), failure to control for this potential confound may bias our coefficient of interest toward zero. This variable also has no missing data for our sample.

In all specifications, we also include a control for the lagged value of our transparency index. We do so for several reasons. For one, in any given year, in any given country, the best predictor of the level of transparency is the level of transparency in that same country in the previous year. Also, including this term renders our empirical model dynamic. Any given control (say GDP per capita) may have an immediate effect on transparency levels, but it may also have an effect that plays out gradually over time. This assumption seems warranted on both practical grounds and due to specific features of our transparency measure. First, any government that seeks to increase rates of disclosure is unlikely to be able to do so instantaneously; rather we would expect to see gradually rising disclosure rates over a period of years. Second, the HRV index is a slow-moving time-series: shifts in transparency values tend to occur gradually. In part, this is by construction – recall from Chapter 3 that our measurement model uses a "random walk" prior, which smooths shifts in index values over time.

Thus we control for (1) level of development – both because of its correlation with regime type and because it proxies for state capacity, (2) international surveillance as proxied by participation in IMF programs, and (3) lagged transparency. Table 9.1 reports the summary statistics of the variables described above.

---

[13] *Manual on Fiscal Transparency*, the International Monetary Fund, page 6, www.imf.org/external/np/pp/2007/eng/101907m.pdf, accessed August 8, 2017.

TABLE 9.1. *Summary statistics.*

Variable Name	Mean	Std. Dev.	Min.	Max.
HRV transparency index	1.18	2.30	−10.9	9.98
Democracy	0.47	0.50	0	1
GDP per capita	8.98	11.3	0.16	65.9
Under IMF	0.39	0.49	0	1

9.3.3 Empirical Model and Results

We assess the relationship between democracy and disclosure through a series of varying intercepts hierarchical models. The unit of observation is the regime-spell-year, where a regime-spell is one or more years of continuous autocratic or democratic rule. Our models assume the following functional form:

$$transparency_{i,t} = \alpha_i + \rho transparency_{i,t-1} + \mathbf{X}_{i,t-1}\beta + \epsilon_{i,t}$$
$$\alpha_i = \zeta_0 + \zeta_1 democracy_i + \nu_i$$

where i denotes regime-spell, t denotes year, and $\mathbf{X}_{i,t-1}\beta$ is a data vector of controls multiplied by their associated coefficients. Our parameter of theoretical interest ζ_1 is estimated based on the variation at the upper level of the hierarchy – that is, at the regime-spell level. Regime spells are defined using the DD definition of democracy. We estimate this model using MCMC, placing separate diffuse multivariate normal priors on the β and ζ terms, and placing an informative normal prior on the ρ term ($\rho \sim N(0.5, 1)$).

In our simplest specifications, we estimate a model including only the democracy variable and the lag of transparency. (As these are varying intercepts models, all regime-spells receive their own intercept term in all specifications.) We also estimate models including the GDP per capita and IMF controls, as well as cubic polynomials of time to adjust for underlying trends. Results of these specifications are reported in Table 9.2.

Table 9.2 reveals a statistically significant correlation between democracy and HRV transparency. In the bivariate model (models 3 and 4), a change from an autocracy to a democracy, by the DD definition, increases the HRV score by approximately 0.1 units. This, however, is a contemporaneous marginal effect. Recall from the discussion above that the inclusion of the lagged dependent variable renders this specification dynamic. The estimated cumulative long-run impact of a shift from autocracy to democracy is to increase transparency levels by roughly 6 units in most of our models. This is a large marginal effect, equivalent to just under one-quarter the distance from the minimum to maximum observed transparency scores on our index.

IMF programs and GDP per capita have the expected positive associations with the disclosure of data, though the coefficient on the IMF term is measured with considerable error. Our substantive conclusion is straightforward: contested electoral competition is associated with greater transparency.

TABLE 9.2. *The relationship between transparency and the minimalist conception of democracy (DD).*

		Model 1	Model 2	Model 3	Model 4
Regime Spell Level	Democracy	0.1	0.111	0.111	0.111
		[0.057, 0.144]	[0.065, 0.157]	[0.065, 0.157]	[0.065, 0.157]
	Lag Transparency	0.992	0.983	0.983	0.983
		[0.976, 1.008]	[0.967, 0.999]	[0.967, 0.999]	[0.967, 0.999]
Regime Spell-Year Level	GDP per capita	0.02	0.024		
		[0.001, 0.043]	[0.002, 0.047]		
	Under IMF	0.014	0.016		
		[−0.016, 0.045]	[−0.018, 0.045]		
	Cubic Time Polynomial	✓		✓	
	# of Obs.	2983	2983	2983	2983
	# of Regimes	183	183	183	183

Results of a varying intercepts hierarchical regression of transparency levels on the DD definition of democracy. Coefficients on parameters at the upper level of the hierarchy are reported above, those that vary at the regime-spell-year level are reported below. Ninety-five percent credible intervals are reported in brackets.

9.4 CONCLUSION

Despite electoral incentives toward obfuscation, democratic governments are more likely to release policy-relevant data than are autocracies. We provide both theoretical arguments of why this is so as well as evidence from data provided by governments to the World Bank. This finding confirms what has often been taken for granted about democracy and transparency.

Specifically, we argue in this chapter that individual agents can better make economic decisions in an informationally enhanced environment. This argument is central to our understanding of why democratic governments supply more transparency: they seek to improve the overall performance of the economy in order to win election. The intuition is obvious: the greater availability of data reduces uncertainty and risk for investment decisions. The results from the previous chapter support this understanding, showing that positive impact of data dissemination on investment.

Beyond the intrinsic importance of this finding for our inquiry into economic transparency, we would like to highlight two contributions that this chapter makes to the empirical literature on the determinants and consequences of democracy and, respectively, to how scholars define democracy. Regarding the determinants and consequences of democracy, the results of this chapter speak to an important methodological concern. Much of the copious research on the causes and effects of political regime relies on cross-national datasets, like the WDI that we use to construct the HRV index. As our analysis shows, however, the reporting of data is nonrandom with respect to political regime; democracies report more data. The listwise deletion of observations due to missing data on certain variables may, therefore, lead – in a systematic fashion – to the deletion of autocracy observations more so than democracy observations. Analyses that ignore this pattern of data-reporting leave themselves vulnerable to biases.[14] We would thus encourage scholars to think carefully about patterns of missing data when empirically analyzing the correlates of democracy.[15]

The results of this chapter also inform an important debate in political science about the most appropriate measure for political regime. The debate over how to define democracy is waged today in many corners of academia, and the debate stretches back throughout modern political science. Dahl (1971), for example, took issue with the minimalist conception of democracy of Schumpeter (1942) when he first introduced his concept of "polyarchy." Dahl argued that contested elections alone were not sufficient to define democracy, because "responsiveness" was also required. And for there to be responsiveness, Dahl listed several guarantees that were necessary, including, for example, the free

---

[14] See King et al. (2001) and, more recently, Lall (2016).
[15] The work of Ross (2006) represents an excellent example of a study on the effects of regime type that carefully scrutinizes patterns of missing data.

flow of information. Przeworski et al. (2000) proposed a return to the minimalist definition of democracy. They make this suggestion not because other features – such as those listed by Dahl – are unimportant, but because the relationships among these various other features should be examined not assumed. So, for example, rather than require the free flow of information to be a defining feature of democracy, they restrict the definition of democracy to cover only elections.

The results of this chapter suggest that the minimalist approach to defining democracy actually does speak to the concerns about transparency that many scholars have. We demonstrate that there is an intrinsic relationship between elections and information – one that need not be assumed by definition. The most transparent regimes are those in which the key offices of the executive and the legislature are filled through contested elections. This relationship is not simply imposed by the definition of democracy, but rather reflects *the equilibrium behavior of self-interested governments*. We establish that this relationship holds both theoretically and empirically. So the minimalist definition of democracy actually covers more territory than just elections.

Note that this result does not imply that all democracies practice transparency in all policy areas. As previous research shows, democratic governments have incentives to optimize policy choices given varying degrees of opacity across the policy areas (Mani and Mukand 2007; Harding and Stasavage 2014) and these governments may even have incentives to optimize obfuscation itself (Kono 2006; Rejali 2007; Conrad, Hill, and Moore 2014). Part II reveals that some democracies have failed to reach the necessary transparency levels to sustain democratic rule.

Still, we show here that electoral incentives – particularly the phenomenon of economic voting – systematically drive democracies toward ever greater openness. And we demonstrate empirically that the incentives that drive democracies to release data trump whatever motives they have to obfuscate.

However, the results of this chapter deepen the puzzle of autocratic transparency. We have little reason, at this point in the book, to expect autocrats to ever disclose data. Nevertheless, while they may disclose at lower rates than democracies, autocracies do disclose. Part I reveals this pattern with descriptive data, even while Part II shows that doing so can lead to mass unrest. Autocrats risk replacement when they enhance the informational environment. To be sure, Chapter 8 documents economic benefits from transparency in the form of investment, but the results for domestic investment are weaker for autocracies than for democracies. This chapter provides one explanation for this pattern. Democrats have stronger incentives to care about the economic well-being of citizens – it helps them win the mass vote. But, as we saw in Part II, for autocrats, transparency enhances the threat posed to them by the masses.

If survival in office is the central concern of an autocrat, why do autocrats disclose? Chapter 10 provides a political answer to this question. It turns out that when it comes to threats, the masses constitute only one; yet, there is another.

9.5 APPENDIX

9.5.1 Proofs of Theoretical Propositions of the Transparency Model

Proof of Proposition 9.1

Proof. From Equation (9.1), the voters are behaving optimally when they set $a_i = y$ for all i. Consider now the government's payoffs, taking voter behavior as given:

$$E(G(a, g, \alpha)|g) = \Delta E(P(-\eta^2)) + (1 - \Delta) - \frac{1}{2}\alpha^2$$

$$= \Delta \int P(-\eta^2) f(\eta) d\eta + (1 - \Delta) - \frac{1}{2}\alpha^2$$

Consider the exponential distribution with CDF $P(x) = 1 - e^{-\beta x}$ for any $x > 0$. We apply the monotonic transformation, defining $w(a, g) = W(a, g) + C = C - \eta^2 = x > 0$, and we let P instead be a function of $w(a, g)$. Then $P(w(a, g)) = 1 - \beta e^{-\beta C} e^{\beta \eta^2}$. Let f be normal with $f(\eta) = \frac{\sqrt{\alpha}}{\sqrt{2\pi}} e^{-\frac{1}{2}\alpha\eta^2}$. Then

$$E(G(a, g, \alpha)|g) = \Delta \int \beta (1 - e^{-\beta C} e^{\beta \eta^2}) \frac{\sqrt{\alpha}}{\sqrt{2\pi}} e^{-\frac{1}{2}\alpha\eta^2} d\eta + (1 - \Delta) - \frac{1}{2}\alpha^2$$

(9.3)

$$= \Delta \beta \left[1 - e^{-\beta C} \frac{\sqrt{\alpha}}{\sqrt{2\pi}} \int e^{-(\frac{1}{2}\alpha - \beta)\eta^2} d\eta \right] + (1 - \Delta) - \frac{1}{2}\alpha^2$$

(9.4)

Now $\int_{-\infty}^{\infty} e^{-kx^2} dx = \frac{\sqrt{\pi}}{\sqrt{k}}$. Then

$$E(G(a, g, \alpha)|g) = \Delta \beta \left[1 - e^{-\beta C} \left(\frac{\frac{1}{2}\alpha}{\frac{1}{2}\alpha - \beta} \right)^{\frac{1}{2}} \right] + (1 - \Delta) - \frac{1}{2}\alpha^2$$

Maximizing over α, we have $\frac{d}{d\alpha} EG(a, g, \alpha) = -\Delta \beta e^{-\beta C} \frac{d}{d\alpha} \left(\frac{\frac{1}{2}\alpha}{\frac{1}{2}\alpha - \beta} \right)^{\frac{1}{2}} - \alpha$.

Now $\frac{d}{d\alpha} \left(\frac{\frac{1}{2}\alpha}{\frac{1}{2}\alpha - \beta} \right)^{\frac{1}{2}} = -\frac{\beta}{4} \left(\frac{1}{2}\alpha - \beta \right)^{-\frac{3}{2}} \left(\frac{\alpha}{2} \right)^{-\frac{1}{2}}$. Then $\frac{d}{d\alpha} EG(a, g, \alpha) = \frac{\Delta}{4} \beta^2 e^{-\beta C} \left(\frac{1}{2}\alpha - \beta \right)^{-\frac{3}{2}} \left(\frac{\alpha}{2} \right)^{-\frac{1}{2}} - \alpha = 0$.

Solving for α, yields two solutions, $(\beta + \sqrt{\beta^2 + (\Delta \frac{\beta^2}{e^{C\beta}})^{\frac{2}{3}}}, \beta - \sqrt{\beta^2 + (\Delta \frac{\beta^2}{e^{C\beta}})^{\frac{2}{3}}})$. Checking the second order condition $\frac{d}{d\alpha} \frac{d}{d\alpha} EG(a, g, \alpha) =$

$\frac{\Delta}{8}\beta^2 e^{-\beta C}(\alpha - 2\beta)^{-\frac{5}{2}}\alpha^{-\frac{3}{2}}(\beta - 2\alpha) - 1$. A sufficient condition for this to be negative is $\alpha - 2\beta > 0$. Then of the two solutions, only $\beta + \sqrt{\beta^2 + \left(\Delta\frac{\beta^2}{e^{C\beta}}\right)^{\frac{2}{3}}}$ satisfies $\alpha - 2\beta > 0$. $\square$

Proof of Proposition 9.2

Proof. From the government's first order condition, $\frac{d}{d\alpha}EG(a, g, \alpha) = 0$. Totally differentiating this yields $\frac{d}{d\alpha}\frac{d}{d\alpha}EG(a, g, \alpha)d\alpha + \frac{d}{d\Delta}\frac{d}{d\alpha}EG(a, g, \alpha)d\Delta = 0$. Then $\frac{d\alpha^*}{d\Delta} = -\frac{\frac{d}{d\Delta}\frac{d}{d\alpha}EG(a,g,\alpha)}{\frac{d^2}{d\alpha^2}EG(a,g,\alpha)}$. From the previous proof, $\alpha - 2\beta > 0$ is sufficient for $\frac{d^2}{d\alpha^2}EG(a, g, \alpha) < 0$. Hence $sign \frac{d\alpha^*}{d\Delta} = sign\left(\frac{1}{4}\beta^2 e^{-\beta C}\left(\frac{1}{2}\alpha - \beta\right)^{-\frac{3}{2}}\left(\frac{\alpha}{2}\right)^{-\frac{1}{2}}\right) > 0$ which again follows from $\alpha - 2\beta > 0$. $\square$

10

Why Autocrats Disclose

Opacity provides benefits for autocrats. A closed informational environment serves as a means to obscure rent-seeking and other malfeasance, enabling autocrats to reap augmented financial rewards from their position of power. Non-transparency also hinders the coordination necessary for popular unrest and thus preserves the autocratic regime.

Yet, autocracies vary widely in the extent to which they disclose economic information to their publics. Some autocrats choose to disclose. Given the economic and political rewards of opacity, why would any autocrat choose transparency? We contend that they do so because transparency offers economic and political benefits too – even for autocrats.

As seen in the previous chapters, the dissemination of data encourages investor confidence, which boosts economic performance. If the consequences of transparency were purely economic, the trade-off would be clear – an autocrat would simply set a level of data disclosure where the marginal costs from transparency, owing to reduced opportunities for rent-seeking, match the marginal benefits, flowing from increased investment.

We have stressed throughout the book, however, that the logic of long-run political survival may weigh more heavily in the calculus of an autocrat than shorter-term material gain. To the extent that transparency causes mass-unrest, which can lead to the ouster of an autocrat, dictatorships should eschew the dissemination of economic data.

What if, however, transparency acts as a double-edged sword politically? Autocrats face many risks to their survival beyond mass unrest, and these other risks may respond quite differently to transparency. Indeed, the very prospect of the mass unrest caused by transparency may reduce the risk of other real threats to the survival of an autocrat.

Consider the interests and desires of members of a leader's inner circle: this elite may include potential rivals for the leadership. Usually loyal allies, inner-circle elites sometimes seek to overturn their leader through a coup. Recall the example of South Korea's President Park Chung Hee, who was assassinated by someone within his clique – his own intelligence chief (Adesnik and Kim 2008: 1). Rival members of the elite can successfully take advantage of such opportunities only under certain circumstances. If masses of opposition groups have coordinated, they may seize on a moment of regime disunity to strike out for regime change. When the assassination of Park took place, mass opposition to the dictatorship existed – but it was fragmented and disorganized (Im 1995: 136). Thus elite disunity did not bring down the regime – only the leader.

But, when the masses are organized and the political environment is charged, elites tend to remain loyal to their leader. Steps to oust the leader in such an environment may spark organized protests by the masses.[1] If these protests are successful, they will likely take down the entire regime, including the members of the inner circle. The prospect of mass unrest may therefore heighten the loyalty of the inner circle.

Take the Tiananmen Square incident of 1989. In the early and mid-1980s, elite members of the Chinese Communist Party disagreed on the future trajectory of economic and political policy in China (Baum 2011: 337). Among the controversies, inner-circle elites disagreed over "the tolerable limits of free market activity and private accumulation of wealth . . . and the proper boundaries of free expression for artists, writers, and other creative intellectuals" (Baum 2011: 337). The disagreements were not merely academic – Deng Xiaoping's path to holding the controlling stake in the Chinese government was not an obvious one and many contending veteran cadres proved recalcitrant toward withdrawing from political life (Baum 2011: 344).

By 1989, Deng had lost confidence in key members of the elite, including, importantly, Zhao Ziyang, the general secretary of the Central Committee of the Communist Party of China (Baum 2011: 424).[2] As transparency increased throughout the 1980s (recall Figure 3.6 from Chapter 3), so did organized mass opposition, culminating in the Tiananmen Square demonstrations in June of 1989. Arguably, data dissemination was part of other liberalization efforts that encouraged protesters (following the logic of Chapter 5). How did the disunited elite react to these protests?

The regime united behind the crushing of protestors and has survived intact ever since.[3] Arguably, this outcome may have been the whole point of

---

[1] We note that the incentives of the elite may differ if large-scale protests *already* have the potential to bring down the regime, in which case elites' best chance of survival may be to side with the protesters and abandon the regime (Casper and Tyson 2014; Dragu and Polborn 2013).

[2] Prior to this, Deng had facilitated Zhao's rise to power when he sacked Hu Yaobang from the general secretary position after student demonstrations had led to the public burning of the *Beijing Daily* (Baum 2011: 397). See also Fewsmith (2001) and Fravel (forthcoming).

[3] While data dissemination continued at high levels and even increased after 1989, information on the Tiananmen Square incident remains opaque inside of China to this day. For a study of China's continued opacity in international relations, see Mastro (2016).

facilitating protest in the first place. Indeed, Deng effectively placed part of the blame for the Tiananmen Square incident on Zhao Ziyang, who was subsequently marshalled out of power, arrested for aiding and abetting a "counter-revolutionary rebellion" (Baum 2011: 342). Party leaders then undertook "energetic efforts...to keep up the appearance of political unity and consensus" (Baum 2011: 342).[4]

The above story illustrates that potential mass unrest – which can be facilitated by transparency – may decrease the chances of problems from within the inner circle. Ironically, just as transparency increases the prospect of one threat, it may decrease the likelihood of another, such as a coup. Transparency may therefore offer a political benefit in terms of autocratic leader survival.

To understand the mechanism, note that elite disunity may encourage the population to overthrow an entire regime. For example, the masses may coordinate to overthrow a regime in the wake of an elite-led *coup d'état*. There are different reasons the masses may strike in such a situation. For instance, the populace may favor the (ousted) leader and view the coup as an indication of policy changes in an undesired direction. Conversely, mass coordination might occur because the policies of the incumbent regime are generally despised and the coup is seen as a moment of regime weakness to be exploited. Either way, elite disunity can incentivize mass unrest.

Now, recall from Part II that transparency serves to enhance the mobilizational capacity of the broad populace. An individual citizen becomes more likely to engage in protest when she recognizes that others share her perceptions of the regime – that is, when the informational environment is relatively rich. Elites recognize that introducing disunity into a high-information environment could spell disaster for them. Would-be coup plotters from within the inner-circle elite must therefore take the informational environment into account. If they stage a coup under conditions of high transparency, mass unrest may result – taking down the entire political order. Casper and Tyson (2014), for example, demonstrate that the correlation between protests and coups grows increasingly strong in high information environments.

Aware of this possibility, a rival elite is less likely to act against the regime leader when he chooses to increase transparency. Transparency essentially acts as a tool through which leaders use the threat posed by the masses to cow recalcitrant rival members of the regime. To borrow a phrase from Padró i Miquel (2007), the "politics of fear" brought on by the threat of popular revolt inspires cohesion within the regime, and increases a leader's freedom of maneuver (for a related result, see Di Lonardo and Tyson 2016).

Leaders, therefore, are most likely to disclose when they perceive threats as emerging from within their ruling coalition, rather than from the populace. We argue that risks to a leader from within his ruling coalition are higher when

---

[4] Subsequent leaders in China have allowed for public protest to gain leverage over international opponents (see Weiss 2014).

the rival elites enjoy some independence from the leader – when the rival's power does not depend on the leader. Disclosing data in these situations, and thereby increasing the risk of mass protest, can shore up the loyalty of an inner circle that might otherwise seek the ouster of a leader. By contrast, leaders who control a dependent elite face low risks from within the ruling coalition (see Svolik 2012: ch. 3). In these situations, disclosing data to increase the threat of mass protest is an unnecessary risk because the leader can already count on inner-circle loyalty.

In this chapter, we examine the logic of these claims rigorously. We then present empirical tests of our hypotheses. We provide empirical evidence that increasing transparency reduces the likelihood of coups, and that autocratic leaders increase transparency when they have more to fear from their inner circle than from the masses.

In what immediately follows, we show how our work on the role of elite support for the survival of autocracy connects to a rich and growing body of scholarship on authoritarian regimes. We then develop the intuition of our argument in a game-theoretic model. Subsequently, we present empirical tests of our theory.

10.1 TWIN THREATS TO AUTOCRATIC SURVIVAL

The core of our argument follows this intuition: any attempt by the inner-circle elite to discipline autocratic leaders might also destabilize the entire regime, and hence such action risks the elite's continued grasp on their privileged positions. The argument takes its inspiration from the work of Bueno de Mesquita et al. (2003) and Besley and Kudamatsu (2007). Padró i Miquel (2007) builds on this logic, contending that this "politics of fear" among elites allows leaders to expropriate from their winning coalition.[5]

Autocratic leaders must navigate twin threats: those emerging from the mass populace and those from rival elites within the regime. The populace may resort to mass unrest to overturn a regime because of languishing economic performance or perhaps because they seek greater civil and political liberties or more accountability from government. Elites may oust the leader through coups – whether of the palace or military varieties. The leader and the elite may differ in their preferences over government policy, whether because of the implications of policies for the divvying of rents, because of divergent primitive preferences over the direction of government, or because the elite doubt the competence of the leader. Elites attempt to discipline the leader and ensure he adopts their

---

[5] Di Lonardo and Tyson (2016) develop a related argument in which an external threat diminishes group infighting as applied to a terrorist group rather than an autocratic regime. For an ironic twist to theories that emphasize leader strength versus the strength of legislatures, where presidential strength paves the way to democracy, see Opalo (2012) and Opalo (2015).

preferred policies through the threat of a coup. If the leader fails to deliver, the elite may seek to replace him with a more palatable alternative.

Scholars have considered the consequences of these twin threats from various angles. Svolik (2013b) shows how attempts to curb pressure from the populace enhances the threat of military intervention in politics. Simply put, reducing the threat of mass unrest causes an increase in the threat from the inner circle. Slater (2010), like us, considers the role of a popular threat in unifying the elite. He argues that the presence of a coherent opposition at the moment of regime founding allows for the formation of elite "protection pacts," in which substantial authority and resources are delegated to the leadership. In a different piece, Slater (2009) considers the twin threats from a different direction, arguing that opposition by communal elites may facilitate unrest and lead to democratization (see also Kim and Slater 2017). In other words, elite disunity may increase the threat from the masses. Casper and Tyson (2014) argue that mass and elite threats are correlated – and that this correlation follows an informational logic. The signal provided by the emergence of one threat (protest, coup) may help galvanize other actors (elites, citizens) to coordinate in the enacting the alternative form of threat.

We focus on the way in which an authoritarian leader may reduce the inner-circle threat by increasing the mobilizational capacity of the populace. Following Bueno de Mesquita and Smith (2009), we consider the role of public goods (in our case, data disclosure) that enhance the ability of the populace to coordinate – and thus serve as a threat to keep the elites in line.

We connect the "twin threats" literature to the research on the role of political institutions under autocracy. We highlight that these institutions can mitigate the problem facing the inner-circle elites. Gehlbach and Keefer (2011) argue that because autocratic institutions help to limit the risks faced by the regime from deposing the leader, institutionalization promotes the credibility of promises not to expropriate regime elites (see also Gehlbach and Keefer 2012; Myerson 2008).

10.2 INFORMATION PROVISION IN AUTOCRACIES

While it is generally accepted that autocratic governments restrict information more severely than their democratic counterparts, autocrats may wish to allow some forms of information to circulate. We argue in this chapter that autocrats may use disclosure to balance the twin threats to their rule against one another. Other recent pieces examine information provision in autocracies and provide alternative rationales for why autocrats may allow for some openness to information. Though, these pieces typically examine forms of information distinct from the disclosure of aggregate data pertaining to social welfare.

Our argument also speaks to scholarship on the role of transparency under autocracy. Most existing studies along this line focus on the role of mass media. Accounts by Egorov, Guriev, and Sonin (2009) and Lorentzen (2014) argue that autocrats can effectively outsource the role of monitoring their agents to the media. Autocratic leaders can spare themselves some of the costs of monitoring regional or bureaucratic officials by relying on investigative media reports. The media may therefore help curb corruption and other behavior that can harm the regime as a whole. These benefits must be traded off against the risk that a free media may promote mass public opposition. In an innovative series on the "Great Firewall" of China, King, Pan, and Roberts (2013, 2014) find supportive evidence of this argument: online censors permit criticism of local government corruption and other forms of mis-governance, but delete calls for protest. In complementary theoretical explorations of media control under autocracy, Gehlbach and Sonin (2014) and Shadmehr and Bernhardt (2015) examine the incentive of autocrats to engage in media censorship, given that citizens rationally update to discount good news about the regime or interpret no news as bad news. Guriev and Treisman (2015) examine the trade-offs dictators face between employing censorship, propaganda, and the co-optation of elites.[6]

While this work on the media shares our focus on information dissemination under autocratic rule, the conception of transparency differs fundamentally from ours. Rather than focusing on the media, we emphasize the role of *government* disclosures of information to the public – as we have throughout the book. In our formulation, increasing transparency does little to enhance monitoring of lower-level public officials because there is no outsourcing of information-collection to the media. And while closer government monitoring of subordinates may be associated with the collection of more information which can be disclosed, there is no need for an autocratic government to make the results of such monitoring public. In our model, the key question is whether autocrats choose to disclose this information to the public.

Boix and Svolik (2013) also examine the role of a form of transparency under autocratic rule. Like us, they conclude that higher levels of transparency are associated with a reduced risk of coup – but, again, the conception of transparency differs from ours. In their model, transparency relates to the ability of members of the regime to observe efforts by autocratic leaders to amass greater authority and power – the clarity of the "rules of the game." As the authority vested in an autocratic leader becomes more clearly defined, conflict is less likely to emerge between these leaders and members of their ruling coalition.[7] While the clarity of the rules of the game may involve the availability of economic

---

[6] For an excellent review of the literature on information problems in nondemocracies, see Wallace (2014). For a remarkable experiment on the impact of the media control following a coup, showing that putschist-controlled broadcasting can increase identity salience and willingness to delay elections, but not increase approval for the junta, see Bleck and Michelitch (2017).

[7] Myerson (2008) and Gehlbach and Keefer (2011) are similarly concerned with elite coordination against a leader and the way in which the existence of coordination mechanisms within the elite may allow dictators to credibly commit to redistribute toward regime members.

information – for instance, information regarding the budget – the critical concern for Boix and Svolik (2013) is the role of information *available to the elite*. By contrast, we focus on the information made available *to the wider public*. If a given piece of information is revealed to the public, it must perforce also be accessible to members of the regime elite – so, these two notions of transparency must be at least somewhat correlated. However, there is no reason to expect that the reverse holds – considerable amounts of information are likely circulated among autocratic elites and not disclosed to the broader public.

Our story involves data disclosure by the government that enables the mass populace to update their higher-order beliefs about the broad distribution of discontent with the regime. Transparency thereby facilitates collective action against the regime. As we detail in the next section, the resulting increased threat of mass insurrection can serve to reduce the twin threat coming from elites – by consolidating elite support for the leader. The leader ironically prolongs his tenure by increasing the threat of destabilization of the regime.

10.3 THE MODEL

Having sketched our argument discursively, we introduce heightened logical rigor using a game-theoretic approach. Our model builds on the framework introduced by Besley and Kudamatsu (2007), who construct a model of autocratic accountability involving both moral hazard and adverse selection. Like us, they examine an interaction in which steps by elite regime-members to discipline their leaders threaten the stability of regime. Our model incorporates disclosure, which both acts as a signal to the elite of the preferences of the leader and serves to increase the risk of mass unrest.

Our argument is counterintuitive and requires mathematical rigor. The mathematics that follow are advanced and we encourage readers to study them with care. Readers who struggled with our previous models, however, may prefer to skim this section before reading our empirical tests in the subsequent section.

10.3.1 Model Primitives

Consider an interaction between an autocratic leader L and a group of elite regime-members R. We also consider the actions of a mass of citizens M, though these actors are nonstrategic in this model.[8] The game proceeds for two periods. In the first period, L must decide whether to disclose $d \in \{0, 1\}$, and in each period he must make a policy decision $e_t \in \{0, 1\}$, where t denotes the period of play $t \in \{1, 2\}$. Regime elites R, after witnessing the outcome of the leader's

---

[8] To remain consistent, we use the male pronoun to refer to autocratic leaders. We ascribe female pronouns to both R and M.

policy decision, must determine whether to retain him in office. We denote this decision $v \in \{0, 1\}$, where $v = 1$ denotes a decision to remove. Leaders may be of one of two types $\theta \in \{0, 1\}$. When $\theta = 1$, leaders are "convergent" – they have a primitive preference for setting e_t equal to the value that maximizes the welfare of the group in power. When $\theta = 0$, leaders are "divergent" – they have a primitive preference for setting e_t equal to a value viewed as suboptimal by the group in power. The prior probability that L is a convergent type is defined as π (i.e., $Pr(\theta = 1) = \pi$).

Following the conclusion of the first period of play, a contest for power takes place between members of the regime and the populace. If members of the regime chose to keep L in place, the probability that the regime falls is given by $p(d)$, where $1 > p(1) > p(0) > 0$. Define the effect of disclosure on mobilizational capacity as $\rho \equiv p(1) - p(0)$. We thus make a primitive assumption that disclosure increases the danger of mass unrest, as is consistent with the theory in Chapter 5 and the evidence in Chapters 6 and 7. Alternatively, one may think of this contest as emerging with positive probability, where disclosure boosts the probability that mass mobilization takes place.

If L was replaced before this contest takes place, we assume that the probability the regime falls is given by $\omega p(d)$, where $\omega \in (1, \frac{1}{p(1)})$. Note that the ω-term reflects the tendency of inner-circle strife to destabilize the regime. One can think of ω as reflecting the strength of L vis-à-vis R: low-ω leaders face a strong, independent, and threatening elite, while high-ω leaders exercise control over an elite that is dependent on the leader.

To anticipate the empirical flavor of ω, one way to interpret this parameter follows the approach of Bueno de Mesquita et al. (2003): ω is an increasing function of L's time in power, during which he entrenches himself and cultivates an R with increasing levels of dependency and loyalty (see Chapter 3 in Svolik 2012). Alternatively, Besley and Kudamatsu (2007) interpret the ω-parameter as the degree to which the autocracy is personalistic, in the Geddes, Wright, and Frantz (2012) sense. In low-ω autocracies, autocratic succession is institutionalized, and R enjoys some power independent of L. The risk of regime collapse following the removal of the leader is higher in high-ω autocracies, where the regime's legitimacy depends on a cult of personality surrounding L. Or one can conceive of ω as reflecting L–R relations along the lines of Gandhi (2008) – that is, in autocracies with a strict inner-circle hierarchy (military dictatorships and monarchies), L enjoys high-ω, whereas in autocracies where L power over the elites is more precarious (civilian autocracies) ω is low.

Continuing with the logic of how the game proceeds, if L was removed, either by members of the regime or by the victory of the populace, we assume a new leader is selected from the same distribution as described above (i.e., $Pr(\theta = 1) = \pi$). If the whole regime is overthrown (L and R are removed), we assume M takes over as a new regime.

Denote national income, or disposable resources, as $y > 0$. Both members of the elite and leader enjoy λy if when in office, where $\lambda \in (\frac{1}{2}, 1)$ reflects the disproportionate flow of resources to members of the regime. In the first period of play, M receives a share of resources given by $(1 - \lambda)y$. In the second period of play, this also denotes the resources flowing to whichever group $\{L, M\}$ loses the contest for power.

Members of the regime want to remain in power, and so continue to gain the larger share λ of resources. R also has preferences over policy. Specifically, R wants the policy e_t to be set equal to a value that is randomly determined at the start of each period, but known to all players, $s_t \in \{0, 1\}$. If policy is set in line with R's preferences, they receive an additional utility bonus $\Delta > 0$. R's utility is thus given by:

$$u_{R,t}(e_t, s_t) = \begin{cases} I_t[\Delta + \lambda y] + (1 - I_t)(1 - \lambda)y & \text{if } e_t = s_t \\ I_t \lambda y + (1 - I_t)(1 - \lambda)y & \text{otherwise} \end{cases} \qquad (10.1)$$

where $I_t \in \{0, 1\}$ is an indicator variable equal to 1 if R is in power at time t and equal to zero if M is in power. Note that R always begins the game in power, hence $I_1 = 1$, whereas I_2 is determined by the contest for power that takes place at the end of the first period of play.

Members of the populace derive utility only based on their share of national income $(1 - \lambda)y$ in the first period of play. Should they come to power in the second period, they will gain in their share of national income – which will rise to λy – and they will become concerned about the leader's choice of policy. The utility of the populace is thus given by:

$$u_{M,t}(e_t, s_t) = \begin{cases} I_t(1 - \lambda)y + (1 - I_t)[\Delta + \lambda y] & \text{if } e_t = s_t \\ I_t(1 - \lambda)y + (1 - I_t)\lambda y & \text{otherwise} \end{cases} \qquad (10.2)$$

where I_t is as defined above. Note that expression 10.2 is essentially identical to the utility of R, save that M is only in power if $I_t = 0$ and R is only in power if $I_t = 1$.

L's utility depends on his type. Convergent types ($\theta = 1$) share the policy preferences of the members of those elites in power (hence "convergent"). Divergent types ($\theta = 0$), however, have primitive preferences opposed to sitting regime members. Specifically, we assume that divergent types derive benefits from setting $e_t \neq s_t$, and we define these benefits as r_t. To ensure that divergent types do truly prefer an alternative policy, we assume that $r_t > \Delta$. The benefits to defying the elite exceed those from adhering to the elites' policy concerns. Moreover, we assume that r_t is known to L, but known only in expectation to all other players. To accomplish this, we assume that r_t is a random variable drawn from a CDF $G(\cdot)$. $G(\cdot)$ has support on $\mathbb{R}_+$ such that $G(\Delta) = 0$ (i.e., $r_t \in (\Delta, \infty)$) and has expected value μ.

Leaders also derive utility from the share of national income flowing to the elite. Thus, leader utility is given by:

$$u_{L,t}(e_t, s_t; \theta) = \begin{cases} \Delta + \lambda y & \text{if } e_t = s_t \text{ and in power} \\ \lambda y & \text{if } e_t \neq s_t, \ \theta = 1 \text{ and in power} \\ r_t + \lambda y & \text{if } e_t \neq s_t, \ \theta = 0 \text{ and in power} \\ 0 & \text{if out of power.} \end{cases} \qquad (10.3)$$

The order of play is as follows:

1. Nature draws the leader's type $\theta \in \{0, 1\}$, the state variable s_1 and the value of rents r_1, which are revealed to the leader but not to any citizen.
2. The leader chooses $d \in \{0, 1\}$ and the value of e_1.
3. Members of the regime observe the choice of d and the realization of the policy outcome. They choose whether to unseat the leader $v \in \{0, 1\}$.
4. A contest for power between R and M takes place. M prevails with probability $p(d)$ if the leader was previously retained and with probability $\omega p(d)$ if the leader was previously removed.
5. a. If M prevails, it is in power in round 2 and a new leader is chosen by Nature. This leader is of type $\theta = 1$ with probability π.
   b. If R prevails after ousting the leader, a new leader is chosen by Nature. This leader is of type $\theta = 1$ with probability π.
   c. Otherwise, L remains in office.
6. Nature chooses values of s_2 and r_2, which are revealed to the sitting leader, but not to any other player.
7. The sitting leader chooses e_2. All payoffs are realized and the game ends.

10.3.2 Equilibrium

We characterize a perfect Bayesian equilibrium (PBE) to this game (Fudenberg and Tirole 1991). As is common in signaling games, this interaction can give rise to multiple such equilibria. We narrow the pool of such equilibria by focusing on PBE in pure strategies in which L chooses to disclose whenever indifferent over this choice. Within this narrowed pool of equilibria, we focus on a semi-separating PBE. This particular equilibrium has some nice properties – specifically, within the (narrowed) pool of equilibria defined above, it uniquely satisfies the intuitive criterion refinement proposed by Cho and Kreps (1987). (A proof is in the appendix to this chapter.)

A PBE in pure strategies consists of two elements: (1) a strategy profile specifying the actions for all players at each stage of the game, and (2) a set of posterior beliefs for members of the regime about the type of leader they are facing.

A strategy for L consists of a choice of an action pair over both policy and disclosure (e_1, d) in the first period of play, where (e_1, d) is a mapping from (determined by) his type θ and the realization of the value of rents r_1, $(e_1, d) : \{0, 1\} \times (\Delta, \infty) \to \{0, 1\} \times \{0, 1\}$. His strategy further consists of a policy choice in the second period of play, e_2, which is a mapping from his type, $e_2 : \{0, 1\} \to \{0, 1\}$.

A strategy for R consists of a mapping from her posterior beliefs over L's type and the choice of disclosure d into her decision of whether to oust the leader $v : [0, 1] \times \{0, 1\} \to \{0, 1\}$. And R's posterior beliefs are updated according to Bayes' rule and are consistent with the strategy profile.[9]

To characterize a semi-separating PBE, we require several definitions.

Definition 10.1. *Define $\bar{\omega}$ and $\underline{\omega}$ such that:*

$$\pi \Delta = \frac{p(0)y(\bar{\omega} - 1)(2\lambda - 1)}{1 - \bar{\omega}p(0)}$$

$$\pi \Delta = \frac{p(1)y(\underline{\omega} - 1)(2\lambda - 1)}{1 - \underline{\omega}p(1)}.$$

It is straightforward to demonstrate that both thresholds exist and are uniquely defined by these expressions. Moreover, it follows that $\bar{\omega} > \underline{\omega}$. If $\omega > \bar{\omega}$, the risks of ousting the leader are too high for members of the regime to bear, regardless of that leader's actions in office. If $\omega > \underline{\omega}$, the risks of ousting the leader will again be too high to warrant a coup, but only if the leader chooses to disclose information. We return to these thresholds in detail below.

We further define a threshold in r_1, which we term $\bar{r}$. This threshold is a function of the parameter ω.

Definition 10.2. *Define $\bar{r}(\omega)$ such that:*

$$\bar{r}(\omega) = \begin{cases} \Delta + [1 - p(0)][\mu + \lambda y] & \text{if } \omega < \underline{\omega} \\ \Delta + \rho[\mu + \lambda y] & \text{if } \omega \in [\underline{\omega}, \bar{\omega}] \\ \Delta & \text{if } \omega > \bar{\omega}. \end{cases}$$

Recall that μ is the expected value of Δ. This threshold thus determines if "divergent" leaders prefer to defy their regime. If $r > \bar{r}$, the leader holds very strongly divergent policy preferences from elites, and so acts on these preferences. If, by contrast, $r < \bar{r}$, the leader may be induced to follow the wishes of other regime members. Again, we return to this threshold below.

We can now characterize the semi-separating PBE to this game in the following proposition.

Proposition 10.1. *A semi-separating PBE to this game consists of the following strategies and beliefs:*

---

[9] M is nonstrategic in this game, given that the interaction terminates after two periods. Even if M comes to power, members of the new regime cannot remove their sitting leader from power.

1. For L:

$$(e_1, d) = \begin{cases} (\neg s_1, 1) & \text{if } r_1 \geq \bar{r}(\omega), \ \omega \leq \bar{\omega} \text{ and } \theta = 0 \\ (\neg s_1, 0) & \text{if } r_1 \geq \bar{r}(\omega), \ \omega > \bar{\omega} \text{ and } \theta = 0 \\ (s_1, 0) & \text{otherwise.} \end{cases}$$

$$e_2 = \begin{cases} \neg s_2 & \text{if } \theta = 0 \\ s_2 & \text{otherwise.} \end{cases}$$

2. For R:

$$v = \begin{cases} 0 & \text{if } \omega > \bar{\omega} \\ 0 & \text{if } \omega > \underline{\omega} \text{ and } d = 1 \\ 0 & \text{if } (e_1, d) = (s_1, 0) \\ 1 & \text{otherwise.} \end{cases}$$

3. R's beliefs are given (with some abuse of notation) by $Pr(\theta = 1|e_1 = s_1, d = 0) > \pi$ and $Pr(\theta = 1|e_1, d) = 0$ for all other realizations of (e_1, d).

10.3.3 Intuitions

In the final period of play, the sitting L sets his policy decision e_2 according to type. That is $e_2 = s_2$ if $\theta = 1$ and $e_2 \neq s_2$ if $\theta = 0$. This is a dominant strategy.

Given this strategy by the leader, R must make her decision regarding retention weighing her expectations about L's future policy choice and the consequences of removal for regime survival. R prefers to keep the leader in place if she believes him to be a convergent type. If she believes L to be a divergent type, R prefers to evict, but may be dissuaded from doing so by the threat of mass unrest.

R can update her beliefs based on the leader's previous decisions over policy and disclosure (e_1, d), and we denote these beliefs, with some abuse of notation, as $Pr(\theta = 1|e_1, d)$. Thus, R can expect policy returns of $Pr(\theta = 1|e_1, d)\Delta$ from retaining the leader – since a convergent leader will always set $e_2 = s_2$ in the second period – and returns of $\pi\Delta$ from replacing the leader with an alternative – since the probability a new leader is convergent is given by π. Removal, however, also has consequences for regime survival. If the leader is retained, the regime is removed with probability $p(d)$ – if he is removed, the regime is ousted with probability $\omega p(d)$. Weighing these various concerns, we can state that R sets $v = 1$ iff:

$$\omega p(d)(1 - \lambda)y + [1 - \omega p(d)][\pi \Delta + \lambda y] > p(d)(1 - \lambda)y + [1 - p(d)][Pr(\theta = 1|e_1, d)\Delta + \lambda y]. \tag{10.4}$$

Because of the adverse consequences of leader removal for the survival of the regime, circumstances can arise under which R chooses to retain their leader even if certain that the leader is a divergent type. That is, $v = 0$ even if

$Pr(\theta = 1|e_1, d) = 0$. The risks incurred by removing the leader simply are not worth the expected benefits $(\pi \Delta)$ from securing a more desirable dictator. Substituting $Pr(\theta = 1|e_1, d) = 0$ into expression 10.4 and simplifying yields the values of $\bar{\omega}$ and $\underline{\omega}$ as defined in Definition 10.1.

So, for $\omega > \bar{\omega}$, regardless of the actions of L in the first period, regime elites choose $v = 0$. The risks of removing the leader simply are not worth any possible policy gains that might be derived from doing so. We refer to autocracies with values of $\omega > \bar{\omega}$ as *entrenched* – either due to their long tenure in power (Bueno de Mesquita et al. 2003), the personalistic nature of the regime (Geddes, Wright, and Frantz 2012), or the strict inner-circle hierarchy (Gandhi 2008).

For $\omega \in [\underline{\omega}, \bar{\omega}]$, leaders can guarantee their retention if they disclose, but are not offered any such guarantee otherwise. Because disclosure heightens the risk of public mobilization, it also renders ousting the leader more risky. Elites are thus less willing to remove when $d = 1$ than when $d = 0$.

We can now consider L's decision over policy and disclosure (e_1, d) in the first period of play. When $\omega > \bar{\omega}$, L can make this decision free of any consideration of the regime's response. Each type of L thus acts on his primitive preference: $e_1 = s_1$ if $\theta = 1$ and not otherwise. Similarly, the leader can act on his primitive preference over disclosure, which is always not to disclose $(d = 0)$. In the model, disclosure acts only to increase the mobilizational capacity of the populace. For leaders who are already secure from elite accountability, disclosure offers only a cost with no benefit.

In a semi-separating equilibrium, a convergent type of leader also acts on his primitive preferences, setting $e_1 = s_1$ and $d = 0$ for all values of $\omega < \bar{\omega}$. So long as elites correctly interpret this behavior as a positive signal of L's type, this maximizes a convergent leader's utility. The question, then, is whether a divergent type would choose to mimic convergent types and set $e_1 = s_1$ and $d = 0$, or choose to separate. A divergent leader bases this decision on the realization of the rents that he receives from deviating from the preferences of the elite, that is, r_1.

Recall that a divergent type earns rents r_1 from setting $e_1 \neq s_1$, where r_1 is a random variable and $r_1 > \Delta$. Hence, divergent types always have some incentive to separate from convergent, and – for a sufficiently high realization of r_1 – this will be a dominant strategy. Since convergent types set $(e_1, d) = (s_1, 0)$, whereas divergent types may choose not to do so, $Pr(\theta = 1|e_1 = s_1, d = 0) > \pi$. Substituting these beliefs into expression 10.4 reveals that R always strictly prefers to retain given the action pair $(s_1, 0)$. A divergent type thus knows that he will be retained with certainty by mimicking convergent types.

The value of rents necessary to induce a divergent type to separate is given by $\bar{r}(\omega)$. For $r_1 > \bar{r}(\omega)$, the leader's policy gains from defying his winning coalition outweigh the benefits from certain retention by the elite. For any value of $\omega < \bar{\omega}$, when a divergent leader chooses to so defy his elite, he also chooses to disclose. This is because, for $\omega \in [\underline{\omega}, \bar{\omega}]$ disclosure guarantees the elite's quiescence. The leader is able to free himself from elite accountability via disclosure. For $\omega < \underline{\omega}$, disclosure does not insulate the leader from regime backlash. But, since the leader anticipates that the elite will mobilize for his removal, the consequences of disclosure will only be felt by his successor. The leader is indifferent between disclosing and not and – in an act of *Schadenfreude* – punishes his winning coalition for their disloyalty. We return to the manner in which disclosure correlates with defiance of (much of) the regime in our discussion of empirical cases, specifically the case of the Soviet Union. Others have also noted that increases in autocratic transparency tend to go hand-in-hand with reforms that alienate large portions of the regime (Chen and Xu 2015). We highlight this point in the following remark:

Remark 10.1. *When $\omega < \bar{\omega}$, if L chooses to defy the policy preferences of the elite ($e_1 \neq s_1$), he also chooses to disclose $d = 1$.*

Combining these strategies and beliefs, we are left with the PBE characterized by Proposition 10.1. Convergent types always act according to their primitive preferences over both policy and disclosure, which are also the preferences of the elite. Divergent types only act according to their primitive preferences over both disclosure and policy if they are entrenched. If not, they may choose to act on their preference over policy if the rents from doing so are sufficiently high. However, if they so separate themselves from convergent types, they must also choose to disclose. Members of the elite, responding to these equilibrium strategies, oust the leader when $(e_1, d) \neq (s_1, 0)$ and $\omega < \underline{\omega}$, and choose to retain otherwise.

10.3.4 Comparative Statics

We advance two empirical claims based on our theory. The first pertains to leader removal – leaders who disclose more readily should be at a reduced threat of removal via coup. The second examines the circumstances under which autocratic leaders choose to disclose – we should witness less disclosure when autocratic institutions are entrenched, and greater disclosure when the leadership is new to office (Bueno de Mesquita et al. 2003), the leader does not enjoy personalistic power (Geddes, Wright, and Frantz 2012), or when the inner circle is not governed by a strict hierarchy (Gandhi 2008).

Our claims regarding the insulating effects of disclosure, however, cannot be examined via a conventional comparative static. The decision to disclose is endogenous, and hence cannot be manipulated like an exogenous parameter. This is true despite the fact that, in a partial equilibrium analysis, it is clear that R's decision over removal is influenced by disclosure, such that she is less likely to set $v = 1$ when $d = 1$.

We instead, therefore, compare the equilibrium defined in Proposition 10.1 to an analogous semi-separating equilibrium in a game isomorphic to that above, save only that L does not possess the option to disclose. Practically, autocrats face a number of obstacles to increasing disclosure, particularly within a short time frame. The disclosure of economic information requires nontrivial amounts of bureaucratic expertise, which must be amassed over time, in addition to large-scale data collection efforts. As argued in Part I, we might imagine that autocratic leaders vary in their capacity to disclose – or in their capacity to increase levels of disclosure. In the following proposition, we demonstrate that – when autocratic leaders possess a greater capacity to disclose, and hence disclose more frequently – they survive for a greater range of parameter values than would be the case where they cannot disclose.

Proposition 10.2. *In a semi-separating equilibrium to a model without disclosure, when $\omega \in [\underline{\omega}, \bar{\omega}]$ and $r_1 > \Delta + [1 - p(0)][\mu + \lambda y]$, divergent types of L are removed by the elite with certainty. For the same set of parameter values, in a semi-separating equilibrium where disclosure is possible, divergent types of L are retained with certainty and choose $d = 1$.*

Empirically, we interpret Proposition 10.2 as indicating that – conditional on institutional covariates – disclosure should be associated with a reduced risk of leader removal via coup. For this range of parameter values, leaders who are able to disclose survive – and their survival results directly from their disclosure decision. The increased risk of popular mobilization cows the elite.

Proposition 10.3. *L chooses $d = 1$ for a wider range of realizations of r_1 and θ when $\omega \leq \bar{\omega}$ than when $\omega > \bar{\omega}$.*

Proposition 10.3 tells us which autocrats should be most prone to disclose. Disclosure should be greater when $\omega \leq \bar{\omega}$ – that is, when the leader is not entrenched – than otherwise. Here, ω represents the balance of power within the regime – specifically the risk leader removal poses for regime survival. This risk increases in ω. Where the risk to the elite is low – when the leader is new, nonpersonalistic, or civilian – we expect the leader to increase the risk for the elites from undertaking a coup by disclosing data.

10.4 SUMMARIZING THE ARGUMENT AND ITS EMPIRICAL IMPLICATIONS

Our contention that leaders trade off the threat of coup against that of mass protest rests on the assumption that coup attempts tend to destabilize the regime *as a whole*. Attempts to unseat the leader from within the ruling clique may serve as a focal point for mobilizing mass unrest. This unrest has the potential to lead to the upending of the regime more generally. Thus, if a leader suspects a lack of fidelity among his ruling clique, he may seek to provoke the masses so as to entice elite loyalty.

Part of this argument is foreshadowed by the evidence presented in Chapter 7, where we show that regime collapse brought on by a coup becomes less likely when autocratic leaders disclose. In the empirical section of this chapter, we push this line of testing further.

Of course, not all leaders face the same level of threat from the inner-circle elites. Under certain types of autocracies, the elites maintain high levels of loyalty to the leader – come what may – while in others, the elites may be more rebellious against a leader who does not serve their interests. This observation is an important one for our argument: if the elites pose but a minor threat, the leader has little reason to facilitate mass mobilization. Why risk popular unrest if the danger posed by the elites is minimal? Gambling on mass unrest becomes necessary only when the elites pose a substantial threat, which, in turn, depends on how much the removal of an autocratic leader upsets the overarching order in society.

The extent to which removing an autocratic leader destabilizes the regime is a function of the power relationship between the leader and the elites. Where the leader exerts great control over the elites, he need not gamble on mass unrest to maintain elite loyalty. Where the leader's grip on power over the elites is more precarious, he may resort to facilitating mass unrest through transparency in order to keep the elites in line.

We propose using three features of authoritarian systems to measure the power relationship between the leader and the elites (ω): time in power, personalistic versus institutionalized autocracy, and hierarchical versus precarious regimes.

1. Time in Power

Bueno de Mesquita et al. (2003) observe that the risk of leader removal in autocracies declines precipitously over time. They argue that entrenched leaders enjoy increasing levels of loyalty from elites over time because they become dependent on the leader for the continued spoils of autocratic rule. This empirical regularity has been supported and explored by the work of many scholars (see Besley and Kudamatsu 2007; Gehlbach and Malesky 2010; Little 2017; Svolik 2012; Francois, Rainer, and Trebbi 2014).

This empirical regularity, we argue, arises because of the extent to which a coup is likely to spark unrest. The removal of a leader who recently assumed office is less likely to provoke mass unrest than the removal of a long-serving autocrat. New leaders have had little time to build up a patronage network within the regime, hence their removal is unlikely to require sweeping purges of official ranks. New leaders are less likely to have built up personal authority or a cult of personality with the mass public than leaders who have long been ensconced in power.

Bueno de Mesquita et al. (2003: 37, 65) term this tendency a "loyalty norm," which, they argue, develops among the elite toward their leader because of the routinized payoffs they receive from him. They do not wish to upset his rule, lest they also upset the private payoffs they receive by supporting the regime. Focusing specifically on leaders in Africa, Francois, Rainer, and Trebbi (2014) also find that the hazard functions of autocrats decrease monotonically over time. Guriev and Treisman (2015) argue that this pattern follows an informational logic – a dictator's survival in office causes the public to update positively with regard to his competence. Little (2017) offers a similar informational logic – leaders who survive past challenges must be inferred to be "strong," and so face fewer future challenges (see also Svolik 2012: ch. 3). The work of these scholars suggests that a leader's legitimacy and the negative consequences of his removal for the ruling clique are both rising over time.

We predict, therefore, that time in power is negatively related to disclosure. The longer the autocrat has survived in office, the greater is the degree of loyalty accorded to the leader and the lower is the potential coup threat. There is less of a need to discipline the elite members with threats of removal from below – and less incentive to disclose to the general public. In terms of our formal model, ω increases with leader tenure.

2. Personalistic versus Institutionalized Autocracy

Following Geddes, Wright, and Frantz (2012), we consider "personalistic" regimes, where the regime's legitimacy derives from the identity of the leader himself, versus "institutionalized" regimes, where lines of succession are determined by rules rather than personal power.

Under personalistic regimes, leaders have less to fear from elites. In terms of our model, ω is high under personalistic regimes. A changing-of-the-guard in a personalistic regime would reflect a moment of regime weakness with intense intra-regime conflict. Change of a personalistic leader can thus readily provide a focal point for unrest, producing mass protest or setting in motion conflicts likely to upend the regime as a whole (Geddes 1999). The personalistic leader knows this, and thus enjoys a higher level of loyalty from the elites. We predict lower levels of data disclosure under personalistic regimes because the leader need not gamble on mass unrest to keep the elites in line.

Under institutionalized regimes (low-ω), elites do not rely on the leader for the continued legitimacy of the regime. Regimes with highly institutionalized rules of succession face a low risk of mass unrest following a change in leadership. The leader has a designated successor, regime officials have a formal voice in government, and legitimacy comes from institutional positions rather than the leader's personal authority. Leadership replacement in such regimes follows regularized procedures and need not send a signal to the public of intra-regime conflict or weakness. A leader of such a regime may therefore be tempted to use transparency to increase the fear – and thus the loyalty – of the elites to the leader.

3. Hierarchical versus Precarious Regimes

Hadenius and Teorell (2007) reject "personalism" as a distinct category of authoritarian regimes because the trait exists, to varying degrees, across all autocracies. Still, the importance of how an autocratic leader deals with the potential threat of usurpers from within the elite is too important to ignore.

Recognizing that the ruling elite pose a major threat to autocrats, Gandhi (2008) has proposed categorizing autocracies precisely according to the institutionalized relationships between the leader and the elite: "to mitigate the threat posed by elites, dictators frequently establish inner sanctums where real decisions are made and potential rivals are kept under close scrutiny" (Cheibub, Gandhi, and Vreeland 2010: 84). Gandhi's coding of authoritarian regimes therefore distinguishes the relationship between the leader and the elite – specifically the inner sanctums – with attention to how these sanctums determine leadership removal and succession. Her categories include military dictatorships and monarchies, which have strict hierarchies, and civilian-ruled autocracies, which do not.

Military dictators typically "harness the organizational apparatus of the armed forces to consolidate their rule" (Cheibub, Gandhi, and Vreeland 2010: 85). While internecine fighting across branches of the military is common, each branch follows a strong hierarchy. Monarchs, similarly, "rely on their family and kin networks very strongly in the governance of their regimes" (Cheibub, Gandhi, and Vreeland 2010: 84). Succession lines are clear and are rarely broken without the approval of the kin network.

By contrast, civilian rulers face the greatest challenge from the elite clique. Civilian rulers "can not appeal to the armed forces in the way that a military dictator can," and they "do not have sufficient family and kin networks to establish permanent dynastic succession" (Cheibub, Gandhi, and Vreeland 2010: 86). Civilian rulers typically attempt to organize the ruling elite through a political party, but their position, generally, is more "precarious" because they do not enjoy a ready-made hierarchy – they must invent one (Cheibub, Gandhi, and Vreeland 2010: 86).

Applying Gandhi's logic to our theoretical model, we would expect military dictators (high-ω) to fear the least from their highly disciplined inner circle. Monarchs (also high-ω) similarly enjoy some loyalty from their kin-based ruling elite. These military and monarchical leaders have the least to gain from the mass unrest unleashed by transparency, and the most to lose. We therefore expect these regimes to exhibit lower levels of transparency. Civilian rulers (low-ω), by contrast, have the most to gain by keeping elites loyal through the fear of mass unrest facilitated by transparency. We consequently predict civilian rules to disclose at higher levels.[10]

Summarizing, inner-circle members of an autocratic regime may attempt to remove their leader. Removing the leader opens up the possibility that his replacement will prove more amenable to the elite. This is risky business.

---

[10] A measure of political party strength of civilian rulers would be useful, but such coding would likely be driven by a tautology – those who survive would be coded as the strongest.

Removing the leader also increases the change of regime collapse – from the threat of mass unrest – potentially costing these same elite individuals their privileged positions (Besley and Kudamatsu 2007; Bueno de Mesquita et al. 2003; Gehlbach and Malesky 2010; Padró i Miquel 2007; Di Lonardo and Tyson 2016). These risks to elites are particularly high in Geddes's personalized regimes, Gandhi's hierarchical regimes, and those long under established leadership. By contrast, elites have less to fear from leaders in Geddes's institutionalized autocracies, Gandhi's civilian autocracies, or under newly established leadership (Bueno de Mesquita et al. 2003). Elites in this later set of autocracies may well win the gamble when they seek to overthrow leaders.

Transparency alters this decision calculus of elites. Transparency increases the mobilizational capacity of the populace, boosting the probability that attempts to remove the leader will cause the regime to collapse (Casper and Tyson 2014). As such, transparency pushes members of the elite toward inaction. As the danger of insurrection mounts, members of the elite grow more complacent in the face of an uncooperative leadership. Indeed, transparency can induce loyalty to a leader – even one who acts against the general interest of the elites.

As detailed in Part II, transparency facilitates mass mobilization by the populace against autocratic regimes. This increased mobilizational capacity of the populace boosts the risk that an internal coup hold for inner-circle elites. Coups carried out by the ruling clique act as signals to the citizenry of (1) incipient policy changes and (2) intra-regime conflict and weakness. Since mass mobilization entails strategic complementarities, citizens are only likely to take to the streets following a coup when they recognize that others share their perception of the implications of the coup – for example, the desirability of policy change or the level of disdain for the regime (the "distribution of discontent"). Herein lies the key to our argument. Since transparency helps ensure that these perceptions are (1) widely shared and (2) *known* to be widely shared, citizens are more likely to respond to an internal coup with protest in a transparent environment than in an opaque one. A coup is always a risky endeavor for members of the autocratic elite, transparency increases these risks by providing oxygen for a popular response sparked by the ouster of the leader.

Autocratic leaders, we contend, determine the level of data disclosure with these effects in mind. Disclosure constitutes a gamble for such a leader. On the positive side, transparency renders elites more complacent by virtue of the increased mobilizational capacity of the populace. Yet, empowering the populace in this manner is obviously hazardous – citizens may depose the regime even as the elite toes the leadership's line.

10.5 DESCRIPTIVE DATA AND EXAMPLES

Our game-theoretic model makes two claims that we can test empirically. Proposition 10.2 contends that transparency ensures the retention of a leader whom elites would remove from power in the absence of transparency. Thus, transparency has a negative effect on the probability of a coup. Proposition 10.3 asserts that leaders can choose opacity when there is a high probability that the whole regime (including, importantly, the inner-circle elites) will topple if the leader falls. Thus, leaders who enjoy a dominant position of power over the inner-circle elites are less likely to disclose data.

We test Proposition 10.2 by examining patterns of transparency and leader removal via coups. We focus on coups here – in contrast to the mass unrest studied in Chapters 6 and 7 – because we wish to examine the actions of elite actors. Coups, in contrast to other forms of autocratic removal – such as democratization or popular uprisings – involve careful planning by tightknit, clandestine operatives from the ranks of the elite, often including a leader's most trusted advisors. Note that, in focusing on coups, we likely undercount the forms of leader removal pertinent to our theoretical model, which include any attempts by regime members to replace the acting leadership, whether or not this involves violence or the threat thereof. One might imagine that we particularly undercount instances of leader removal in more institutionalized autocracies, where such ousters may be achieved through more orderly processes. Coefficients on the measures of autocratic institutions – particularly on the Geddes, Wright, and Frantz (GWF) proxies for ω – in our empirical models of the risk of coup are likely to be biased relative to the effect of theoretical interest. In particular, these coefficients are likely to be biased downward relative to the true frequency of elite-driven usurpations in institutionalized regimes.

We test Proposition 10.3 using the three distinct empirical approaches of Bueno de Mesquita et al. (2003), Geddes, Wright, and Frantz (2012), and Cheibub, Gandhi, and Vreeland (2010) to approximate ω, as detailed previously in the chapter. An autocratic leader's time in power, following the logic of Bueno de Mesquita and colleagues, is predicted to have a negative effect on the level of transparency; Geddes's personalistic autocracies are also predicted to have a negative effect; and Gandhi's hierarchical autocracies are predicted to have a similar negative effect.

We consider first some descriptive data and then present some examples to illustrate the logic of our argument. We reserve more rigorous analysis of the data for the subsequent section.

10.5.1 Descriptive Data of Coups by Transparency Level

Consider first the observed number of coups in our dataset as a function of the level of transparency. Figure 10.1 presents the frequency with which leaders are removed by coup for various levels of transparency. We group together leader-year observations based on transparency quartiles in our sample of autocratic leader-years, where the groupings, ordered by increasing levels of transparency, are presented on the x-axis. The frequency with which leaders are removed

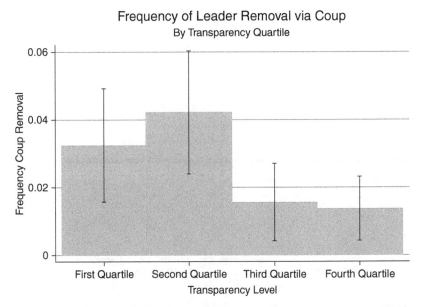

FIGURE 10.1. Frequency of leader removal via coup by transparency quartile. Autocratic leader years are grouped by transparency quartile, which is plotted on the x-axis. The frequency of successful coups within each quartile is plotted on the y-axis. Whiskers denote 95 percent confidence intervals around these frequencies. The figure shows that increased transparency is associated with fewer coups.

via coup in each quartile is presented on the y-axis, and the whiskers denote 95 percent confidence intervals around these frequencies.

A striking relationship is present in Figure 10.1: autocratic leaders with transparency levels in the 50th percentile or below are removed via coups far more often than those autocratic leaders with transparency levels above the sample median. Between 3 and 4 percent of leader years witness a successful coup when transparency is below its median value. This falls to just above 1 percent of leader-years when transparency is above its median value.

Conclusion: More transparency is associated with fewer (successful) coups.

10.5.2 Descriptive Data of Disclosure by ω

Having shown that transparent autocracies are less vulnerable to coups, we now consider which autocracies pursue such transparency. Recall that leaders facing low-level threats from elites (high-ω) are least likely to disclose, while those facing high-level threats from elites (low-ω) are most likely to disclose.

Entrenched autocrats have little to fear from inner-circle elites. Bueno de Mesquita et al. (2003: 296) show that when autocrats first come into power,

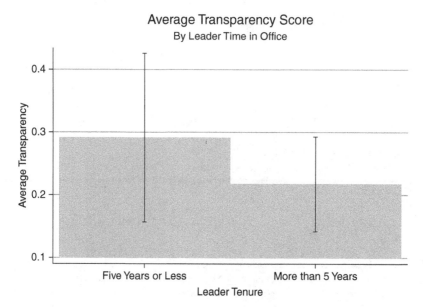

FIGURE 10.2. Transparency score by leader tenure as measured by the leader's number of years in office. Autocratic leader years are categorized based on whether a leader has been in power for 5 years or less (to the left) or more than five years (to the right), along the x-axis. The y-axis depicts average transparency scores. Whiskers denote 95 percent confidence intervals. The figure shows that long-tenured autocracies disclose less data on average.

they face extraordinarily high failure rates: "Leaders from small-coalition systems find it hard to survive the first few years in office but subsequently find it easier to survive than leaders from large-coalition systems." They go on to say "By the end of 5 years, 28 percent of leaders with small coalitions and 20 percent of leaders with large coalitions remain in office. At the ten-year mark the comparative numbers are 16 percent and 6 percent ... It would appear that leaders of small-coalition systems really do have an incumbency advantage over their large-coalition counterparts, but this advantage takes time to become stabilized" (Bueno de Mesquita et al. 2003: 294).

Thus, while new autocrats might pursue transparency in order to keep the inner-circle elites in line, a long-serving leader need not resort to this tactic. We therefore expect transparency levels to drop with a leader's time in office.

Figure 10.2 presents an easy manner in which to examine this relationship. We divide autocratic regimes into those in which the leader has served 5 years in office or less, and those in which the leader has served for more than five years. These two categories are plotted along the x-axis. The height of the bars depicts the average transparency score in all autocratic regimes in our sample in each respective category. Whiskers denote 95 percent confidence intervals.

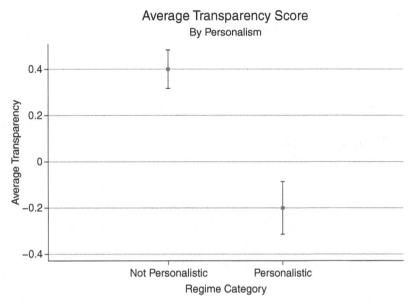

FIGURE 10.3. Transparency scores by personalism of regime measured as a function of the classification of the Geddes, Wright, and Frantz (2012) dataset. Regime classifications are plotted on the x-axis and average transparency scores are plotted on the y-axis. The dots depict the average transparency scores within each category, whiskers depict 95 percent confidence intervals around this average. The figure shows that personalistic autocracies disclose less data on average.

We see in Figure 10.2 that regimes under relatively new leaders – plotted to the left – have higher transparency scores than those with entrenched leaders – plotted to the right. These values vary greatly within each category, but this variance is reduced when other explanatory variables are introduced to the analysis. We return to this analysis below.

Conclusion: Entrenched autocrats (high-ω), who have little to fear from inner-circle elites, have the lowest levels of transparency.

Next we look at autocracies by Geddes's classification: personalistic or not.

Figure 10.3 plots the average transparency score for nonpersonalist and personalist regimes, respectively. Transparency scores are plotted on the y-axis, while regime category is plotted on the x. Dots denote average transparency values, while whiskers are 95 percent confidence intervals. As is clear from the graph, personalistic regimes, on average, have substantially and significantly lower transparency scores than their nonpersonalistic counterparts.

Conclusion: Personalistic autocracies, who have the least to fear from inner-circle elites (high-ω), have the lowest levels of transparency.

Finally we consider which of Gandhi's types of autocracies pursue such transparency. Recall that Gandhi defines inter-elite relations in autocracies as

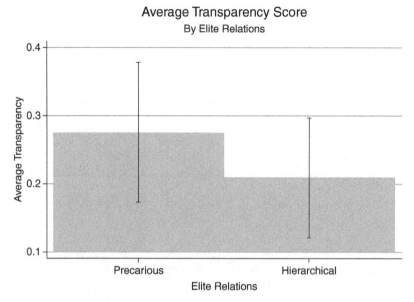

FIGURE 10.4. Transparency score by inter-elite relations as measured by regime classification from Cheibub, Gandhi, and Vreeland (2010). Regime categories – precarious or hierarchical – are plotted on the x-axis. Average transparency scores are plotted on the y-axis. Whiskers denote 95 percent confidence intervals. The figure shows that hierarchical autocracies disclose less data on average.

either hierarchical – as in military or monarchical regimes – or precarious – in civilian-led regimes. Figure 10.4 presents these two categories on the x-axis. The height of the bars for each respective category depicts the average transparency score in each. Whiskers denote 95 percent confidence intervals.

As is clear from Figure 10.4, hierarchical regimes, on average, are less transparent than their precarious counterparts. These differences in the raw data, however, are smaller than the distinction between personalistic and nonpersonalistic regimes, presented in Figure 10.3, and are imprecisely estimated. Applying regression techniques below improves the precision of these estimates, such that the difference between hierarchical and precarious regimes grows statistically significant.

Conclusion: The hierarchical autocracies of military dictatorships and monarchies, who have the least to fear from inner-circle elites (high-ω), have lower levels of transparency than precarious civilian rulers.

The descriptive data in Figures 10.1–10.4 illustrate the two main empirical implications of our model: (1) Compared with autocracies that disclose data at low rates, autocracies with higher rates of data disclosure face lower risks of coups. (2) High-ω leaders, who enjoy high levels of elite loyalty, disclose data at lower rates than do low-ω leaders, whose control over elites is more tenuous.

While we reserve more rigorous testing for later in the chapter, the descriptive data presented here are consistent with our main hypotheses. We observe an association between autocratic leaders disclosing data to the public and a reduced threat of a coup from within the ruling clique. We also see that low-ω leaders (measured in three different ways) disclose more data than high-ω leaders.

10.5.3 Another Tale of Two Countries

To further illustrate the logic of our argument, we present two examples. First we return to an example from Chapter 6: South Korea under Presidents Park and Chun. Then we introduce a new example: the USSR under Mikhail Gorbachev.

South Korea

Recall from Chapter 6 how the autocratic leaders of South Korea navigated the twin threats of mass protest and elite disloyalty. Our argument and the descriptive evidence suggest that President Park Chung Hee effectively navigated the risk of popular revolt in 1979 by keeping transparency low. There were protests, but they suffered from a lack of organizational unity and did not pose a serious threat to the survival of the regime (Im 1995; Adesnik and Kim 2008). This was, arguably, the logical strategy. As a military dictator, who enjoyed a cult of personality and had been entrenched in power since 1963, he should have had little to fear from elites.

But perhaps Park erred too much against the threat of mass unrest and not enough against the disloyalty of his ruling clique. In 1979, he was shot to death by Kim Jae Kyu, his own intelligence chief (Adesnik and Kim 2008: 1). Arguably, had the protests in the streets posed a greater threat, the elites would have rallied to support their leader, rather than kill him.

Indeed, Park's protégé and successor, General Chun Doo Hwan, rapidly and steadily increased transparency, and perhaps, as a result, instilled loyalty – through fear of the masses – among the ruling elite. A newly installed leader, Chun needed to shore up the loyalty of elites. The approach appears to have succeeded to an extent. Though he came to power through martial law without formal procedures, he ruled for nearly a decade without facing serious coup attempts or domestic assassination attempts.[11] As noted by Adesnik and Kim (2008: 10), "Chun was deeply disturbed by the violent end of the Park dictatorship." His inner circle remained loyal, and they had good reason. As discussed in Chapter 6, mass protest steadily rose throughout Chun's rule. If the elites had acted against him, the increasingly organized opposition may have been able to topple the entire regime.

---

[11] Although, through luck, he survived an assassination attempt by the North Korean government while visiting Burma in 1983 (Kihl 1985: 66).

In this case, however, the leader may have erred too much against the threat of elite disloyalty and not enough against the threat of mass unrest. Mass protests for democracy forced Chun to allow for direct presidential elections and the restoration of civil liberties (Adesnik and Kim 2008: 10–12). He would also abide by the seven-year term limit established in the constitution. Note, however, that he had imposed this constitution himself – back in 1980 (Adesnik and Kim 2008: 4). Of course, he sought to continue restricting civil liberties and to see his hand-picked successor to achieve power through indirect "elections." These autocratic goals eluded Chun due to the successful mass protests.

Nevertheless, despite being "embarrassed by his surrender to the opposition's demands [for direct presidential elections and the restoration of civil liberties], Chun achieved his critical objectives of presiding over the first orderly transfer of power in the history [of South Korea] while retaining that power in the hands of a reliable ex-general, namely Roh," who actually won the presidential election in direct, contested elections (Adesnik and Kim 2008: 15). Note that the decision of Roh Tae Woo, Chun's designated successor, to allow for direct elections to determine the presidency "did not result from compromise and bargaining among the elites," but rather took them by surprise; it was the mass unrest in the streets that led to democracy (Bermeo 1997: 314).

Considering the fate of his assassinated predecessor, Chun left power rather unscathed even as the country experienced a transition to democracy. Transparency may have facilitated the mass unrest, which ended his leadership of the country, but he kept the elites at bay. Following our argument, the leader who increased transparency escaped his predecessor's violent death and maintained inner-circle loyalty.

The USSR

The mechanisms of our argument are perhaps even better illustrated by one of the best known leaders of the twentieth century: Soviet General Secretary Mikhail Gorbachev. Gorbachev implemented the famous *glasnost* and *perestroika* reforms in the former Soviet Union between 1985 and 1991.[12] We do not contend that these reforms were *only* the result of the mechanisms we describe in our model – for instance, Gorbachev was also likely motivated by a desire to reduce bureaucratic slack among subordinate officials (Egorov, Guriev, and Sonin 2009).[13] Yet, he also appears to have made his regime more transparent in an explicit attempt to provoke the potential threat of mass unrest and thus curb rival members of the elite.

Gorbachev came to power in 1985 facing a stagnating economy and popular ideological disaffection (Dallin 1992; Kotz and Weir 1997). As a newly installed

---

[12] *Glasnost* can be translated as "openness." The term *perestroika* may be translated either as "restructuring" or "reconstruction." For a thorough treatment of the period and the subsequent collapse of the Soviet Union, see Beissinger (2002).

[13] We thank Scott Gehlbach for bringing this argument to our attention.

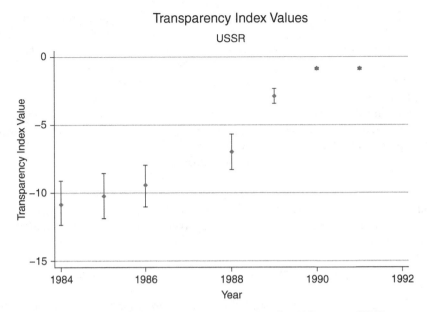

FIGURE 10.5. HRV transparency scores time series: the USSR. Mean HRV transparency index scores and 95 percent credible intervals are plotted on the y-axis. Time, measured annually, is plotted on the x-axis. HRV index values range from −10.9 to 10, in the full sample of 125 country years from 1980 to 2010, with higher scores denoting greater disclosure. The figure shows that the HRV index tracks well with historical accounts of *glasnost* and *perestroika*.

civilian ruler who did not enjoy a personalistic following, Gorbachev faced a variety of threats, both internal and external to the regime. To address potential threats arising from economic stagnation and rising balance of payments difficulties, Gorbachev promoted a series of economic and political reforms – called *perestroika*. Through these reforms, Gorbachev sought to reduce the authority of the Soviet industrial ministries over state enterprises, introduce limited marketization of the economy, and decentralize authority within the ruling Communist Party (Brown 2007; Whitefield 1993). Coupled with these structural reforms, Gorbachev instituted a variety of moves aimed at political liberalization. These policies, which were grouped under the rubric of "socialist democracy," would come to include multicandidate elections and increased transparency and freedom to debate (*glasnost*) (Kotz and Weir 1997). We argue that these reforms aimed to stem the internal threat to Gorbachev's rule.

The HRV index reflects the impact of these reforms on data disclosure. We plot these scores, from 1984 to 1991, in Figure 10.5. Over this period, the USSR substantially increases its transparency score, from the lowest levels in the sample of country-years to levels more consistent with the average nondemocracy.

Remark 10.1 holds that leaders choose to disclose in equilibrium if, and only if, they adopt policies viewed unfavorably by (large portions of) regime members. As is consistent with Remark 10.1, scholars have interpreted *glasnost* and socialist democracy as, in part, an attempt to overcome resistance among Party members to the economic restructuring entailed in *perestroika*. For instance, Kotz and Weir (1997: 96) state that, "As resistance mounted to [the leadership's] program of economic and social reform, Gorbachev apparently concluded that democratization was the way to break this resistance and prevent perestroika from being stopped in its tracks" (see also Brown 2007; Reddaway and Glinski 2001; Whitefield 1993).

Such "democratization" helped to ensure the compliance of Party members through two methods. First, Gorbachev attempted to employ newly available avenues of mobilization to rally the populace to his reformist cause and against recalcitrant elites. Second, the creation of such avenues of mobilization created the risk that opposition groups might form within the populace and threaten continued Soviet rule. As these threats emerged, conservative Party elites were less able to take action against Gorbachev without endangering their own positions.

Scholars agree that Gorbachev's liberalizing reforms played a critical role in giving rise to a popular opposition. Aleksandr Yakovlev, Politburo member, chief of ideology, and close associate of Gorbachev, remarked that in their efforts at reform, "We [the leadership] created an opposition to ourselves" (as quoted in Reddaway and Glinski 2001: 122). Brown (2007: 18–19) describes *perestoika* as a reform "from above," and notes that prior to these reforms "[n]either a mass movement for reform nor (still less) a revolution was remotely in the cards." Brown (2007: 92–93) further notes that *glasnost* was a "double-edged" sword which aided reformers, led by Gorbachev, by publicizing the deficiencies of the Soviet state, but that greater access to information also risked increasing public discontent and mobilization against the leadership.

Nor were these risks merely incidental – the dangers posed by a popular opposition increased Gorbachev's authority within the Communist Party. At times, it seems that Gorbachev acted to deliberately increase these threats.

For instance, one of the most radical opposition voices belonged to Boris Yeltsin, who would come to play a pivotal role in the eventual collapse of the Soviet regime. Gorbachev had the opportunity to sideline Yeltsin in 1987, when Yeltsin was forced to resign as the Moscow party secretary. Yet, Gorbachev merely reassigned Yeltsin to a somewhat less prominent position. Later, Gorbachev failed to remove Yeltsin from electoral ballots, following the introduction of multicandidate elections in 1988. Reddaway and Glinski (2001) (and Yeltsin himself) attribute Gorbachev's actions to his desire to use Yeltsin's radicalism as a threat to ensure the quiescence of conservative opponents.

Similarly, Reddaway and Glinski (2001: 160) contend that Gorbachev "covertly encouraged" organizers of a rally by Democratic Russia in 1990, as a means of threatening more conservative opponents and ensuring the passage of reforms creating a Soviet presidency. As Brown (2007: 128) argued of the rise of a popular opposition, "Gorbachev and the progress of perestroika now have liberal as well as conservative critics. While in some ways this makes life even tougher for the Soviet leader, on balance it is to his political advantage."

The presence of a popular opposition and, more generally, the opening of the informational environment following Gorbachev's reforms increased the mobilizational potential of the populace. As the public became better able to mobilize, members of the Soviet elite faced a greater risk in moving against Gorbachev. Any destabilization of the leadership posed an increased risk of giving rise to popular unrest and consequently to the collapse of the regime as a whole.

Despite these risks, conservative members of the elite did move to depose Gorbachev through a coup in August of 1991.[14] Consistent with the mechanisms of our theory, this coup gave rise to a counter-coup led by Boris Yeltsin in his capacity as the newly created president of the Russian Republic. This counter-coup led to the ouster of the putschists and gave rise to processes leading to the collapse of the Soviet regime and the dissolution of the Union.[15]

We intend these anecdotes to serve as illustrations of how the logic of our game-theoretic model might unfold in the real world. Competing explanations, however, would offer alternative accounts for the strategic actions of Park, Chun, and Gorbachev. The descriptive data offered earlier in this section further support our reading of these events, but here too competing explanations might reveal our correlations to be driven by other factors. To offer more convincing evidence, accounting for alternative explanations, we turn to regression analysis.

10.6 REGRESSION ANALYSIS

We now adopt more rigorous methods of testing our central hypotheses. Our formal model suggests that transparency should reduce the likelihood of elite disunity (Proposition 10.2). We test this proposition by looking at the relationship between the HRV index and coups. Our model further contends that leaders who have less to fear from elites (where $\omega > \tilde{\omega}$) should be less likely to disclose (Proposition 10.3). As in the descriptive data section above, we use three approaches to identify autocracies as having $\omega > \bar{\omega}$.

10.6.1 The Effect of Transparency on Coups

We have so far shown with descriptive data that transparency is associated with a lower frequency of coups, consistent with Proposition 10.2 from our theoretic model. We now further test this claim, controlling for autocratic institutions,

---

[14] The proximate cause of the coup was the negotiation of a new union treaty giving increased independent authority to the 15 constituent republics of the USSR.

[15] Technically inclined readers should note that this outcome – in which a leader is removed despite the decision to disclose – does occur on the equilibrium path described in Proposition 10.1.

economic factors, past history of coups, and duration in power. If our argument is on target, we should find that, controlling for alternative explanations, transparency insulates leaders from coups.

Similar to the approach employed in Chapter 7, we estimate the relationship between the hazard of autocratic leader removal via coup and transparency using a series of Cox competing hazards specifications. Here, the event of interest is leader removal via coup, and the competing hazards are alternate forms of leader removal. Leaders are counted as "at risk" from the moment they enter into office. If a leader is removed via coup, the date of that removal enters our dataset as a "failure," the hazard of which is to be estimated. If a leader is removed by a method other than a coup, he is "censored" from the dataset following his removal.[16] Leaders are similarly censored if they survive to the end of the time period of observation. The unit of observation is the autocratic leader-year, where leader identities and the methods and dates of leader removal are defined by Svolik (2012).

Note, however, that here our outcome of interest – leader removal via coup – subtly departs from the outcomes measured in Chapters 6 and 7 – regime collapse, through a variety of methods, including coups. There, we follow Svolik (2012) in defining instances of regime collapse, which take place when *both* of the following hold: (1) an autocratic leader is ousted from power, and (2) his replacement is unaffiliated with the ruling regime. Here our interest is not in regime collapse, but merely leader removal. Hence, only the first of these two conditions need be satisfied for a coup to enter our dataset. Though, in Chapter 7, we also find a negative association between transparency and regime collapses brought on via coups.

Again following the approach of Chapter 7, we adjust for the possibility that past successful coups predict future coups – we stratify the baseline hazard rate in our Cox estimates based on two measures of coup history (Box-Steffensmeier and Zorn 2002). The first is a simple indicator variable $\{0, 1\}$, equal to one if any past autocratic leader was removed via a coup. The second is an ordered variable $\{0, 1, 2, 3\}$, which denotes the number of past autocratic leaders removed via coup and, if equal to 3, denotes that more than two previous leaders have been removed via coup. We thus fit specifications of the following form:

$$h_l(t, c_l) = h_0(t, c_l)exp(\delta Transparency_{l,t-1} + \mathbf{X}_{l,t-1}\beta) \tag{10.5}$$

where l denotes autocratic leader, t denotes time, c_l is an indicator for coup history, $\mathbf{X}_{l,t-1}\beta$ is a vector of time-varying controls and associated coefficients, and $h_0(t, c_l)$ captures the risk of a coup when all explanatory variables in the model

---

[16] The leader is "censored" with respect to a coup because we do not know how long he would have avoided a coup had he survived the risk that took him down. See Goemans (2008) for an alternative application of the competing hazards model. This approach assumes that the hazard of one form of removal is conditionally independent of alternative forms of removal (Gordon 2002).

are set to 0. We estimate $h_0(t, c_l)$ nonparametrically within each stratum, based on the fraction of observations that experience a coup at time t as compared to the number of observations at risk (leaders who have not yet been removed for *any* reason). Duration dependence is thus factored out of the likelihood function, while a history of coups may shift both the shape and level of the baseline hazard function (Beck, Katz, and Tucker 1998; Box-Steffensmeier and Zorn 2002). We use the HRV index to measure *Transparency* in these regressions. Our hypothesis holds that the coefficient on transparency, δ, should be negative.

The control variables include several measures of autocratic institutions, drawn from the Autocratic Regimes dataset of Geddes, Wright, and Frantz (2012) (the GWF dataset). This dataset partitions autocracies into four categories: (1) personalistic dictatorships, (2) single party regimes, and (3) nonpersonalistic military regimes or monarchies.[17] We control for binary indicators of single party (*Party*) and personalistic regimes (*Personal*) in all specifications presented in Table 10.1. Thus, we estimate hazard rates relative to the residual category, nonpersonalistic military/monarchical. These controls are necessary given substantial evidence that autocratic regime survival is conditioned by institutional features (Boix and Svolik 2013; Gandhi 2008; Gandhi and Przeworski 2007; Geddes 1999).[18]

Alternatively, we employ the Gandhi (2008) approach to coding leader–elite relations as a test of robustness in Table 10.2. We construct a binary indicator, *Hierarchical*, which codes the hierarchical autocracies – all military dictatorships and all monarchies – as 1, and the civilian-ruled autocracies as 0.

In both Tables 10.1 and 10.2, we additionally control for economic covariates drawn from the Penn World Table version 7.1 (Heston, Summers, and Aten 2012). Specifically, we control for levels of economic growth in real PPP GDP, measured in percentage points (*Growth*). We also control for real GDP per capita, measured in thousands of constant 2005 PPP adjusted US dollars (*GDP per capita*). The former control is necessary given substantial evidence that poor economic growth precipitates regime instability under autocratic rule (Haggard and Kaufman 1995; Przeworski et al. 2000). The latter is included given the findings of a large literature on the role of economic development in destabilizing autocracies (Boix 2003; Boix and Stokes 2003; Epstein et al. 2006).

Results using the GWF controls are presented in Table 10.1, while those using the DD controls are presented in Table 10.2. Results in which the baseline hazard is stratified based on whether there was a previous coup are

---

[17] There are only eight monarchical regimes in our sample, constituting less than 10 percent of the total in both sets of empirical results. We thus treat military regimes and monarchies as a single reference category.

[18] In all specifications employing the GWF controls, we interact the single party indicator with time, to adjust for violations of the proportional hazards assumption indicated by tests of the residuals (Box-Steffensmeier and Jones 2004; Keele 2010).

TABLE 10.1. *Hazard of leader removal via coup.*

	Past Coup Strata	Coup Experience Strata	Past Coup Control
Transparency	−0.248	−0.282	−0.240
	[−0.480,−0.016]	[−0.531,−0.033]	[−0.461,−0.019]
Growth	−0.003	−0.005	−0.000
	[−0.031,0.026]	[−0.042,0.032]	[−0.029,0.029]
GDP per capita	−0.110	−0.094	−0.117
	[−0.208,−0.012]	[−0.175,−0.013]	[−0.229,−0.005]
Party	−1.793	−1.709	−1.735
	[−2.595,−0.991]	[−2.451,−0.967]	[−2.661,−0.810]
Party × t	0.113	0.112	0.109
	[0.045,0.181]	[0.049,0.175]	[0.037,0.182]
Personal	−0.807	−0.676	−0.809
	[−1.609,−0.004]	[−1.437,0.084]	[−1.592,−0.025]
Ever Past Coup			−0.047
			[−0.908,0.814]
# of Subjects	89	89	89
# of Failures	36	36	36

Results from Cox competing hazards regressions of leader removal via coup on transparency and controls. Results in the leftmost column are from a model in which the baseline hazard rate is stratified based on whether there was a previous leader removal via coup in the sample; results in the center column are from a model in which the baseline hazard is stratified based on an ordered variable based on the frequency of past coups; results in the rightmost column do not stratify the baseline hazard, and simply control for an indicator for past coups (95 percent confidence intervals are reported in brackets).

presented in the leftmost column; those stratified based on the ordered indicator of coup history are presented in the center column; and results that do not stratify the baseline hazard, but simply control for an indicator of past coups (*Ever Past Coup*), are presented in the rightmost column.

In all specifications, the coefficient on the transparency term is negative, with 95 percent confidence intervals bounded away from zero. Point estimates indicate that a one standard deviation increase in the HRV index is associated with a roughly 35 percent fall in the hazard of a coup.

To ease interpretation of these results, we present plots of smoothed estimates of the hazard function from Table 10.1 in Figure 10.6. The solid line depicts the smoothed hazard when the HRV index is at its 10th percentile in the sample, while the dashed line presents the same when the HRV index is at its 90th percentile. In the former instance, the hazard that a newly seated leader is ousted via a coup during the first year of his reign is roughly 3.25 percent. When transparency is at its 90th percentile, this falls to a hazard of roughly 1.75 percent.

Figure 10.6 also reveals that the hazard rate declines over time, particularly over the first 20 years of a leader's rule. This pattern is consistent with our

TABLE 10.2. *Hazard of removal via coup (DD controls).*

	Past Coup Strata	Coup Experience Strata	Past Coup Control
Transparency	−0.202	−0.228	−0.217
	[−0.401,−0.002]	[−0.450,−0.006]	[−0.420,−0.014]
Growth	−0.008	−0.006	−0.006
	[−0.035,0.019]	[−0.040,0.028]	[−0.033,0.021]
GDP per capita	−0.073	−0.071	−0.078
	[−0.145,−0.001]	[−0.138,−0.004]	[−0.154,−0.002]
Hierarchical	0.410	0.280	0.430
	[−0.196,1.017]	[−0.311,0.871]	[−0.182,1.041]
Ever Past Coup			−0.126
			[−0.969,0.717]
# of Subjects	94	94	94
# of Failures	37	37	37

Results from Cox competing hazards regressions of leader removal via coup on transparency and controls. Results in the leftmost column are from a model in which the baseline hazard rate is stratified based on whether there was a previous leader removal via coup in the sample; results in the center column are from a model in which the baseline hazard is stratified based on an ordered variable based on the frequency of past coups; results in the rightmost column do not stratify the baseline hazard and simply control for an indicator for past coups (95 percent confidence intervals are reported in brackets).

empirical interpretation of the parameter ω, which we believe is rising over a leader's tenure in office. Personalist regimes also suffer a lower risk of coup than monarchical/military regimes, which is also consistent with our interpretation of ω. Party-based regimes also suffer a lower risk of coup when a leader is new to office, but this advantage declines over time. Moreover, since the Cox model assumes that a shift in covariate values shifts the hazard rate by a constant *percentage* value, this implies that the absolute size of the relationship between transparency and coup risk diminishes as ω rises ($\omega > \bar{\omega}$), as is consistent with Proposition 10.3. We should stress, however, that this result derives from assumptions undergirding the functional form of the Cox model. While proportional hazards tests do not reject this functional form assumption, this constitutes a weak test of our theoretical claim, and thus we return to testing Proposition 10.3. Coefficients on Gandhi's definition of hierarchical regimes are imprecisely estimated, and their sign is inconsistent with our interpretation of ω. Hierarchical regimes are, if anything, at a slightly increased risk of coup as compared to precarious regimes – though this difference is very imprecisely estimated and likely arises due to chance.

Our central term of interest, the coefficient on the transparency term, however, remains negative, significant at the 95 percent level or above, and is of similar magnitude to the results using the GWF measure (in Table 10.1). We conclude that data disclosure reduces the threat of coups.

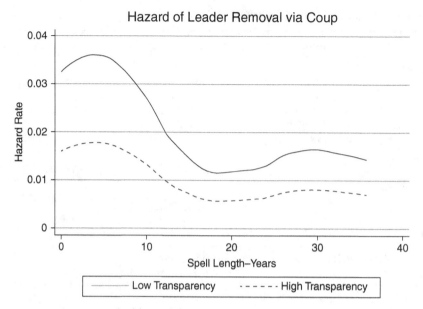

FIGURE 10.6. Smoothed hazard function of leader removal via coup. Estimates of the smoothed hazard function from the model in the third column of Table 10.1. The solid line depicts the hazard of coup when transparency is at its 10th percentile in the sample. The dashed line depicts the corresponding hazard when transparency is at its 90th percentile. Estimated hazards are for the nonpersonalistic, nonparty residual category in the Geddes, Wright, and Frantz (2012) dataset (military/monarchical regimes) that has not previously experienced leader removal via a coup. Spell length indicates how long a leader has survived in power without succumbing to a coup. The figure shows that transparency reduces the risk of a coup, especially for new leaders.

10.6.2 Autocracy and Transparency

In addition to advancing claims about the relationship between transparency and the frequency of coups, our theory offers predictions about which autocratic regimes are likely to disclose information. Proposition 10.3 contends that disclosure is less likely when $\omega > \bar{\omega}$. We treat this proposition as advancing an empirical claim that (1) leaders become less willing to disclose once entrenched in office and are more willing to disclose when new to office (Bueno de Mesquita et al. 2003), (2) GWF's personalistic regimes disclose less than other autocracies, and (3) DD's hierarchical leaders disclose less than civilian-ruled autocracies (note that the DD dataset of Cheibub, Gandhi, and Vreeland [2010] includes the update to the data of Gandhi [2008]).

In this section, we assess Proposition 10.3 through a series of varying intercepts hierarchical regression models of the HRV index on a series of institutional and time-varying characteristics. Specifically, we estimate models of the following form:

$$transparency_{i,t} = \rho transparency_{i,t-1} + \alpha_i + \mathbf{X}_{i,t-1}\beta + \epsilon_{i,t}$$
$$\alpha_i \sim N(\mathbf{Z}_i\gamma, \sigma_\alpha^2) \tag{10.6}$$

where i denotes a given autocratic regime, t denotes the year, $\mathbf{X}_{i,t-1}$ is a vector of time-varying controls, α_i is a regime-specific intercept term, and $\mathbf{Z}_i$ is a vector of regime-level (time-invariant) controls.[19]

Our definition of an autocratic regime is drawn from the dataset of Svolik (2012) in which an autocratic regime consists of the continuous succession of autocratic leaders affiliated with a given ruling clique. This dataset also provides our definition of a leader's time in office. We code an indicator *New Leader* $\in$ $\{0, 1\}$, which is set equal to one if a leader has been in power for 5 years or less. Since newly installed autocrats are likely to face greater threats of coup and intra-regime discipline (Bueno de Mesquita et al. 2002; Francois, Rainer, and Trebbi 2014), we would expect that new leaders disclose more readily than entrenched leaders. It is the new, rather than entrenched, leaders who require insulation from their elite.

As compared to the models above, we draw several additional economic controls from the Penn World Table, version 7.1 (Heston, Summers, and Aten 2012). We include controls chain-series *GDP*, in addition to *GDP per capita*, both measured in PPP adjusted 2005 US dollars. These controls are included given that larger economies and more developed states may simply be more able to disclose data than less developed ones. We additionally control for *Ec. Openness* ($\frac{Exports+Imports}{GDP}$), given that more open economies may be subject to more pressure to disclose from international markets. We also add a control for *Government Consumption* as a percent of GDP, given that statist economies may face less pressure to disclose information to the general public. We also include an indicator for states that are currently subject to an IMF program, as a control, given that the IMF often requires governments to disclose economic information. (Also recall our discussion about controlling for IMF participation in Chapter 9.)

All regressions additionally include an indicator for fuel exporters, drawn from Easterly and Sewadeh (2001). We include this term given the findings of Egorov, Guriev, and Sonin (2009), who find that natural resource exporters are more opaque than other autocracies.

The regime classifications (of both GWF and Gandhi) and the fuel exporter indicator constitute the time-invariant regime characteristics $\mathbf{Z}_i$, from Equation 10.6. The *New Leader* indicator, IMF control, and economic covariates constitute the time-varying terms $\mathbf{X}_{i,t-1}$.

---

[19] In Hollyer, Rosendorff, and Vreeland (forthcoming), we examine alternative empirical specifications – including a difference-in-differences specification – with analogous results.

We additionally control for the lagged value of the HRV index to capture model dynamics (Beck and Katz 2011). Dynamics are of concern on both theoretical and empirical grounds. Empirically, transparency evolves according to a smooth (slow-moving) process – indeed, the HRV index is constructed in a manner that includes a nonparametric inter-temporal smoother (Hollyer, Rosendorff, and Vreeland 2014). Theoretically, it is implausible to assume that, for instance, a new leader aiming to increase levels of disclosure will be able to achieve this increase within the space of a single year. Rather, one would expect this increase to play out over a period of several years. Where such dynamics are present, excluding the lagged dependent variable would result in model misspecification.

All variables that are neither binary indicators nor time counters have been standardized by subtracting the mean and dividing by the standard deviation.[20] The results from models based on Equation 10.6 are presented in Tables 10.3 and 10.4.

Across the two tables, the coefficient on the *New Leader* indicator is positive in all specifications. The 95 percent credible intervals on this term are bounded away from zero across all six specifications. Recall further that the presence of the lagged dependent variable renders these models dynamic. We simulate the estimated marginal effect of a new leader over time, based on the results from our baseline specification – Model 1 in Table 10.3 – in Figure 10.7. In the figure, the system is assumed to be in equilibrium in time $t = 0$ and a new leader is introduced in time $t = 1$. We then examine how transparency is expected to evolve, based on this "shock," over the ensuing ten years.

The estimated marginal effect of a new leader is small in absolute terms. The introduction of a new leader in time $t = 0$ is anticipated to increase transparency scores by roughly 0.12 standard deviations by time $t = 5$. However, our transparency scores tend to vary little within autocratic regimes over time. On average, the standard deviation of the (standardized) transparency measure within an autocratic regime is 0.28. Thus, a new leader (that is, a leader with low-ω) is predicted to increase transparency scores by roughly $\frac{1}{3}$ to $\frac{1}{2}$ their overtime standard deviation by the conclusion of his first five years in office. The qualitative results are similar in Table 10.4.

The coefficient on the GWF indicator for personalist regimes in Table 10.3 is consistently negative. The result falls in line with our theoretical expectations about high-ω leaders. The 95 percent credible intervals are bounded away from zero in our most parsimonious specification, which drops insignificant controls. The 90 percent credible intervals (unreported) are bounded away from zero in all specifications. The estimated contemporaneous marginal effect of changing from a military to a personalistic regime is a decline of between 0.038 and

---

[20] We estimate the model described in Equation 10.6 via MCMC in JAGS 3.3.0. We place separate diffuse multivariate normal priors on the coefficients on regime-level variables γ and the regime-year level variables β, respectively. We place an informative prior on $\rho \sim N(0, 1)$.

TABLE 10.3. *Models of disclosure: GWF data.*

		Model 1	Model 2	Model 3
Regime Predictors	Party	−0.002	−0.002	−0.003
		[−0.043, 0.035]	[−0.04, 0.041]	[−0.043, 0.032]
	Personalistic	−0.038	−0.037	−0.04
		[−0.082, 0.006]	[−0.083, 0.008]	[−0.085, 0]
	Fuel Exporter	−0.025	−0.027	−0.029
		[−0.07, 0.027]	[−0.075, 0.017]	[−0.077, 0.01]
Regime-Year Predictors	Lag Transparency	0.959	0.958	0.961
		[0.939, 0.975]	[0.939, 0.975]	[0.943, 0.979]
	GDP per capita	0	−0.001	
		[−0.019, 0.018]	[−0.019, 0.017]	
	GDP	0.003	0.004	
		[−0.013, 0.017]	[−0.01, 0.018]	
	Ec. Openness	−0.006		
		[−0.021, 0.01]		
	Growth	−0.002		
		[−0.013, 0.009]		
	Gov't Consumption	−0.011	−0.011	
		[−0.026, 0.003]	[−0.027, 0.003]	
	Under IMF	−0.008	−0.007	−0.007
		[−0.035, 0.017]	[−0.032, 0.02]	[−0.033, 0.019]
	New Leader	0.027	0.028	0.029
		[0.001, 0.05]	[0.001, 0.05]	[0.005, 0.055]
	Cubic Time Polynomial	✓	✓	✓
	# Obs	1404	1404	1404
	# Regimes	117	117	117

Results from a hierarchical varying-intercepts linear regression of HRV transparency index scores on listed covariates. Covariates that shift the intercept term are described as "Regime Predictors," while those that directly shift predicted transparency values are listed as "Regime-Year Predictors." All covariates that are neither indicators terms nor time counters have been standardized by subtracting the mean and dividing by the standard deviation (95 percent credible intervals are presented in brackets).

0.04 standard deviations in the HRV index. Given the dynamics of the model, however, the long-term equilibrium association between regime classification and transparency is considerably larger. The long-term equilibrium difference between personalistic and military regimes is roughly 0.95 standard deviations.

Table 10.4 presents similar results for the DD proxy for high-ω leaders. The coefficient on the indicator for hierarchical regimes is consistently negative – following our theoretical expectations. The 95 percent credible intervals are bounded away from zero in all models bar Model 1. The estimated contemporaneous marginal effect of changing from a civilian to a hierarchical regime

TABLE 10.4. *Models of disclosure: DD data.*

		Model 1	Model 2	Model 3
Regime predictors	Single party	−0.014 [−0.077, 0.047]		
	Multi-party	0.025 [−0.031, 0.073]		
	Legislature	0.042 [−0.003, 0.084]		
	Hierarchical	−0.024 [−0.061, 0.005]	−0.036 [−0.064, −0.009]	−0.034 [−0.062, −0.004]
	Communist	0.021 [−0.04, 0.08]		
	Fuel exporter	−0.003 [−0.054, 0.045]	−0.024 [−0.068, 0.016]	−0.023 [−0.066, 0.019]
Regime-year predictors	Lag transparency	0.957 [0.939, 0.976]	0.962 [0.947, 0.979]	0.965 [0.948, 0.98]
	GDP per capita	0.008 [−0.009, 0.026]	0.002 [−0.013, 0.019]	
	GDP	0 [−0.015, 0.014]	0.004 [−0.01, 0.017]	
	Ec. openness	−0.012 [−0.027, 0.002]		
	Growth	−0.004 [−0.015, 0.007]		
	Gov't consumption	−0.017 [−0.029, −0.002]	−0.017 [−0.031, −0.003]	
	Under IMF	−0.011 [−0.038, 0.012]	−0.009 [−0.033, 0.017]	−0.009 [−0.034, 0.014]
	New leader	0.032 [0.007, 0.054]	0.03 [0.006, 0.055]	0.03 [0.007, 0.056]
	Cubic time Polynomial	✓	✓	✓
	# Obs	1481	1481	1481
	# Regimes	131	131	131

Results from a hierarchical varying-intercepts linear regression of HRV transparency index scores on listed covariates. Covariates that shift the intercept term are described as "Regime Predictors," while those that directly shift predicted transparency values are listed as "Regime-Year Predictors." All covariates that are neither indicators terms nor time counters have been standardized by subtracting the mean and dividing by the standard deviation (95 percent credible intervals are presented in brackets).

is a decline of between 0.024 and 0.036 standard deviations in the HRV index. Given the dynamics of the model, however, the long-term equilibrium association between regime classification and transparency is considerably larger. The long-term equilibrium difference between hierarchical and civilian autocracies is between 0.6 and 0.9 standard deviations in the transparency index.

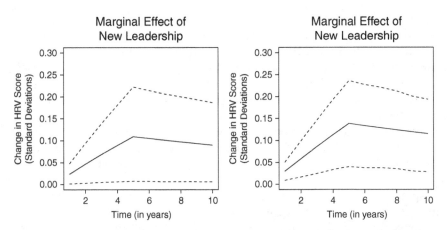

FIGURE 10.7. Marginal effect of a new leader over a 10-year period. Standardized HRV transparency index scores are plotted on the y-axis. Time, measured in years, is plotted on the x-axis. Solid lines depict mean estimated marginal effects and dotted lines depict 95 percent credible intervals. A new leader is predicted to increase transparency scores by roughly $\frac{1}{3}$ to $\frac{1}{2}$ their over-time standard deviation by the conclusion of his first five years in office. Panel to the left depicts regressions using GWF data, that to the right depicts results using DD data.

As for our control variables, the coefficient on the *fuel exporter* indicator is negative in every model estimated as is consistent with Egorov, Guriev, and Sonin (2009). These results are not typically significant, though; p-values just exceed 0.10 in all specifications. Interestingly, coefficients on economic covariates are consistently small and imprecisely estimated in all models.

We conclude that these rigorous statistical models, which account for other factors and explanations, uphold our preliminary evidence that high-ω leaders are less likely to disclose.

10.7 CONCLUSION

Leaders in transparent autocracies enjoy a reduction in the risk of a coup. Across a variety of statistical specifications, an increase of one standard deviation in HRV index scores is associated with a roughly 35 percent reduction in the hazard of a coup. While such leaders are more insulated from threats that emerge from within their regime, existing results indicate that they suffer an increased risk from the masses. Autocrats are thus placed in a delicate position when deciding whether or not to disclose: they must trade off the threats they face from within their regime against those from without.

Taken together with the theory and evidence from Part II, this chapter introduces a theoretical argument prefaced on such a balancing act. Transparency insulates leaders from internal threats, we argue, precisely *because* it exposes them to increased external threats. The common threat to both the leader and the autocratic elite posed by mass unrest ensures greater cohesion within the regime (Padró i Miquel 2007; Di Lonardo and Tyson 2016). Autocratic leaders, therefore, can manipulate this threat to ensure greater freedom of maneuver vis-à-vis their winning coalition. Transparency serves as one mechanism to gain this freedom.

Accordingly, this chapter contends that autocrats should be most prone to disclose information when the internal balance of power tends to favor the autocratic elite over the leader. When the elites pose a threat to the leader, he stands to benefit most from additional freedom to maneuver. Increasing transparency makes it easier for the masses to protest, and this increased threat to the regime enables the leader to reduce the threat from the elites, who must increase their loyalty lest the masses take them all down. Leaders facing little or no threat from within the inner circle, however, need not risk mass mobilization; such leaders can maintain low levels of transparency. Consistent with this argument, entrenched, personalistic, and hierarchical autocrats are, empirically, less prone to transparency than their counterparts.

There is a growing literature on information provision in autocracies. Much of this work focuses on interactions between the regime and the public, or between central and regional officials. In contrast, our approach examines conflicts at the intra-elite level. Our focus does not imply that other interactions are unimportant – to the contrary, our argument is indeed premised on the role transparency plays in mass politics. Rather, this chapter offers a novel dimension over which the politics of information may have an effect and advances the notion that elite and mass politics within autocracies are closely connected.

The intuition that elite and mass politics in autocracies interact has important implications for the study of autocratic politics more generally. Here we offer the suggestion that the public acts as a threat against the regime as a whole and that this threat can be manipulated to the benefit of leaders. Cunning leaders may employ such tactics to escape some of the constraints placed on them by autocratic institutions. Intriguingly, dictators may have an incentive to destabilize their own regimes.

10.8 APPENDIX

Proofs of Lemmas and Propositions

Proof of Proposition 10.1.   A PBE, in pure strategies, consists of (1) a strategy profile in which all actors adopt best responses given their beliefs, and (2) a set of beliefs that is weakly consistent with the strategy profile and updated according to Bayes' rule, wherever possible (Fudenberg and Tirole 1991). A semiseparating PBE in pure strategies to this game involves a first period strategy for L in which, for some range of realizations of r_1, different values of θ lead to different signals (e_1, d).

We begin via backward induction. In the final period of play, L has a dominant strategy, conditional on his type θ. $e_2 = s_2$ if $\theta = 1$ and $e_2 \neq s_2$ if $\theta = 0$.

Given this strategy for all types of L, we can now characterize R's decision over $v \in \{0, 1\}$. If L is retained, and the regime survives, R receives an expected utility of $Pr(\theta = 1 | e_1, d)\Delta + \lambda y$. However, the regime only survives with probability $1 - p(d)$. With probability $p(d)$ the regime collapses, in which case R is guaranteed a utility of $(1 - \lambda)y$. Hence, the expected utility of retention is $p(d)(1 - \lambda)y + [1 - p(d)][Pr(\theta = 1 | e_1, d)\Delta + \lambda y]$.

If R sets $v = 1$ and the regime survives, she receives expected utility of $\pi \Delta + \lambda y$, where π denotes the probability with which Nature chooses $\theta = 1$. However, following $v = 1$, the regime survives with probability $1 - \omega p(d)$. Hence, the expected utility of removal is $\omega p(d)(1 - \lambda)y + [1 - \omega p(d)][\pi \Delta + \lambda y]$.

Comparing these two utilities yields expression 10.4 in the text. $v = 1$ iff:

$$\omega p(d)(1 - \lambda)y + [1 - \omega p(d)][\pi \Delta + \lambda y] > p(d)(1 - \lambda)y$$
$$+ [1 - p(d)][Pr(\theta = 1 | e_1, d)\Delta + \lambda y]$$

Notice that the RHS of expression 10.4 is monotonic and increasing in $Pr(\theta = 1 | e_1, d)$, while the LHS is invariant in this term. Therefore, if the expression fails to hold when $Pr(\theta = 1 | e_1, d) = 0$, it will never hold. Substituting $Pr(\theta = 1 | e_1, d) = 0$ and rearranging yields:

$$\pi \Delta > \frac{p(d)y(\omega - 1)(2\lambda - 1)}{1 - \omega p(d)}$$

which defines the two thresholds $\bar{\omega}$ and $\underline{\omega}$ in Definition 10.1. If $\omega > \bar{\omega}$ this expression can never hold for any value of d, so R has a strictly dominant strategy of setting $v = 0$. If $\omega > \underline{\omega}$, the expression can never hold so long as $d = 1$. So, R must respond to $d = 1$ by setting $v = 0$.

Notice further that, given $\omega > 1$ and $\lambda > \frac{1}{2}$, the inequality in expression 10.4 can never hold for $Pr(\theta = 1 | e_1, d) \geq \pi$. Hence, for any $Pr(\theta = 1 | e_1, d) \geq \pi$, R must set $v = 0$.

Given these preliminaries, we can now consider L's strategy in the first period of play. Clearly, for $\omega > \bar{\omega}$, L has a dominant strategy, conditional on type. For $\theta = 1$, it must be the case that $(e_1, d) = (s_1, 0)$. Analogously, for $\theta = 0$, it must be the case that $(e_1, d) = (\neg s_1, 0)$.

Consider, now, values of $\omega \leq \bar{\omega}$. Let L play a strategy of $(e_1, d) = (s_1, 0)$ when $\theta = 1$ as is consistent with his primitive preference. Given this strategy when $\theta = 1$, R must hold beliefs such that $Pr(\theta = 1|e_1 = s_1, d = 0) \geq \pi$, hence sending this signal pair guarantees $v = 0$ for all types of L.

We must now consider the strategy for L when $\theta = 0$. Let us first consider the case when $\omega \in [\underline{\omega}, \bar{\omega}]$. He can guarantee retention by adopting the action pair $(s_1, 0)$, in which case his expected utility is given by $\Delta + \lambda y + [1 - p(0)][\mu + \lambda y]$. Notice that, for $\omega \in [\underline{\omega}, \bar{\omega}]$, a divergent L may also guarantee retention by setting $d = 1$. If he does this, he also strictly prefers to follow his primitive preference over policy by setting $e_1 \neq s_1$. (Analogously, if he chooses to separate by setting $e_1 \neq s_1$, he strictly prefers to set $d = 1$ and guarantee $v = 0$ rather than $v = 1$.) By setting $(e_1, d) = (\neg s_1, 1)$, L obtains $r_1 + \lambda y + [1 - p(1)][\mu + \lambda y]$. Hence, for $\theta = 0$ and $\omega \in [\underline{\omega}, \bar{\omega}]$, L chooses $(\neg s_1, 1)$ if $r_1 > \Delta + \rho[\mu + \lambda y]$, where $\rho \equiv p(1) - p(0)$, and chooses $(s_1, 0)$ otherwise.

Let us now consider the case when $\omega < \underline{\omega}$. Here, L can guarantee retention by adopting $(s_1, 0)$, but faces certain removal for any other signal pair. His expected utility from $(s_1, 0)$ is identical to that given above. His utility from any alternative in which $e_1 \neq s_1$ is given by $r_1 + \lambda y$. (Clearly, the signal $(s_1, 1)$ is dominated.) L thus prefers to choose $e_1 \neq s_1$ if $r_1 > \Delta + [1 - p(0)][\mu + \lambda y]$, and to choose $(s_1, 0)$ otherwise. L is indifferent between $(\neg s_1, 1)$ and $(\neg s_1, 0)$. As noted above, we assume $d = 1$ whenever L is indifferent, such that L adopts the signal $(\neg s_1, 1)$ when $r_1 > \Delta + [1 - p(0)][\mu + \lambda y]$, $\theta = 0$ and $\omega < \underline{\omega}$.

We can summarize these cut-points in r_1 by $\tilde{r}(\omega)$, as defined in Definition 10.2. Given this strategy by L, R must believe $Pr(\theta = 1|e_1 = s_1, d = 0) > \pi$ and, when $\omega > \bar{\omega}$, must believe $Pr(\theta = 1|e_1 \neq s_1, d = 0) = 0$, when $\omega \leq \bar{\omega}$, must believe $Pr(\theta = 1|e_1 \neq s_1, d = 1) = 0$. Other messages remain off the path of play and beliefs are unrestricted. We set these beliefs to be $Pr(\theta = 1|e_1, d) = 0$ for all off-path messages (e_1, d). Given these beliefs, R's best response is to set $v = 0$ when $(e_1, d) = (s_1, 0)$. As noted above, her best response is also to set $v = 0$ whenever $\omega > \bar{\omega}$ or $\omega \geq \underline{\omega}$ and $d = 1$. R's best response is to set $v = 1$ in all other cases. This completes the characterization of the semi-separating equilibrium.   □

Proof that the Semi-Separating Equilibrium Uniquely Satisfies the Intuitive Criterion. This proof consists of two requirements. First, we must demonstrate that the semi-separating equilibrium satisfies the intuitive criterion refinement. Second, we must demonstrate that no alternative pure strategy PBE, in which L discloses whenever indifferent, satisfies the intuitive criterion refinement. We take each of these steps in turn.

We begin by demonstrating that the PBE characterized by Proposition 10.1 satisfies the intuitive criterion refinement. There are information sets that are never hit in equilibrium, though which information sets are not hit depends on the value of the parameter ω. For $\omega > \bar{\omega}$, the messages $(s_1, 0)$ and $(\neg s_1, 0)$ are observed in equilibrium, while $(s_1, 1)$ and $(\neg s_1, 1)$ are never observed. Trivially, however, both off-path messages are equilibrium dominated for both types of L – since, when $\omega > \bar{\omega}$, both types of L have a dominant strategy. Hence, the intuitive criterion does not limit off equilibrium path beliefs, and the equilibrium survives.

For $\omega \leq \bar{\omega}$, the messages $(s_1, 0)$ and $(\neg s_1, 1)$ are observed in equilibrium, while the messages $(s_1, 1)$ and $(\neg s_1, 0)$ are not. The message $(s_1, 0)$ equilibrium dominates both off path messages for convergent types of L, since $(s_1, 0)$ returns the highest possible utility for L when $\theta = 1$. Given that this is the case, either the intuitive criterion (1) does not limit beliefs for these off-path messages (the off-path message is equilibrium dominated for all types of L) or (2) the intuitive criterion requires that these off-path beliefs are such that $Pr(\theta = 1 | e_1, d) = 0$ (the off-path message is equilibrium dominated when $\theta = 1$, but not when $\theta = 0$). Given that we specify $Pr(\theta = 1 | e_1, d) = 0$ for $(e_1, d) = \{(s_1, 0), (\neg s_1 1)\}$ in the semiseparating equilibrium, these beliefs are consistent with the intuitive criterion refinement.

We now must demonstrate that alternative pure strategy PBE, in which L discloses whenever indifferent, do not satisfy an intuitive criterion refinement. To accomplish this task, we must first characterize the alternative pure strategy PBE to this game.

First, notice that there cannot exist any PBE in which divergent types adopt a pure strategy of setting $e_1 = s_1$. No such equilibrium can exist because, for a sufficiently high realization of the rents term r_1, divergent types have a dominant strategy of setting $e_1 \neq s_1$ – i.e., they will do so regardless of R's beliefs.

Notice further that, for $\omega > \bar{\omega}$, both types of L have a dominant strategy. In any PBE, it must be the case that for $\omega > \bar{\omega}$, L chooses $(s_1, 0)$ when $\theta = 1$ and $(\neg s_1, 0)$ when $\theta = 0$. We therefore confine our attention to equilibrium strategies when $\omega \leq \bar{\omega}$.

These restrictions rule out any equilibrium in which all types of L pool on the action $e_1 = s_1$ when $\omega \leq \bar{\omega}$. The intuitive criterion rules out any equilibrium in which, for some range of values of ω, both types of leader pool on the either the message $(\neg s_1, 1)$ or $(\neg s_1, 0)$. For any range of parameter values such that both types of L pool on $(e_1, d) \in \{(\neg s_1, 1), (\neg s_1, 0)\}$, R's posterior belief on witnessing this signal must be such that $Pr(\theta = 1 | e_1, d) = \pi$, which, in turn, guarantees that her best response to this message is $v = 0$. Since either equilibrium message then satisfies L's preferences over both policy and retention when $\theta = 0$, either message will equilibrium dominate any off path message $(e_1 = s_1, d = \cdot)$ when $\theta = 0$. However, the equilibrium message cannot equilibrium dominate any off path message $(e_1 = s_1, d = \cdot)$ for convergent types, since $e_1 = s_1$ satisfies L's policy preference when $\theta = 1$. Thus, the intuitive criterion requires that R hold off-path beliefs $Pr(\theta = 1 | e_1 = s_1, d = \cdot) = 1$. Given these off-path beliefs, convergent types prefer to deviate from the equilibrium – that is, any such equilibrium must fail the intuitive criterion refinement.

There remains one additional scenario to consider – an alternative semiseparating PBE in which convergent types adopt the strategy of sending the message $(s_1, 1)$. Divergent types pool with this message for values of $r_1 < \bar{r}(\omega)$ when $\omega < \underline{\omega}$, and will deviate to $(\neg s_1, 1)$ otherwise, where $\bar{r}(\omega)$ is as defined in

Definition 10.2. In this equilibrium, R's beliefs are defined such that $Pr(\theta = 1 | e_1 = s_1, d = 1) > \pi$ and $Pr(\theta = 1 | e_1, d) = 0$ for any other message pair. Given this, R's strategy is to set $v = 0$ if $(e_1, d) = (s_1, 1)$; $v = 0$ if $d = 1$ and $\omega > \underline{\omega}$; and $v = 1$ otherwise.

In this equilibrium, the off-path message $(s_1, 0)$ is equilibrium dominated for divergent types for all $\omega > \underline{\omega}$ and when $\omega < \underline{\omega}$ and $r_1 \geq \bar{r}(\omega)$. This off-path message is not, however, equilibrium dominated for convergent types. Hence, R's beliefs on witnessing $(s_1, 0)$ must be such that $Pr(\theta = 1 | s_1, 0) > \pi$ – and R must respond to these belief by setting $v = 0$ on witnessing $(s_1, 0)$. However, if R adopts this strategy, convergent types of L strictly prefer to deviate from the equilibrium, and send the message $(s_1, 0)$. The equilibrium does not survive an intuitive criterion refinement.

We have thus considered all alternative pure strategy PBE, in which L discloses where indifferent, to the game. The semiseparating equilibrium characterized by Proposition 10.1 survives the intuitive criterion refinement. Alternative pure strategy PBE does not. Hence, the equilibrium characterized by Proposition 10.1 is the unique pure strategy PBE to satisfy the intuitive criterion.   □

Proof of Proposition 10.2. To complete this proof, we first must construct an analogous semi-separating equilibrium to that specified in Proposition 10.1 to a game isomorphic to that above, save that disclosure is not an option. That is, the game is identical, except that d is fixed and equal to zero.

As in the original game, L has a dominant strategy of playing according to type in the final period of play. Given this, R's retention decision is identical to the original model, and her best response is given by expression 10.4. As in the original game, we can therefore characterize a value of $\bar{\omega}$ to the alternative game, and this value is given by Definition 10.1. There is no analogue to the value $\underline{\omega}$, however.

We can now consider L's strategy regarding his policy decision in the first period of play e_1. This is now his only message. Clearly, if $\omega > \bar{\omega}$, because R has a dominant strategy of setting $v = 0$, L also has a dominant strategy of playing according to type – that is, $e_1 = s_1$ if $\theta = 1$ and $e_1 \neq s_1$ if $\theta = 0$.

As in the original semiseparating equilibrium, we consider an equilibrium in which, when L is a convergent type, $e_1 = s_1$ when $\omega \leq \bar{\omega}$ as well. Given that this pure strategy by convergent types of L, R's belief on witnessing $e_1 = s_1$ must be such that $Pr(\theta = 1 | e_1 = s_1) \geq \pi$ – in which case R's best response is to set $v = 0$.

Divergent types of L thus have a choice of whether to pool with convergent types when $\omega \leq \bar{\omega}$ – and enjoy guaranteed retention – or to separate and gain rents at the expense of removal. A divergent type gains expected utility $\Delta + \lambda y + [1 - p(0)][\mu + \lambda y]$ from setting $e_1 = s_1$. He gains expected utility $r_1 + \lambda y$ from setting $e_1 \neq s_1$. Hence, divergent types will set $e_1 \neq s_1$ if $r_1 > \Delta + [1 - p(0)][\mu + \lambda y]$ and will set $e_1 = s_1$ otherwise.

We can now characterize a semiseparating equilibrium to the alternative game:

1. For L:

$$e_1 = \begin{cases} \neg s_1 & \text{if } \theta = 0 \text{ and } \omega > \bar{\omega} \\ \neg s_1 & \text{if } \theta = 0 \text{ and } r_1 > \Delta + [1 - p(0)][\mu + \lambda y] \text{ and } \omega \leq \bar{\omega} \\ s_1 & \text{otherwise} \end{cases}$$

and

$$e_2 = \begin{cases} \neg s_s & \text{if } \theta = 0 \\ s_2 & \text{otherwise.} \end{cases}$$

2. For R:

$$v = \begin{cases} 0 & \text{if } \omega > \bar{\omega} \\ 0 & \text{if } e_1 = s_1 \\ 1 & \text{otherwise.} \end{cases}$$

3. R's beliefs are given by $Pr(\theta = 1 | e_1 \neq s_1) = 0$ and $Pr(\theta = 1 | e_1 = s_1) > \pi$.

Comparing these two equilibria, it is apparent that, in the alternative model, for $\omega \leq \bar{\omega}$, any decision to set $e_1 \neq s_1$ results in removal. This is not true in the original model, where the message $(\neg s_1, 1)$ results in retention for $\omega \in [\underline{\omega}, \bar{\omega}]$. In the alternative model, divergent types choose to set $e_1 \neq s_1$ when $\omega \leq \bar{\omega}$ iff $r_1 > \Delta + [1 - p(0)][\mu + \lambda y]$. In the original model, divergent types choose to send the message $(\neg s_1, 1)$ for $\omega \in [\underline{\omega}, \bar{\omega}]$ for $r_1 > \Delta + \rho[\mu + \lambda y]$ where $1 - p(0) > \rho$.

Hence, we can say, that in the alternative model, leaders are removed for $\omega \in [\underline{\omega}, \bar{\omega}]$ when $r_1 > \Delta + [1 - p(0)][\mu + \lambda y]$; whereas, in the original model, such leaders would choose to disclose and would be retained. □

Proof of Proposition 10.3. This proposition follows trivially from the equilibrium definition in Proposition 10.1. □

CONCLUSION

11

Consequences of Transparency

Truth never damages a cause that is just.

– Mohandas (Mahatma) K. Gandhi[1]

Popular enthusiasm for transparency abounds. Many readers might therefore expect the authors of a book on transparency to conclude with an unadulterated endorsement of transparency and its zealous supporters. Indeed, our original measure of transparency, focusing on data disclosure, could even be used as a metric to shame and pressure governments that lag behind in the quest to produce ever-increasing amounts of data on the functioning of their economies.[2]

Instead, however, we caution readers against the wholesale embrace of transparency as a goal in and of itself. Data disclosure offers many benefits – economic and political. It also entails costs. In this chapter, we consider, in a methodical fashion, the benefits and costs of transparency identified by our research. For democracies, we do recommend transparency. For autocracies, however, our conclusions are nuanced.

11.1 ECONOMIC BENEFITS

Economically, data disclosure appears to benefit society. Broadly speaking, transparency increases investment. The effect of transparency on foreign direct

---

[1] From Merton (1965: 33).

[2] On the mechanism driving the demand to produce data, see Kelley and Simmons (2015). On the question of transparency and international legitimacy, see Hafner-Burton, Steinert-Threlkeld, and Victor (2016). For an example showing that too much concern for transparency can lead to bad outcomes, see the discussion of Kalyanpur and Newman (2017) on the international response to the Asian financial crisis.

investment (FDI) holds across both democracies and autocracies. Interestingly, the effect on domestic investment – while evident when we examine both political regimes together – is weaker under authoritarianism. We suggest in Chapter 8 that this weaker effect on domestic gross capital formation results from the privileged position of economic elites under autocratic political regimes. Because of their especially intimate ties to the ruling leadership, wealthy investors under autocracy may have access to economic data even in the absence of full public disclosure. The effect of making economic data public is lessened, therefore, because key economic actors have access to the relevant information either way.

This is not to say that transparency has no effect on investment under autocracy, but rather that the economic benefits of data disclosure appear, overall, more convincing for democracies. Even as we focus on the economic benefits of transparency, differences emerge across political regimes.

11.2 TRANSPARENCY AND DEMOCRACY

Of course, the logic of political survival differs across regime types. Unlike their autocratic counterparts, who survive by cultivating a loyal elite constituency, democrats survive in office by winning elections. Pursuing policies that promote the welfare of large segments of society therefore serves to help keep them in power.

Not surprisingly, then, Chapter 9 shows that democracies tend to disclose data at higher rates than do autocracies. Because of economic benefits through increased investment, transparency helps governments win elections. Transparency causes investment, investment leads to a more prosperous electorate, and a prosperous electorate is more likely to retain incumbent governments. Thus voters reward their government for the benefits of transparency and, if aware of the benefits that transparency might bring, perhaps might directly base their voting decisions on the government's record of disclosure.

States, however, require tremendous resources to collect and codify complicated economic interactions and generate aggregate economic indicators across a range of hundreds of factors. Richer countries have greater capacity to gather national-level data. Not surprisingly, therefore, we find that data disclosure trends upward with economic development. Moreover, democracies tend to be richer than autocracies (Lipset 1959; Przeworski et al. 2000), opening the possibility that the difference in rates of disclosure across regime-types arises due to differences in capacity. Instead, however, we find that democracies provide more data than do their autocratic counterparts at every level of GDP per capita. We believe that this is so because transparency is good for democratic leaders.

As suggested by the theory of Chapter 5, democracy also "works" better under higher levels of transparency. Voting under high levels of data disclosure empowers voters to reelect incumbents who best serve the economic well-being of society, and to throw the rascals out of office. The public disclosure of economic data enables voters to base their electoral decisions on aggregate economic performance. To the extent that the median voter benefits from the overall strong economic performance of her country, she can best decide whether to reelect incumbent leaders when she is fully informed about how the economy is performing.

Furthermore, when economic data is publicly shared, the voter can rest assured that other citizens are similarly casting their votes having received credible information about the country's overall economic performance. Data disclosure thus affirms the *legitimacy* of the democratic approach to selecting leaders. The voter knows that her fellow citizens are relatively well informed when making their electoral decisions. By contrast, in democracies suffering from opacity surrounding economic outcomes, voters rely much more on their personal economic situation when making a voting decision or may rely on heuristics, such as voting along ethnic lines. Elections become less able to select better leaders, and the legitimacy of the democratic system becomes questionable. Citizens may seek to alter the democratic order or even support coup attempts by anti-democratic elites. Low levels of data disclosure can potentially cause the collapse of democracy.

Consistent with our theory that transparency consolidates and legitimizes democratic rule, Chapters 6 and 7 show that democracy is more likely to survive when transparency increases. To put it another way, democracy collapses under low levels of data disclosure. This finding holds when we control for numerous other factors that scholars have shown to influence the survival of democracy.

The effect of the HRV index even outperforms the famous effect of GDP per capita in consolidating democracy. We do not mean to suggest that other studies showing that democracies survive at high levels of GDP per capita are misguided. Data disclosure and GDP per capita are positively correlated, and, to be sure, part of the story of democratic survival is economic. We suggest, however, that the causal mechanism by which democracies survive at high income levels may run – at least in part – through the disclosure of aggregate economic data.

Transparency thus offers benefits to the democratic order. From the perspective of a democratically elected government, transparency improves the economy, which helps win reelection – and, of course, transparency reduces opportunities for rent-seeking. From the perspective of voters, transparency helps democracy function more efficiently. By improving economic outcomes and creating a better informed electorate, transparency appears to hold only benefits for a democratic society. Transparency is good for democracies.

Given that most of the world's citizens now live under democracy, these findings should confirm the intuitions and experiences of most of the world's citizens: life gets better as transparency increases. For democracies, this book stresses only advantages from data disclosure. In this sense, our book provides theoretical and empirical support for the transparency fad – for citizens of democratic countries.

11.3 TRANSPARENCY AND INSTABILITY UNDER AUTOCRACY

Yet, billions of people still live under autocratic forms of government – and under autocracy, the effects of transparency are not so clear-cut. Our central thesis contends that the disclosure of economic data facilitates mass protest against autocratic regimes. Popular protest involves a collective action problem – and if only small numbers of citizens protest, they can easily be jailed, or worse. One problem potential protestors face involves coordination. Any single citizen may be dissatisfied with the ruling regime, but she can only guess as to the overall distribution of discontent. Transparency helps to solve this problem, by informing citizens' higher-order beliefs. Not only does data disclosure inform individual citizens of the overall performance of the economy, it also informs them of the beliefs of others, thereby facilitating the coordination required for a mass movement.

How does the facilitation of mass unrest impact political stability under autocracy? We have considered three specific outcomes that are correlated with increasing transparency: (1) a transition to democracy, (2) the replacement of one autocratic regime by another, and (3) the consolidation of the inner circle of autocratic elites, which further entrenches the autocratic regime. Let us consider the multifaceted effects that increasing transparency can have under autocratic rule one by one.

11.3.1 Transitions to Democracy

To the extent that mass unrest leads to democratic transitions, many observers may favor transparency under autocracy. Democracy promotion has been a pillar of US foreign policy, for example, since the end of World War II. The United States invested heavily in democracy promotion in Western Europe, especially in Italy, West Germany, Portugal, and Spain after the war, and this approach was part of the national security blueprints of the Clinton presidency and reemphasized after the terrorist attacks of 9/11, when the Bush administration elevated democratization in the Middle East as a strategic priority (see Bermeo 2017; Bush 2015; L. Howard 2015; Lagon 2011; Doyle 1986). If the goal of foreign policy is democracy promotion, and transparency causes democratic transitions, then encouraging autocratic governments to disclose more economic data would seem good foreign policy.

Many democratic transitions, however, do not last (see Huntington 1968). Recall the transparency "danger zone" from Chapter 6. Table 6.9 identifies 18 countries that experienced multiple regime-type transitions – for example, from autocracy to democracy, back to autocracy – in our sample. Most have reached an above-average level of transparency for autocracies but a below-average level of transparency for democracies. History has witnessed these countries oscillate back and forth from autocracy to democracy. This kind of instability has numerous negative consequences for the citizens who experience them.

Furthermore, the mass unrest facilitated by transparency may not result in democracy but simply the replacement of one autocratic regime by another. We return to this prospect below.

Moreover, while our results indicate quantitatively that transparency facilitates transition to democracy, our theory and the totality of our empirical results suggest that transparency is associated with a particular *kind* of democratic transition. Specifically, transparency promotes democratization that is driven from below. While demands from the citizenry have been the primary force driving democratic transitions in recent years (Bunce 2003), and have played a prominent role throughout history (Przeworski 2009; Wood 2000), many scholars argue that democratization can also be an elite-driven process.[3]

According to such arguments, democratization emerges from the fracturing of the autocratic elite (O'Donnell and Schmitter 1986). Competing elite factions may seek support from the populace (Llavador and Oxoby 2005), or may use elections as a mechanism for resolving distributional disputes (Przeworski 1991; Wantchekon 2004). "Pacted" democratic transitions, involving an alliance between portions of the *ancien regime* and newly empowered elements of the masses, may arise (Karl 1990).

Our theory and empirical results regarding coups suggest that such "pacted" transitions grow *less* likely as transparency rises. Transparency under autocratic rule encourages cohesion within the elite, rendering the types of splits that give rise to pacted transitions less frequent. Transparency's positive association with transitions driven from below must outweigh its negative effect on pacted transitions, since it is positively associated with democratization in total. Yet, this suggests we should expect pressures toward democratization to assume a particular form as transparency rises.

This too has important policy implications for those who seek to promote democracy. In autocracies with a fractious elite, promoting greater disclosure may, counter-intuitively, have adverse consequences. Moreover, when seeking tools to promote democratization, policymakers must decide which process – pressures from below, or fracturing within – is most desirable in bringing about the collapse of the autocratic regime. Pacted transitions can have deleterious results, insofar as nondemocratic elites continue to exercise power well after free and fair elections are first held (Göktepe and Satyanath 2013). These elites may arise again to overthrow the newly established democratic order. However, such transitions involve less direct confrontation that those that are driven from below, and so, intuitively, may be less likely to dissolve into violence.

---

[3] Yashar (1997) examines the interaction of elite divisions and popular demands.

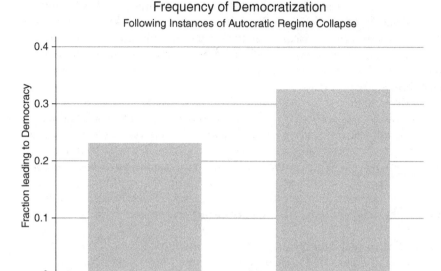

FIGURE 11.1. Transition to democracy versus autocratic instability. The proportion of instances of autocratic collapse that lead to democratization as a function of transparency. The y-axis depicts the fraction of cases of autocratic regime collapse that lead to democratization. The x-axis depicts the level of transparency, where "low" transparency corresponds to a level at or below the autocratic median and "high" transparency corresponds to a level above the autocratic median. More often, in either case, mass unrest under autocracy leads to a new autocratic regime – not to a democratic transition.

11.3.2 Replacement of One Autocracy by Another

Figure 11.1 shows the percentage of cases in which the collapse of an autocratic regime leads to democratization at various levels of transparency. Autocratic regime collapse is defined following Svolik (2012) as the replacement of a given autocrat by a successor unaffiliated with the sitting ruling clique. As can be seen, increasing transparency does not always result in a democratic transition. When transparency is below the autocratic median, only 23 percent of instances of regime collapse lead to democratization. Increasing levels of transparency boost this percentage, but modestly so: 33 percent of instances of regime collapse lead to democratization when transparency is above the autocratic median. More often, in either case, mass unrest under autocracy leads to a new autocratic regime – not to a democratic transition.

So, increasing transparency in the pursuit of democratic transitions faces at least two risks. (1) Even if democracy emerges, it may not be stable and autocracy may subsequently reemerge. (2) Democracy may not emerge at all, but instead mass unrest may simply cause the fall of one autocracy and the rise of another. And still there is another risk.

11.3.3 Entrenchment

Transparency under autocracy has an insidious side. Even as data disclosure encourages mass unrest, the fear of mass unrest can help an autocratic leader to increase the loyalty of inner-circle elites.

Chapter 10 explores the strategic logic of facilitating mass unrest to increase the loyalty of elites. The chapter also documents empirical evidence supporting the theory. Even as mass unrest increases with transparency under autocracy, the risk of coups is reduced. We suggest that this is because coup-plotters typically come from within the elite ranks of an autocratic regime and when they depose a leader under high levels of transparency they run the risk that the masses will coordinate on the obvious elite disunity and topple all members of the regime. This risk increases under high levels of transparency because of the effect of transparency on facilitating mass unrest.

So increasing transparency can be used by autocratic leaders as a tool to further entrench their regimes. As argued above, this may lessen the likelihood of a certain *type* of democratic transition – a pacted transition. Transparency instead fosters democratization that is driven by the masses – the most common form of transition in our data. Elite cohesion may be undesirable from a policy standpoint, even if democratization is not an end goal, if – for instance – a particular autocratic leader is unduly repressive or belligerent and cannot be checked by elites within his regime. All told, increasing transparency under autocracy can lead to a range of outcomes – many of them objectionable.

11.4 POLICY ADVICE: PROMOTE DEMOCRATIC STABILITY, NOT AUTOCRATIC INSTABILITY

Our research comes to two conclusions: (1) increasing transparency helps consolidate democracy and (2) increasing transparency can lead to various outcomes under autocracy, including democratization, but also the establishment of new autocracies or the entrenchment of old ones. Unrest certainly becomes more likely as transparency rises under autocratic rule and thus destabilization is possible. But, democratization is far from guaranteed. For advocates and policymakers interested in promoting democracy around the world, therefore, we offer rather straightforward advice: rather than attempt to influence levels of transparency under autocracy, invest in transparency in existing democracies. New democracies, those that have just transitioned from autocracy, should be particularly fruitful targets for such an intervention.

BOX 11.1. Likely cases of democratic collapse.

Burundi
Guinea-Bissau
Liberia
Madagascar
Malawi
Mali*
Mauritius
Niger
Nigeria
Papua New Guinea
Sierra Leone
* Democracy collapsed in Mali in 2012.

11.4.1 Promoting Democracy

Democracy exists in many poor countries where the survival of democratic rule is uncertain. Przeworski et al. (2000) famously identified Argentina in 1975 as the highest-income country where democracy ever collapsed. Below that level of income, however, democracy has collapsed more than five dozen times in over 40 countries around the world. At present, more than 50 democracies exist at levels of per capita income below that of Argentina in 1975 (for a list, see Cheibub and Vreeland 2016: 18–19). There is good reason to believe that the next time democracy collapses, it will fall in one of these countries. Indeed, at this writing, the last two democracies to fall were Mali (in 2012) and Thailand (in 2014) – both had incomes below that of Argentina 1975 (measured in purchasing power parity terms).

For what it is worth, Thailand in 2006 had the highest level of transparency for any democratic to autocratic transition in our sample, with a score of 3.79. The average transparency score for years in which a democracy collapses is 0.53 (with a median value of −0.11), as compared to an average score during years in which democracies survive of 2.60 (with a median of 2.56). Only 20 percent of country years in our sample of instances in which democracies survive have a transparency score as low as the average in which democracies collapse.

In Box 11.1, we list all of the democracies in existence in 2008 (the conclusion of our sample) that, over the period since 2000, had an average level of transparency below the median value for democracies that collapsed (−0.11). We suggest that democracies on this list face particular risks of collapse due to their relatively low levels of transparency. (And, indeed, several countries on this list – for example, Burundi and Mali – are currently experiencing or are in imminent danger of autocratic backsliding.)

We suggest that policymakers interested in promoting democracy should focus on encouraging the governments of these countries – with financial and technical assistance – to increase the amount of aggregate economic data that they collect and disseminate.

The results of our study suggest that transparency can help democracy-promotion efforts by contributing to the survival of democracy where it currently exists. A policy that specifically targets poorer democracies, those at risk of collapse, may have the biggest impact. International organizations and foreign governments should help improve the capacity of these democracies to collect and disseminate economic data. We expect that democratically elected governments will welcome such assistance and if some elements of ruling governments resist, policy conditionality can be used to incentivize these governments to adopt broader data-disclosure policies.

Our results suggest that transparency promotion may pay particularly large dividends in newly transitioned democracies. Recall from our discussion in Chapter 6, and specifically Figure 6.11, countries that experience a stable autocratic-to-democratic transition tend to see a sustained increase in levels of disclosure in the immediate wake of democratization. Contrastingly, those new democracies that subsequently revert back to autocracy tend to remain stuck in the "danger zone," with high levels of transparency relative to autocracies, but low levels when compared to other democracies. Their transparency scores stagnate in the five-year period following democratization.

Now, this empirical regularity may not be entirely causal. New democracies that better resolve tensions between powerful social actors may have greater capacity to increase disclosure following transition. Increases in transparency may be a sign that elections are already working well.

However, the logic we advance throughout this book suggests this relationship is at least partially driven by a causal mechanism. New democracies, which have just experienced a transition, are likely to introduce elections to a relatively information-poor environment – since their autocratic predecessors tend to disclose at low levels when compared to entrenched democracies. That is, new democracies are likely to reside in the "danger zone" with high levels of disclosure relative to entrenched autocracies and low levels relative to entrenched democracies. By boosting disclosure, these regimes might escape the danger zone, imbue their electoral processes with greater legitimacy, and help to consolidate democracy. Such states should therefore prove particularly important targets for policy interventions.

11.4.2 Avoiding Autocratic Instability

While the results of our study would support the provision of technical assistance to help existing democracies to disclose increasing levels of aggregate economic data, we would draw a contrast between democracy promotion for existing democracies with democracy creation – that is, seeking to *create* democracy where it currently does not exist. We caution that pressuring autocratic

TABLE 11.1. *Transparency scores among Arab MENA countries in 2010.*

Widespread Unrest		Limited/No Unrest	
Country	HRV Score	Country	HRV Score
Egypt	1.467	Algeria	−0.344
Jordan	2.039	Kuwait	−0.632
Libya	−0.697	Lebanon	1.148
Morocco	1.302	Iraq	−0.635
Syria	1.773	Oman	−0.640
Tunisia	0.873	Saudi Arabia	−0.516
		United Arab Emirates	−0.889

Transparency scores of Arab MENA countries, classified by level of unrest during the Arab uprisings. Unrest classifications from the "resistance" index of Korotayev et al. (2014: 164), where "Widespread Unrest" corresponds to a score of 3 or less on their Resistance index. Mean HRV index scores are to the right of the relevant country name.

governments to become more transparent, so that information flows freely in their societies, could result in outcomes far from idyllic democratic rule.

Consider recent historical events. We began this book project in the shadow of mass protests spreading across the Middle East in 2010. We recall the West's enthusiasm for this so-called Arab Spring, which was facilitated by the spread of information through social and traditional media, in a manner not unlike the causal mechanism we have identified in this book.[4] In fact, among the Middle East and North African countries, those that had the lowest HRV scores in 2010 were – with the notable exception of Libya – less likely to experience protests. See Table 11.1.

Table 11.1 lists the HRV scores in 2010 for all countries in our sample that are located in the Middle East and North Africa.[5] The level of unrest is defined by Korotayev et al. (2014: 164), with "Widespread Unrest" corresponding to a score of 3 or less on their scale.[6] It is clear from a casual examination of

---

[4] Aday et al. (2012) argue that traditional media – specifically *Al-Jazeera* – played a bigger role than social media for most protests, for example, by announcing upcoming events. On the diffusion of information during the Arab uprisings, see Schwedler (2013). For a discussion of the later coup attempt in Turkey, see Hollyer, Rosendorff, and Vreeland (2016).

[5] Formally, all Arab countries that are in regions 6 and 11 by the ACLP definition in Cheibub, Gandhi, and Vreeland (2010).

[6] Korotayev et al. (2014) begin their piece by acknowledging that "quantitative analysis of the Arab Spring events is a rather difficult task." Their Resistance index approximates how resistant given regimes were to instability during the Arab uprisings (Korotayev et al. 2014: 158). At one extreme (a score of 7), the political system "has shown a very high degree of resistance, the pan-Arab wave of destabilization was manifested only in some small-scale protest actions" (Korotayev et al. 2014: 158). At the other extreme (a score of 1), the political system exhibited

Table 11.1 that those countries that experienced widespread protest during the so-called Arab Spring period tended to have higher levels of transparency from those that did not. Indeed, of the countries with a negative HRV score, only Libya experienced widespread protest stemming from the Arab uprisings. All other low-transparency autocracies avoided mass unrest. The democracy on the list – Lebanon – was similarly insulated. Yet no autocracy with a positive HRV score managed to avoid widespread protest during this period.

Time magazine's person of the year in 2011 was "The Protestor," who embodied the protestors throughout the Middle East and Tunisia in particular.[7] After images of a fruit seller's self-immolation spread over Facebook and *Al Jazeera*, Tunisians took to the streets, and the tweet directed at Tunisia's dictator, "Get out, Ben Ali" is said to have inspired millions across the Arab world.

Many observers lauded these events as the first coming of democracy to the Arab world. One of us even witnessed the eruption of spontaneous applause at a faculty meeting when the news of the collapse of the Mubarak regime in Egypt broke. The overwhelming sentiment among the professors (other than the more sanguine political scientists and economists in the room) was a celebration of the end of a military dictatorship and the emergence of democracy.

Mass protest turned into an organized armed rebellion in Libya, but seemed doomed to fail until US, French, and British forces intervened under the mandate of a "no fly zone" established by the United Nations Security Council.[8] Again, many of observers were supportive, seeing the action as an important test of the United Nations, principle of "responsibility to protect" (R2P), where the sovereignty of a state could be violated if doing so would prevent human rights atrocities.[9] In light of subsequent events, it is now clear that greater skepticism was warranted.[10]

"Extremely low resistance: a successful revolution" (Korotayev et al. 2014: 158). We break the scale at 3, where political systems exhibited "Low resistance: powerful anti-government protests with violent collisions that shattered the power (strength of anti-government forces is comparable with the one of the pro-government forces)" (Korotayev et al. 2014: 158). A score of 4 is categorized as below average resistance: "large-scale and prolonged antigovernment protests with individual violent clashes" (Korotayev et al. 2014: 158). On their index, Egypt, Libya, and Tunisia are scored 1, Syria is score 2, and Jordan and Morocco are scored 3. By contrast, Algeria, Kuwait, and Lebanon are scored 4, Oman is scored 5, and Iraq and Saudi Arabia are scored 6.

[7] See http://content.time.com/time/specials/packages/completelist/0,29569,2101745,00.html, accessed August 31, 2016.

[8] For a discussion of the vote, see Vreeland and Dreher (2014: 22–23).

[9] See *The Economist* (2011). On R2P, see Thakur and Weiss (2009); Hehir (2013); Badescu and Weiss (2010). On R2P as a legacy of the nineteenth century free press, see Bass (2008).

[10] President Obama identified the Libya intervention and its fallout as the "worst mistake" of his administration. See "The Legacy of Obama's 'Worst Mistake,'" by Dominic Tierney, *The Atlantic*, April 15, 2016, www.theatlantic.com/international/archive/2016/04/obamas-worst-mistake-libya/478461/, accessed August 11, 2017.

While increased information flows may facilitate collective action against autocratic regimes and lead to the possibility of democratic transitions, they may also simply lead to instability and bloodshed. Successful transitions to democracy may subsequently be overturned. Autocracies that collapse may simply be replaced by new undemocratic regimes. Mass unrest against a unified regime may devolve into violence and civil war. And, in some instances, increasingly unified autocratic elites may head off any incipient challenges that might emerge from the public.

The uprisings associated with the so-called Arab Spring have indeed resulted in this full range of outcomes (Haddad and Schwedler 2013: 212). Only in Tunisia, where the uprising originated, do we observe a successful transition to democracy. President Zine El Abidine Ben Ali, who had ruled the country since 1987, fled the country in January 2011, opening the door to contested elections.[11] The National Constituent Assembly, formed through multiparty elections in October 2011, elected President Moncef Marzouki, the leader of a secular center-left party (Zavis 2011). A human rights activist and former dissident, Marzouki had formerly been imprisoned and then exiled under the Ali regime. Alternation in power took place in 2014, when Marzouki lost in direct presidential elections to Béji Caïd Essebsi, of a moderate secular political party (Nidaa Tounes).[12] So far, the Arab uprisings can count this example as a successful democratic transition.

By contrast, Egypt saw the emergence of democracy, but many did not like the results of the election and the democratically elected government was subsequently ousted in a coup. President Hosni Mubarak, who had ruled Egypt since 1981, was deposed by his own Armed Forces Supreme Council in February 2011, amidst uncontrollable mass protest in the streets. The Armed Forces Supreme Council acted as a caretaker government until voters chose, in June 2012, President Mohamed Morsi of the Muslim Brotherhood's political party as the first democratically elected president in the history of Egypt.[13] Many Egyptians were dissatisfied by the election of someone from a religious party, and they took to the streets in protest of his administration – the chief of the military, Abdel Fattah el-Sisi, ousted Morsi in July 2013.[14] In June of 2014, Sisi became president of Egypt.[15] The former military chief won a contested election over an opposition candidate; the Muslim Brotherhood's political party was banned from participating. President Sisi has vowed to wipe out the Muslim Brotherhood, and Morsi currently sits in prison and has been sentenced to death.[16]

---

[11] See http://rulers.org/rult.html, accessed May 25, 2016.

[12] Again, see http://rulers.org/rult.html, accessed May 25, 2016, as well as Tavana and Russell (2014).

[13] See www.cnn.com/2012/06/30/world/africa/egypt-morsi/, accessed August 31, 2016.

[14] See www.bbc.com/news/world-middle-east-24772806, accessed August 31, 2016.

[15] See rulers.org/rule.html, accessed August 31, 2016.

[16] Again, see www.bbc.com/news/world-middle-east-24772806, accessed August 31, 2016.

While representing a failed democratic transition, at least the country of Egypt persists as a whole and stable state. The Arab spring has achieved less in Libya and Syria. When protests turned to armed struggle in Libya, the country's leader, who had been in power since 1969, "vowed to fight until the last drop of his blood" (Saleh and England 2011). Colonel Muammer Gaddafi urged his supporters to "cleanse Libya house by house," rooting out protesters, whom he described as "rats" (Saleh and England 2011). Experts predicted a "bloodbath" in the opposition stronghold city of Benghazi with a population of 700,000 people (*The Economist* 2011). Then the United Nations intervened, under the leadership of the United States, France, and the United Kingdom. Reaching beyond the establishment of the UN-mandated "no-fly zone" over the country, they began bombing and offered the help of on-the-ground military advisors to the rebels fighting against the Gaddafi regime (Kuperman 2015). In October 2011, Gaddafi was killed and a National Transitional Council governed until July 2012, when elections were held amid growing violence.[17] Factionalism has grown and thousands have been killed and displaced from their homes. At this writing, rival governments exist in the east and west of the country – and the terrorist organization known as the Islamic State has taken over neighborhoods in major cities throughout the country (Wehrey 2016).

Syria has had it worse: more than a quarter of a million people have lost their lives since the dawning of the Arab Spring.[18] In March of 2011, protests emerged in the city of Deraa after police arrested some teenagers for painting revolutionary slogans on a school. Unrest soon emerged throughout Syria, with protesters calling for the resignation of President Assad, who had ruled the country since 2000. The government tried but failed to put down the protests, which grew increasingly violent and organized. Rebel forces took control of territory in the northwest and southwest of the country, but the regime has held on to much territory in the west, with the assistance of Russia and Hezbollah forces from Lebanon. Vast expanses of territory in the eastern part of the country have been taken over by the Islamic State.[19] Meanwhile, the core security services have remained closely tied to Assad and have resisted peace talks predicated on his abdication.

So, while mass unrest led to democracy in the case of Tunisia, an old autocracy was replaced with a new one in Egypt, and Libya and Syria have descended into chaos.[20] These examples seem to fit the logic of Chapter 5. In the meantime, many autocratic regimes successfully survived the protests of the Arab Spring.

---

[17] See www.theguardian.com/world/2012/jul/01/libyan-militia-storm-election-office, accessed August 31, 2016.

[18] This timeline comes from BBC (2016).

[19] On the establishment of the modern Syrian state, see Neep (2012, 2017). For a discussion of its partition, see Daoudy (2016).

[20] The future of the democratic regime is questionable in Tunisia, where, at this writing, there are some worrisome signs. See, for example, Chomiak (2016); International Crisis Group (2017); Marzouki and Meddeb (2015); and Marzouki (2015).

When protests emerged in Jordan in 2011, the Hashemite monarchy led by King Abdullah II quickly reached a consensus. They took the opportunity to reorganize elite-level politics, sacking his entire cabinet, including the prime minister, dissolving the parliament, and holding new elections (Andoni 2011). The monarchy also agreed to meet with opposition groups – but a set of anti terror laws makes any bold public protest still subject to prosecution (Yom 2015). Arguably, the Hashemite monarchy has emerged strengthened by the protests of the Arab Spring because leaders of opposition groups fear what unrest could bring, as seen in neighboring Syria (Yom 2015). Protests similarly emerged in Morocco, where King Mohammed VI had been under pressure to implement reforms – relinquishing some of his absolutist power – that had been stalled since terrorist attacks in 2003. Mohammed responded to protesters by issuing proposed constitutional changes, which increased the power of the elected government over day-to-day matters, but which also maintained his (the King's) control over the military and status as the "commander of the faithful" in religious matters. These reforms proved sufficient to placate both internal and external critics and allowed Mohammed's rule to survive intact.[21] These examples appear to fit the logic of Chapter 10.

The region's low-transparency examples – Algeria, Kuwait, Iraq, Oman, Saudi Arabia, and the United Arab Emirates – saw limited unrest. Saudi Arabia and Oman placated protesters by promising limited reforms.[22] The Kingdom of Saudi Arabia reportedly distributed more than 100 billion dollars in domestic incentives to buy off opposition (Jones 2011: 44) and played an active role in neighboring Bahrain, which saw more widespread pro-democracy protests. With the help of Saudi Arabia, Bahrain's monarchy successfully crushed the rebellion.[23] More recently, the Kingdom consolidated power at home, following the (natural) death of King Abdullah in January 2015.[24] Indeed, the majority of Arab regimes survived the Spring movements unscathed.

---

[21] "Morocco King Proposes Limited Steps to Democracy," by Steven Erlanger, *New York Times*, June 17, 2011, www.nytimes.com/2011/06/18/world/africa/18morocco.html?_r=1&src=me& ref=world.

[22] See The Arab Awakening, *Aljazeera*, February 22, 2011, www.aljazeera.com/indepth/spotlight/2011/02/2011222121213770475.html, accessed August 31, 2016.

[23] Again, see www.aljazeera.com/indepth/spotlight/2011/02/2011222121213770475.html, accessed August 31, 2016. Note that Bahrain is not in our HRV index sample because its population did not exceed 500,000 during the full 1980–2010 period. Recall from Chapter 3 that micro-states are excluded from our analysis. For a discussion of how state-level analysis obscures some of the dynamics of the uprisings and calls for focus at the micro-level and analysis of interconnections across the region, see Schwedler (2015).

[24] The new ruler, King Salman bin Abdulaziz Al Saud (Abdullah's half brother) shook up the line of succession, replacing his anointed heir (Muqrin bin Abdulaziz) with his nephew (Mohammed bin Nayef), and naming his own son (Mohammed bin Salman) as the second in line to the throne (Naylor and Sly 2015).

11.4.3 Policy Options

In discussing the Arab Spring examples, we do not wish to appear overly pessimistic about the democratization that transparency can bring. Instead, we offer them as a cautionary tale of what transparency can cause under autocracy. We thus seek to temper the wild enthusiasm for transparency with methodical nuance. Moreover, we offer another option for pro-democracy advocates. Rather than use transparency to cause democracy to emerge out of preexisting autocracies, we stress that transparency can best be used as a tool to consolidate and strengthen preexisting democracies.

When the West or an international organization pressures a recalcitrant authoritarian government to release increasing levels of economic data, we should question (1) why does the government resist pressure to disclose data and (2) what will be the consequences of increased transparency? Policymakers may often assume that the government's reluctance is due to limited data-collection capacity and thus their pressure may simply seem to incentivize higher effort. On the other hand, policymakers may be well aware that the climate of opacity advantages a corrupt elite and they may seek to undermine this corruption. But doing so may undermine the very stability of the state. While we do not advocate that policymakers should ignore corruption, we do encourage careful consideration of the larger questions of political instability. The main take-aways from our work on transparency under autocracy are (1) transparency causes unrest among the masses and (2) transparency increases loyalty among regime elites. If a poor country already faces economic problems, will policies that implicitly encourage mass protest compound these problems? If the problem is corruption, will a consolidation of elite loyalty around a now more entrenched leader really help?

While we trace out with logical and empirical rigor the various paths to different outcomes, any outcome is possible under autocracy as transparency increases: a new but perhaps unstable democracy, a new autocracy, or an entrenched autocracy. Transitions to democracy are never obvious. They are rare, idiosyncratic, and often fraught with dire consequences for citizens living through them. The bottom line is that we should thus be cautious with autocracies.

And why expend limited resources to promote transparency under autocracy, where the results are not obvious, when we have such a clear use for transparency in another set of regimes? Transparency can be used as a policy tool to strengthen existing – and particularly newly emergent – democracies.

We see nothing but upsides from enhancing transparency in a country that is already democratic. Like much of the transitions literature, we suggest that we know much more about how to help democracy survive than how to create one out of an autocracy. The most prominent finding in that literature is that democracy survives at higher levels of economic development. Of course, this finding often leaves people wondering how to promote economic development – a subject of wide debate. Our book offers a hint. We find that the highly robust effect of GDP per capita in sustaining democracy disappears when we introduce our measure of transparency. Because our HRV index is positively correlated with GDP per capita, we do not suggest that the original GDP per capita finding is misguided. Rather, we believe that we have discovered one of the mechanisms through which per capita income has this consolidating effect. We offer policy advice that is clear-cut: promote transparency in democratic countries.

11.5 ADVANCING THE SCHOLARLY DEBATE ON TRANSPARENCY AND STABILITY

Skepticism strengthens science. Accordingly, we welcome doubts about all aspects of our project. We highlight, however, that this project offers an original conceptualization and measurement of transparency, which has been employed to test original theories about democracy, investment, and the stability of political regimes. Rigorous testing, as well as anecdotal evidence, confirm the validity of our measurement and our hypotheses. So, while we concede that skeptical readers can certainly raise objections to any single characteristic of our research, we would contend that one should not dismiss this book's full arsenal of theoretical and empirical findings *in toto*.

For example, some readers may not like our approach to measuring transparency. They may contend that our focus on data dissemination ignores other important facets of transparency, such as the transparency of the policymaking process or the freedom of the media to investigate the government or the ability of the media to share information with the public. We recognize that other facets of transparency play important roles in political economy. Yet we ask our readers to recognize, further, that:

1. Our measure focuses on an important facet of transparency – data dissemination – that should not be ignored.
2. The measure comprehensively incorporates the reporting of important economic data in a systematic and sophisticated manner.
3. The HRV index reflects the well-known qualitative experiences of important cases that we have raised. Throughout the chapters, we have explored the qualitative validity of the index by examining two dozen countries, including: Argentina, Bangladesh, Bulgaria, Cambodia, the Central African Republic, Chile, China, Côte d'Ivoire, Guinea-Bissau, Hungary, Mexico, Nepal, Paraguay, the Philippines, Poland, Romania, Somalia, South Korea, the Soviet Union/Russia, Tanzania, Uganda, Vietnam, Zambia, and Zimbabwe.
4. We have shown that the index tracks with other phenomena that are central to comparative political economy, including: (a) democratic political

institutions, (b) the survival of democracy itself, (c) transitions to democracy, (d) incidents of mass unrest under autocracy, (e) investment – both foreign and domestic, and (f) the reduction of coups against autocratic governments.

Regarding these empirical findings, the skeptical reader may dismiss any one of them, of course. But rejecting them all out of hand does not strike us as sensible, for several reasons. First, we stress that before delving into empirical patterns, we derived hypotheses supported by rigorous theory, using game-theoretic reasoning and mathematical proofs. One should always be dubious about jumping from correlation to causation because the latter can never be observed and thus requires theory. All of our work rests on theory, applying a standard assumption of political economy – that rational individuals take actions designed to achieve desired outcomes – to stylized settings, varying political institutions and levels of transparency.

Second, we acknowledge that endogeneity looms over our findings – as it does over all observational research in the social sciences. It is possible that any one of our findings is driven by an endogenous relationship between our explanatory variable and outcome variable resulting in a correlation between the independent variable and the error term. Such endogeneity may be due to omitted variable bias or mutual causation between the independent and dependent variables. We would find it hard to believe, however, that our full set of discoveries could all owe to endogeneity. We have attempted to include all relevant control variables throughout the project. For example, the level of economic development has been shown to be among the most prominent correlates of democracy and we control for GDP per capita throughout our work. Indeed, while GDP per capita is perhaps the most robust predictor of the survival of democracy, the statistical significance of its effect disappears when we include our data dissemination measure of transparency.

Regarding autocracy, we have introduced surprises. Some readers, informed by a rich and growing literature on the logic of political survival under autocracy, may have come to this project with the expectation that transparency would help co-opt groups into an autocratic regime, thereby prolonging autocratic rule. We affirm this expectation with our finding that transparency reduces coups. But we also confront these readers with our finding that transparency encourages mass unrest. Other readers, informed by events such as the Arab Spring or the break down of the Soviet Bloc, may have opened our book with a presumption that transparency destabilizes autocratic rule. Our work on transparency and unrest affirms this expectation, but our work on transparency and coups challenges it. Thus, for each of these sets of readers, we hope to have introduced surprises and nuance into their thinking about transparency and autocracy.

11.6 CONCLUSION

We therefore conclude our book with two sets of messages – one for academic research on the determinants and consequences of transparency and one for policymakers.

For our academic audience, we ask that researchers think carefully about the mechanisms undergirding various theories of transparency. At a minimum, this project should inform researchers to use a measure of transparency that closely maps onto their theoretical mechanisms. Several measures – capturing rather different facets of transparency – are available to researchers. Hence, it should be no longer sufficient for researchers to simply rely on some nebulous measure of "transparency." Researchers should choose the measure that best fits the theoretical facet of transparency identified by the theory to be tested.

This book also offers a method to generate new measures of transparency. If existing measures do not correspond well to a researcher's theoretical mechanism, she should work toward creating one that does. At some level, transparency always involves the dissemination of specific information to a specific audience. Rather than rely on survey-based measures, which may incorporate prejudice in favor or against different cultures, the approach of this book centers on the measurement of data reporting, and offers a method to aggregate the objective reporting of data on various factors. Our approach here is broad – considering economic data on 240 variables. Subsets or completely different sets of variables may prove more appropriate for future studies.

In many cases, however, our specific measure of transparency – the HRV index – may stand as an appropriate measure to test theory. In these cases, we invite scholars to make use of our original measure.

As for the enormous literature on political regime transitions, we have introduced a new factor that should be incorporated into future work on the subject. We have shown that transparency, as measured by the HRV index, predicts both the emergence and survival of democracy. The role that the index plays in the survival of autocracy is also central, if nuanced. We note that our measure, in some specifications, outperforms the canonical control variable in the literature, GDP per capita.

For scholars who study investment, we suggest that transparency plays a role in informing both domestic and foreign investors. The finding depends on political institutions. Transparency plays a more systematic role in informing domestic investors under democracy. As for foreign direct investment, transparency has a positive impact regardless of regime type.

The upshot of this advice is that researchers should not see missing data simply as an obstacle to overcome. In many cases, missing data are a phenomenon worthy of explanation.

Finally, we turn to the policymaking audience, whose interest lies in improving the material conditions of living for people living under different political systems. We warn against the unquestioned embrace of transparency as a panacea.

When dealing with democratic governments, particularly in newly transitioned democracies, our findings support the enthusiasm for transparency. Democratic governments should wish to pursue higher levels of data dissemination (following the logic presented in Chapter 9), and doing so should help democracy to function better and endure (as argued throughout Part II). Data dissemination should also provide the additional benefit of greater investment (as shown in Chapter 8) which may improve the overall level of a country's economic development. Thus, policymakers should absolutely promote data disclosure under democracy by providing resources and incentives to democratically elected governments.

When dealing with autocracies, our findings suggest caution. In contrast to the literature on democracy, where consensus exists that it survives under strong economic conditions, the literature on the stability of autocracy is fraught with disagreement. Our work offers a new explanation as to why. Even while we can identify specific mechanisms by which transparency can stabilize (by reducing coups) and destabilize (by encouraging mass unrest), the bottom line is that transparency can have multiple effects under autocracy. Often old autocracies are replaced by new, or the old ones become entrenched; only sometimes do we witness transitions to democracy and often these eventually collapse back into autocracy. Too much blood has been spilt by well-intentioned foreign governments intervening in countries hoping to bring about better governance. The time has come to recognize that we have little control as to the outcome when pursuing such goals in autocratic countries. Instead, we suggest focusing on an attainable goal supported by scientific research. Democracy promotion is best achieved by helping to consolidate democratic rule in existing democracies. This book offers a new method to do so: promote data disclosure under democracy.

References

Abbott, Kenneth W. and Duncan Snidal. 1998. "Why States Act through Formal International Organizations." *Journal of Conflict Resolution* 42(1):3–32.

Abdelal, Rawi, Mark Blyth, and Craig Parsons. 2015. *Constructing the International Economy*. Ithaca, NY: Cornell University Press.

Abrajano, Marisa and Zoltan L. Hajnal. 2015. *White Backlash: Immigration, Race, and American Politics*. Princeton, NJ: Princeton University Press.

Acemoglu, Daron. 2008. "Oligarchic versus Democratic Societies." *Journal of the European Economic Association* 6(1):1–44.

Acemoglu, Daron and James A. Robinson. 2000. "Why Did the West Extend the Franchise? Democracy, Inequality, and Growth in Historical Perspective." *Quarterly Journal of Economics* 115(4):1167–1199.

Acemoglu, Daron and James A. Robinson. 2006. *Economic Origins of Dictatorship and Democracy*. New York: Cambridge University Press.

Acemoglu, Daron, Simon Johnson, and James A. Robinson. 2001. "The Colonial Origins of Comparative Development: An Empirical Investigation." *American Economic Review* 91(5):1369–1401.

Acemoglu, Daron, Simon Johnson, James Robinson, and Pierre Yared. 2008. "Income and Democracy." *American Economic Review* 98(3):808–842.

Aday, Sean, Henry Farrell, Marc Lynch, John Sides, and Deen Freelon. 2012. "Blogs and Bullets II: New Media and Conflict After the Arab Spring." Technical report, United States Institute of Peace.

Adesnik, A. David and Sunhyuk Kim. 2008. "If at First You Don't Succeed: The Puzzle of South Korea's Democratic Transition." CDDRL Working Papers No. 83.

Adserà, Alícia, Carles Boix, and Mark Payne. 2003. "Are You Being Served? Political Accountability and Quality of Government." *Journal of Law, Economics & Organization* 19(2):445–490.

Ahsan, Zayadul and Pavitra Banavar. 2009. "Who Are the Militants?" In *Political Islam and Governance in Bangladesh*, ed. Ali Riaz and C. Christine Fair. New York: Routledge, pp. 71–90.

Ai, Chunrong and Edward C. Norton. 2003. "Interaction Terms in Logit and Probit Models." *Economic Letters* 80(1):123–129.

Albertus, Michael. 2015. *Autocracy and Redistribution: The Politics of Land Reform.* New York: Cambridge University Press.

Alesina, Alberto and Allan Drazen. 1991. "Why Are Stabalizations Delayed?" *American Economic Review* 81(5):1170–1188.

Al Jazeera. 2011. "Timeline: Ivory Coast," November 30. www.aljazeera.com/news/africa/2010/12/2010121971745317811.html, accessed February 5, 2018.

Almeida, Paul, Robert Grant, and Anupama Phene. 2002. "Knowledge Acquisition through Alliances: Opportunities and Challenges." In *The Blackwell Handbook of Cross-Cultural Management*, ed. Martin J. Gannon and Karen L. Newman. Oxford: Blackwell, pp. 67–76.

Alt, James, David Dreyer Lassen, and Shanna Rose. 2006. "The causes of fiscal transparency: evidence from the US states." *IMF Staff Papers* 53 (Special Issue):30–57.

Alt, James, David Dreyer Lassen, and Joachim Wehner. 2014. "It Isn't Just about Greece: Domestic Politics, Transparency and Fiscal Gimmickry in Europe." *British Journal of Political Science* 44(4):707–716.

Alvarez, Mike, José Antonio Cheibub, Fernando Limongi, and Adam Przeworski. 1996. "Classifying Political Regimes." *Studies in Comparative International Development* 31(2):3–36.

Andoni, Lamis. 2011. "Jordanians Demand Change." *Al Jazeera.* www.aljazeera.com/indepth/opinion/2011/02/2011220105658153939.html, accessed May 27, 2016.

Angeletos, George-Marios and Ivan Werning. 2006. "Crises and Prices: Information Aggregation, Multiplicity, and Volatility." *American Economic Review* 96(5):1720–1736.

Angeletos, George-Marios, Christian Hellwig, and Alessandro Pavan. 2007. "Dynamic Global Games of Regime Change: Learning, Multiplicity, and the Timing of Attacks." *Econometrica* 75(3):711–756.

Ansell, Ben and David Samuels. 2010. "Inequality and Democratization: A Contractarian Approach." *Comparative Political Studies* 43(12):1543–1574.

Arias, Eric, James R. Hollyer, and B. Peter Rosendorff. Forthcoming. "Cooperative Autocracies, Leader Survival, Creditworthiness and Bilateral Investment Treaties." *American Journal of Political Science.*

Arnold, R. Douglas. 2013. *Congress, the Press, and Political Accountability.* Princeton, NJ: Princeton University Press.

Ashworth, Scott and Ethan Bueno de Mesquita. 2014. "Is Voter Competence Good for Voters? Information, Rationality and Democratic Performance." *American Political Science Review* 108(3):565–587.

Aumann, Robert J. 1995. "Backward Induction and Common Knowledge of Rationality." *Games and Economic Behavior* 8(1):6–19.

Baccini, Leonardo, Pablo M. Pinto, and Stephen Weymouth. 2017. "The distributional consequences of preferential trade liberalization: Firm-level evidence." *International Organization* 71(2):373–395.

Badescu, Cristina G. and Thomas G. Weiss. 2010. "Misrepresenting R2P and Advancing Norms: An Alternative Spiral?" *International Studies Perspectives* 11(4):354–374.

Bailey, Michael A., Anton Strezhnev, and Erik Voeten. 2017. "Estimating Dynamic State Preferences from United Nations Voting Data." *Journal of Conflict Resolution* 61(2):430–456.

Baker, Scott R., Nicholas Bloom, and Steven J. Davis. 2016. "Measuring Policy Uncertainty." *Quarterly Journal of Economics* 131(4):1593–1636.

Banks, Arthurs S. 1979. "Cross-National Time-Series Data Archive." Center for Social Analysis, State University of New York at Binghamton.

Banks, Jeffrey S. and Rangarajan K. Sundaram. 1993. "Adverse Selection and Moral Hazard in a Repeated Elections Model." In *Political Economy: Institutions, Competition and Representation*, ed. William A. Barnett, Melvin J. Hinich, and Norman J. Schofield. New York: Cambridge University Press, pp. 295–312.

Barnett, Michael N. and Martha Finnemore. 1999. "The Politics, Power, and Pathologies of International Organizations." *International Organization* 53(4):699–732.

Barro, Robert J. 1973. "The Control of Politicians: An Economic Model." *Public Choice* 14(1):19–42.

Barro, Robert J. and Jong Wha Lee. 1996. "International Measures of Schooling Years and Schooling Quality." *American Economic Review* 86(2):218–223.

Bartels, Larry M. 2008. *Unequal Democracy: The Political Economy of the New Guilded Age*. Princeton, NJ: Princeton University Press.

Bass, Gary J. 2008. *Freedom's Battle: The Origins of Humanitarian Intervention*. New York: Knopf.

Baum, Richard. 2011. "The Road to Tiananmen: Chinese Politics in the 1980s." In *The Politics of China: Sixty Years of The People's Republic of China*, 3rd edn. ed. Roderick MacFarquhar. New York: Cambridge University Press, pp. 337–467.

Bayes, Thomas and Richard Price. 1763. "An Essay towards Solving a Problem in the Doctrine of Chances." *Philosophical Transactions of the Royal Society of London* 53:370–418.

Baylies, Carolyn and Morris Szeftel. 1992. "The Fall and Rise of Multi-Party Politics in Zambia." *Review of African Political Economy* 54:75–91.

BBC. 2011. "Ivory Coast's Laurent Gbagbo Arrives in The Hague." *BBC News*. www.bbc.com/news/world-15946481, accessed February 16, 2016.

BBC. 2016. "Syria: The story of the conflict." *BBC News*. www.bbc.com/news/world-middle-east-26116868, accessed May 27, 2016.

Beck, Nathaniel and Jonathan N. Katz. 2011. "Modeling Dynamics in Time-Series–Cross-Section Political Economy Data." *Annual Review of Political Science* 14:331–352.

Beck, Nathaniel, Jonathan N. Katz, and Richard Tucker. 1998. "Taking Time Seriously: Time-Series–Cross-Section Analysis with a Binary Dependent Variable." *American Journal of Political Science* 42(4):1260–1288.

Beissinger, Mark R. 2002. *Nationalist Mobilization and the Collapse of the Soviet State*. New York: Cambridge University Press.

Beitz, Charles R. 1989. "Covert Intervention as a Moral Problem." *Ethics & International Affairs* 3:45–60.

Benhabib, Jess, Alejandro Corvalan, and Mark M. Spiegel. 2011. "Reestablishing the Income-Democracy Nexus." NBER Working Paper No. 16832.

Berger, Daniel, William Easterly, Nathan Nunn, and Shanker Satyanath. 2013. "Commercial Imperialism? Political Influence and Trade during the Cold War." *American Economic Review* 103(2):863–896.

Berliner, Daniel. 2014. "The Political Origins of Transparency." *Journal of Politics* 76(2):479–491.

Berliner, Daniel and Aaron Erlich. 2015. "Competing for Transparency: Political Competition and Institutional Reform in Mexican States." *American Political Science Review* 109(1):110–128.

Bermeo, Nancy. 1997. "Myths of Moderation: Confrontation and Conflict during Democratic Transitions." *Comparative Politics* 29(3):305–322.

Bermeo, Sarah Blodgett. 2017. "Aid Allocation and Targeted Development in an Increasingly Connected World." *International Organization* 71(4):735–766. doi: 10.1017/S0020818317000315.

Bernhard, Michael, Timothy Nordstrom, and Christopher Reenock. 2001. "Economic performance, institutional intermediation, and democratic survival." *Journal of Politics* 63(3):775–803.

Berry, William D., Jacqueline H. R. DeMeritt, and Justin Esarey. 2010. "Testing for Interaction Effects in Binary Logit and Probit Models: Is an Interaction Term Necessary." *American Journal of Political Science* 54(1):248–266.

Besley, Timothy. 2006. *Principled Agents? The Political Economy of Good Government.* New York: Oxford University Press.

Besley, Timothy and Robin Burgess. 2002. "The Political Economy of Government Responsiveness: Theory and Evidence from India." *Quarterly Journal of Economics* 117(4):1415–1451.

Besley, Timothy and Masayuki Kudamatsu. 2007. "Making Autocracy Work." LSE STICERD Research Paper No. DEDPS48.

Besley, Timothy and Torsten Persson. 2007. "The Origins of State Capacity: Property Rights, Taxation, and Politics." NBER Working Paper.

Bierman, Frank and Bernd Siebenhuner, eds. 2009. *Managers of Global Change: The Influence of International Environmental Bureaucrats.* Cambridge, MA: MIT Press.

Birney, Mayling. 2014. "Decentralization and Veiled Corruption under China's 'Rule of Mandates.'" *World Development* 53:55–67.

Bleck, Jaimie and Kristin Michelitch. 2017. "Capturing the Airwaves, Capturing the Nation? A Field Experiment on State-Run Media Effects in the Wake of a Coup." *Journal of Politics* 79(3):873–889.

Bloom, Nick. 2009. "The Impact of Uncertainty Shocks." *Econometrica* 77(3):623–685.

Blyth, Mark. 2002. *Great Transformations: Economic Ideas and Institutional Change in the Twentieth Century.* New York: Cambridge University Press.

Bohlken, Anjali Thomas. 2016. *Democratization from Above: The Logic of Local Democracy in the Developing World.* New York: Cambridge University Press.

Boix, Carles. 2003. *Democracy and Redistribution.* New York: Cambridge University Press.

Boix, Carles and Susan C. Stokes. 2003. "Endogenous Democratization." *World Politics* 55(4):517–549.

Boix, Carles and Milan W. Svolik. 2013. "The Foundations of Limited Authoritarian Government: Institutions, Commitment, and Power-Sharing in Dictatorships." *Journal of Politics* 75(2):300–316.

Borzel, Tanja A., Meike Dudziak, Tobias Hofmann, Diana Panke, and Carina Sprungk. 2007. "Recalcitrance, Inefficiency, and Support for European Integration: Why Member States Do (Not) Comply with European Law." Center for European Studies Working Paper Series 153.

Box-Steffensmeier, Janet M. and Bradford S. Jones. 2004. *Event History Modeling: A Guide for Social Scientists.* New York: Cambridge University Press.

Box-Steffensmeier, Janet M. and Christopher Zorn. 2002. "Duration Models for Repeated Events." *Journal of Politics* 64(4):1069–1094.

Box-Steffensmeier, Janet M., Dan Reiter, and Christopher Zorn. 2003. "Nonproportional hazards and event history analysis in international relations." *Journal of Conflict Resolution* 47(1):33–53.

Bradshaw, Richard. 1997. "Ending a Central African Mutiny." *Christian Science Monitor*, January 10. www.csmonitor.com/1997/0110/011097.opin.opin.1.html, accessed February 25, 2016.

Bratton, Michael. 1992. "Zambia Starts Over." *Journal of Democracy* 3(2):81–94.

Bratton, Michael. 1998. "Second Elections in Africa." *Journal of Democracy* 9(3): 51–66.

Bremmer, Ian. 2006. *The J Curve: A New Way to Understand Why Nations Rise and Fall*. New York: Simon & Schuster.

Brown, Archie. 2007. *Seven Years that Changed the World: Perestroika in Perspective*. New York: Oxford University Press.

Brown, Nathan J. and Amr Hamzawy. 2010. *Between Religion and Politics*. Washington, DC: Carnegie Endowment.

Broz, J. Lawrence. 2002. "Political System Transparency and Monetary Commitment Regimes." *International Organization* 56(4):861–887.

Broz, J. Lawrence. 2007. "Replication Data for: Political System Transparency and Monetary Commitment Regimes." https://dataverse.harvard.edu/dataset.xhtml?persistentId=hdl:1902.1/10299&tab=files&studyListingIndex=0_082f4c2e620d79d32bd7770b68a6, accessed February 5, 2018.

Broz, J. Lawrence and Jeffry A. Frieden. 2001. "The Political Economy of International Monetary Relations." *Annual Review of Political Science* 4:317–343.

Broz, J. Lawrence, Jeffry Frieden, and Stephen Weymouth. 2008. "Exchange Rate Policy Attitudes: Direct Evidence from Survey Data." *IMF Staff Papers* 55(3):417–444.

Brunetti, Aymo and Beatrice Weder. 2003. "A Free Press Is Bad News for Corruption." *Journal of Public Economics* 87(7):1801–1824.

Bueno de Mesquita, Bruce and Alastair Smith. 2009. "Political Survival and Endogenous Institutional Change." *Comparative Political Studies* 42(2):167–197.

Bueno de Mesquita, Bruce, James D. Morrow, Randolph M. Siverson, and Alastair Smith. 2002. "Political Institutions, Policy Choice and the Survival of Leaders." *British Journal of Political Science* 32(4):559–590.

Bueno de Mesquita, Bruce, Alastair Smith, Randolph M. Siverson, and James D. Morrow. 2003. *The Logic of Political Survival*. Cambridge, MA: MIT Press.

Bueno de Mesquita, Ethan. 2007. "Politics and the Suboptimal Provision of Counterterror." *International Organization* 61(1):9–36.

Bueno de Mesquita, Ethan. 2010. "Regime Change and Revolutionary Entrepreneurs." *American Political Science Review* 104(3):446–466.

Bunce, Valerie. 2003. "Rethinking Recent Democratization: Lessons from the Postcommunist Experience." *World Politics* 55(2):167–192.

Bunce, Valerie J. and Sharon L. Wolchik. 2011. *Defeating Authoritarian Leaders in Postcommunist Countries*. New York: Cambridge University Press.

Burkhart, Ross E. and Michael S. Lewis-Beck. 1994. "Comparative Democracy: The Economic Development Thesis." *American Political Science Review* 88(4):903–910.

Busch, Marc L. 2000. "Democracy, Consultation, and the Paneling of Disputes Under GATT." *Journal of Conflict Resolution* 44(4):425–446.

Bush, Sarah Sunn. 2015. *The Taming of Democracy Assistance: Why Democracy Promotion Does Not Confront Dictators*. New York: Cambridge University Press.

Büthe, Tim and Helen V. Milner. 2008. "The Politics of Foreign Direct Investment into Developing Countries: Increasing FDI through International Trade Agreements?" *American Journal of Political Science* 52(4):741–762.

Campello, Daniela and Cesar Zucco Jr. 2016. "Presidential Success and the World Economy." *Journal of Politics* 78(2):589–602.

Canes-Wrone, Brandice and Jee-Kwang Park. 2012. "Electoral Business Cycles in OECD Countries." *American Political Science Review* 106(1):103–122.

Carlsson, Hans and Eric van Damme. 1993. "Global Games and Equilibrium Selection." *Econometrica* 61(5):989–1018.

Carmines, Edward G. and Richard A. Zeller. 1979. *Reliability and Validity Assessment*. London: SAGE.

Carnes, Matthew E. 2014. *Continuity Despite Change: The Politics of Labor Regulation in Latin America*. Palo Alto, CA: Stanford University Press.

Casar, M. Amparo. 2002. "Executive-Legislative Relations: The Case of Mexico (1946–1997)." In *Legislative Politics in Latin America*, ed. Scott Morgenstern and Benito Nacif. New York: Cambridge University Press, pp. 114–144.

Casper, Brett Allen and Scott A. Tyson. 2014. "Popular Protest and Elite Coordination in a Coup d'état." *Journal of Politics* 76(2):548–564.

Cavaillé, Charlotte and Jeremy Ferwerda. 2017. "How Distributional Conflict over Public Spending Drives Support for Anti-immigrant Parties." CAGE Online Working Paper Series.

Chandra, Kanchan. 2004. *Why Ethnic Parties Succeed*. New York: Cambridge University Press.

Chandra, Kanchan. 2005. "Ethnic Parties and Democratic Stability." *Perspectives on Politics* 3(2):235–252.

Chandra, Kanchan. 2006. "What is Ethnic Identity and Does It Matter?" *Annual Review of Political Science* 9:397–424.

Chapman, Terrence L. 2011. *Securing Approval: Domestic Politics and Multilateral Authorization for War*. Chicago: University of Chicago Press.

Cheibub, José Antonio. 2007. *Presidentialism, Parliamentarism, and Democracy*. New York: Cambridge University Press.

Cheibub, José Antonio and James Raymond Vreeland. 2011. "Economic Development and Democratization." In *The Dynamics of Democratization: Dictatorship, Development, and Diffusion*, ed. Nathan Brown. Baltimore, MD: Johns Hopkins University Press, pp. 145–182.

Cheibub, José Antonio and James Raymond Vreeland. 2016. "Modernization Theory: Does Economic Development Cause Democratization?" In *The Oxford Handbook of Politics of Development*, ed. Carol Lancaster and Nicolas van de Walle. New York: Oxford University Press. doi: 10.1093/oxfordhb/9780199845156.013.26.

Cheibub, José Antonio, Zachary Elkins, and Tom Ginsburg. 2011. "Latin American Presidentialism in Comparative and Historical Perspective." University of Chicago Public Law and Legal Theory Working Paper, No. 361.

Cheibub, José Antonio, Jennifer Gandhi, and James Raymond Vreeland. 2010. "Democracy and Dictatorship Revisited." *Public Choice* 143(1–2):67–101.

Chen, Jidong and Yiqing Xu. 2015. "Information Manipulation and Reforms in Authoritarianism." Presented at the 2015 MPSA Conference.

Cho, In-Koo and David M. Kreps. 1987. "Signaling Games and Stable Equilibria." *Quarterly Journal of Economics* 102(2):179–222.

Choi, Seung-Whan. 2009. "The Effect of Outliers on Regression Analysis: Regime Type and Foreign Direct Investment." *Quarterly Journal of Political Science* 4(2):153–165.

Chomiak, Laryssa. 2016. "The Revolution in Tunisia Continues." Technical report Middle East Institute. www.mei.edu/content/map/revolution-in-tunisia-continues, accessed February 23, 2018.

Chortareas, Georgios, David Stasavage, and Gabriel Sterne. 2002. "Does it Pay to Be Transparent? International Evidence from Central Bank Forecasts." *The Federal Reserve Bank of St. Louis Review* 84(4):99–118.

Chwe, Michael Suk-Young. 2013. *Rational Ritual: Culture, Coordination, and Common Knowledge*. Princeton, NJ: Princeton University Press.

Chwieroth, Jeffrey. 2007. "Neoliberal Economists and Capital Account Liberalization in Emerging Markets." *International Organization* 61(2):443–463.

Clark, William R. Roberts and Mark Hallerberg. 2000. "Mobile Capital, Domestic Institutions, and Electorally-Induced Monetary and Fiscal Policy." *American Political Science Review* 94(2):323–346.

Clark, William Roberts, Matt Golder, and Sona N. Golder. 2017. "The British Academy Brian Barry Prize Essay: An Exit, Voice and Loyalty Model of Politics." *British Journal of Political Science* 47(4):719–748. doi: 10.1017/S0007123416000442.

Clinton, Joshua and David E. Lewis. 2008. "Expert Opinion, Agency Characteristics, and Agency Preferences." *Political Analysis* 16(1):3–20.

Clinton, Joshua, Simon Jackman, and Douglas Rivers. 2004. "The Statistical Analysis of Roll Call Data." *The American Political Science Review* 98(2):355–370.

Clore, Mathison and Michael McGrath. 2015. "The Domestic Benefits of Economic Transparency." International Political Economy Research Lab, School of Foreign Service, Georgetown University.

Cogley, Nathaniel Terence. 2013. "The Logic of Political Cessation: Social Esteem and Executive Tenure in Africa." PhD thesis, Yale University.

Colgan, Jeff D. and Jessica L. P. Weeks. 2015. "Revolution, Personalist Dictatorships, and International Conflict." *International Organization* 69(1):163–194.

Conrad, Courtenay R. and Emily Hencken Ritter. 2013. "Treaties, Tenure, and Torture: The Conflicting Domestic Effects of International Law." *Journal of Politics* 75(2):397–409.

Conrad, Courtenay, R. Daniel W. Hill, and Will H. Moore. 2014. "Political Institutions, Plausible Deniability, and the Decision to Hide Torture." SSRN. http://ssrn.com/abstract=2481762, accessed February 23, 2018.

Constable, Pamela and Arturo Valenzuela. 1991. *A Nation of Enemies: Chile Under Pinochet*. New York: W. W. Norton.

Cooray, Arusha and Krishna Chaitanya Vadlamannati. 2015. "Do Transparency Initiatives Work? Assessing the Impact of the Special Data Dissemination Standard (SDDS) on Data Transparency." CAMA Working Paper 24/2015.

Copelovitch, Mark, Christopher Gandrud, and Mark Hallerberg. 2018. "Financial Data Transparency, International Institutions, and Sovereign Borrowing Costs." *International Studies Quarterly* 62(1): 23–41.

Coremberg, Ariel. 2004. "Measuring Argentina's GDP Growth." *World Economics* 1 (1):1–32.

Cox, Robert and Harold Jacobson. 1973. *The Anatomy of Influence: Decision-Making in International Organization.* New Haven, CT: Yale University Press.

Crawford, Vincent P. and Joel Sobel. 1982. "Strategic Information Transmission." *Econometrica* 50(6):1431–1451.

Cull, Robert and Lixin Colin Xu. 2003. "Who Gets Credit? The Behavior of Bureaucrats and State Banks in Allocating Credit to Chinese State-owned Enterprises." *Journal of Development Economics* 71(2):533–559.

Culpepper, Pepper D. 2010. *Quiet Politics and Business Power: Corporate Control in Europe and Japan.* New York: Cambridge University Press.

Dahl, Robert A. 1971. *Polyarchy: Participation and Opposition.* New Haven, CT: Yale University Press.

Dallin, Alexander. 1992. "Causes of the Collapse of the Soviet Union." *Post-Soviet Affairs* 8(4):279–302.

Daoudy, Marwa. 2016. "Syrian Lives Matter." openDemocracy, March 24. www.opendemocracy.net/north-africa-west-asia/marwa-daoudy/syrian-lives-matter, accessed February 23, 2018.

Darden, Keith A. 2009. *Economic Liberalism and Its Rivals: The Formation of International Institutions among the Post-Soviet States.* New York: Cambridge University Press.

Davenport, Christian. 2007. "State Repression and the Tyrannical Peace." *Journal of Peace Research* 44(4):285–504.

Diamond, Larry. 1994. "Toward Democratic Consolidation." *Journal of Democracy* 5(3):4–17.

Diamond, Larry. 1999. *Developing Democracy: Toward Consolidation.* Baltimore, MD: Johns Hopkins University Press.

Di Lonardo, Livio and Scott A. Tyson. 2016. "Deterrence and Counterdeterrence in the Fight Against Global Terror." SSRN. https://www.princeton.edu/rppe/speaker-series/TysonDET.pdf, accessed March 19, 2018.

Diskin, Abraham, Hanna Diskin, and Reuven Y. Hazan. 2005. "Why Democracies Collapse: The Reasons for Democratic Failure and Success." *International Political Science Review* 26(3):291–309.

Di Tella, Rafael and Ernesto Schargrodsky. 2003. "The Role of Wages and Auditing During a Crackdown on Corruption in the City of Buenos Aires." *Journal of Law, Economics & Organization* 46(1):269–292.

Djankov, Simeon, Edward Glaeser, Rafael La Porta, Florencio Lopez de Silanes, and Andrei Shleifer. 2003. "The New Comparative Economics." *Journal of Comparative Economics* 31:595–619.

Doom, Ruddy and Koen Vlassenroot. 1999. "Kony's Message: A New Koine? The Lord's Resistance Army in Northern Uganda." *African Affairs* 98(390):5–36.

Downs, Anthony. 1957. *An Economic Theory of Democracy.* New York: Harper & Row.

Doyle, Michael W. 1986. "Liberalism and World Politics." *American Political Science Review* 80(4):1151–1169.

Dragu, Tiberiu and Mattias Polborn. 2013. "The Administrative Foundation of the Rule of Law." *Journal of Politics* 75(4):1038–1050.

Dreher, Axel. 2006. "Does Globalization Affect Growth? Evidence from a New Index of Globalization." *Applied Economics* 38(10):1091–1110.

Dreher, Axel, Stephan Klasen, James Raymond Vreeland, and Eric Werker. 2013. "The Costs of Favoritism: Is Politically Driven Aid Less Effective?" *Economic Development and Cultural Change* 62(1):157–191.

Dreher, Axel, Jan-Egbert Sturm, and Jakob de Haan. 2010. "When Is a Central Bank Governor Replaced? Evidence Based on a New Data Set." *Journal of Macroeconomics* 32(3):766–781.

Drezner, Daniel W. 2008. *All Politics is Global: Explaining International Regulatory Regimes.* Princeton, NJ: Princeton University Press.

Dube, Oeindrila and Juan Vargas. 2013. "Commodity Price Shocks and Civil Conflict: Evidence from Colombia." *Review of Economic Studies* 80(4):1384–1421.

Duch, Raymond M. and Randolph T. Stevenson. 2008. *The Economic Vote: How Political and Economic Institutions Condition Election Results.* New York: Cambridge University Press.

Ear, Sophal. 2007. "The Political Economy of Aid and Governance in Cambodia." *Asian Journal of Political Science* 15(1):68–96.

Easterly, William and Mirvat Sewadeh. 2001. "Global Development Network Growth Database." World Bank Economic and Development Research Group, Washington, DC.

Economist, The. 2007. "The Coup that Dare Not Speak Its Name: The Army, Not the Politicians, Now Runs Bangladesh," January 18. www.economist.com/node/8560006, accessed February 11, 2016.

Economist, The. 2011. "Responsibility to Protect: The Lessons of Libya." May 19. https://www.economist.com/node/18709571, accessed May 25, 2016.

Edmond, Chris. 2013. "Information Manipulation, Coordination, and Regime Change." *Review of Economic Studies* 80(4):1422–1458.

Edwards, Martin, Kelsey Coolidge, and Daria Preston. 2012. "Who Reveals? Transparency and the IMF's Article IV Consultations." Presented at the Annual Meetings of the Political Economy of International Organizations, January 26–28, Villanova University.

Egorov, Georgy and Konstantin Sonin. 2012. "Incumbency Advantages in Non-Democracies." Paper Presented at the 2011 MPSA Annual Meeting.

Egorov, Georgy, Sergei Guriev, and Konstantin Sonin. 2009. "Why Resource-poor Dictators Allow Freer Media: A Theory and Evidence from Panel Data." *American Political Science Review* 103(4):645–668.

Epstein, David L., Robert Bates, Jack Goldstone, Ida Kristensen, and Sharyn O'Halloran. 2006. "Democratic Transitions." *American Journal of Political Science* 50(3):551–569.

Fairfield, Tasha. 2010. "Business Power and Tax Reform: Taxing Income and Profits in Chile and Argentina." *Latin American Politics and Society* 52(2):37–71.

Fearon, James D. 1995. "Rationalist Explanations for War." *International Organization* 49(3):379–414.

Fearon, James D. 1999. "Electoral Accountability and the Control of Politicians: Selecting Good Types versus Sanctioning Poor Performance." In *Democracy, Accountability, and Representation,* ed. Adam Przeworski, Susan C. Stokes, and Bernard Manin. New York: Cambridge University Press, pp. 55–97.

Fearon, James D. 2011. "Self-Enforcing Democracy." *Quarterly Journal of Economics* 126(4):1661–1708.

Fearon, James D. and David Laitin. 2003. "Ethnicity, Insurgency, and Civil War?" *American Political Science Review* 97(1):75–90.

Ferejohn, John. 1986. "Incumbent Performance and Electoral Control." *Public Choice* 50(1):5–25.

Ferejohn, John. 1999. "Accountability and Authority: Toward a Theory of Political Accountability." In *Democracy, Accountability and Representation*, ed. Adam Przeworski, Susan C. Stokes, and Bernard Manin. New York: Cambridge University Press, pp. 131–153.

Fernandez, Raquel and Dani Rodrik. 1991. "Resistance to Reform: Status Quo Bias in the Presence of Individual-Specific Uncertainty." *American Economic Review* 81(5):1146–1155.

Fernández-Vásquez, Pablo, Pablo Barberá, and Gonzalo Rivero. 2016. "Rooting Out Corruption or Rooting for Corruption? The Heterogenous Electoral Consequences of Scandals." *Political Science Research and Methods* 4(2):379–397.

Ferraz, Claudio and Frederico Finan. 2008. "Exposing Corrupt Politicians: The Effects of Brazil's Publically Released Audits on Electoral Outcomes." *Quarterly Journal of Economics* 123(2):703–745.

Ferraz, Claudio and Frederico Finan. 2011. "Electoral Accountability and Corruption: Evidence from the Audits of Local Governments." *American Economic Review* 101(4):1274–1311.

Ferreira, Patrícia M. 2004a. "Guinea-Bissau: Between Conflict and Democracy." *African Security Review* 13(4):45–56.

Ferreira, Patrícia M. 2004b. "Guinea-Bissau: Perspectives on the Up-coming Elections." Institute for Security Studies: Situation Report.

Fewsmith, Joseph. 2001. *China since Tiananmen: The Politics of Transition*. New York: Cambridge University Press.

Fforde, Adam and Stefan de Vylder. 1996. *From Plan to Market: The Economic Transition in Vietnam*. Boulder, CO: Westview Press.

Fiorina, Morris P. 1981. *Retrospective Voting in American National Elections*. New Haven, CT: Yale University Press.

Flores, Thomas Edward and Irfan Nooruddin. 2016. *Elections in Hard Times: Building Stronger Democracies in the 21st Century*. New York: Cambridge University Press.

Foweraker, Joe and Todd Landman. 2002. "Constitutional Design and Democratic Performance." *Democratization* 9(2):43–66.

Francois, Patrick, Ilia Rainer, and Francesco Trebbi. 2014. "The Dictator's Inner Circle." NBER Working Paper.

Frank, Richard W and Ferran Martínez i Coma. 2017. "How Election Dynamics Shape Perceptions of Electoral Integrity." *Electoral Studies* 48:153–165.

Fravel, M. Taylor. Forthcoming. *Active Defense: China's Military Strategy Since 1949*. Princeton, NJ: Princeton University Press.

Freeman, John R. and Dennis P. Quinn. 2012. "The Economic Origins of Democracy Reconsidered." *American Political Science Review* 106(1):58–80.

Frieden, Jeffry A. 1991. "Invested Interests: The Politics of National Economic Policies in a World of Global Finance." *International Organization* 45(4):425–451.

Fudenberg, Drew and Jean Tirole. 1991. *Game Theory*. Cambridge, MA: MIT Press.

Gandhi, Jennifer. 2008. *Political Institutions under Dictatorship*. New York: Cambridge University Press.

Gandhi, Jennifer and Ellen Lust-Okar. 2009. "Elections Under Authoritarianism." *Annual Review of Political Science* 12:403–422.

Gandhi, Jennifer and Adam Przeworski. 2006. "Cooperation, Cooptation, and Rebellion Under Dictatorships." *Economics and Politics* 18(1):1–26.

Gandhi, Jennifer and Adam Przeworski. 2007. "Authoritarian Institutions and the Survival of Autocrats." *Comparative Political Studies* 40(11):1279–1301.

Ganguly, Sumit and Brian Shoup. 2005. "Nepal: Between Dictatorship and Anarchy." *Journal of Democracy* 16(4):129–143.

Gassebner, Martin, Michael J. Lamla, and James Raymond Vreeland. 2013. "Extreme Bounds of Democracy." *Journal of Conflict Resolution* 57(2):171–197.

Geddes, Barbara. 1999. "What Do We Know about Democratization after Twenty Years?" *Annual Review of Political Science* 2:115–144.

Geddes, Barbara, Joseph Wright, and Erica Frantz. 2012. "Authoritarian Regimes: A New Data Set." Unpublished data set in progress.

Gehlbach, Scott and Philip Keefer. 2011. "Investment without Democracy: Ruling-party Institutionalization and Credible Commitment in Autocracies." *Journal of Comparative Economics* 39(2):123–139.

Gehlbach, Scott and Philip Keefer. 2012. "Private Investment and the Institutionalization of Collective Action in Autocracies: Ruling Parties and Legislatures." *Journal of Politics* 74(2):621–635.

Gehlbach, Scott and Edmund Malesky. 2010. "The Contribution of Veto Players to Economic Reform." *Journal of Politics* 72(4):957–975.

Gehlbach, Scott and Konstantin Sonin. 2014. "Government Control of the Media." *Journal of Public Economics* 118:163–171.

Gelman, Andrew and Jennifer Hill. 2006. *Data Analysis Using Regression and Multilevel/Hierarchical Models*. New York: Cambridge University Press.

Gelman, Andrew, Yuri Goegebeur, Francis Tuerlinckx, and Iven van Mechelen. 2000. "Diagnostic Checks for Discrete Data Regression Models Using Posterior Predictive Simulations." *Journal of the Royal Statistical Society: Series C (Applied Statistics)* 49(2):247–268.

Gilardi, Fabrizio. 2002. "Policy Credibility and Delegation to Independent Regulatory Agencies: A Comparative Empirical Analysis." *Journal of European Public Policy* 9(6):873–893.

Gilens, Martin and Benjamin I. Page. 2014. "Testing Theories of American Politics: Elites, Interest Groups, and Average Citizens." *Perspectives on Politics* 12(3):564–581.

Gilligan, Michael J. 1997. *Empowering Exporters: Reciprocity, Delegation, and Collective Action in American Trade Policy*. Ann Arbor: University of Michigan Press.

Gilligan, Thomas W. and Keith Krehbiel. 1987. "Collective Decisionmaking and Standing Committees: An Informational Rationale for Restrictive Amendment Procedures." *Journal of Law, Economics, and Organization* 3(2):287–335.

Girod, Desha M., Megan A. Stewart, and Meir R. Walters. 2016. "Mass Protests and the Resource Curse: The Politics of Demobilization in Rentier Autocracies." *Conflict Management and Peace Science*. doi: 10.1177/0738894216651826.

Goemans, Hein. 2006. "Archigos: A Database on Political Leaders." Paper Presented at the Annual Meeting of the American Political Science Association.

Goemans, Hein E. 2008. "Which Way Out? The Manner and Consequences of Losing Office." *Journal of Conflict Resolution* 52(6):771–794.

Goemans, Hein E., Kristian Skrede Gleditsch, and Giacomo Chiozza. 2009. "ARCHIGOS: A Data Set on Leaders 1875–2004, Version 2.9." Rochester University.

Göktepe, Gökçe and Shanker Satyanath. 2013. "The Economic Value of Military Connections in Turkey." *Public Choice* 155(3–4):531–552.

Gordon, Sanford C. 2002. "Stochastic Dependence in Competing Risks." *American Journal of Political Science* 46(1):200–217.

Gourevitch, Peter. 1978. "The Second Image Reversed: The International Sources of Domestic Politics." *International Organization* 32(4):881–912.

Gray, Julia. 2009. "International Organization as a Seal of Approval: The European Union Accession and Investor Risk." *American Journal of Political Science* 53(4):931–949.

Greene, William. 2010. "Testing Hypothesis about Interaction Terms in Nonlinear Models." *Economic Letters* 107(2):291–296.

Grief, Avner. 2006. *Institutions and the Path to the Modern Economy: Lessons from Medieval Trade*. New York: Cambridge University Press.

Grossman, Gene M. and Elhanan Helpman. 1994. "Protection for Sale." *American Economic Review* 84(4):833–850.

Grossman, Gene M. and Elhanan Helpman. 2001. *Innovation and Growth in the Global Economy*. Cambridge, MA: MIT Press.

Gruber, Lloyd. 2000. *Ruling the World: Power Politics and the Rise of Supranational Institutions*. Princeton, NJ: Princeton University Press.

Guardado, Jenny. 2017. "Corruption and the Returns to Public Office: Evidence from the Spanish Empire." Manuscript, Georgetown University.

Guriev, Sergei and Daniel Treisman. 2015. "How Modern Dictators Survive: An Informational Theory of the New Authoritarianism." NBER Working Paper.

Gurr, Ted R. 1970. *Why Men Rebel*. Princeton, NJ: Princeton University Press.

Haas, Peter M. 1992. "Introduction: Epistemic Communities and International Policy Coordination." *International Organization* 46(1):1–35.

Haber, Stephen, Herbert S. Klein, Noel Maurer, and Kevin J. Middlebrook. 2008. *Mexico Since 1980 (The World Since 1980)*. New York: Cambridge University Press.

Habyarimana, James, Macartan Humphreys, Daniel N. Posner, and Jeremy M. Weinstein. 2009. *Coethnicity: Diversity and the Dilemmas of Collective Action*. New York: Russell Sage Foundation.

Haddad, Bassam and Jillian Schwedler. 2013. "Editors' Introduction to Teaching about the Middle East since the Arab Uprisings." *PS: Political Science & Politics* 46(2):211–216.

Hadenius, Axel and Jan Teorell. 2007. "Pathways from Authoritarianism." *Journal of Democracy* 18(1):143–156.

Hafner-Burton, Emilie M. 2012. "International Regimes for Human Rights." *Annual Review of Political Science* 15:265–286.

Hafner-Burton, Emilie M., Zachary C. Steinert-Threlkeld, and David G. Victor. 2016. "Predictability Versus Flexibility: Secrecy in International Investment Arbitration." *World Politics* 68(3):413–453.

Haggard, Stephan and Robert R. Kaufman. 1995. *The Political Economy of Democratic Transitions*. Princeton, NJ: Princeton University Press.

Hardin, Russell. 1999. *Liberalism, Constitutionalism, and Democracy*. New York: Oxford University Press.

Harding, Robin and David Stasavage. 2014. "What Democracy Does (and Doesn't Do) for Basic Services: School Fees, School Inputs, and African Elections." *Journal of Politics* 76(1):229–245.

Hathaway, Oona. 2007. "Why Do Countries Commit to Human Rights Treaties?" *Journal of Conflict Resolution* 51(4):588–621.

He, Baogang and Mark E. Warren. 2011. "Authoritarian Deliberation: The Deliberative Turn in Chinese Political Development." *Perspectives on Politics* 9(2):269–289.

Heckman, James J. 1979. "Sample Selection Bias as a Specification Error." *Econometrica* 47(1):153–161.

Heder, Steve. 2005. "Hun Sen's Consolidation: Death or Beginning of Reform?" *Southeast Asian Affairs* 2005(1):111–130.

Hehir, Aidan. 2013. "The Permanence of Inconsistency: Libya, the Security Council, and the Responsibility to Protect." *International Security* 38(1):137–159.

Heitzman, James. 1989. "Government and Politics." In *Bangladesh: A Country Study*, ed. James Heitzman and Robert L. Worden. Washington, DC: Library of Congress, pp. 149–200.

Hellwig, Christian, Arijit Mukherji, and Aleh Tsyvinski. 2006. "Self-fulfilling Currency Crises: The Role of Interest Rates." *American Economic Review* 96(5): 1769–1787.

Helpman, Elhanan. 1984. "A Simple Theory of International Trade with Multinational Corporations." *Journal of Political Economy* 92(3):451–471.

Herron, Michael C. 1999. "Postestimation Uncertainty in Limited Dependent Variable Models." *Political Analysis* 8(1):83–98.

Heston, Alan, Robert Summers, and Bettina Aten. 2009. "Penn World Table Version 6.3." Center for International Comparisons of Production, Income and Prices at the University of Pennsylvania.

Heston, Alan, Robert Summers, and Bettina Aten. 2012. "Penn World Table Version 7.1." Center for International Comparisons of Production, Income and Prices at the University of Pennsylvania.

Hibbs, Douglas A., Jr. 1982. "President Reagan's Mandate from the 1980 Elections: A Shift to the Right?" *American Politics Research* 10(4):387–420.

Hibbs, Douglas A., Jr. 2000. "Bread and Peace Voting in U.S. Presidential Elections." *Public Choice* 104(1):149–180.

Hoffman, Barak D. 2011. "The Politics of Transparency in Kenya and Tanzania." Manuscript, Georgetown University.

Hoftun, Martin, William Raeper, and John Whelpton. 1999. *People, Politics and Ideology: Democracy and Social Change in Nepal*. Kathmandu, Nepal: Mandala Book Point.

Hollyer, James R. 2010. "Conditionality, Compliance and Domestic Interests: State Capture and EU Accession Policy." *Review of International Organizations* 5(4):387–431.

Hollyer, James R. forthcoming. "Measuring Governance: Objective and Perceptions-based Governance Indicators." In *The Governance Report 2017*, ed. Helmut Anheier, Matthias Haber, and Mark Kayser. New York: Oxford University Press.

Hollyer, James R. and B. Peter Rosendorff. 2011. "Why Do Authoritarian Regimes Sign the Convention Against Torture? Signaling, Domestic Politics, and Non-Compliance." *Quarterly Journal of Political Science* 6(3–4):275–327.

Hollyer, James R. and B. Peter Rosendorff. 2012. "Leadership Survival, Regime Type, Policy Uncertainty and PTA Accession." *International Studies Quarterly* 56(4):748–764.

Hollyer, James R., B. Peter Rosendorff, and James Raymond Vreeland. 2011. "Democracy and Transparency." *Journal of Politics* 73(4):1–15.

Hollyer, James R., B. Peter Rosendorff, and James Raymond Vreeland. 2014. "Measuring Transparency." *Political Analysis* 22(4):413–434.

Hollyer, James R., B. Peter Rosendorff, and James Raymond Vreeland. 2015. "Transparency, Protest and Autocratic Instability." *American Political Science Review* 109(4):764–784.

Hollyer, James R., B. Peter Rosendorff, and James Raymond Vreeland. 2016. "What makes governments resistant to coups? Transparency with voters." *Washington Post*, August 5.

Hollyer, James R., B. Peter Rosendorff, and James Raymond Vreeland. 2018. "Transparency, Protest and Democratic Stability." *British Journal of Political Science.* doi: 10.1017/S0007123417000308.

Hollyer, James R., B. Peter Rosendorff, and James Raymond Vreeland. Forthcoming. "Why Do Autocrats Disclose? Economic Transparency and Inter-elite Politics in the Shadow of Mass Unrest." *Journal of Conflict Resolution.*

Holman, Michael. 2005. "Powerful Personality Who as PM Twice Failed Uganda." *Financial Times*, October 12.

Horst, René Harder. 2003. "Consciousness and Contradiction: Indigenous Peoples and Paraguay's Transition to Democracy." In *Contemporary Indigenous Movements in Latin America*, ed. Erick D. Langer and Elena Munoz. Wilmington, DE: Scholarly Resources, pp. 103–134.

Howard, Lise Morjé. 2015. "US Foreign Policy Habits in Ethnic Conflict." *International Studies Quarterly* 59(4):721–734.

Howard, Marc Morjé. 2002. "The Weakness of Postcommunist Civil Society." *Journal of Democracy* 13(1):157–169.

Huber, Evelyne, Dietrich Rueschemeyer, and John D. Stephens. 1993. "The Impact of Economic Development on Democracy." *Journal of Economic Perspectives* 7(3):71–86.

Huber, John D. and Nolan McCarty. 2004. "Bureaucratic Capacity, Delegation and Political Reform." *American Political Science Review* 98(3):481–494.

Huntington, Samuel P. 1968. *Political Order in Changing Societies.* New Haven, CT: Yale University Press.

Huntington, Samuel P. 1991. *The Third Wave: Democratization in the Late Twentieth Century.* Norman, OK: University of Oklahoma Press.

Hutchcroft, Paul D. and Joel Rocamora. 2003. "Strong Demands and Weak Institutions: The Origins and Evolution of the Democratic Deficit in the Philippines." *Journal of East Asian Studies* 3(2):259–292.

Hyde, Susan and Nikolay Marinov. 2014. "Information and Self-Enforcing Democracy: The Role of International Election Observers." *International Organization* 68(2):329–359.

Im, Hyug-Baeg. 1995. "Politics of Democratic Transition from Authoritarian Rule in South Korea." *Korean Social Science Journal* 21(1):134–151.

International Crisis Group. 2017. "La transition bloquée: corruption et régionalisme en Tunisie." Technical report, Rapport Moyen-Orient et Afrique du Nord No. 177, May 10.

IRIN. 2003. "Army ousts president who kept delaying elections," September 14. www.irinnews.org/report/46145/guinea-bissau-army-ousts-president-who-kept-delaying-elections, accessed February 24, 2016.

Irwin, Timothy. 2012. "Accounting Devices and Fiscal Illusions." IMF Staff Discussion Note.

Islam, MD. Shamsul. 2009. "Political Violence in Bangladesh." In *Political Islam and Governance in Bangladesh*, ed. Ali Riaz and C. Christine Fair. New York: Routledge, pp. 27–45.

Islam, Roumeen. 2006. "Does More Transparency Go Along with Better Governance?" *Economics & Politics* 18(2):121–167.

Jackman, Simon. 2009. *Bayesian Analysis for the Social Sciences*. Chichester, UK: Wiley.

Jacobs, Lawrence R. and Desmond King. 2016. *Fed Power: How Finance Wins*. New York: Oxford University Press.

Jamal, Amaney A. 2009. *Barriers to Democracy: The Other Side of Social Capital in Palestine and the Arab World*. Princeton, NJ: Princeton University Press.

Jensen, Nathan M. 2003. "Democratic Governance and Multinational Corporations: Political Regimes and Inflows of Foreign Direct Investment." *International Organization* 57(3):587–616.

Jensen, Nathan M. 2006. *Nation States and the Multinational Corporation: A Political Economy of Foreign Direct Investment*. Princeton, NJ: Princeton University Press.

Jensen, Nathan M. 2007. "Firm-Level Responses to Politics: Political Institutions and the Operations of U.S. Multinationals." 2007 Conference on the Political Economy of International Finance, Atlanta, GA.

Jensen, Nathan and Leonard Wantchekon. 2004. "Resource Wealth and Political Regimes in Africa." *Comparative Political Studies* 37(7):816–841.

Jensen, Nathan M., Edmund Malesky, and Stephen Weymouth. 2014. "Unbundling the Relationship Between Authoritarian Legislatures and Political Risk." *British Journal of Political Science* 44(3):655–684.

Jerven, Morten. 2013. *Poor Numbers: How We Are Misled by African Development Statistics and What to Do about It*. Ithaca, NY: Cornell University Press.

Jinnah, Sikina. 2014. *Post-Treaty Politics: Secretariat Influence in Global Environmental Governance*. Cambridge, MA: MIT Press.

Johns, Leslie. 2007. "A Servant of Two Masters: Communication and the Selection of International Bureaucrats." *International Organization* 61(2):245–275.

Johnson, Juliet. 2016. *Priests of Prosperity: How Central Bankers Transformed the Post-communist World*. Ithaca, NY: Cornell University Press.

Johnson, Tana. 2011. "Guilt by Association: The Link between States? Influence and the Legitimacy of Intergovernmental Organizations." *Review of International Organizations* 6(1):57–84.

Johnson, Tana. 2014. *Organizational Progeny: Why Governments are Losing Control over the Proliferating Structures of Global Governance*. New York: Oxford University Press.

Johnson, Tana and Johannes Urpelainen. 2014. "International Bureaucrats and the Formation of Intergovernmental Organizations: Institutional Design Discretion Sweetens the Pot." *International Organization* 68(1):175–208.

Johnston, Alastair Iain. 2001. "Treating International Institutions as Social Environments." *International Studies Quarterly* 45(4):487–515.

Jones, Toby Craig. 2011. "Saudi Arabia Versus the Arab Spring." *Raritan: A Quarterly Review* 31(2):43–59.

Jusko, Karen Long and W. Phillips Shively. 2005. "Applying a Two-Step Strategy to the Analysis of Cross-National Public Opinion Data." *Political Analysis* 13(4): 327–344.

Kalck, Pierre. 2004. *Historical Dictionary of the Central African Republic*, 3rd edn. Lanham, MD: Scarecrow Press.

Kalyanpur, Nikhil and Abraham Newman. 2017. "Form over Function in Finance: International Institutional Design by Bricolage." *Review of International Political Economy* 24(3):363–392.

Karl, Terry Lynn. 1990. "Dilemmas of Democratization in Latin America." *Comparative Politics* 23(1):1–21.

Karlekar, Karin Deutsch and Jennifer Dunham. 2014. *Press Freedom in 2013: Media Freedom Hits Decade Low*. Washington, DC: Freedom House.

Karns, Margaret and Karen Mingst. 1990. *International Organizations: The Politics and Processes of Global Governance*. Boulder, CO: Lynne Reiner Publishers.

Kasfir, Nelson. 2006. "'No-party Democracy' in Uganda." *Journal of Democracy* 9(2):49–63.

Katsiaficas, George. 2012. *Asia's Unknown Uprisings Volume 1: South Korean Social Movements in the 20th Century*. Oakland, CA: PM Press.

Kaufmann, Daniel and Ana Bellver. 2005. "Transparenting Transparency: Initial Empirics and Policy Applications." SSRN paper. https://ssrn.com/abstract=808664, accessed March 18, 2018.

Kayser, Mark Andreas and Michael Peress. 2012. "Benchmarking Across Borders: Electoral Accountability and the Necessity of Comparison." *American Political Science Review* 106(3):661–684.

Keefer, Philip and David Stasavage. 2003. "The Limits of Delegation: Veto Players, Central Bank Independence, and the Credibility of Monetary Policy." *American Political Science Review* 97(3):407–423.

Keele, Luke. 2010. "Proportionally Difficult: Testing for Nonproportional Hazards in Cox Models." *Political Analysis* 18(2):189–205.

Kelley, Judith G. and Beth A. Simmons. 2015. "Politics by Number: Indicators as Social Pressure in International Relations." *American Journal of Political Science* 59(1):55–70.

Kelliher, Daniel. 1997. "The Chinese Debate over Village Self-Government." *The China Journal* 37:63–86.

Kerner, Andrew and Charles Crabtree. 2018. "The IMF and the Political Economy of GDP Data Production." SocArXiv, January 16. https://osf.io/preprints/socarxiv/qsxae/, accessed March 18, 2018.

Kerner, Andrew and Jane Lawrence. 2014. "What's the Risk? Bilateral Investment Treaties, Political Risk and Fixed Capital Accumulation." *British Journal of Political Science* 44(1):107–121.

Keynes, John Maynard. 2011. *The General Theory Of Employment, Interest, And Money*. Charleston, SC: CreateSpace Independent Publishing Platform. Originally published 1936.

Khemani, Stuti. 2007. Can Information Campaigns Overcome Political Obstacles to Serving the Poor? In *The Politics of Service Delivery in Democracies: Better Access for the Poor*, ed. Shantayanan Devarajan and Ingrid Widlund. Stockholm: Ministry for Foreign Affairs, pp. 56–69.

Kihl, Young Whan. 1985. "North Korea in 1984: 'The Hermit Kingdom?' Turns Outward!" *Asian Survey* 25(1):65–79.

Kim, Diana and Dan Slater. 2017. "War, Opium, and the Selective State: Legibility and Legitimacy in Asian Empires." Oxford University Workshop on Understanding Insurgencies.

King, Gary, James Honaker, Anne Joseph, and Kenneth Scheve. 2001. "Analyzing Incomplete Political Science Data: An Alternative Algorithm for Multiple Imputation." *American Political Science Review* 95(1):49–69.

King, Gary, Jennifer Pan, and Margaret E. Roberts. 2013. "How Censorship in China Allows Government Criticism but Silences Collective Expression." *American Political Science Review* 107(2):326–343.

King, Gary, Jennifer Pan, and Margaret E. Roberts. 2014. "Reverse-Engineering Censorship in China: Randomized Experimentation and Participant Observation." *Science* 345(6199):1–10.

King, Gary, Ori Rosen, Martin Tanner, and Alexander F. Wagner. 2008. "Ordinary Economic Voting Behavior in the Extraordinary Election of Adolf Hitler." *Journal of Economic History* 68(4):951–996.

King, Stephen J. 2003. *Liberalization against Democracy: The Local Politics of Economic Reform in Tunisia*. Bloomington: Indiana University Press.

Kiondo, Andrew. 1992. "The Nature of Economic Reforms in Tanzania." In *Tanzania and the IMF: The Dynamics of Liberalization*, ed. Horace Campbell and Howard Stein. Boulder, CO: Westview Press, pp. 21–42.

Klašnja, Marko. 2015. "Corruption and the Incumbency Disadvantage: Theory and Evidence." *Journal of Politics* 77(4):928–942.

Knight, Alan. 2007. Mexico's Three Fin de Siècle Crises. In *Cycles of Conflict, Centuries of Change: Crisis, Reform, and Revolution in Mexico*, ed. Elisa Servín, Leticia Reina, and John Tutino. Durham, NC: Duke University Press, pp. 153–183.

Knorr-Held, Leonhard. 1999. "Conditional Prior Proposals in Dynamic Models." *Scandinavian Journal of Statistics* 26(1):129–144.

Kono, Daniel Y. 2006. "Optimal Obfuscation: Democracy and Trade Policy Transparency." *American Political Science Review* 100(3):369–384.

Kono, Daniel Y. and Stephanie J. Rickard. 2014. "Buying National: Democracy and Public Procurement." *International Interactions* 40(5):657–682.

Korotayev, Andrey V., Leonid M. Issaev, Sergey Yu Malkov, and Alisa R. Shishkina. 2014. "The Arab Spring: A Quantitative Analysis." *Arab Studies Quarterly* 36(2):149–169.

Kosack, Stephen and Archon Fung. 2014. "Does Transparency Improve Governance?" *Annual Review of Political Science* 17:65–87.

Kotz, David M. and Fred Weir. 1997. *Revolution from Above: The Demise of the Soviet System*. New York: Routledge.

Kramer, Gerald H. 1983. "The Ecological Fallacy Revisited: Aggregate- versus Individual-level Findings on Economics and Elections, and Sociotropic Voting." *American Political Science Review* 77(1):92–111.

Kuperman, Alan J. 2015. "Obama's Libya Debacle: How a Well-Meaning Intervention Ended in Failure." *Foreign Affairs* 94(2):66–77.

Kuran, Timur. 1991. "Now Out of Never: The Element of Surprise in the East European Revolution of 1989." *World Politics* 44(1):7–48.

Lagon, Mark P. 2011. "Promoting Democracy: The Whys and Hows for the United States and the International Community." Council on Foreign Relations.

Lake, David A. 2009. "Open Economy Politics: A Critical Review." *Review of International Organizations* 4(3):219–244.

Lake, David A. and Matthew A. Baum. 2001. "The Invisible Hand of Democracy: Political Control and the Provision of Public Services." *Comparative Political Studies* 34(6):587–621.

Lall, Ranjit. 2016. "How Multiple Imputation Makes a Difference." *Political Analysis* 24(4):414–433.

Landry, Pierre. 2008. *Decentralized Authoritarianism in China: The Communist Party's Control of Local Elites in the Post-Mao Era*. New York: Cambridge University Press.

Leblang, David and Shanker Satyanath. 2006. "Institutions, Expectations, and Currency Crises." *International Organization* 60(1):245–262.

Lee, Melissa M. and Nan Zhang. 2017. "Legibility and the Informational Foundations of State Capacity." *Journal of Politics* 79(1):118–132.

Levitsky, Steven and Lucan A. Way. 2002. "The Rise of Competitive Authoritarianism." *Journal of Democracy* 13(2):51–65.

Levitz, Philip and Grigore Pop-Eleches. 2009. "Why no Backsliding? The European Union's Impact on Democracy and Governance Before and After Accession." *Comparative Political Studies* 20(10):1–29.

Lewis, Joanna I. 2007. "China's Strategic Priorities in International Climate Change Negotiations." *The Washington Quarterly* 31(1):155–174.

Lewis-Beck, Michael S. 1988. *Economics and Elections: The Major Western Democracies*. Ann Arbor: University of Michigan Press.

Lewis-Beck, Michael S. and Mary Stegmaier. 2009. "Competing for Transparency: Political Competition and Institutional Reform in Mexican States." *Electoral Studies* 28(4):625–631.

Li, Quan. 2009. "Outlier, Measurement, and the Democracy-FDI Controversy." *Quarterly Journal of Political Science* 4(2):167–181.

Li, Quan and Adam Resnick. 2003. "Reversal of Fortunes: Democratic Institutions and Foreign Direct Investment Inflows to Developing Countries." *International Organization* 57(1):175–211.

Lijphart, Arend, ed. 1992. *Parliamentary Versus Presidential Government*. New York: Oxford University Press.

Linsi, Lukas and Daniel K. Mügge. 2017. "Harmonized Inaccuracy: International Economic Statistics in the Age of Globalization." Manuscript, University of Amsterdam.

Linz, Juan J. 1978. "Crisis, Breakdown, and Reequilibration." In *The Breakdown of Democratic Regimes*, ed. Juan J. Linz and Alfred Stepan. Baltimore, MD: Johns Hopkins University Press, pp. 3–87.

Linz, Juan J. and Alfred Stepan. 1996. *Problems of Democratic Transition and Consolidation: Southern Europe, South America, and Post-Communist Europe*. Baltimore, MD: Johns Hopkins University Press.

Lipscy, Phillip Y. 2017. *Renegotiating the World Order: Institutional Change in International Relations*. New York: Cambridge University Press.

Lipset, Seymour Martin. 1959. "Some Social Requisites of Democracy: Economic Development and Political Legitimacy." *American Political Science Review* 53(1):69–105.

Little, Andrew T. 2012. "Elections, Fraud and Election Monitoring in the Shadow of Revolution." *Quarterly Journal of Political Science* 7(3):249–283.

Little, Andrew T. 2016. "Communication Technology and Protest." *Journal of Politics* 68(1):152–166.

Little, Andrew T. 2017. "Coordination, Learning and Coups." *Journal of Conflict Resolution* 61(1):204–234.

Little, Andrew T., Joshua A. Tucker, and Tom LaGatta. 2015. "Elections, Protest, and Alternation of Power." *Journal of Politics* 77:1142–1156.

Lizzeri, Alessandro and Nicola Persico. 2004. "Why Did the Elites Extend the Suffrage? Democracy and the Scope of Government, with an Application to Britain's 'Age of Reform.' " *Quarterly Journal of Economics* 119(2):707–764.

Llavador, Humberto and Robert J. Oxoby. 2005. "Partisan Competition, Growth, and the Franchise." *Quarterly Journal of Economics* 119(3):1155–1189.

Loggins, Kenny, Giorgio Moroder, and Tom Whitlock. 1986. "Danger Zone." *Top Gun* available: www.youtube.com/watch?v=siwpn14IE7E, accessed February 2, 2016.

Lohmann, Susanne. 1993. "A Signaling Model of Informative and Manipulative Political Action." *American Political Science Review* 87(2):319–333.

Lohmann, Susanne. 1994. "Dynamics of Informational Cascades: The Monday Demonstrations in Leipzig, East Germany, 1989–1991." *World Politics* 47(1):42–101.

Londregan, John B. and Keith T. Poole. 1996. "Does High Income Promote Democracy?" *World Politics* 49(1):1–30.

Looney, Kristen Elizabeth. 2012. "The Rural Developmental State: Modernization Campaigns and Peasant Politics in China, Taiwan and South Korea." PhD thesis, Harvard University.

Lorentzen, Peter. 2014. "China's Strategic Censorship." *American Journal of Political Science* 58(2):402–414.

Lorentzen, Peter, Pierre Landry, and John Yasuda. 2010. "Transparent Authoritarianism? An Analysis of Political and Economic Barriers to Greater Government Transparency in China." Presented at the 2010 Annual Meeting of the American Political Science Association, Washington, DC.

Luo, Zhaotian and Arturas Rozenas. 2018. "The Election Monitor's Curse." *American Journal of Political Science* 62(1):148–160.

Luo, Zhaotian and Arturas Rozenas. Forthcoming. "Strategies of Election Rigging: Trade-Offs, Determinants, and Consequences." *Quarterly Journal of Political Science*.

Lust-Okar, Ellen. 2006. "Elections Under Authoritarianism: Preliminary Lessons from Jordan." *Democratization* 13(3):456–471.

Lynch, Colum and William Branigin. 2011. "Ivory Coast Strongman Arrested after French Forces Intervene." *Washington Post*, April 11. www.washingtonpost.com/world/ivory-coast-strongman-arrested-after-french-forces-intervene/2011/04/11/AFOBaeKD_story.html?utm_term=.be1aa5efd197, accessed February 5, 2018.

Magaloni, Beatriz. 2006. *Voting for Autocracy: Hegemonic Survival and its Demise in Mexico.* New York: Cambridge University Press.

Mahdavi, Paasha. 2017. "Nationalization and Governance: The Politics of State Control over Natural Resources." Manuscript, Georgetown University.

Mainwaring, Scott and Matthew Soberg Shugart. 1997. *Presidentialism and Democracy in Latin America.* New York: Cambridge University Press.

Majone, Giandomenico. 1994. "The Rise of the Regulatory State in Europe." *West European Politics* 17(3):77–101.

Majone, Giandomenico. 1997. Independent Agencies and the Delegation Problem: Theoretical and Normative Dimensions. In *Political Institutions and Public Policy*, ed. Bernard Steunenberg and Frans van Vught. Dordrecht, Netherlands: Kluwer Academic Publishers, pp. 139–156.

Malesky, Edmund. 2008. "Straight Ahead on Red: How Foreign Direct Investment Empowers Subnational Leaders." *Journal of Politics* 70(1):97–119.

Malesky, Edmund. 2009. "Gerrymandering Vietnam Style: Escaping the Partial Reform Equilibrium in a Non-Democratic Regime." *Journal of Politics* 71(1):132–159.

Mani, Anandi and Sharun Mukand. 2007. "Democracy, Visibility and Public Good Provision." *Journal of Development Economics* 83(2):506–529.

Manin, Bernard. 1997. *The Principles of Representative Government.* New York: Cambridge University Press.

Mansfield, Edward D. and Eric Reinhardt. 2008. "International Institutions and the Volatility of International Trade." *International Organization* 62(4):621–652.

Mansfield, Edward D., Helen V. Milner, and B. Peter Rosendorff. 2000. "Free to Trade: Democracies, Autocracies and International Trade." *American Political Science Review* 94(2):305–322.

Mansfield, Edward D., Helen V. Milner, and B. Peter Rosendorff. 2002. "Why Democracies Cooperate More: Electoral Control and International Trade Agreements." *International Organization* 56(3):477–513.

Markus, Gregory B. 1988. "The Impact of Personal and National Conditions on the Presidential Vote: A Pooled Cross-Sectional Analysis." *American Journal of Political Science* 32(1):137–154.

Markusen, James R. 1984. "Multinationals, Multi-plant Economies, and the Gains from Trade." *Journal of International Economics* 16(3–4):205–226.

Marshall, Monty G. and Keith Jaggers. 2005. "POLITY IV Project: Dataset users' manual." George Mason University, Center for Global Policy, School of Public Policy.

Marshall, Monty G. and Keith Jaggers. 2013. "Polity IV Project: Political Regime Characteristics and Transitions, 1800–2009." Center for International Development and Conflict Management at the University of Maryland, College Park.

Martin, Andrew D. and Kevin M. Quinn. 2002. "Dynamic Ideal Point Estimation via Markov Chain Monte Carlo for the U.S. Supreme Court, 1953–1999." *Political Analysis* 10(10):134–153.

Martin, Lisa L. and Beth A. Simmons. 1998. "Theories and Empirical Studies of International Institutions." *International Organization* 52(4):729–757.

Marzouki, Nadia. 2015. "Tunisia's Rotten Compromise." Technical report Middle East Research and Information Project, available www.merip.org/mero/mero071015, accessed February 5, 2018.

Marzouki, Nadia and Hamza Meddeb. 2015. "Tunisia: Democratic Miracle or Mirage?" Technical report Jadaliyya, available www.jadaliyya.com/Details/32181/Tunisia-Democratic-Miracle-or-Mirage, accessed February 5, 2018.

Masoud, Tarek. 2011. "The Road to (and from) Liberation Square." *Journal of Democracy* 22(3):20–34.

Mastro, Oriana Skylar. 2016. "The Vulnerability of Rising Powers: The Logic Behind China's Low Military Transparency." *Asian Security* 12(2):63–81.

Mbadinga, Moussounga Itsouhou. 2001. "The Inter-African Mission to Monitor the Implementation of the Bangui Agreements (MISAB)." *International Peacekeeping* 8(4):21–37.

McCargo, Duncan. 2005. "Cambodia: Getting Away with Authoritarianism?" *Journal of Democracy* 16(4):98–112.

McCoy, Alfred W. 1999. *Closer Than Brothers: Manhood at the Philippine Military Academy.* New Haven, CT: Yale University Press.

McFaul, Michael. 2005. "Transitions from Postcommunism." *Journal of Democracy* 16(3):5–19.

McGillivray, Fiona. 1997. "Party Discipline as a Determinant of the Endogenous Formation of Tariffs." *American Journal of Political Science* 41(2):584–607.

McNamara, Kathleen R. 1998. *The Currency of Ideas*. Ithaca, NY: Cornell University Press.

Mearsheimer, John J. 1994. "The False Promise of International Institutions." *International Security* 19(3):5–49.

Meredith, Martin. 2007. *Mugabe: Power, Plunder, and the Struggle for Zimbabwe*. New York: Public Affairs.

Merton, Thomas, ed. 1965. *Gandhi on Non-violence: Selected Texts from Mohandas K. Gandhi's Non-violence in Peace and War*. New York: New Directions Publishing.

Meyer, Lorenzo. 2007. "The Second Coming of Mexican Liberalism: A Comparative Perspective." In *Cycles of Conflict, Centuries of Change: Crisis, Reform, and Revolution in Mexico*, ed. Elisa Servín, Leticia Reina, and John Tutino. Durham, NC: Duke University Press, pp. 271–304.

Michalski, Tomasz and Gilles Stoltz. 2013. "Do Countries Falsify Economic Data Strategically? Some Evidence That They Might." *Review of Economics and Statistics* 95 (2):591–616.

Milner, Helen V. 1997. *Interests, Institutions, and Information*. Princeton, NJ: Princeton University Press.

Milner, Helen V. 2006a. "The Digital Divide: The Role of Political Institutions in Technology Diffusion." *Comparative Political Studies* 39(2):176–199.

Milner, Helen V. 2006b. Why Multilateralism? Foreign Aid and Domestic Principle-Agent Problems. In *Delegation and Agency in International Organizations*, ed. Darren G. Hawkins, David A. Lake, Daniel L. Nielson, and Michael J. Tierney. New York: Cambridge University Press, pp. 107–139.

Milner, Helen V. and Dustin Tingley. 2015. *Sailing the Water's Edge: The Domestic Politics of American Foreign Policy*. Princeton, NJ: Princeton University Press.

Mmuya, Max and Amon Chaligha. 1992. *Towards Multiparty Politics in Tanzania*. Dar es Salaam, Tanzania: Dar es Salaam University Press.

Moene, Karl Ove and Michael Wallerstein. 2006. "Social Democracy as a Development Strategy." In *Globalization and Egalitarian Redistribution*, ed. Pranab Bardhan, Samuel Bowles, and Michael Wallerstein. Princeton, NJ: Princeton University Press, pp. 148–168.

Mohsin, Amena and Meghna Guhathakurta. 2007. "The Struggle for Democracy in Bangladesh." In *Democracy in Muslim Societies: The Asian Experience*, ed. Zoya Hasan. London: SAGE, pp. 46–74.

Moore, Barrington, Jr. 1966. *Social Origins of Dictatorship and Democracy: Lord and Peasant in the Making of the Modern World*. Boston, MA: Beacon Press.

Morris, Stephen D. 2011. "Forms of Corruption." *CESifo DICE Report* 2/2011:10–14.

Morris, Stephen and Hyun Song Shin. 1998. "Unique Equilibrium in a Model of Self-fulfilling Currency Attacks." *American Economic Review* 88(3):587–597.

Morris, Stephen and Hyun Song Shin. 2001. "Global Games: Theory and Application." Cowles Foundation Discussion Paper No. 1275R.

Morris, Stephen and Hyun Song Shin. 2002. "Social Value of Public Information." *American Economic Review* 92(5):1521–1534.

Mosley, Layna. 2000. "Room to Move: International Financial Markets and National Welfare States." *International Organization* 54(4):737–773.

Mosley, Layna. 2003. "Attempting Global Standards: National Governments, International Finance, and the IMF's Data Regime." *Review of International Political Economy* 10(2):331–362.

Myerson, Roger B. 2008. "The Autocrat's Credibility Problem and Foundations of the Constitutional State." *American Political Science Review* 102(1):125–139.

Nagler, Jonathan. 1991. "The Effect of Registration Laws and Education on U.S. Voter Turnout." *American Political Science Review* 85:1393–1405.

Naughton, Barry. 2006. *The Chinese Economy: Transitions and Growth.* Cambridge, MA: MIT Press.

Naylor, Hugh and Liz Sly. 2015. "In a Surprise Move, Saudi Arabia's Monarch Shakes up Line of Succession." *Washington Post*, April 29.

Neep, Daniel. 2012. *Occupying Syria under the French Mandate: Insurgency, Space, and State Formation.* New York: Cambridge University Press.

Neep, Daniel. 2017. *The Nation Belongs to All: The Making of Modern Syria.* London: Allen Lane.

Nelson, Stephen C. 2014. "Playing Favorites: How Shared Beliefs Shape the IMF's Lending Decisions." *International Organization* 68(2):297–328.

Nepal, Mani, Alok K. Bohara, and Kishore Gawande. 2011. "More Inequality, More Killings: The Maoist Insurgency in Nepal." *American Journal of Political Science* 55(4):886–906.

Nolan, Jonathan and Christopher Nolan. 2008. "The Dark Knight." Manuscript. https://stephenfollows.com/resource-docs/scripts/dark_knight._The_.pdf, accessed August 5, 2017.

Nolan, Jonathan and Christopher Nolan. 2012. "The Dark Knight Rises." Manuscript. www.imsdb.com/scripts/Dark-Knight-Rises,-The.html, accessed September 1, 2017.

Nooruddin, Irfan and Nita Rudra. 2014. "Are Developing Countries Really Defying the Embedded Liberalism Compact?" *World Politics* 66(4):603–640.

North, Douglass C. 1990. *Institutions, Institutional Change and Economic Performance.* New York: Cambridge University Press.

North, Douglass C. and Barry R. Weingast. 1989. "Constitutions and Commitments: The Evolution of Institutions Governing Public Choice in Seventeenth-Century England." *Journal of Economic History* 49(4):803–832.

Oatley, Thomas. 1999. "How Constraining is Capital Mobility? The Partisan Hypothesis in an Open Economy." *American Journal of Political Science* 43(4):1003–1027.

O'Donnell, Guillermo. 1996. "Illusions About Consolidation." *Journal of Democracy* 7(2):34–51.

O'Donnell, Guillermo A. 1979. *Modernization and Bureaucratic-Authoritarianism: Studies in South American Politics.* Berkeley, CA: Institute of International Studies, University of California.

O'Donnell, Guillermo and Philippe C. Schmitter. 1986. *Transitions from Authoritarian Rule: Tentative Conclusions About Uncertain Democracies.* Baltimore, MD: Johns Hopkins University Press.

Ofcansky, Thomas P. 1996. *Uganda: Tarnished Pearl of Africa.* Boulder, CO: Westview Press.

Olson, Mancur. 1971. *The Logic of Collective Action: Public Goods and the Theory of Groups.* Cambridge, MA: Harvard University Press.

Olson, Mancur. 1993. "Dictatorship, Democracy, and Development." *American Political Science Review* 87(3):567–576.

Opalo, Kennedy Ochieng'. 2012. "African Elections: Two Divergent Trends." *Journal of Democracy* 23(3):80–93.

Opalo, Kennedy Ochieng'. 2015. "The Politics of Institutional Change: The Case of African Legislatures." PhD thesis, Stanford University.

Owen, Erica and Dennis P. Quinn. 2016. "Does Economic Globalization Influence the US Policy Mood? A Study of US Public Sentiment, 1956–2011." *British Journal of Political Science* 46(1):95–125.

Padró i Miquel, Gerard. 2007. "The Control of Politicians in Divided Societies: The Politics of Fear." *Review of Economic Studies* 74(4):1259–1274.

Parker, Christopher S. and Matt A. Barreto. 2014. *Change They Can't Believe In: The Tea Party and Reactionary Politics in America*. Princeton, NJ: Princeton University Press.

Pemstein, Daniel, Stephen A. Meserve, and James Melton. 2010. "Democratic Compromise: A Latent Variable Analysis of Ten Measures of Regime Type." *Political Analysis* 18(4):426–449.

Pepinsky, Thomas B. 2009. *Economic Crises and the Breakdown of Authoritarian Regimes: Indonesia and Malaysia in Comparative Perspective*. New York: Cambridge University Press.

Pepinsky, Thomas B. 2013. "The Domestic Politics of Financial Internationalization in the Developing World." *Review of International Political Economy* 20(4):848–880.

Persson, Torsten, Gérard Roland, and Guido Tabellini. 1997. "Separation of Powers and Political Accountability." *Quarterly Journal of Economics* 112(4):1163–1202.

Persson, Torsten, Gérard Roland, and Guido Tabellini. 2000. "Comparative Politics and Public Finance." *Journal of Political Economy* 108(6):1121–1161.

Piccolino, Giulia. 2014. "Ultranationalism, Democracy and the Law: Insights from Côte d'Ivoire." *Journal of Modern African Studies* 52(1):45–68.

Plummer, Martyn. 2003. "JAGS: A Program for Analysis of Bayesian Graphical Models Using Gibbs Sampling." *Proceedings of the 3rd International Workshop on Distributed Statistical Computing*, March 20–22, Vienna, Austria.

Plümper, Thomas and Vera E. Troeger. 2007. "Efficient Estimation of Time-Invariant and Rarely Changing Variables in Finite Sample Panel Analyses with Unit Fixed-Effects." *Political Analysis* 15(2):124–139.

Posner, Daniel N. and David J. Simon. 2002. "Economic Conditions and Incumbent Support in Africa's New Democracies: Evidence from Zambia." *Comparative Political Studies* 35(3):313–336.

Posner, Elliot. 2009. "Making Rules for Global Finance: Transatlantic Regulatory Cooperation at the Turn of the Millennium." *International Organization* 63(4):665–699.

Power, Timothy J. and Mark J. Gasiorowski. 1997. "Institutional Design and Democratic Consolidation in the Third World." *Comparative Political Studies* 30(2):123–155.

Prat, Andrea. 2005. "The Wrong Kind of Transparency." *American Economic Review* 95(3):862–877.

Prunier, Gérard. 1996. "Somalia: Civil War, Intervention and Withdrawal." *Refugee Survey Quarterly* 15(1):35–85.

Przeworski, Adam. 1991. *Democracy and the Market*. New York: Cambridge University Press.

Przeworski, Adam. 1998. Deliberation and Ideological Domination. In *Deliberative Democracy*, ed. John Elster (Cambridge Studies in the Theory of Democracy). New York: Cambridge University Press, pp. 140–160.

Przeworski, Adam. 2005. "Democracy as an Equilibrium." *Public Choice* 123(3):253–273.

Przeworski, Adam. 2009. "Conquered or Granted? A History of Suffrage Extensions." *British Journal of Political Science* 39(2):291–321.

Przeworski, Adam. 2010. *Democracy and the Limits of Self-Government*. New York: Cambridge University Press.

Przeworski, Adam and Fernando Limongi. 1997. "Modernization: Theories and Facts." *World Politics* 49(2):155–183.

Przeworski, Adam, Michael E. Alvarez, José Antonio Cheibub, and Fernando Limongi. 2000. *Democracy and Development: Political Institutions and Well-Being in the World, 1950–1990*. New York: Cambridge University Press.

Przeworski, Adam, Susan C. Stokes, and Bernard Manin, eds. 1999. *Democracy, Accountability, and Representation*. New York: Cambridge University Press.

Putnam, Robert D. 1993. *Making Democracy Work: Civic Traditions in Modern Italy*. Princeton, NJ: Princeton University Press.

Rahman, Waliur. 2007. "Is Bangladesh Heading towards Disaster?" *BBC News*, January 8. https://news.bbc.co.uk/2/hi/south_asia/6241263.stm, accessed February 11, 2016.

Rakner, Lise, Nicolas van de Walle, and Dominic Mulaisho. 1999. "Aid and Reform in Zambia: Country Case Study." Final Report: Aid and Reform in Africa Project.

Rauch, Bernhard, Max Göttsche, Gernot Brähler, Stefan Engel. 2011. "Fact and Fiction in EU-Governmental Economic Data." *German Economic Review* 12 (3):243–255.

Reddaway, Peter and Dmitri Glinski. 2001. *The Tragedy of Russia's Reforms: Market Bolshevism Against Democracy*. Washington, DC: United States Institute of Peace Press.

Reina, Leticia, Elisa Servín, and John Tutino. 2007. "Introduction: Crises, Reforms, and Revolutions in Mexico, Past and Present." In *Cycles of Conflict, Centuries of Change: Crisis, Reform, and Revolution in Mexico*, ed. Elisa Servín, Leticia Reina, and John Tutino. Durham, NC: Duke University Press, pp. 1–22.

Reinalda, Bob and Bertjan Verbeek, eds. 1998. *Autonomous Policy Making by International Organizations*. London: Routledge.

Rejali, Darius M. 2007. *Torture and Democracy*. Princeton, NJ: Princeton University Press.

Riaz, Ali and Subho Basu. 2007. *Paradise Lost? State Failure in Nepal*. Lanham, MD: Lexington Books.

Riaz, Ali and C. Christine Fair. 2009. "Introduction." In *Political Islam and Governance in Bangladesh*, ed. Ali Riaz and C. Christine Fair. New York: Routledge, pp. 1–6.

Riedel, James and William S. Turley. 1999. "The Politics and Economics of Transition to an Open Market Economy in Viet Nam." OECD Development Centre Working Papers 152.

Ritter, Emily Hencken and Courtenay R. Conrad. 2016. "Human Rights Treaties and Mobilized Dissent Against the State." *Review of International Organizations* 11(4):449–475.

Rivera, Temario C. 2002. "Transition Pathways and Democratic Consolidation in Post-Marcos Philippines." *Contemporary Southeast Asia* 24(3):466–483.

Rivera, Temario C. 2011. "Southeast Asian Middle Classes: Prospects for Social Change and Democratization." In *The Middle Classes and Democratization in the Philippines: From the Asian Crisis to the Ouster of Estrada*, ed. Abdul Rahman Embong. Bangi, Malaysia: Penerbit Universiti Kebangsaan Malaysia, pp. 230–261.

Roberts, D. 2003. "From 'Communism' to 'Democracy' in Cambodia: A Decade of Transition and Beyond." *Communist and Post-Communist Studies* 36(2):245–258.

Roberts, Jordan and Juan Fernando Tellez. 2017. "Freedom House's Scarlet Letter: Negative Assessments and Verbal Conflict." Manuscript, Duke University.

Rodrik, Dani. 1991. "Policy Uncertainty and Private Investment in Developing Countries." *Journal of Development Economics* 36(2):229–242.

Rodrik, Dani. 1995. "Why is there International Lending?" NBER Working Paper.

Rogowski, Ronald. 1987. "Political Cleavages and Changing Exposure to Trade." *American Political Science Review* 81(4):1121–1137.

Roodman, David. 2007a. "The Anarchy of Numbers: Aid, Development, and Cross-Country Empirics." *World Bank Economic Review* 21(2):255–277.

Roodman, David. 2007b. "Macro Aid Effectiveness Research: A Guide for the Perplexed." Working Paper no. 135, Center for Global Development, Washington, DC.

Rosendorff, B. Peter. 2001. "Choosing Democracy." *Economics & Politics* 13(1):1–29.

Rosendorff, B. Peter and Kong Joo Shin. 2012. "Importing Transparency: The Political Economy of BITs and FDI Flows." Manuscript, Wilf Department of Politics, New York University.

Rosendorff, B. Peter and Kong Joo Shin. 2015. "Regime Type and International Commercial Agreements." *International Journal of Economic Theory* 11(1):107–119.

Ross, Michael 1999. "The Political Economy of the Resource Curse." *World Politics* 51:297–322.

Ross, Michael. 2006. "Is Democracy Good for the Poor?" *American Journal of Political Science* 50(4):860–874.

Rudra, Nita and Ida Bastiaens. Forthcoming. *Democracies in a Conundrum? Globalization, Democracy, and the Poor*. New York: Cambridge University Press.

Rudra, Nita and Siddharth Joshi. 2011. "Good for the Goose, Bad for the Flock? FDI in Developing Countries (with Special Focus on India)." Paper prepared for the 2011 IPEC Conference: Globalization and the Politics of Poverty and Inequality.

Rustow, Dankwart A. 1970. "Transitions to Democracy: Toward a Dynamic Model." *Comparative Politics* 2(3):337–363.

Sachs, Jeffrey D. and Andrew Warner. 1995. "Economic Reform and the Process of Global Integration." Brookings Papers on Economic Activity.

Saiegh, Sebastian. 2004. "The 'Sub-national' Connection: Legislative Coalitions, Cross-Voting and Policymaking in Argentina." In *The Argentine Crisis at the Turn of the Millennium: Causes, Consequences and Explanations*, ed. Flavia Fiorucci and Marcus Klein. Amsterdam: Aksant Academic Publishers, pp. 145–158.

Saint-Paul, Gilles and Thierry Verdier. 1993. "Education, Democracy and Growth." *Journal of Development Economics* 42(2):399–407.

Saleh, Hebah and Andrew England. 2011. "Defiant Gaddafi vows fight to death." *Financial Times*, February 23.

Samuels, David J. and Matthew S. Shugart. 2010. *Presidents, Parties, and Prime Ministers*. New York: Cambridge University Press.

Scacco, Alexandra. 2008. "Who Riots? Explaining Individual Participation in Ethnic Violence." PhD thesis, Columbia University.

Schedler, Andreas. 1998. "What is Democratic Consolidation?" *Journal of Democracy* 9(2):91–107.

Schedler, Andreas. 2012. "The Measurer's Dilemma: Coordination Failures in Cross-National Data Collection." *Comparative Political Studies* 45(2):237–266.

Scheve, Kenneth F. and Matthew J. Slaughter. 2001. "What Determines Individual Trade-Policy Preferences?" *Journal of International Economics* 54(2):267–292.

Schmitter, Phillippe C. 1992. "The Consolidation of Democracy and Representation of Social Groups." *American Behavioral Scientist* 35(4/5):422–449.

Schoenfeld, David. 1982. "Partial Residuals for the Proportional Hazards Regression Model." *Biometrika* 69(1):239–241.

Schumpeter, Joseph A. 1942. *Capitalism, Socialism, and Democracy*. New York: Harper & Brothers Publishers.

Schwartzberg, Melissa. 2014. *Counting the Many: The Origins and Limits of Supermajority Rule*. New York: Cambridge University Press.

Schwedler, Jillian. 2013. "Spatial Dynamics of the Arab Uprisings." *PS: Political Science & Politics* 46(2):230–234.

Schwedler, Jillian. 2015. "Comparative Politics and the Arab Uprisings." *Middle East Law and Governance* 7(1):141–152.

Semo, Enrique. 2007. "The Left in the Neoliberal Era." In *Cycles of Conflict, Centuries of Change: Crisis, Reform, and Revolution in Mexico*, ed. Elisa Servín, Leticia Reina, and John Tutino. Durham, NC: Duke University Press, pp. 346–362.

Sen, Amartya. 1999. *Development as Freedom*. New York: Oxford University Press.

Servín, Elisa. 2007. "Another Turn of the Screw: Toward a New Political Order." In *Cycles of Conflict, Centuries of Change: Crisis, Reform, and Revolution in Mexico*, ed. Elisa Servín, Leticia Reina, and John Tutino. Durham, NC: Duke University Press, pp. 363–392.

Shadmehr, Mehdi and Dan Bernhardt. 2011. "Collective Action with Uncertain Payoffs: Coordination, Public Signals, and Punishment Dilemmas." *American Political Science Review* 105(4):829–851.

Shadmehr, Mehdi and Dan Bernhardt. 2015. "State Censorship." *American Economic Journal: Microeconomics* 7(2):280–307.

Shadmehr, Mehdi and Dan Bernhardt. 2017. "When Can Citizen Communication Hinder Successful Revolution." *Quarterly Journal of Political Science* 12(3):301–323.

Shadmehr, Mehdi and Dan Bernhardt. n.d. "Vanguards in Revolution: Sacrifice, Radicalism and Coercion." Manuscript, University of Miami.

Shambaugh, George E. and Elaine B. Shen. 2017. "A Clear Advantage: The Benefits of Transparency to Crisis Recovery." Manuscript, Georgetown University.

Shapiro, Ian. 2003. *The Moral Foundations of Politics*. New Haven, CT: Yale University Press.

Shen, Elaine and Mike Sliwinski. 2015. "A Clear Advantage: The Benefits of Transparency to Foreign Direct Investment." *International Public Policy Review* 9(2):26–36.

Shugart, Matthew Soberg and John M. Carey. 1992. *Presidents and Assemblies: Constitutional Design and Electoral Dynamics*. New York: Cambridge University Press.

Siddiqi, Dina Mahnaz. 2009. "Political Culture in Contemporary Bangladesh: Histories, Ruptures and Contradictions." In *Political Islam and Governance in Bangladesh*, ed. Ali Riaz and C. Christine Fair. New York: Routledge, pp. 7–26.

Simmons, Beth. 1994. *Who Adjusts: Domestic Sources of Foreign Economic Policy During the Interwar Years*. Princeton, NJ: Princeton.

Sithole, Masipula. 2001. "Fighting Authoritarianism in Zimbabwe." *Journal of Democracy* 12(1):160–169.

Slater, Dan. 2009. "Revolutions, Crackdowns, and Quiescence: Communal Elites and Democratic Mobilization in Southeast Asia." *American Journal of Sociology* 115(1):203–254.

Slater, Dan. 2010. *Ordering Power: Contentious Politics and Authoritarian Leviathans in Southeast Asia*. New York: Cambridge University Press.

Solow, Robert M. 1957. "Technical Change and the Aggregate Production Function." *Review of Economics and Statistics* 39(3):312–320.

Stasavage, David. 2003a. *Public Debt and the Birth of the Democratic State: France and Great Britain, 1688–1789*. New York: Cambridge University Press.

Stasavage, David. 2003b. "Transparency, Democratic Accountability, and the Economic Consequences of Monetary Institutions." *American Journal of Political Science* 47(3):389–402.

Stasavage, David. 2004. "Open Door or Closed Door? Transparency in Domestic and International Bargaining." *International Organization* 58(4):667–703.

Stasavage, David. 2011. *States of Credit: Size, Power, and the Development of European Polities*. Princeton, NJ: Princeton University Press.

Stigler, Stephen M. 2013. "The True Title of Bayes's Essay." *Statistical Science* 28(3):283–288.

Stiglitz, Joseph. 2002. Transparency in Government. In *The Right to Tell: The Role of Mass Media in Economic Development*, ed. World Bank (WBI Development Studies). Washington, DC: World Bank Publications, pp. 27–44.

Stokes, Susan. 2001. *Mandates and Democracy: Neoliberalism by Surprise in Latin America*. New York: Cambridge University Press.

Stone, Randall W. 2008. "The Scope of IMF Conditionality." *International Organization* 62(4):589–620.

Summers, Robert and Alan Heston. 1991. "The Penn World Table (Mark 5): An Expanded Set of International Comparisons, 1950–1988." *Quarterly Journal of Economics* 106(2):327–368.

Svolik, Milan. 2008. "Authoritarian Reversals and Democratic Consolidation." *American Political Science Review* 102(2):153–168.

Svolik, Milan. 2012. *The Politics of Authoritarian Rule*. New York: Cambridge University Press.

Svolik, Milan. 2013a. "Incentives, Institutions, and the Challenges to Research on Authoritarian Politics." *APSA Comparative Democratization Newsletter* 11(2):7–11.

Svolik, Milan. 2013b. "Contracting on Violence: The Moral Hazard in Authoritarian Repression and Military Intervention in Politics." *Journal of Conflict Resolution* 57(5):765–794.

Svolik, Milan. 2013c. "Learning to Love Democracy: Electoral Accountability and the Success of Democracy." *American Journal of Political Science* 57(3):685–702.

Svolik, Milan. 2015. "Which Democracies will Last? Coups, Incumbent Takeovers, and the Dynamic of Democratic Consolidation." *British Journal of Political Science* 45(4):715–738.

Tajima, Yuhki. 2014. *The Institutional Origins of Communal Violence: Indonesia's Transition from Authoritarian Rule*. New York: Cambridge University Press.

Tallberg, Jonas, Thomas Sommerer, Theresa Squatrito, and Christer Jonsson. 2013. *The Opening Up of International Organizations: Transnational Access in Global Governance*. New York: Cambridge University Press.

Tangri, Roger and Andrew M. Mwenda. 2010. "President Museveni and the Politics of Presidential Tenure in Uganda." *Journal of Contemporary African Studies* 28(1):31–49.

Tavana, Daniel and Alex Russell. 2014. *Tunisia's Parliamentary and Presidential Elections*. Washington, DC: Project on Middle East Democracy.

Taylor, Scott D. 2007. *Business and the State in Southern Africa: The Politics of Economic Reform*. Boulder, CO: Lynne Rienner.

Thakur, Ramesh and Thomas G. Weiss. 2009. "R2P: From Idea to Norm – and Action?" *Global Responsibility to Protect* 1(1):22–53.

Thompson, Mark R. 2004. *Democratic Revolutions: Asia and Eastern Europe*. New York: Routledge.

Tiernay, Michael. 2011. "Battle Outcomes and Peace Agreements." Unpublished manuscript.

Tobin, Jennifer L. and Marc L. Busch. 2010. "A BIT is Better than a Lot: Bilateral Investment Treaties and Preferential Trade Agreements." *World Politics* 62(1):1–42.

Tobin, Jennifer L. and Susan Rose-Ackerman. 2011. "When BITs Have Some Bite: The Political-Economic Environment for Bilateral Investment Treaties." *Review of International Organizations* 6(1):1–32.

Treier, Shawn and Simon Jackman. 2008. "Democracy as a Latent Variable." *American Journal of Political Science* 52(1):201–217.

Treisman, Daniel. 2004. "Stabilization Tactics in Latin America: Menem, Cardoso, and the Politics of Low Inflation." *Comparative Politics* 36(4):399–419.

Truex, Rory. 2016. *Making Autocracy Work: Representation and Responsiveness in Modern China*. New York: Cambridge University Press.

Tsai, Kellee S. 2007. *Capitalism without Democracy: The Private Sector in Contemporary China*. Ithaca, NY: Cornell University Press.

Tsai, Lily L. 2007. "Solidarity Groups, Informal Accountability, and Local Public Goods Provision in Rural China." *American Political Science Review* 101(2):355–372.

Tsebelis, George. 2002. *Veto Players: How Political Institutions Work*. New York: Princeton University Press.

Tucker, Joshua A. 2006. *Regional Economic Voting: Russia, Poland, Hungary, Slovakia, and the Czech Republic, 1990–99*. New York: Cambridge University Press.

Tucker, Joshua A. 2007. "Enough! Electoral Fraud, Collective Action Problems, and Post-Communist Colored Revolutions." *Perspectives on Politics* 5(3):535–551.

Tutino, John. 2011. "Capitalismo global, estado nacional, y los límites de la Revolución: Tres momentos claves en el siglo XX mexicano." *Foro Internacional* 51(3–4):5–40.

Tutino, John. 2018. *The Mexican Heartland: How Communities Shaped Capitalism, a Nation, and World History, 1500–2000*. Princeton, NJ: Princeton University Press.

Vachudova, Milada Anna. 2005. *Europe Undivided: Democracy, Leverage, & Integration After Communism*. New York: Oxford University Press.

Vadlamannati, Krishna Chaitanya, Arusha Cooray, and Samuel Brazys. 2017. "Nothing to Hide: Commitment to, Compliance with, and Impact of the Special Data Dissemination Standard." Unpublished manuscript.

Vadlamannati, Krishna Chaitanya, and Indra de Soysa. 2015. "Do Rulers of Natural Resource Wealth Welcome Transparency? An Empirical Analysis of Institutional Change." Manuscript, Norwegian University of Science and Technology.

Van der Linden, Wim J. and Ronald K. Hambleton, eds. 1997. *Handbook of Modern Item Response Theory*. New York: Springer.

Van der Walt, Lucien. 1998. "Trade Unions in Zimbabwe: For Democracy, Against Neo-Liberalism." *Capital and Class* 22(3):85–117.

Vander Weyden, Patrick. 2000. "Parliamentary Elections in Cambodia 1998." *Electoral Studies* 19(4):615–646.

Van de Walle, Nicolas. 2002. "Africa's Range of Regimes." *Journal of Democracy* 13(2):66–80.

Vanhanen, Tatu. 2000. "A New Dataset for Measuring Democracy, 1810–1998." *Journal of Peace Research* 37(2):251–265.

Veeraraghavan, Rajesh. 2015. "Open Governance and Surveillance: A Study of the National Rural Employment Program in Andhra Pradesh, India." PhD thesis, University of California, Berkeley.

Vidal, Claudine. 2003. "La brutalisation du champ politique ivoirien, 1990–2003." *African Sociological Review/Revue Africaine de Sociologie* 7(2):45–57.

von Soest, Christian. 2007. "How Does Neopatrimonialism Affect the African State's Revenues? The Case of Tax Collection in Zambia." *Journal of Modern African Studies* 45(4):621–645.

Vreeland, James Raymond. 2003a. "A Continuous Schumpeterian Conception of Democracy." Presented at the Annual Meetings of the Public Choice Society and Economic Science Association, March 21–23, Nashville, Tennessee.

Vreeland, James Raymond. 2003b. *The IMF and Economic Development*. New York: Cambridge University Press.

Vreeland, James Raymond. 2003c. "Why Do Governments and the IMF Enter into Agreements? Statistically Selected Case Studies." *International Political Science Review* 24(3):321–343.

Vreeland, James Raymond. 2008. "Political Institutions and Human Rights: Why Dictatorships Enter into the United Nations Convention Against Torture." *International Organization* 62(1):65–101.

Vreeland, James Raymond and Axel Dreher. 2014. *The Political Economy of the United Nations Security Council: Money and Influence*. New York: Cambridge University Press.

Wacziarg, Romain and Karen Horn Welch. 2008. "Trade Liberalization and Growth: New Evidence." *World Bank Economic Review* 22(2):187–231.

Wallace, Jeremy L. 2014. "Information Politics in Dictatorships." Manuscript, The Ohio State University.

Wallace, Jeremy L. 2016. "Juking the Stats? Authoritarian Information Problems in China." *British Journal of Political Science* 46(1):11–29.

Walter, Stefanie. 2008. "A New Approach for Determining Exchange-Rate Level Preferences." *International Organization* 62(3):405–438.

Wantchekon, Leonard. 2004. "The Paradox of 'Warlord' Democracy: A Theoretical Investigation." *The American Political Science Review* 98(1):17–33.

Wehrey, Frederic. 2016. "Why Libya's transition to democracy failed." *Washington Post*, February 17.

Wei, Shang-Jin and Tao Wang. 1997. "The Siamese Twins: Do State-owned Banks Favor State-owned Enterprises in China?" *China Economic Review* 8(1):19–29.

Weingast, Barry R. 1997. "The Political Foundations of Democracy and the Rule of Law." *American Political Science Review* 91(2):245–263.

Weiss, Jessica Chen. 2014. *Powerful Patriots: Nationalist Protest in China's Foreign Relations*. New York: Oxford University Press.

Whitefield, Stephen. 1993. *Industrial Power and the Soviet State*. New York: Oxford University Press.

Williams, Andrew. 2009. "On the Release of Information by Governments: Causes and Consequences." *Journal of Development Economics* 89(1):124–138.

Wintrobe, Ronald. 1998. *The Political Economy of Dictatorship*. New York: Cambridge University Press.

Wood, Elisabeth Jean. 2000. *Forging Democracy from Below: Insurgent Transitions in South Africa and El Salvador*. New York: Cambridge University Press.

World Bank. 2011. *The State of World Bank Knowledge Services: Knowledge For Development 2011*. Washington, DC: The World Bank.

World Bank. n.d. *World Development Indicators*. Washington, DC: The World Bank.

Wright, Joseph. 2008a. "Do Authoritarian Institutions Constrain? How Legislatures Affect Economic Growth and Investment." *American Journal of Political Science* 52(2):322–343.

Wright, Joseph. 2008b. "Political Competition and Democratic Stability in New Democracies." *British Journal of Political Science* 38(2):221–245.

Yashar, Deborah J. 1997. *Demanding Democracy: Reform and Reaction in Costa Rica and Guatemala, 1870s–1950s*. Palo Alto, CA: Stanford University Press.

Yom, Sean. 2015. "Arab Civil Society after the Arab Spring: Weaker but Deeper." *Middle East Institute*, October 22. www.mei.edu/content/map/arab-civil-society-after-arab-spring-weaker-deeper, accessed May 27, 2016.

Zavis, Alexandra. 2011. "Former Dissident Sworn in as Tunisia's President." *Los Angeles Times*, December 13. latimesblogs.latimes.com/world_now/2011/12/tunisia-president-moncef-marzouki.html, accessed May 25, 2016.

Name Index

Subject Index

accountability: aggregate outcomes of policy and, 35–37; electoral, 10, 97n8, 256 (*see also* democratic dissemination of data); facets of transparency and, 7–8; formal heuristic for studying transparency and, 32–33; policy choices and, 34; policy/ outcomes linkage and, 35; publicness/ higher-order beliefs and, 37–38
adverse selection problems, 97, 99n11, 275
Afghanistan, 57, 70
Albania, 57, 70
Algeria, 70, 326–327, 330
Angola, 57, 70
Arab Spring, 326–330
Archigos data set, 149, 168, 205
Argentina, 1, 66–68, 70, 324, 332
assassinations, 146–149, 152, 157, 191, 193–195
Australia, 58, 70
Austria, 57, 70
autocracies: danger zone of transparency in, 164, 166–167, 320, 325; data disclosure in, HRV scores vs. log GDP per capita, 85–87; dynamics of change in, 24; elite and mass politics, interaction of, 308; entrenchment of regimes, transparency and, 323; hierarchical vs. precarious, 285–286; higher-order beliefs and collective action in, 38; inner-circle elites in, 129; investment and regime type, 243–245; investors in, elites/regime insiders as, 219, 224–225; personalistic vs. institutionalized, 285; power relations

between leader and elites, 284–286; stability of and the informational environment, 17–18, 23; threats to, types of, 145–148, 272–273; transparency in, impact of, 2, 4–5; transparency in, reasons for, 21–23 (*see also* autocratic dissemination of data; disclosure, reasons for)
autocratic dissemination of data: alternative accounts of, 273–275; coups and transparency, analysis of, 297–302; coups and transparency, descriptive data of, 288–289; as a double-edged sword, 269–272; empirical implications from a game theoretic model of, summary of, 283–284, 287; equilibrium for a game theoretic model of, 278–280; game theoretic model of, 275–283; intuitions from a game theoretic model of, 280–282; mass unrest/elite management, examples of, 293–297; power relationship between leader and elites, measures of, 284–286; primitives for a game theoretic model of, 275–278; propositions/empirical claims, proofs of, 308–313; propositions/ empirical claims from a game theoretic model of, 282–283, 292; propositions/ empirical claims from a game theoretic model of, testing the, 287–288; puzzle of, 215–216, 245–246, 266–267; twin threats to autocratic survival and, 272–273, 307–308; type of autocracy and transparency, analysis of, 302–307; type